TEXAS FURNITURE

THE CABINETMAKERS AND THEIR WORK, 1840–1880

TEXAS

by Lonn Taylor and David B. Warren

FURNITURE

The Cabinetmakers and Their Work   1840-1880

Foreword by Miss Ima Hogg

UNIVERSITY OF TEXAS PRESS

Austin and London

Published with the cooperation of the Bayou Bend Collection,
Museum of Fine Arts, Houston, and the Winedale Museum,
University of Texas at Austin, and the assistance of the
Varner–Bayou Bend Heritage Fund.

Library of Congress Cataloging in Publication Data

Taylor, Lonn, 1940–
    Texas furniture.
    Bibliography: p.
    Includes index.
    1. Furniture industry and trade—Texas—History.
2. Furniture, American. I. Warren, David B.,
1937–   joint author. II. Title.
TS806.T4T39   749.2′764   75-20391
ISBN 0-292-73801-3

FOR MISS IMA HOGG, 1882–1975,

who dreamed of this book for a decade,

AND FOR HARVEY PATTESON, 1921–1974,

who put the final year of his life into its making

Contents

Illustrations

The advertisements pictured in the text appear in the *Texas Almanac*, 1859 (p. 2); the *Northern Standard*, June 14, 1845, and the *Neu-Braunfelser Zeitung*, May 16, 1856 (p. 12); the *Standard*, March 3, 1855 (p. 38); the *Colorado Tribune*, July 21, 1851, and the *Texas Weekly Quid Nunc*, July 25, 1865 (p. 272).

Foreword

Ten years ago a publication on early Texas cabinetmaking would have been somewhat of a surprise to most Texans. Few people would have dreamed that enough pieces of Texas-made furniture could be found to make a serious study of the subject worthwhile.

The Index of American Design, first published in 1950, had a few photographs of Texas furniture which were generally regarded as unique. Before this, the earliest and most discerning authority on Texas cabinetmaking, Miss Jean Pinckney of Austin, had begun, with her sister, Miss Pauline Pinckney, to collect and explore the folk art of Texas, its furniture and paintings, as early as 1927. I hardly think they realized, though, the vast quantity and scope of the furniture which existed. And Mr. Ted James of San Antonio could tell a fascinating story of how, over twenty-five years ago, he came to collect furniture in New Braunfels made by Johann Michael Jahn. His search reads like a veritable mystery story.

I myself was aware of a West Columbia gunsmith named Dance who fashioned some furniture. There was also a wheelwright, Heinrich Jansen, who made furniture by hand for his family. The Varner-Hogg Plantation house has a charmingly well made cedar four-post tester bedstead made by him, the gift of his grandson, Philip Gupton. Fredericksburg had several well-remembered furniture makers, the most prominent of whom was Johann Peter Tatsch. In Washington County, I had purchased a locally made naïve bed of Southern ash, as well as a really sophisticated walnut slant-top desk. It had never occurred to me to look further.

When the Winedale Museum was dedicated in April, 1967, Dr. Charles van Ravenswaay, director of the Henry Francis du Pont Winterthur Museum, was one of our distinguished guests. Upon learning that one of the former owners of the museum property, Mr. Lee Wagner, had some furniture made in the vicinity of Round Top, Dr. van Ravenswaay was anxious to see the pieces. He found a table and chest of drawers, very well designed and made, of a style influenced by the Central European Biedermeier period. From these pieces and from Dr. van Ravenswaay's appreciation and remarks, the idea for a book on Texas furniture was born.

Dr. van Ravenswaay had made a study of the German trek up the Mississippi Valley. His findings stimulated my curiosity about Texas and prompted me to approach the University of Texas Press to see if there would be interest in publishing research on early Texas cabinetmaking. I suggested a many-sided approach to the subject, with consulting editors who were expert in cabinetmaking and well versed in the history of the early settlers in Texas. The Press approved the plan and consented to publish such a work. This was nearly seven years ago. We thank the Press staff for their encouragement and patience in waiting these many years for the completion of our material.

My part of the work was preliminary and started at once from scratch. First, we appealed to Dr. Chester Kielman, director of the archives at the University of Texas, for certain census lists from 1850 through 1870. We began with the lists from the areas in Texas where immigrants from Central Europe had settled. As the project expanded, we read every census list from every county in Texas. We found that men who made furniture were registered not only as cabinetmakers but also as wheelwrights, carpenters, builders, and so on. We tried to trace their descendants by name. We inquired whether they had examples of any pieces made in the family. Our success was gratifying. We asked for and received snapshots as well as answers to a detailed questionnaire. As the snapshots arrived, we slipped them into albums and made a card index file with pertinent information given from the questionnaire.

Some pieces pictured appeared primitive, others sophisticated; all had charm and showed a creative quality, with an innate attempt to make something of beauty. Furniture and amenities often had to be made in Texas, since the immigrants from Europe—and the Anglo-Americans, too (who had come to Texas earlier)—had arrived either by sailing vessel or by covered wagon, with little space in many cases for more than the family trunk. At that time Texas was a frontier territory, rough though enticing for those seeking a home with expanse of land.

A novice at bookmaking, I presume, is destined to meet with many frustrations. One incident is worth recording. A friend, having seen the volumes containing the finest examples of cabinetmaking, asked to borrow them over the weekend. The Sunday papers, however, became hopelessly entangled with the albums, and they were thrown out with the family debris—never to be recovered. Had it not been for our card index, so painstakingly annotated by Miss Blake Anderson of Houston, we would have been in a shocking situation. As it was, much time was lost in retracing our steps.

The time soon came when we had to consider the heart of the book, the background history of the immigrants and the early settlers in Texas. Many facets of furnituremaking would have to be investigated. Two obvious scholars were at hand. Mr. Lonn Taylor was a natural, a professional researcher and editor, director of the Winedale Museum of the University of Texas. Mr. David B. Warren, then curator of the Bayou Bend Collection of the Houston Museum of Fine Arts and now associate director of the museum, was an authority on furnituremaking, especially the furniture of the United States. We sought to have the publication a joint effort of the Winedale Museum of the University of Texas and the Houston Museum of Fine Arts. Mr. Mike McLanahan, president of the Houston Museum of Fine Arts, when approached, readily consented, seeing at once the prestige which would accrue to the museum if Mr. Warren were to take the necessary part. Mr. Taylor agreed not only to do the research and writing but also to act as editor in chief. Mr. Warren agreed to do the analyses of the furniture and supervise the actual photography.

Since we started our book, much general interest has recently been engendered by the brilliant exhibition on Texas cabinetmakers by the Witte Museum of San Antonio in 1973 and by the publication of the catalogue of this exhibition.

We wish to express appreciation for some important early research given Mr. Taylor by Mr. James McReynolds of Nacogdoches.

No endeavor upon which I launch can ever come to fruition without the counsel and assistance of my invaluable secretary, Mrs. Jane Zivley.

Ima Hogg

Acknowledgments

We will never be able to express adequately our debt of gratitude to Miss Ima Hogg of Houston, who conceived this book, conducted much of the original research, made funds available for continuing research and photography, and is, in the larger sense, the true author of the work. It is our hope that furniture collectors everywhere will recognize their debt not only to her philanthropy but to her scholarship as well.

Hundreds of people across Texas have helped her and us in compiling this work. We would particularly like to thank the owners of furniture who permitted us to come into their homes and photograph pieces and who are recognized in the chapter on Furniture of the Frontier. Mrs. Charles Bybee of Round Top, Mr. and Mrs. Robin Elverson of Houston, Mr. Ted James of San Antonio, and Mr. Robert Quill Johnson of Castroville were particularly patient and helpful. Others gave generously of their time to help us with research on a particular cabinetmaker; among those whom we now number not only as informants but also as valued friends are Mrs. Hugo Biesele of New Braunfels, Mrs. Ferdinand Blumberg of New Braunfels, Mr. and Mrs. Joe Carriker of West Columbia, Mr. Roger Conger of Waco, Mr. Oscar Haas of New Braunfels, Mrs. Lyne Lewis Harper of Fredericksburg, Mrs. Gloria Hill of Houston, Mrs. Sadie Hoel of Clifton, Mrs. Walter D. Kleine of Gonzales, Mr. and Mrs. Knight Parker of San Augustine, Misses Jean and Pauline Pinckney of Austin, Mr. and Mrs. Ed Schulze of Fredericksburg, Mr. Hugo Schulze of Hilda, Mr. William Spalding of Waxahachie, Mrs. Hannah Steinhagen of Anderson, Mr. and Mrs. Marshall Steves of San Antonio, Dr. and Mrs. O. A. Stratemann of New Braunfels, and Mr. and Mrs. Nath Winfield of Chappell Hill.

V. A. Patterson and Nora Comstock read and transcribed the census returns upon which the Checklist of Texas Cabinetmakers is based, and that part of the book is really theirs. They share it with Janis Robertson, Gloria Jaster, Rosa Lee Hinze, and Verlie Wegner, who tabulated and proofread it. Mrs. May Schmidt of the Austin–Travis County Collection, Austin Public Library, has followed this project with interest and directed us to a number of important sources. James McReynolds did invaluable work at the beginning of this project, and we would like to acknowledge our debt to him.

Lonn Taylor owes a special debt of thanks to Mary Elizabeth Johnson for extending to him the hospitality of the Greene Ranch, outside Lytle, over the past three years.

Finally, we would both like to thank our wives, whose collaboration has gone beyond the usual bounds of wifely devotion: Babette Warren as photographer and Diane Taylor as editor and proofreader.

L. T.
D. B. W.

TEXAS FURNITURE

THE CABINETMAKERS AND THEIR WORK, 1840–1880

J. M. JONES.

J. B. ROOT.

B. R. DAVIS.

JONES, ROOT & CO.,

HOUSE-FURNISHING DEPOT,

No. 8 STRAND STREET, GALVESTON.

Wholesale and Retail Dealers in Furniture, House-Furnishing and Fancy Goods, Clocks, Watches, Jewelry, Blank-Books, Stationery, Printing-Paper, etc.

Furniture Manufactory,

MARKET STREET, west of Theatre, GALVESTON.

I. F. W. AHRENS,

Manufacturer and General Dealer in Cabinet Furniture, Chairs, Sofas, Bedsteads, and every description of Furniture of the most modern styles.

Families furnishing houses can have his services by applying at his Manufactory.

Mid-Nineteenth-Century Texas:
The Coast and the Hinterland

More than any other time and place in the American past, except possibly the Boston of the 1770's, mid-nineteenth-century Texas is still with us. It exists as a myth in the popular mind, created by a century of cowboy stories and illustrated Western novels and reinforced by fifty years of Hollywood films. To most Americans, Texas during the forty years between 1840 and 1880—years between independence from Mexico and the beginning of real integration into the Union—was a land of ranches and loading pens; small towns with muddy streets, board sidewalks, and false-fronted buildings; longhorn cattle and Spanish ponies; gunfights, mesquite, prickly pear, Mexicans, and Comanches. Those of us who are Texans may carry a different variety of stereotype in our minds, formed from remembered fragments of high-school textbooks and the experiences, real or imagined, of our ancestors: Austin's colonists felling trees and building log cabins in the wilderness; Davy Crockett at the Alamo; a grandfather leaving home at fourteen to fight for Southern rights; an aged great-uncle born in slavery. As a result our images of the past are more varied, but no truer: Texas was a land of slave plantations, cotton bales, steamboats, and elegant balls; or a land of hardy, God-fearing pioneers; or a land of pain, misery, and backbreaking labor. In some places, pieces of nineteenth-century Texas continued to exist in reality until well into the 1950's: black men plowing with mules or yokes of oxen;

farms without electricity, where children slept in lofts on corn-shuck mattresses and mothers made soap from lard on Saturday mornings; a certain attitude about personal dignity and the right to carry pistols. These bits of reality served to confirm the appropriate stereotype, and so most Texans share with their fellow Americans a distorted view of their past.

But nineteenth-century Texas is with us in more immediate ways: in the words written by the people who lived in it and in the objects that they made and used. This book is about one class of those objects, furniture, and the men who made and sold it, and, by extension, the people who used it and the kind of society they lived in. The picture of that society that emerges from this kind of study is infinitely more complex than any of the stereotypes, though it embraces all of them.

Basically, it is a picture of a semicolonial agrarian culture, exporting one major crop, cotton, and dependent upon the sale of that crop for its durable goods. It is a picture that is recognizable all around the rim of the Gulf of Mexico, from Florida to Yucatán, that very Golden Circle that so many Texans of the fifties dreamed of welding into a slave empire: a society with an aristocracy based on landownership, congregating in coastal cities like Mobile and Pensacola and New Orleans, Galveston and Veracruz, Campeche and Mérida, Havana and Port au Prince, looking to the Northeast or to Europe for its cultural standards; with an interior rich in fertile agricultural land, but difficult of access; with a free laboring class anxious to become aristocrats and a servile laboring class held in legal bondage by the darkness of their skin; and with a need to import many of the necessities of life and nearly all of the luxuries.

In Texas, this culture was particularly characterized by its isolation: isolation, on the one hand, from the rest of the United States and, on the other hand, of the settlements within its boundaries from each other. At first the isolation was political and psychological as well as geographic: Texas was part of exotic, Catholic Mexico, a refuge of pirates and filibusters; later, it was an independent republic, with its own bent for empire; always it was a haven for people wishing to cut ties with the old states. As immigration from those states increased, the physical aspects of isolation did not diminish. It was a long, dismal journey into Texas by land, across the bayous of western Louisiana and through the Piney Woods; it was quicker but infinitely more dangerous to come by water: five days to three weeks from New Orleans, with the possibility of shipwreck or running aground on Galveston Island at the end of the journey.[1]

Once at Galveston, the Texas immigrant found himself in the state's largest seaport and major commercial center, an island town of two-story white houses with broad verandas, green-shuttered windows, high-ceilinged rooms with punkah fans, and wide stairways, surrounded by gardens filled with oleanders, poinsettias, bougainvillaea, and palm trees. Houston, the jumping-off spot for the interior, lay across a wide, shallow bay, from which northers sometimes blew most of the water, and then eight hours by steamboat up narrow, winding Buffalo Bayou. From Houston, it was thirty to fifty miles across a strip of almost uninhabited coastal prairie to the beginning of the densely populated cotton settle-

ments. In the winter and spring this mosquito-infested lowland, known to Texans as the "wet prairies," was often covered with water; in 1833 the Brazos and Colorado rivers overflowed and met there, so that one could travel the forty miles between them in a skiff. Even as an old man, John Holland Jenkins remembered the misery of trying to cross them in the spring of 1836: "After crossing the Brazos, we had to raft across two or three bayous, and all along we worked up to our knees in mud and water . . . it took us a whole day to traverse the Brazos bottom, a distance of *four miles.*"[2]

For years these prairies were a barrier to communication between Texas's major coastal cities and her rich hinterland settlements. Freight wagons crept across them at a rate of eight miles a day, if they did not have to be unloaded and reloaded several times to drag them out of bogs; a planter living on the other side of them was as effectively isolated from the luxuries and society of the coast as if he lived in the interior of Yucatán. Small wonder that there was rejoicing in the backlands when the Buffalo Bayou, Brazos, and Colorado Railroad was completed from Houston to Alleyton in 1860, and its advertisements blared, "THE WET PRAIRIES ARE BRIDGED!"[3]

West of the wet prairies, and north of Houston through the Piney Woods toward the Red River, lay the hinterland settlements, divided by those who spoke of them into Eastern Texas and Middle Texas. In the late thirties there were tiny Anglo-American communities in this hinterland: San Augustine, Clarksville, Jonesborough, and Liberty in Eastern Texas; San Felipe, Washington, Bastrop, and Brazoria in Middle Texas; each separated from the others by miles, in some cases hundreds of miles, of pine forest or prairie. Jonesborough, for instance, was so far from the rest of Texas that it was represented in the Arkansas legislature in 1837. By the mid-forties these communities, scatterings of log cabins along a road, had grown into villages, and other villages grew up between them as the population of Texas doubled in the forties and tripled in the fifties. Places like Jefferson, Marshall, Henderson, Crockett, Tyler, Huntsville, Montgomery, La Grange, Rutersville, and Columbus were bustling communities of the fifties, and there were many smaller places, crossroads with a store and a church and a blacksmith shop.[4]

Communication between these communities was as difficult as travel across the wet prairies. The towns were linked by roads that were usually passable to horsemen but generally impassable to wagons. There were few ferries and fewer bridges; as late as 1846 there was neither across the Brazos at Nashville, and travelers paid a fee to swim their horses through the river beside a canoe. Yet the hinterland was part of an international economy: the economy of cotton. Farmers and planters all over Eastern and Middle Texas sold their cotton to merchants in these communities, who in turn consigned it to cotton factors in Galveston and Houston, who placed it on the market in New Orleans or New York or Europe. Cotton bales moved from the hinterland to Galveston by wagon or, if possible, by raft or barge and sometimes by steamboat. (Texas steamboat captains had a reputation for pushing their boats up rivers and bayous into "water that wouldn't float an alligator" to take cotton out.) Credit flowed back to the village merchants and was passed on by them to the farmers and planters. Little cash was involved; it was a credit-barter system, typical of colonial countries and underdeveloped areas in the twentieth century as well as the nineteenth.[5]

Although the residents of the hinterland participated in an international economy, their isolation meant that they lived in a local one, a tiny but intense economy that supplied most, but by no means all, of their material needs. Round Top, in northeastern Fayette County, was a typical hinterland cotton community of the type that grew up in the fifties. It was not the county seat, but it was the principal place within its precinct, or "beat,"[6] supplying farms and plantations within at least a ten-mile radius. It was an unincorporated village, laid out in lots and square blocks on top of the bluff where the road from Brenham to Austin crossed Cummins Creek. In 1860 it was not ten years old; yet it had an academy, a church, a post office, and several stores, and there were thirty-seven different professions and occupations represented on its census return, including a gunsmith, a shoemaker, three blacksmiths, three wagonmakers, a baker, a saddler, a chairmaker, a tinner, a cigarmaker, a bookbinder, a shinglemaker, a mechanic, and an engineer. There were also five merchants, their shelves stocked with "store goods": sugar, coffee, salt, candles, bolts of cloth, china and glassware, log chains and bulk iron castings—as well as a few things that could also be made locally: boots and shoes, bridles, hoes, axes, plows. The neighboring farmers and planters drove their wagons to town on Saturday to buy their essentials from local artisans: wagons from the wagonmaker, plows and harrows from the blacksmith, harnesses from the saddler, furniture from the chairmaker, and shoes from the shoemaker. The merchants bought their cotton and acted as their bankers, accepting the store orders with which customers on their ledgers paid for goods and services purchased elsewhere; provided them with the small luxuries they could not obtain from local craftsmen; and frequently went bankrupt through overstocking store goods.[7]

Thus, while the financial sinews of the antebellum hinterland were international, its essential durable goods were produced by a network of isolated local economies, ranged in circles of a half-day's wagon trip from places like Round Top and sometimes separated by wide expanses of uninhabited prairie and forest.

To the west, beyond the Colorado River, still another Texas stretched away to the Rio Grande: Western Texas. This was Mexican Texas—a good half of it still Mexico, in the view of some of its residents, until the end of the forties[8]—a place of mesquite-covered prairies, limestone hills, tangled chaparral, and ranchos, dependent not on cotton but on hides and cattle. Its towns were even fewer and farther between than those to the east: Gonzales and Goliad and Victoria along its still fertile eastern edge; then the adobe-lined streets and plazas of San Antonio de Béxar astride the road to Mexico, surrounded by crumbling missions and full of strange sights and smells for the Anglo; and then two hundred miles of chaparral and a few little adobe towns, solidly Mexican in population and character, clustered along the Rio Grande. In the fifties, after statehood, Western Texas was given some coherence by the military. San Antonio became a quartermaster depot and Fort Brown (at Brownsville) a permanent post at the mouth of the Rio Grande, and military roads fanned out from the two across the brush country and up the river. An Anglo population, centered around San Antonio, Corpus Christi, and Gonzales, began to speak of the interests of Western Texas in the legislature, but, even then and, indeed, well into this century, the majority of the region's sparse population felt little connection, cultural, economic, or otherwise, with the plantation economy that developed on the other side of the Colorado. They were isolated from it by language, by religion, by custom, and by resentment of wrongs, real or imagined. The Spanish-speaking ranchers of the brush country looked southward to Mexico for cultural sustenance, and thence to Paris; and the merchants of the river towns, Brownsville and Roma and Rancho Davis, looked across the Rio Grande for customers: the ledgers of wholesale firms like José San Ramón's in Brownsville show twice as many orders from northern Mexico as from Texas.

The Mexican *vaqueros* and sheepherders participated in Anglo society as employees, and the Anglo ranchers who employed them were always conscious of living in an alien environment; their own interests and affections reached back through the brush to San Antonio, and beyond to Houston and Galveston and Saint Louis.[9]

While the Anglos found the native population of Western Texas alien, there were immigrant groups in the region that were even more foreign to them: groups that came from Europe, took root in Western Texas, and flourished in its isolation. They retained their languages and their customs to a greater degree, perhaps, than immigrants who made their homes in parts of Texas already settled and tamed by Anglos.

Far to the north of San Antonio, west of the line of settlement on the Comanche frontier, a colony of Norwegians lodged themselves among the low hills of Bosque County.[10] West of Bexar, across the Medina River, a French promoter settled some five hundred Alsatian families and nearly that many single men at Castroville, Lacoste, Quihi, and D'Hanis. Frederick Law Olmsted, who visited Castroville ten years after its implantation, said that its whole aspect was "as far from Texan as possible . . . It might sit for a portrait of one of the poorer villages of the upper Rhone valley."[11]

The Germans, however, were by far the most numerous European immigrants to Western Texas and the ones who made the most impact on the state as a whole. They were part of a great population movement, the nineteenth-century *Auswanderung* (emigration), during which hundreds of thousands of families left Germany and came to the New World, settling not only in Texas but also in the Ohio and Mississippi valleys and in Mexico, Central America, and Brazil. Most of those who reached Texas were small farmers and village artisans who had left Germany for economic reasons, but a literate and influential minority were impoverished aristocrats no longer able to live *standesgemäss* (according to the requirements of their station) in the old country, or young university graduates or army officers looking for the *vaqueros* and "squatter-regulators" of Karl Postl's Texas novels.[12]

They began coming to Texas in the 1830's, settling along the middle Brazos and Colorado, and within ten years so much interest in emigration to Texas had been generated in Germany that a Society for the Protection of German Immigrants in Texas was formed by a group of princes and nobles. The *Adelsverein,* as the society was called in Texas, brought several thousand families to its settlements in the Western Texas Hill Country. By the mid-1850's the towns they founded there, New Braunfels and Fredericksburg, were sizable cities in which virtually everyone spoke German. Olmsted described New Braunfels in a chapter entitled "An Evening Far from Texas," in which he said: "I never in my life, except perhaps in awakening from a dream, met with such a sudden and complete transfer of associations. Instead of loose boarded or hewn log walls with crevices stuffed with rags or daubed with mortar, . . . instead even of four bare, cheerless sides of whitewashed plaster, . . . we were—in short, we were in Germany."[13]

The influence of the German settlements in Western Texas was not limited to New Braunfels and Fredericksburg or even to the surrounding countryside. The Hill Country settlements were sustained by channels to Europe that ran back through Middle Texas, through the German settlements of the lower Brazos-Colorado region and, later, through the settlements along the Guadalupe below Seguin, to the ports of Indianola (founded by the *Adelsverein* as Carlshafen) and Galveston. German merchants in Galveston sold cotton and maintained credit for the inland German settlements, and by the outbreak of the Civil War there was an influential German element in that city. Germans on the way to the Western settlements were enticed by their compatriots to remain in Middle Texas, and the German population there swelled. San Antonio, too, had an important German community, much of it an overflow from the hills. By the 1870's there was a distinctly *Bürgerlich* atmosphere about that city's social life, which revolved around the German Casino; and families like the Grosses, Altgelts, and Guenthers dominated the city's commerce. Teutonic influence spread far beyond these areas. All over Texas, German artisans read German newspapers published in New Braunfels, San Antonio, and Galveston. For a time, the proceedings of the legislature were published in German. At least one former member of the Frankfort Parliament sat in the state senate, a graduate of the University of Giessen served as land commissioner, and one of his classmates represented Texas in Congress. Robert Justus Kleberg, the son of one of the first Germans to come to Texas, became manager and administrator of the ranch that symbolized the cattle kingdom—the King Ranch.[14]

Mid-nineteenth-century Texas, then, was a society that was both isolated and fragmented. It was far from the sources of everything but its own wealth, cotton: on the rim of fashion, on the outer reaches of the industrial revolution, lacking railroads, canals, factories—all of those things that made the nineteenth century a synonym for progress in other places. It had port cities and coastal settlements with shipping connections to the rest of the world, but those towns existed, like all seaports, in a world of their own: Galveston had more in common with Havana, or possibly even Singapore, than with Huntsville or San Antonio. The settled interior was dotted with small communities of Anglo-American farmers and slaveholders, cut off from the coast and from each other, and interspersed, in some sections, with colonies of Europeans. It is a picture that little resembles the Hollywood myth and is distant even from the Texan stereotype.

The material culture of such a society was extremely complex, so complex that it is impossible to generalize about it and say, "Texans in the 1850's had thus and so." There is an understandable tendency among furniture collectors and restorationists to concentrate on the homes and furnishings of the wealthy, and this has been as much the case in Texas as in the rest of the United States. Yet in 1860 only 263 men in the state could claim a total personal estate of more than $100,000.[15] The bulk of the state's citizens lived at other economic levels; they were farmers, artisans, merchants, storekeepers, clerks, hired hands, and slaves; and they surrounded themselves with material objects that reflected their station in life. This was especially true of the quality and variety of furniture that they owned.

The picture is further complicated by the ethnic mosaic. The material culture of the Spanish-speaking population of Western Texas and that of the black slaves of Middle and Eastern Texas have not been adequately investigated, but it is evident that many of the German settlers used objects that were peculiarly German. Although one of the goals of the *Adelsverein* was to relieve pauperism in Germany, the immigrants were not always poor, nor did they always come to Texas empty-handed. The price of land in Germany was artificially high in the forties, and even the smallest farm could be transformed into enough cash to finance fairly elaborate preparations for a family migration. The Germans had a strong sense of the deprivations of a new, wild land and little experience with the difficulties of freighting heavy objects from the coast to the interior. Although many immigrants arrived in Texas with little more than a family trunk, others brought along a great variety of belongings. The literature of their immigration is rich with references to barrels of china, pewter plates, walnut furniture, pianos, paintings, mirrors, wheeled plows, mill machinery, and even a flock of Saxon Merino sheep, all brought across the water to Texas. The homes of German settlers in Texas contained many things that were unfamiliar to their American neighbors: Ottilie Fuchs Goethe remembered that a rumor circulated that her father's family ate off silver plates because they used pewter tableware brought from Germany; and Caroline Mackensen Romberg recalled the incongruity of a huge, gilt-framed German mirror, embellished with cherubs, that hung on one wall of her family's log cabin in Bell County. Models brought from Europe existed for the production of similar objects by German craftsmen in Texas, and much of the furniture made in Western Texas shows the influence of these models.[16]

On the other hand, the Anglo-Americans, experienced movers, traveled light and brought little with them in the way of material goods: a buggy, a wagon, trunks, bedding, tools, and weapons formed their essential baggage. Tables, chairs, and beds were made in Texas and, at least in the thirties, a rough democracy of furnishing prevailed. As Mary Austin Holley said, "Tables are made by the house carpenter, which answer the purpose very well, where nobody has better, and the chief concern is to get something to put upon them. The maxim here is nothing for show, but all for use."[17] Even in the forties and fifties, the majority of Anglo houses in Texas were scantily furnished. Most administrators' inventories, especially in the interior counties, reflect a spartan attitude toward furniture and a tendency to acquire more land instead. For example, Robert Ligon, a respectable Fayette County farmer who died in 1853, left a section of land valued at $2,580 and five adult slaves worth another $2,500, but his furniture consisted of two bedsteads and bedding, a bureau and bookcase, half a dozen chairs, two pine tables, a clock, a set of silver spoons and a ladle, a skillet, two pots, a Dutch oven, three tubs, two stoneware jars, a churn, and a sieve.[18] There were many others like him, rich in land but poor in material goods.

Christopher Columbus Goodman, a Leon County farmer, wrote a series of letters to his brother in New York describing his life in the interior of Texas in the mid-forties. In one of them he said, "The houses are made of logs, and when you go into them you will find the furniture very scarce and very indifferent," and then went on to prove his point by giving a detailed description of the main room in his own two-room cabin:

In the southwest and southeast corners of my house stands each a bed with white bleached domestic toilets hanging to them. The bedsteads are of my own manufacture and are made from the timber of the woods. Between the two beds and in the south end of the house is a window, or that is what we call it here. It is a hole about four feet square, made by sawing out three or four of the logs, and has no glass in it. Wife has a string stretched across the top of it with some white rags hanging to it. Over the window is a shelf. Two holes bored in the logs and wooden pins make the shelf. On this shelf I count from where I am sitting eleven quilts, three shawls, two bolts of calico, four dress patterns, and a lot of other fixings, I don't know what they are. I see two of Perriller's dresses, one hanging from each side of the shelf, with some other little things hanging against the wall. Over the bed and against the wall on the west side hangs all the Presidents of the States up to date. There is another shelf with some more quilts on it and some pictures hanging about. Over the door on the same side of the house is another shelf. On top of it is our family Bible, two testaments, two hymn books, besides a host of other books, papers, etc. On the same side in a corner next to the fireplace stands a box about four feet square covered with wall paper. I am sitting by it at this time writing to you.

Over my head are two more shelves covered with curtain calico. On top of one is a looking glass. On each side of it are two pictures in gilt frames. One of them is the Apostle Jude baptising someone, I don't know who. The other is on the same order, but I don't know what it represents. On the same shelf are nine tumblers, one sugar bowl, three blue bowls, one of them full of guinea and hen's eggs. On the shelf below that I see two broken tumblers, one blackjack bottle, razor strop and razor, and another

bowl. In the center of the mantelpiece stands a clock which says it is about time for me to quit. On one side of it sits a looking glass. The shelf is covered with jars, bottles, lamps, candlesticks, and so on.

On the east side over the door is one picture. On the left side of the door next to the fireplace against the wall, hangs what Perriller calls a wall towel. It is a piece of bleached domestic about four and a half feet long and three feet wide. At the bottom of it are some lace and fringe. In the center of it is a little round red thing. Perriller sticks her needles and pins in it. The rest of the wall is hung with turkey tails, turkey wings and clothing. I have now given you a very fair description of my place. I will sum up the balance in a very few words. In fact, my house in your country would hardly make a good stable for a cow.[19]

In contrast to Goodman, a few wealthy Texans, especially those in Galveston and Houston, lived in elaborately furnished houses. The inventory made in 1839 of the house furnishings used by George Fisher, a Houston commission merchant, could easily have been compiled in a merchant's home in Baltimore or New York. It begins:

> One large gilt framed mirror, valued $300
> One mahogany bookcase in two parts, with glass doors
> One pier table with marble slab top
> One centre table, mahogany, with marble slab top
> One washstand, mahogany, with marble slab top
> One mahogany wardrobe
> Thirteen mahogany chairs, hair bottomed
> One mahogany rocking chair, hair bottomed
> Two large mahogany sofas, hair bottomed
> Three mahogany card tables
> Two cherry dining tables
> Twelve curl'd maple cane bottom chairs
> One cane bottomed rocking chair
> One mahogany easy chair
> Three high posted bedsteads, and two teasters [sic]
> Two mahogany washstands

One mahogany hat rack
One cast iron umbrella stand, brass mounted
One tinned and wooden framed safe
One pine bookcase in two parts, imitation mahogany
One large gilt framed looking glass
One mahogany framed looking glass
One small mahogany framed looking glass
One small mahogany writing desk
One large mahogany sideboard with looking glass
One large mahogany bureau with oval looking glass
One small mahogany bureau with square looking glass

The list continues through several pages of tableware, bedding, candlesticks, fireplace equipment, cooking utensils, mosquito nets, and a tin bath tub, "painted green and white."[20]

Such magnificence was seldom available in the interior, however, even to those who could afford it. Not only were the freight rates exorbitantly high, but in addition freighters were careless and slow, wagons overturned, and fragile objects suffered from frequent reloading. Sam Houston, living at Huntsville while serving as United States senator from Texas, ordered a shipment of furniture from a Galveston commission agent. When it arrived, Houston wrote a scathing letter to the agent, a Mr. Sarla:

I have received a small cooking stove without any pipe. One large bedstead without Tiester [sic] (as it was too large to send), one of the bedposts split at the top and roughly filled with wax or putty—no side rails, and further I have not looked at the thing. It is of no use as it is to anyone. The bureau came also, and the locks all off it. The scatchings of the key holes are handsomely fixed with wax or putty and the joints wonderful; and taking it all in all surpasses anything that I have ever seen, except the side-board—that is infamous beyond all things else. The veneering is broken and split. Wherever it needed it, and I should say at least twenty places, it has been puttied (for wax was not strong enough nor hard enough) and varnished.

The looking glass was broken before it left Houston, and hardly a splinter reached here. One end of the sideboard was split for near a foot and filled with wax. I have not told you all, nor is it worth the trouble. I called on a cabinetmaker and asked him what the lot, except the stove, was worth, and he said the whole was not worth more than seventy dollars. He said twelve dollars was the full worth of the sideboard. I passed by the table. It came the naked stand without leaves. And here they all are, and the freight upwards of $22.00. I am willing to lose that, and let the furniture be sold for what it will bring, and if it was good it ought to bring at least 25 per cent higher here than in Galveston.[21]

Difficulties such as those encountered by General Houston encouraged most of his contemporaries to buy their furniture from the local cabinetmaker, even when they could afford to pay the "25 per cent higher," and to try to obtain most of their other essentials from local craftsmen, too. This reliance on local craftsmen meant that most of the objects in everyday household use, while having a standard form, had individual idiosyncrasies, so that wagons, quilts, saddles, shoes, utensils, and furniture not only expressed the maker's individual taste and desire for community prestige and continued patronage but also summed up the varieties of his own experiences as designer and manufacturer and user. Local craftsmanship made it possible for a number of solutions to the same problem to coexist in one community, embodied in the products of its craftsmen. It may even have meant, in the long run, that the purchaser got a better object for his money than when he bought a factory product. As far as furniture went, there is no doubt that he got a more beautiful, better-made, and probably more useful object.

By the mid-1880's all of this had changed. The isolation that had characterized Texas society twenty years before had all but disappeared. Three competing networks of railroad lines spread over Texas during the years after the Civil War: one fanning out from Houston, one probing Eastern Texas from New Orleans, and one reaching down into Northeast Texas from Saint Louis. The railroads ended the days of wagon transport in Texas forever; shipments that had taken two weeks to reach the interior from the coast now made the trip in two days, at a fraction of the cost. Furthermore, freight rates favored Midwestern manufacturers, and factory-made goods of all sorts, from Grand Rapids furniture to Studebaker wagons, rode down the rails from Saint Louis. No longer was Galveston the interior's only door to the world; now rails tied its communities together, took their cotton out, and brought the industrial revolution to them in all its material abundance.[22]

The communities of the interior, of course, retained their vitality and their unique characters, and the ethnic groups remained intact and continued to speak Norwegian and German, Spanish and Alsatian. But a subtle change took place: the material culture of these communities was altered, and locally made objects, tailored to the needs of the maker and the buyer, were replaced with impersonal, factory-made substitutes. Almost without anyone noticing, the Texas craftsman became first a repairman and then a curiosity.

Cabinetmaking in the Hinterland

During the years from 1830 to the mid-1870's, while the Anglo-American and European settlement of Texas was taking place, a great change occurred in the way that furniture was made in the United States. The development of certain types of machinery—the Blanchard tracing element, by which an irregular form could be produced on a lathe; the carving machine; the mortising machine; the dovetailing machine; the band saw; and the scroll saw—and the coupling of this machinery with animal, water, and steam power were shifting the manufacture of furniture from the shops of traditional craftsmen, in the eighteenth-century sense, to primitive furniture factories. In the traditional shops, a master craftsman and his employees made furniture with hand tools largely on a "to-order" basis for individual shops and private customers, and craftsmen were generally paid by the piece for the furniture they made. In the primitive factories—which first sprang up in New York but quickly spread, in the early 1840's, to the West, to Saint Louis and Cincinnati—furniture was produced by wage-earning cabinetmakers, some of whom even called themselves "mechanics." These men worked in shops specializing in one furniture form, using as many of the new machines as the owner of the shop could afford. At first the machines were hand- or horse-powered; as the middle of the century rolled by, more and more Western shops introduced steam power. The resulting mass-produced furniture was then stockpiled in urban "furniture warerooms" and country stores.[1]

The story of cabinetmaking in Texas is the story of the conflict between these two methods of manufacture; and, on a broader canvas, it is the story of the struggle between small-town Texas craftsmen with a handmade product and urban Midwestern manufacturers with a cheaper, factory-made product. Unfortunately, perhaps, for collectors, the steam-powered machines inevitably won out, and it is safe to say that most of the small amount of furniture still being made in Texas by 1880 was produced by steam-powered machines in establishments that could legitimately be called factories. However, the line between the two methods of production was not always sharply drawn. Machinery, especially hand-powered devices like the mortising machine, filtered slowly into the shops of Texas cabinetmakers. Many craftsmen in both the city and the country tried to compete with the Midwestern factories, using horse and ox power and, in a few cases, steam power; others tried frantically to increase production by hiring more workmen using hand tools. In some cases they were successful, and a few cabinetmakers, like Willet Babcock of Paris, became prosperous furniture manufacturers, but most did not. In the mid-1870's they gave up and became farmers, furniture dealers and repairmen, or (because of their coffin-building abilities) under-

13

takers. But in the brief decades between 1840 and the mid-seventies they made some wonderful furniture.

There were, in those years, an enormous number of cabinetmakers in Texas. A check of the population schedules of the United States censuses for Texas for 1850, 1860, and 1870 yields the names of nearly 900 men who gave their profession as "cabinetmaker"; of these, about 150 appear on the products-of-industry schedules as having an annual product exceeding five hundred dollars. They supplied a large and rapidly growing population with furniture; during those years virtually every settled county of the state had at least one cabinetmaker working in it.

The vast majority of Texas cabinetmakers were American Southerners, who immigrated to Texas as adults from Tennessee, Georgia, Alabama, and Mississippi. A considerable minority, however, were Germans, brought to Texas by the large German migration in the forties and fifties. The German cabinetmakers not only worked in the portions of the state that were settled by Germans but were also found in the predominantly Anglo-American settlements of Eastern and Middle Texas. In 1860, when about 6 percent of the state's population was German-born, exactly one-third of its cabinetmakers were Germans. New Yorkers, Pennsylvanians, and New Englanders also made furniture in Texas, as well as a few Midwesterners, Frenchmen, Englishmen, Scandinavians, Poles, and Bohemians.[2]

Curiously enough, the manuscript census returns list no cabinetmakers with Spanish surnames, even though these names predominated in the counties along the Rio Grande. Since no cabinetmakers at all are listed in these counties, it may be that the accessibility of the better-off residents along the river to furniture imported through Brownsville and the poverty of the rest of the population precluded a need for locally made furniture. It is also possible that English-speaking census enumerators may have failed to record Spanish-speaking cabinetmakers as such but instead entered them as "carpenters," of which quite a few appear in the Valley counties and in San Antonio.

While virtually every settled county in Texas, outside the Valley area, had at least one cabinetmaker, there were six areas of the state that can be described as nineteenth-century cabinetmaking centers (see Map 1); of these, only two, the Hill Country region and the lower Brazos-Colorado river-valley region (Map 2), are familiar to most furniture collectors and are well represented in Texas museums. The other four, Galveston, Austin, the Piney Woods of East Texas, and the rich cotton-and-wheat Blackland Prairie of North Texas, are untouched fields for local studies and systematic collections of furniture.

Galveston, had it been founded at the beginning, rather than the end, of the industrial revolution, might have become a furniture center to rival Boston, Philadelphia, Baltimore, and Charleston. It was the principal city of its region, serving a vast inland trade scattered over an area as large as New England; it boasted a wealthy and cosmopolitan population; and it was a major seaport, with ready access to raw material from all over the world.

Galveston was a major furniture-importing center for Texas during the 1840's and 1850's, when its great wholesale houses bought shipments of furniture from New York cabinet shops and resold them to furniture warerooms as far inland as Gonzales, San Antonio, and Austin.[3] Cobb's House Furnishing Warehouse on Galveston's Tremont Street advertised a typical lot in November, 1847: "Ma-

MAP I. The six major cabinetmaking regions of Texas, 1840–1880. County lines as in 1975.

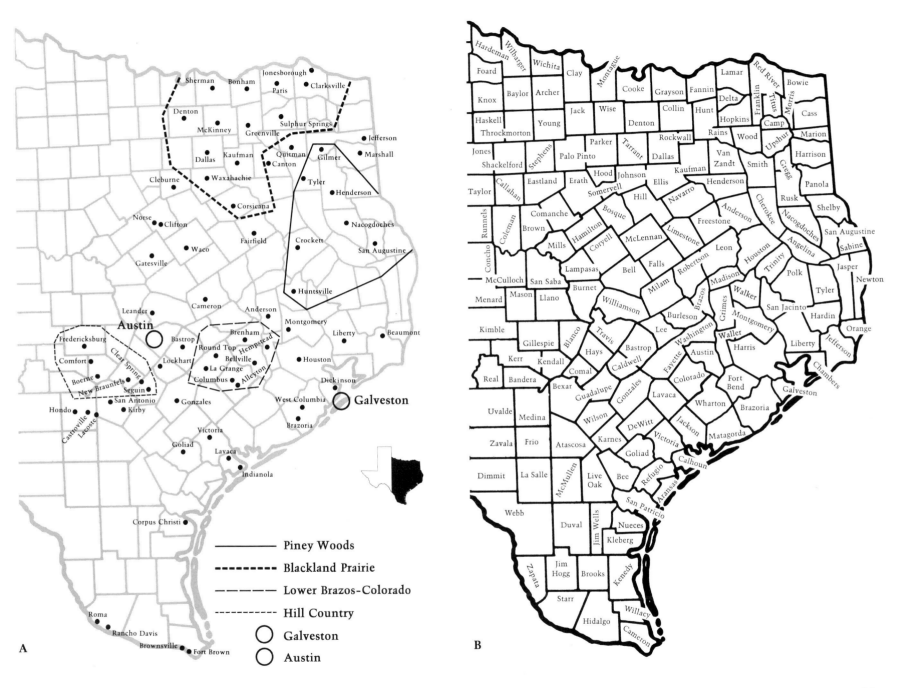

A

Piney Woods

Blackland Prairie

Lower Brazos-Colorado

Hill Country

○ Galveston

○ Austin

B

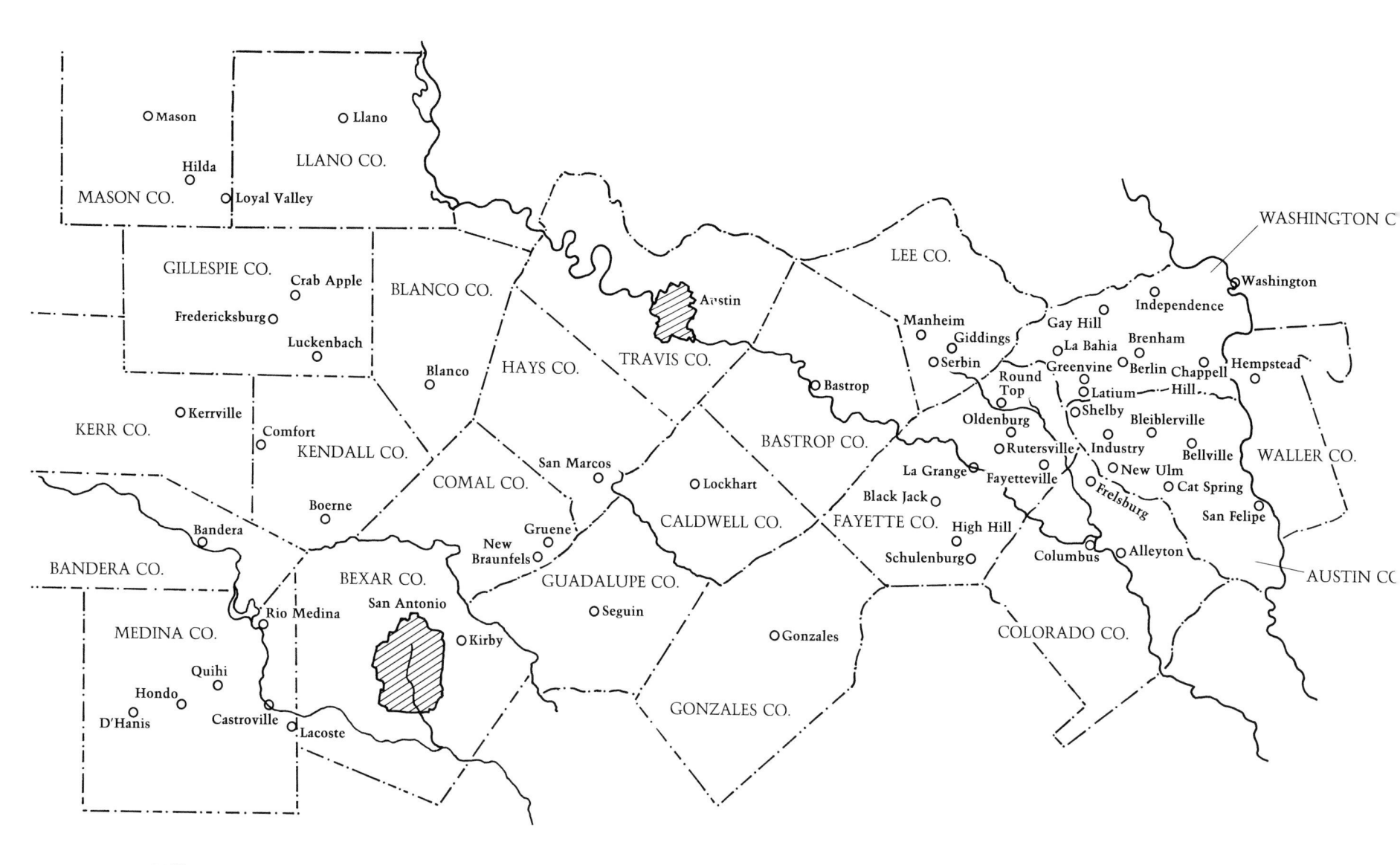

MAP 2. Hill country and lower Brazos-Colorado regions. County lines as in 1975.

hogany sofas, French and 3/4 French Mahogany Chairs, Card Tables, Mahogany Bookcases, Mahogany Wardrobes, Marble and Mahogany top Bureaus, Workstands."[4] A great deal of this furniture, some of it made by New York cabinet shops which specialized in furniture for the Southern market, found its way into Texas before the Civil War. Much of it came knocked down, to be assembled by local furniture dealers who kept cabinetmakers on hand for this task.[5] Undoubtedly, a few of these pieces are today regarded by their owners as "Texas-made furniture."

Furniture was also being manufactured in Galveston during the 1840's. Two of the Tremont Street warerooms advertised that they not only sold imported furniture but would also "make to order and repair furniture on the shortest notice"[6] and that their products were exported to other prosperous Texas communities: citizens of the new town of Corpus Christi were offered a selection of Galveston wardrobes, bureaus, sideboards, presses, safes, cupboards, sofas, settees, couches, center tables, desks, and bedsteads, made to order.[7] In 1848, Galveston's furniture industry truly came of age: a local cabinetmaker invented a hand-powered boring and mortising machine, the first piece of woodworking machinery ever patented by a Texan. Four years later another Galvestonian took out a second furniture patent, "a device for fastening bureau drawers."[8] By 1850 sixteen cabinetmakers, thirteen of them Germans, were producing furniture valued at seven thousand dollars in the city's shops.[9] The largest shop in the city was an establishment that was peculiar, in Texas, to Galveston and Austin and was atypical even in Galveston: a combination lumber yard, livery stable, blacksmith shop, contractor's office, cabinet shop, and workers' barracks, owned by Henry Journey, a New Yorker, who employed twenty men—laborers, carpenters, and cabinet-

makers—and built, according to the census return, "buildings, furniture, etc."[10] Galveston's other shops were more like their New York counterparts: the cabinetmakers worked with hand tools at individual benches, two or three to a shop, earning about a dollar and a half a day.[11] None of the city's cabinetmakers ever used steam power, and water power on low-lying Galveston Island was a practical impossibility.

Galveston cabinetmakers worked under one peculiar disadvantage. There was no supply of native wood on the island, nor any along the nearby coast (see Maps 3 and 4). The difficulties of overland transportation were so great that it was easier to ship pine from Maine, Florida, and Alabama than it was to haul it from Eastern Texas. On the other hand, Galveston cabinetmakers had ready access to mahogany, rosewood, black walnut, and other imported materials.[12]

The late forties and early fifties were the heyday of Galveston cabinetmaking; by 1860 the total value of furniture made in the city had fallen to less than a third of its 1850 level, perhaps because of the constant availability of imported furniture. During the next decade, furniture production rose again to the 1850 level, but this figure appears to have included a good deal of upholstering, repairing, mattress manufacturing, and assembling of knocked-down furniture. By the seventies, Galveston cabinetmakers seem to have turned entirely to gluing together furniture made elsewhere, and the focus of cabinetmaking in the state had shifted away from the coast.[13]

Little furniture made in Galveston seems to have survived; one marked example, labeled "W. Richter & Comp. Moebel fabrik Galveston" (see 3.13), bears out the predominance of Germans in the trade and closely resembles New York furniture of the period.

Texas's other urban furniture center, Austin, had none of Galveston's natural advantages for trade and industry, nor was it a wealthy or cosmopolitan town. Intentionally located on the western frontier in 1839 and seriously threatened by Indian and Mexican incursions in the early forties, Austin had either to produce its own material goods or to haul them by wagon from Houston or Indianola. The expense of freighting furniture overland undoubtedly encouraged Austin cabinetmakers. The city's craftsmen could obtain a good supply of pine lumber from the forest at Bastrop, only thirty miles away, and could cut walnut, cypress, and other hard-

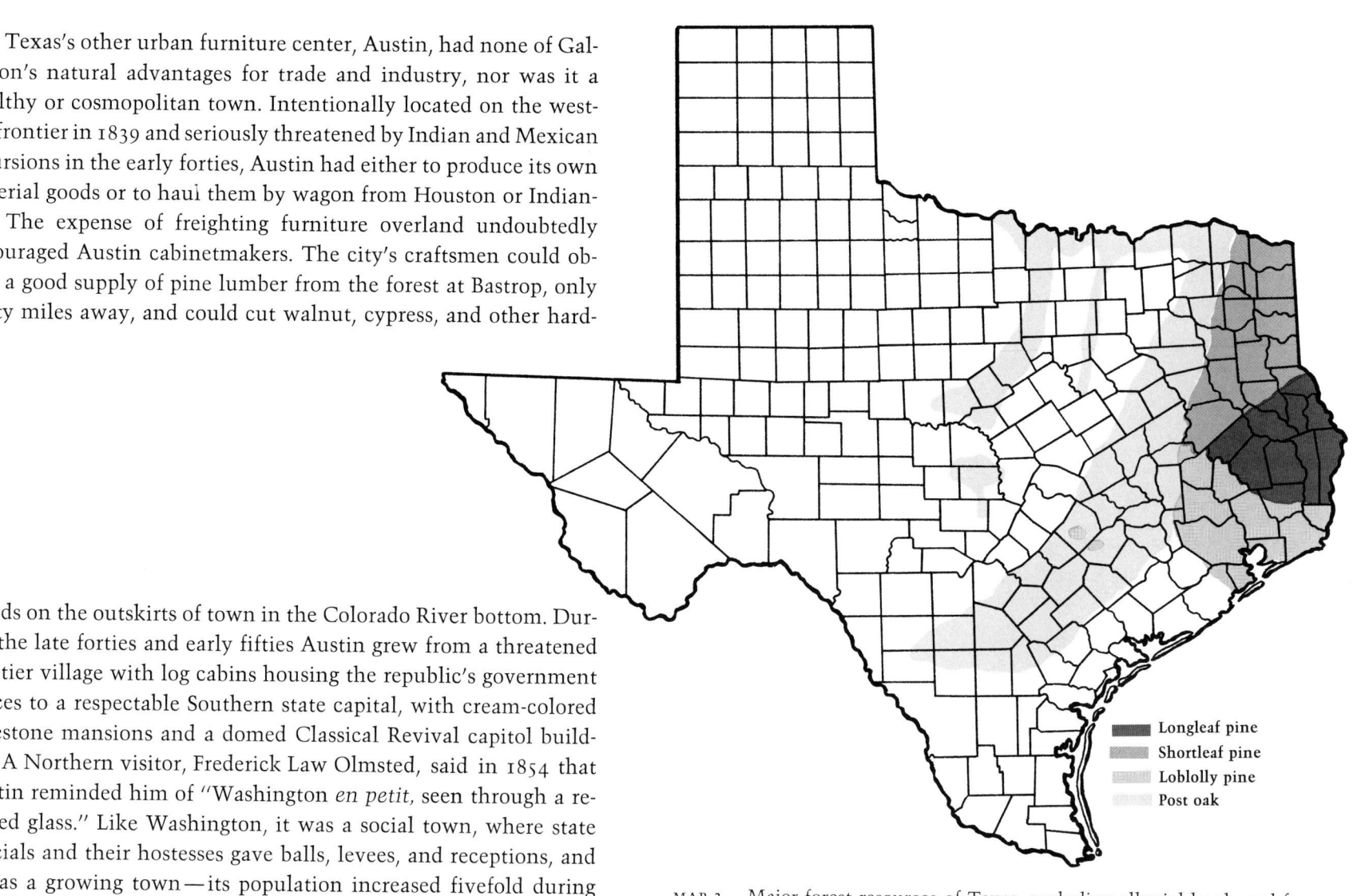

woods on the outskirts of town in the Colorado River bottom. During the late forties and early fifties Austin grew from a threatened frontier village with log cabins housing the republic's government offices to a respectable Southern state capital, with cream-colored limestone mansions and a domed Classical Revival capitol building. A Northern visitor, Frederick Law Olmsted, said in 1854 that Austin reminded him of "Washington *en petit,* seen through a reversed glass." Like Washington, it was a social town, where state officials and their hostesses gave balls, levees, and receptions, and it was a growing town—its population increased fivefold during the fifties and included a sizable German element.[14]

Longleaf pine
Shortleaf pine
Loblolly pine
Post oak

MAP 3. Major forest resources of Texas, excluding alluvial hardwood forests. County lines as in 1975. (Based on William L. Bray, *Forest Resources of Texas.*)

Cabinetmakers arrived in Austin almost as soon as the city was surveyed. The first auction of lots was held in August, 1839, and within eight months the city had two cabinet shops. One was simply a small, two-man "cabinet manufactory" on Pecan Street (now Sixth Street),[15] but the other was an establishment similar to Henry Journey's in Galveston, operated by one H. Ward, who boasted that he had been employed for thirteen years on the public works of the state of New York and was "determined not to be thrown from the track or outdistanced by any" in carrying on "the house, carpenter, and joiner's business in all its branches."[16] Ward's

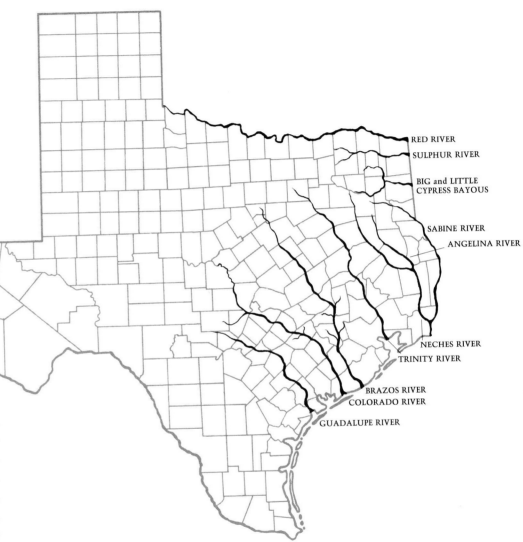

shop employed fifteen to twenty workmen, two of whom were cabinetmakers. They supplied the new citizens of Austin with "tables, stands and desks, China presses, bedsteads and cots, wardrobes and book cases and drawers, milk and meat safes, cupboards and lockers."[17] Both of these shops appear to have closed during the general exodus from Austin in 1842, when the threat of Mexican invasion caused the capital to be temporarily moved to Houston, for during the late forties there were only two small cabinet shops in the city, both operated by Germans.[18]

In the fifties, however, a new type of establishment developed in Austin: a combination furniture wareroom and cabinetmaking

MAP 4. Major alluvial hardwood forest resources of Texas. County lines as in 1975. (Based on William L. Bray, *Forest Resources of Texas*.)

shop. The wareroom displayed furniture shipped from Galveston—
"Sofas; Tete-a-Tetes; Easy, Parlor, Reclining, and Fine Rocking
Chairs, as well as wood seat do.; Centre and extension tables, Music
Stools, Hall Stands, Clock Cradles (a beautiful and novel article),
Basket Stands, Single and Double Bedsteads, Brass Cornices, Fire-
Boards, and other articles too numerous to mention," advertised
one[19]—and there was a workroom in the rear, where the owner and
an employee or partner worked at the lathe and bench. Such shops
were scattered along Congress Avenue and Pecan Street and doubled
as undertaking parlors, their owners not only making coffins but
also preparing corpses for burial and operating hearses. Carl
Nitschke's water-powered sawmill on Bull Creek supplied them
with sawed and seasoned walnut for coffins and furniture, and their
products found their way into many Austin houses and offices, including the Governor's Mansion (see 2.16) and Elisha Pease's Greek
Revival home. At the outbreak of the Civil War, Austin accom-
modated at least ten such cabinetmakers.[20]

A few of these remained in business in the capital after the war,
and a few more shops on the same model opened in the late sixties.
There was a trend, however, toward larger shops and increased
production, although all Austin furniture continued to be made
by hand or with hand-powered machinery well into the seventies.
In 1870, for the first time, there were two cabinet shops in the city
whose annual product was valued at more than five hundred dollars. They resembled those of Galveston in the late forties: an
owner and three or four employees worked with hand tools to produce several thousand dollars' worth of furniture. In one of them,
Joseph W. Hannig and his three men made six thousand dollars'
worth of furniture; it was one of the largest cabinet shops in the
state (see 3.6). Hannig, a German, was well known in Austin as the
husband of Suzanna Dickenson, the survivor of the Alamo.[21]

In 1871 the Houston and Texas Central Railroad reached
Austin,[22] and by the next year V. De Leon, an Austin cabinetmaker,
was pleading that "dealers will find it to their interest to examine
my prices before sending North."[23] But Austin's local cabinet shops,
even though at least one was equipped with a scroll saw, found it
impossible to compete with the large furniture factories, and by
1880 there was no one in the capital city who described himself as
a cabinetmaker.[24]

Of the other centers in the state, the Piney Woods of East Texas
was the oldest. Cabinetmakers here were not concentrated in one
city but were at first scattered through a number of towns and
settlements clustered around the trade center of San Augustine.
They remained, however, village craftsmen: few, if any, Texas cabinetmakers ever worked on isolated farms. Cabinetmaking flourished in the Piney Woods because it was an area of rapid settlement
and relative prosperity, far from a source of imported furniture and
in the middle of a vast supply of timber. Anglo-American settlers
from the Southern states began crossing the Sabine into East Texas
before 1800, traveling along El Camino Real, the Spanish road from
Louisiana to San Antonio. By 1834, Mexican authorities estimated
that six thousand people lived in the area around Nacogdoches and
the new Anglo-American town of San Augustine, thirty miles to
the east. San Augustine, astride the San Antonio road, became an
official port of entry into the Republic of Texas; it was the home
of a university and of many of the republic's leading citizens. To
the east, in the rich Sabine bottoms, settlers developed small farms
into slave plantations and rafted their cotton down the Sabine in
hundred-bale boatloads; to the northwest, planters moved into the
rich valleys and rolling hills of Rusk County, which during the
fifties became the state's most populous county. The cotton-rich

society of Alabama and Mississippi was re-created in the red lands around San Augustine, and it was a society hungry for material goods.[25]

A few wealthy Rusk County planters furnished their homes with factory-made furniture, ordered from Shreveport and shipped to them wrapped in cotton-bagging, but most East Texans patronized cabinetmakers in San Augustine and the surrounding towns —Mount Enterprise, Henderson, and Milam. Though their shops were small and used only hand power, these cabinetmakers did a surprisingly large volume of business. Four cabinetmakers east of San Augustine, in rural Sabine County, turned out $2,400 worth of furniture in 1850, and Abner H. Stith in Henderson made $2,000 worth of "bureaus and other pieces" that same year. Stith was one of eleven cabinetmakers working in Rusk County then; all but two of them were Southerners. In San Augustine the trade was dominated by a German and a New Hampshireman, and in Sabine County the four shops were owned by an Englishman, a German, a Tennessean, and a Pennsylvanian. The customers, however, determined the style, and the style of East Texas furniture reflected the Classical Revival and Restauration ("pillar-and-scroll") styles popular throughout the conservative rural South; one East Texas cabinetmaker, J. M. Whitehead, advertised that he made "all . . . articles of Furniture usually manufactured in a Southern Cabinet Shop." The furniture made in San Augustine may have been more elegant than that from the surrounding area, as the town's leading cabinetmaker, J. George Woldert, reported in 1850 that he used only walnut and cherry lumber, no pine. Unfortunately, few examples of this furniture have been located and identified, although much of it must exist in old homes in and around San Augustine.[26]

During the late forties, pioneers began moving westward from the San Augustine area into what is now Smith County, on the western edge of the Piney Woods. At the same time, the pine forests were being penetrated from the south by settlers coming up the Trinity, opening up the rich bottom lands on both sides of the river in Houston and Walker counties. New towns—Tyler, Crockett, and Huntsville—sprang into being, and the focus of East Texas life shifted slightly to the west. In the fifties, farmers from the cotton states poured into these new lands: the white population of Smith County increased threefold during that decade, the slave population sixfold.[27]

The new immigrants included cabinetmakers, who came in response to a new market, generated by a quickly growing, prospering population and made known to them by published appeals offering "plenty of employment" to "mechanics who have learned useful trades," including "carpenters, gin-wrights, cabinetmakers . . ."[28] Men from Tennessee, North Carolina, Kentucky, Virginia, and Alabama opened cabinet shops in and around Tyler, Huntsville, and Crockett and were soon busy supplying the surrounding countryside with furniture. In 1860, shops at Tyler, Jamestown, Mount Carmel, and Old Canton in Smith County; Crockett in Houston County; and Huntsville, Waverly, and Cincinnati in Walker County produced furniture valued at a total of $13,788.[29] Nearly every one of these shops was operated by one man or (less often) two partners, using hand tools to make a wide variety of furniture: a Jamestown cabinetmaker offered bureaus, wardrobes, secretaries, safes, bedsteads, and center, dressing, dining, and folding tables.[30]

The tools were simple but generally included a lathe and sometimes even the little hand-powered mortising machine developed in the 1830's to aid cabinetmakers in chiseling mortised joints. The administrator of one Huntsville cabinetmaker's estate made an inventory of his tools after his death in 1851; they in-

22

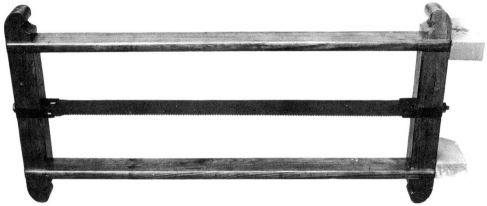

D

C

PLATE I. Cabinetmaker's tools used by Heinrich Scholl in New Braunfels, ca. 1870. (A) Foot-treadle lathe, 9′ 2″ long, built by Scholl. The flywheel on the left could be belted to a horse power. (B) Tool chest, on castors, with rack in front for saws. (C) Hanging wall rack holding Scholl's planes and chisels. Scholl used this rack over his bench. (D) Framed pit saw, 4′ 1″ high, used by the Scholl brothers for ripping planks from logs. (Courtesy of Dr. and Mrs. O. A. Stratemann. Photographs by Jim Bones.)

cluded two workbenches, a lathe, a mortising machine, fourteen planes, a bucksaw, four saws, a keyhole saw, an adze, a drawing knife, three squares, eight chisels, four augers, a brace and bits, three screws (probably gluing clamps), and a glue kettle. A set of chair rounds, a box of screws, some walnut and cherry lumber, a keg of white lead, five bottles of oil, and a "lot of copal varnish" were also in the shop.[31] The planes probably included samples of all three types of cabinetmaker's planes: smoothing planes for smoothing roughly sawed boards, molding planes for making decorative cornices and fluted columns, and rabbet planes for cutting tongue-and-groove joints in boards. Another administrator's inventory of a Walker County shop mentions "match plains; 2 smoothing plains; 1 moulding and rabit plain; 2 fore plains; 2 jack plains";[32] and a Fayette County cabinetmaker owned "one-half set of hollows and rounds, one o.g. [ogee] plane, one astragal plane, two rabbit planes, one fillister [a movable attachment which regulated the distance of a rabbet plane's cut from the edge of a board]."[33]

The presence of lead, oil, and copal varnish in a Huntsville shop provides a clue to the way in which much Texas furniture was finished. A good deal of it, especially if it was pine, was painted or grained; a number of bills and estate inventories list such items as "pine tables, painted red," "painted pine work tables," or "pine bookcase, imitation mahogany."[34] A few of these pieces still exist with their original paint, or traces of it (see 2.20, 2.22, 2.34, 2.39, and 6.31). Walnut furniture was frequently varnished with a glossy copal varnish "to brighten the ornamental appearance of the grain."[35]

An anomaly in the pattern of East Texas cabinet shops was the existence of the convict-operated shop in the state penitentiary at Huntsville, where a cabinet shop, wagon factory, and textile mill were established in accordance with the best nineteenth-century penological principles, which held that convicts should be usefully employed in enterprises profitable to the state. The cabinet shop probably dates back to the penitentiary's establishment in 1849; in 1854 the report of the penitentiary superintendent, which dealt mostly with the establishment of the textile mill, recommended that "the wagon and cabinet shops be continued, and leave adequate force to run the textile machinery, both of which yield a handsome return for the labor." The return was indeed handsome: the profit from the cabinet shop alone in 1855 was $1,340. That year the four convicts employed there produced twenty-one bedsteads, four sets of bedposts, two tables, two washstands, one wardrobe, and one crib.[36] Five years later, in 1860, the shop's production was valued at $1,300.[37] The prison shop seems to have been discontinued after the Civil War, when the whole prison system was in a state of disorganization,[38] but it was apparently reopened in the late 1870's, as it manufactured furniture for state office buildings and elaborate wooden chests; one such chest is in the Winedale collection. Many items made in the prison found their way into private homes in the Huntsville area; they are distinguished by neither design nor craftsmanship. (The cabinet shop is still operating today and is staffed by about forty prisoners; they make brooms and brushes, do cabinet work for state institutions, and occasionally make pieces of furniture.)

Since the economy of rural Texas was less specialized than that of the cities, many East Texas cabinetmakers did more than make furniture. Country living in the nineteenth century demanded that everyone play more than one part: merchants were postmasters, bankers, and saloonkeepers; ministers were teachers, librarians, sextons, and musicians; farmers were carpenters, veterinarians, tanners, farriers, and drovers. Most rural Texas cabinetmakers owned and worked farms on the outskirts of the towns they lived in; they tended to invest their profits in farm land. As farmers they built barns, repaired tools, fixed harnesses, and performed the diverse chores required to manage an unmechanized farm. Robert Minor Wyatt, a Virginian who made furniture all over East Texas before settling in Waxahachie, recorded both his cabinet work and his farm tasks in his diary: "October 6, 1860, Bought two bedsteads and made one, made a trundle bed, made a safe, a table, and have done a good many little jobs." "May 12, 1861: I turned a set of rollers for a cane mill. I harvested the wheat a day or two then cut eight acres of oats and got one acre clear of the rent for my part which was twelve hundred bushels."[39] Some East Texas cabinetmakers doubled as carpenters, framing, raising, and roofing their neighbors' houses as well as making furniture to go in them. A few were not only craftsmen but also mechanics—men who understood the intricacies of machines with moving parts. W. J. Foster, a Crockett artisan of the fifties, advertised that he could supply wardrobes, bedsteads, lounges, safes, cribs, tables, all kinds of household furniture, and "COFFINS . . . at the shortest notice," and then added a note "To FARMERS: From years of experience we feel able to put any repairs needed upon gins, and guarantee satisfaction, if not damaged by unexperienced hands."[40] In 1860 his shop did $3,800 worth of business, of which $500 was gin repairing.[41] Over in San Augustine, Ransom Horn, who is still remembered there as "a natural-born machinist," had a horse-powered factory where he made furniture, shotguns, and gin parts. Horn specialized in making the wooden screws, thirty feet in length, that were the essential part of an animal-powered cotton press. San Augustine old-timers still recall his quick action in replacing a screw that broke during a busy Saturday's ginning: he had some men cut a white oak, shaped it, and within the hour cut the screw threads into it with a broadaxe and had it in place in the press.[42] Another cabinetmaker-mechanic was T. Spotswood Blennerhasset of Bonham, who advertised in 1853 that he made "bedsteads, chairs, and cabinets" and did "Turning in wood or Iron, . . . the repairing of Gins, Thrashing, or Reaping and Cutting Machines, Horse Powers, &c. &c.: Also the placing or setting up of Cylinder or Flue Boilers, on the latest and best plan for draught, and Safety; and with horizontal, perpindicular or Vibrating Cylinders, for Mill purposes, &c., &c."[43] Other cabinetmakers were equally diverse but less mechanical; Gottfried Buescher of New Ulm once signed a contract to build "a carrousel containing twenty wooden horses and two buggies."[44] The point is that, not just in East Texas but in all the rural areas of the state, men whose main business was furniture also turned house columns, repaired farm implements, made wheels, built wagons, and strayed far from furniture making.[45]

Although most East Texas furniture was made with hand tools and foot-powered lathes, a few of the larger shops in the region were mechanized during the late fifties. Mechanization was usually achieved by setting up a "horse power"—a treadmill or a circular sweep turned by a horse, mule, or ox—which was then geared and belted to a lathe. Animal-powered lathes could be turned with much greater force than the usual foot-powered variety, and shops equipped with them could produce a greater volume and variety of turned work. In some shops the horse power was belted to a shaft which ran through the shop, to which more than one lathe could be attached, and at least one cabinetmaker in the state (but not in the East Texas region) reported operating both a lathe and a slitting saw with a horse power. By 1860, a total of six cabinetmakers in Tyler, Crockett, San Augustine, Mount Carmel, and Rusk County reported using horse power.[46]

William Sheppard's shop at Tyler provides an example of how an East Texas shop was mechanized. Sheppard, a Kentuckian, came to Tyler in the mid-fifties, when the town was less than a decade old, and opened a small cabinet shop on the first floor of the Temple Building, where he made wardrobes, tables, lounges, bedsteads, stands, sofas, bookcases, and desks "in a superior, workmanlike manner."[47] By 1860 he had prospered and had gone into partnership with a Tennessean named J. C. Rogers. Rogers and Sheppard described themselves as "Furniture Merchants and Cabinet Makers"; they set up a horse-powered lathe, employed three helpers, and specialized in the manufacture of bedsteads, wardrobes, and bureaus made from local pine and oak. Their retail department carried a variety of other forms: "Sofas, . . . Wash stands, Dining tables, Toilet tables, and every description of furniture usually found in the country," and they also advertised that "orders from a distance will receive prompt attention."[48]

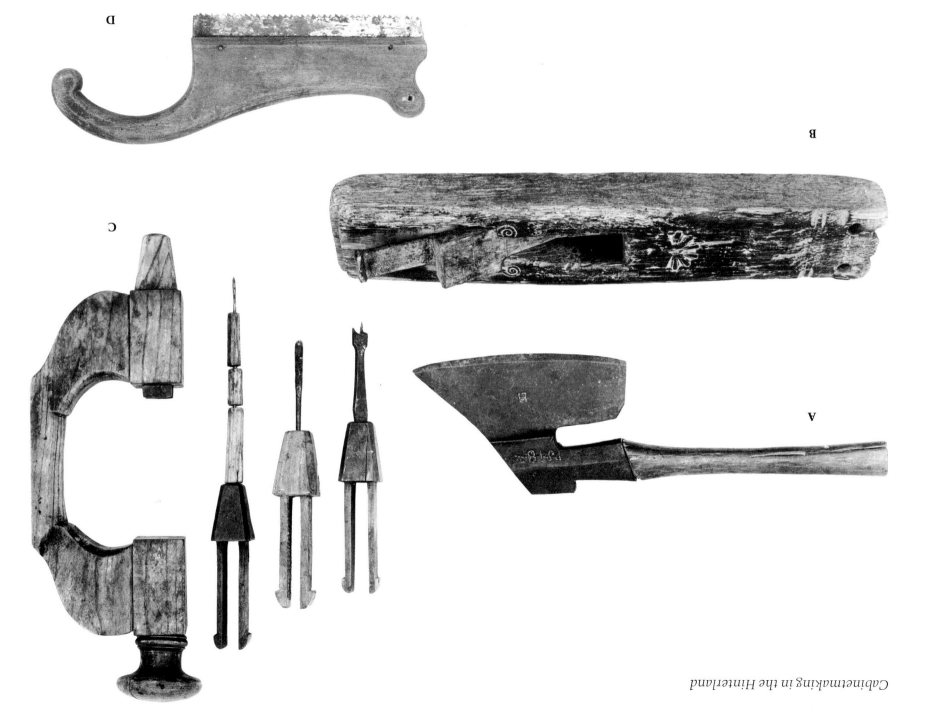

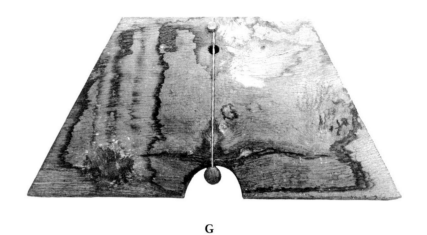

G

E

F

PLATE 2. Cabinetmakers' tools of German origin used in Fredericksburg, ca. 1860. (A) Goose-wing broadaxe used by Jacob Schneider, marked *PS 1829* and *GB*. The axe and handle are 21″ long; the blade face, 12 1/4″. (B) Trying plane used in Fredericksburg in the 1850's; 36 1/2″ long. (C) Brace and bits used by William Leilich. The brace is 15″ long. (D) Grooving saw used by Leilich; 13″ long; a tool peculiar to Europe. (E) An early nineteenth-century fillister plane brought to Fredericksburg from Germany; 12″ long. (F) Another type of nineteenth-century German fillister plane, in which the movable fence is held in place by wedges; 11 1/4″ long. (G) A plumb level used by Johann Peter Tatsch; the forerunner of the spirit level. (Courtesy of the Pioneer Museum, Fredericksburg. Photographs by Jim Bones.)

Although most of their fellow craftsmen, even those with horse-powered machinery, succumbed to the impact of factory-made furniture after the Civil War, Rogers and Sheppard decided to compete with the Midwestern factories. They moved their shop to a site a few miles northeast of Tyler, known as Mechanicsville, and set up a fifteen-horsepower steam engine. By 1870 they had four lathes, two boring machines, and a tenoning machine in operation, and ten employees were using them to make $5,500 worth of furniture in that year. The factory was unsuccessful, however, and today nothing is left of Mechanicsville but the grave of a subsequent owner's child.[49]

The next cabinetmaking region of the state was also a rural one, embracing the county-seat towns and crossroads communities of the great Blackland Prairie which lay to the north and west of the Piney Woods, stretching from the headwaters of the Sabine River westward to the upper reaches of the Trinity.

The first settlers in this region were Southerners, pushing up the valley of the Red River from Arkansas in search of new cotton lands. They founded the town of Clarksville in the late 1830's and gave it a stamp much like that of San Augustine: a wealthy Southern cotton town, a trade center for farms and plantations up and down the fertile Red River valley. Then they moved westward to the edge of the prairie, into Lamar County and Hopkins County, building new towns as they went: Paris and Bright Star. In the early forties, the Peters Colony scheme brought hundreds of families to this area; they were followed by immigrants who came down the Texas road from Missouri through Indian Territory. By 1860 the entire Blackland Prairie, reaching to the Cross Timbers in the west and the edges of the pine forest in the southeast, had been colonized.[50]

The towns of this new region differed from those of East Texas. Clarksville, Paris, and Bright Star (later renamed Sulphur Springs) were Southern towns, but west of Paris the ratio of slave to free population began to fall rapidly. This was a land of frontiersmen, wheat farmers, and stockmen. Collin County voted against secession, as did the seven neighboring counties. Dallas looked across the Trinity to an endless expanse of prairie, upon which a Fourierian socialist colony of Frenchmen had been established. Even Corsicana and Waxahachie, though predominantly Southern in population, were prairie towns, and their merchants looked westward rather than back down the Trinity to the Piney Woods.[51]

Of these towns, Clarksville was the first to attract cabinetmakers, in the forties, and it remained a cabinetmaking center through the seventies. Paris, Bright Star, and Corsicana all came into prominence in the fifties, while McKinney, Dallas, and Waxahachie developed small furniture industries after the Civil War.[52]

The cabinetmakers of this region reflected its cultural differences. While most of the East Texas cabinetmakers were from the lower South, many of their Blackland counterparts were from the upper South, the North, and the new Midwest. The leading cabinetmaker of Clarksville, the most Southern of the Blackland towns, was from New Jersey; in Paris, a New Yorker and a Tennessean dominated the trade; in McKinney, a Kentuckian and a Pennsylvania German from Illinois had the largest shop. In the other towns, men from Connecticut, Virginia, Ohio, Tennessee, Kentucky, and Missouri all played leading roles.[53]

Perhaps because they were supplying furniture to larger areas, the major Blackland shops were larger than the ones in East Texas. They employed three or four hands instead of one or two (the largest shop in Paris reported six hands in 1860) and produced a much larger volume of furniture annually.[54] Many of the workers in these shops apparently worked on a piecework basis, rather than receiving any daily wages. The employer supplied the wood, bench, lathe, and place to work; the employee supplied his own hand tools and was paid so much for each piece of furniture he made. This method was used by John H. Spalding of Waxahachie, whose shop produced $7,500 worth of furniture in 1870.[55] Spalding's ledger for 1873 contains numerous entries concerning payments for piecework:

Henry Manuel: by making two wardrobes price 28.00 each	22.40
Henry Manuel: by one bookcase	5.00
Henry Manuel: by making wardrobe	14.00
Alex Philips: by work	100.00
B. F. Spalding: by making coffin and case	5.00
H. B. Manuel: by two bureaus price 35.00	28.00
H. B. Manuel: by two bureaus price 60.00	48.00
H. B. Manuel: by two washstands 50.00	24.00
B. F. Spalding: by seven stand tables	14.00
B. F. Spalding: by two sofas	19.00[56]

Another Blackland cabinetmaker, Moses A. Mock of Hillsboro, reported to the census taker that he worked "by contract, materials furnished," rather than by wages.[57]

The Blackland cabinetmakers, being farther from a ready supply of pine, relied less on that wood and used a larger variety of native and imported hardwoods than the East Texas craftsmen. Although some pine planking hauled from East Texas sawmills was used, the alluvial hardwood forests of the Red and Trinity rivers and their tributaries provided oak, ash, hickory, pecan, sweet gum, black gum, cottonwood, elm, white maple, magnolia, and black walnut.[58] Clarksville and Paris were particularly close to a rich hardwood supply; the Red River meandered for nearly two hundred miles along the northern edge of Lamar and Red River counties.

When James B. Shanahan opened his cabinet shop in Clarksville in 1844, he advertised that he wished "to purchase 30 or 40,000 feet of black Walnut, Birch, Cherry, and Sycamore lumber," for which he would pay in cabinet ware.[59] Shanahan also imported exotic wood and precut veneer, probably through the Red River port of Jefferson. He announced in the summer of 1848 that he had "lately received a fresh supply of veneer" and was "prepared as heretofore to do any sort of cabinet work, such as book cases, bureaus, wardrobes, tables, bedsteads, etc.... Mahogany, Walnut, Birch and Gum, always on hand for manufacturing purposes."[60] Other Clarksville cabinetmakers advertised periodic arrivals of mahogany and rosewood veneering through the fifties. If it was possible, hardwood lumber was bought in planks at the sawmill and carted to the shop to be dried and seasoned; few cabinetmakers relished the labor of felling trees and sawing planks from them unless it was an absolute necessity.[61]

Probably because of the size of their shops, a few Blackland cabinetmakers were pioneers in the use of steam engines as power sources. A Corsicana shop was using a 2 1/2-horsepower engine to operate woodworking machinery in 1860,[62] and that same year a cabinetmaker at Bright Star, Connecticut-born Watson W. Bell, advertised to "call the attention of the public to his STEAM SHOP," where, "having machinery, he is prepared to do such work as Sash, Door, Blind, and HOUSE FURNITURE cheaper than any other establishment in the country," as well as make wagon hubs on a hub-mortising machine.[63] In the late sixties steam came to Clarksville; a local cabinetmaker entered into a contract with Obadiah Stephens to establish the Stephens and Longe Furniture and Chair Factory, which would produce not only furniture but also "fencing, shingles, sash and blinds, [and] planing lumber."[64] The machinery for this enterprise, which included a 20-horsepower steam engine, was erected a few miles north of Clarksville at a place called Stephens-boro; in 1870 the factory produced two hundred bedsteads and a thousand chairs.[65] At the same time, a second steam engine, a 4-horsepower one, had been set up in a Bright Star shop.[66]

It was in Paris, however, that two Blackland cabinetmakers not only successfully made the transition from craftsmen to manufacturers but also sustained the attempt long enough to be considered successful industrialists. Both Willet Babcock and James W. Rodgers came to Paris in the fifties, and both opened small cabinet shops near the town square. By 1860 both of them had taken partners and prospered to the point that they operated, respectively, the largest and second-largest cabinet shops in Texas, producing, between them, furniture valued at $10,500 in that year. By 1870, both had added horse-powered machinery to their shops.[67] Babcock, who had bought a two-story building in the mid-sixties and opened an opera house on the second floor, installed an eighteen-horsepower steam engine in 1875; he advertised that, "having no rents to pay and running hands who have been with me for years," he was able to sell at low prices and to give wholesale bills prompt attention.[68] In 1880, his Paris factory employed thirty-two hands and produced $25,000 worth of furniture, and he also owned a much smaller factory in Clarksville—perhaps the old Stephens and Longe establishment. Both were evidently closed at Babcock's death in 1881.[69] Rodgers installed a steam engine in his shop in 1879 and moved it down by the railroad tracks, where he also set up a planing mill. He died in 1891, but his company was reorganized as the Rodgers-Wade Furniture Company and continues in business in Paris today, the oldest operating furniture factory in Texas.[70]

Yet another region of the state in which cabinetmaking was an important trade was a relatively small but densely populated area along the lower Brazos and Colorado rivers, including Washington and Austin counties and parts of Fayette and Colorado counties. (Austin County at that time included present-day Waller County.) This country had been the heart of the Anglo-American settlements in Mexican Texas: the capital of Stephen F. Austin's colony was in Austin County; the first capital of the republic was in Washington County. Today it is a fashionable area for weekend homes, restored farmhouses, and antique shopping; of all the cabinetmaking regions in Texas, it is probably the most thoroughly collected. Along with the Hill Country, it boasts a fairly large corpus of furniture that has been attributed to its cabinetmakers; unfortunately, the attributions have not always been well documented or specific.

Settlement began in the lower Brazos-Colorado area in the early 1820's. In the 1840's, and even more so in the 1850's, it became an area of large river plantations, some of them worked by fifty or more slaves, interspersed with small cotton farms. An active planter society, modeled on that of the older Southern states and based on ownership of land and slaves, developed. Economic life centered around small communities like Chappell Hill, Travis, Gay Hill, Independence, Washington, Groce's Landing, and Round Top—crossroads communities with one or two mercantile stores, a blacksmith or wheelwright's shop, a church, and perhaps an academy—as well as the county-seat towns. Many of the artisans and small farmers were Germans, for German immigration into the area began in the 1830's and continued until after the Civil War, resulting in whole communities—Industry, Cat Spring, Frelsburg, Millheim, Shelby, and New Ulm, in particular—that were distinctively Teutonic.[71]

It is unlikely that much furniture was made commercially in the area before the Texas Revolution. The region's first documented cabinet shop was opened at Washington in 1838 by a Baptist minister, Z. N. Morrel; from then until the mid-seventies a steady flow of furniture was turned out from shops in Brenham, Chappell Hill, Gay Hill, Washington, Independence, Cat Spring, New Ulm, Columbus, Round Top, La Grange, Hempstead, and Frelsburg. While a few of the cabinetmakers who made this furniture were immigrants from the old South, the majority of them

PLATE 3. A homemade chairmaker's lathe from Williamson County. The turning head is the top of a brass bedpost filled with lead. (Courtesy of the Winedale Museum, Leslie Hawkins Collection. Photograph by Jim Bones.)

were Germans. Germans especially dominated the trade in the sixties and seventies. The records do not reveal any slave cabinetmakers, even though the area had a large slave population before the Civil War.[72]

The large amount of furniture made in the lower Brazos-Colorado region was a reflection not only of the area's wealth but also of its richness in hardwood timber. The bottoms of both the Brazos and the Colorado were hardwood forests up to six miles wide in some places and were especially abundant in black walnut (*Juglans nigra*), which was much favored by local cabinetmakers because of its durability and the ease with which it could be carved and turned—"like butter," as an elderly Fayette County sawmill man remembered. The ridges between the rivers and their tributaries were covered with eastern red cedar (*Juniperus virginiana*), which was used extensively for wardrobes and chests because its aroma was thought to repel insects. Pine could be obtained from a ninety-thousand-acre "island" of loblolly pine near Bastrop, an isolated section of the East Texas pine forest that extended into western Fayette County.[73]

The quality of many individual pieces of Brazos-Colorado furniture reflects the superior technical training of their makers as well as the desire of their purchasers to be fashionable. Many of the area's German cabinetmakers were men who had served apprenticeships and done journeyman work in Europe; a few held master cabinetmakers' papers. The Umlands of Chappell Hill were representative of this class. Johann and Heinrich Umland, brothers, had owned a large and fashionable cabinet shop in Hamburg, but their business was destroyed in the fire of 1842 and they decided to emigrate. Heinrich arrived in Texas in 1849, purchased land in Austin County, and became a farmer. Johann, who joined him five years later, opened a cabinet shop at Chappell Hill, where several

PLATE 4. Samples of native woods used by Texas cabinetmakers. (A) *Left to right:* shortleaf yellow pine, longleaf yellow pine, longleaf yellow pine, eastern red cedar, cypress, sycamore, sycamore, black gum, white gum, elm. (B) *Left to right:* hackberry, cherry, mulberry, mesquite, magnolia, white oak, ash, black walnut, hickory, pecan. (Photographs by Jim Bones.)

other German cabinetmakers and silversmiths had found a ready market for their products among the local planters. The shop prospered; Johann Umland's furniture was purchased by the wealthiest families of the community, people who might otherwise have imported furniture from Galveston; and he was elected a town alderman.[74] The surviving examples of his furniture not only exhibit a high degree of craftsmanship but also show an awareness of current furniture styles; they include details taken from the Gothic Revival and Renaissance Revival styles then popular in the Northeast and in Europe (see 1.1 and 1.2). Umland was not the only stylish and competent cabinetmaker in the area; a good deal of other furniture from Washington and Austin counties shows the influence of both the revival styles and the Biedermeier style popular in Germany in the forties and is constructed with the carefully framed and beveled panels characteristic of German joinery.

It is also evident from examining furniture with a documented provenance collected in the Brazos-Colorado area that a good many German settlers who were not professional cabinetmakers had the woodworking skills necessary to make fairly complicated pieces of furniture for their own use. One explanation for this may be that German settlers were equipped with these skills by the emphasis placed on joinery and woodworking *(Handwerk)* in Prussian elementary schools, which were compulsory and universal in the early decades of the nineteenth century.[75] The practice of cabinetmaking and turnery was an acceptable middle-class recreation in Germany,[76] and this attitude toward the craft may have encouraged a certain amount of amateur cabinetmaking among Texas Germans. It is a fact that some of the most remarkable pieces of Brazos-Colorado furniture were made by a wheelwright, Christofer Friderich Carl Steinhagen, for pleasure rather than profit (see 1.3, 2.32, 4.1, 5.1, and 6.25). Other examples of documented furniture which cannot be traced to professional cabinetmakers were undoubtedly made by men like Heinrich Umland who, although trained as cabinetmakers in Germany, became farmers in Texas and appear on the census under that occupation.

By the late 1860's, Brenham, Hempstead, and Cat Spring began to replace the smaller communities as cabinetmaking centers, but the rapid extension of railroads into the area in the years following the Civil War quickly snuffed out a developing local furniture industry. A Connecticut Yankee, Leander Mosscross, opened a mechanized furniture factory fitted out with a ten-horsepower steam engine, a lathe, a planer, a mortiser, and two "sawing and bevelling machines" in Hempstead in 1870,[77] but the experiment was a failure, and by the mid-seventies most of the region's cabinetmakers had turned to assembling knocked-down furniture shipped in from Saint Louis and the Midwest. A few, however, continued to produce hand-made furniture for a diminishing clientele until the early years of this century.[78]

The final nineteenth-century cabinetmaking region of Texas, the Hill Country, bore little resemblance to the others. Its terrain was unlike that of any other settled area of the state: geologically the eroded edge of the Edwards Plateau, it was a land of steep, narrow stream valleys interspersed with bare limestone hills, the remnants of the plateau. The streams, fed by springs gushing from the limestone and bordered by giant cypresses, formed tiny, forested, fertile alluvial plains, where settlers could plant a few acres of corn and raise a bale of cotton, and provided tumbling water power for gristmills and sawmills. Between them rose the arid and inhospitable limestone hills, covered with a stunted growth of juniper, mesquite, oaks, prickly pear, and yucca. It was a land of stark juxtaposition: cool, crystal-clear, fern-lined, shaded streams cutting habitable and

tillable valleys into the rim of the desert.[79]

The population was unlike the rest of the state, too, at least in the purity of its strain. In the mid-1840's this region, on the state's western frontier, literally in Comanche country, was colonized by several thousand Germans. Other parts of the state, particularly the lower Brazos-Colorado region, had German settlers, but nowhere else were they as numerous and as little intermingled with Anglo-Americans as in the Hill Country. They were first established there in 1845, when some two hundred colonists brought to Texas by the Society for the Protection of German Immigrants in Texas (*Adelsverein*) founded the city of New Braunfels; by 1850 both New Braunfels and Fredericksburg, sixty miles to the northwest, were flourishing German towns, and German farmsteads had sprung up along the creek valleys between the two and even down the Guadalupe River east of New Braunfels, toward the predominantly Anglo town of Seguin. Three years later the population of Comal County, including New Braunfels, was nearly 60 percent German; Gillespie County, including Fredericksburg, was 85 percent German.[80]

The cabinetmakers of these communities showed a strong tendency to try to reproduce the conditions under which they had worked in Germany. Part of this tendency may have had its origins in an attitude about immigration; as Mack Walker has said, the emigrants of the forties "went to America less to build something new than to regain and conserve something old . . . to till new fields and find new customers, true enough, but ultimately to keep the ways of life they were used to, which the new Europe seemed determined to destroy."[81] Part of it may also have stemmed from the fact that until the seventies they worked in comparative cultural isolation from Anglo-American society; their clients, their employees, and even their tools were largely German.

Possibly because the Hill Country cabinetmakers were making furniture for a community that grew up almost overnight, there were a very large number of them. In 1860, Fredericksburg, with a population of 1,200, reported ten cabinet shops large enough to be listed on the census of manufactures—more shops than any other city in Texas. Each of these shops was operated on a carefully circumscribed scale by one man, using only hand tools and in no case producing more than $1,500 worth of furniture in a year. None of them used even the horse or water power that must have been available to them, although a Mormon community had successfully operated a cabinet shop with a water-powered lathe a few miles from Fredericksburg in the early 1850's. In New Braunfels there were ten cabinetmakers in 1850 and seven in 1860, all producing less than $500 worth of furniture per year, and by 1870 there were five one-man, hand-powered shops, each with an annual production of between $500 and $1,200. There was never a serious attempt to establish a mechanized furniture industry in the Hill Country, as there was in East Texas, the Blackland Prairie, and the lower Brazos-Colorado region, nor did Hill Country cabinetmakers perform the jack-of-all-trades function that rural cabinetmakers did in other parts of the state. No Hill Country cabinetmaker ever described himself as a "mechanic" or set up a steam boiler. They were traditional European village craftsmen, and specialists in their craft.[82]

Virtually all of the older men who made furniture in New Braunfels or Fredericksburg were trained in Europe, and the younger men served abbreviated European-style apprenticeships to the older ones, an almost unknown practice among cabinetmakers in other parts of Texas.[83] The furniture they made showed a strong German influence on design and construction—stronger, even, than is seen in pieces made by German cabinetmakers in the Brazos-Colorado region, where it was tempered by the taste of Anglo-American customers. The bench and chest and the wardrobe (5.11 and 2.15) made by Franz Stautzenberger, who was trained as a craftsman in the household of the Duke of Nassau, and Johann Martin Loeffler's *Brettstuhl* (4.27) might well have been made in Germany rather than in Clear Spring and Fredericksburg. The large number of elegant side chairs made in New Braunfels by Johann Michael Jahn and his fellow craftsmen (4.15–4.24) show a definite Biedermeier influence, as do several New Braunfels sofas and lounges (such as 5.3). As in the Brazos-Colorado region, heavy framed and beveled construction was common in case pieces, rather than the lighter nailed construction used by most Southern cabinetmakers. A few Hill Country cabinetmakers also showed their awareness of fashionable revival styles: the wardrobes made in Fredericksburg by Johann Peter Tatsch (2.28–2.31) are replete with Renaissance Revival pediments and twisted columns; and a bed made by William Arhelger (1.8) exhibits the Elizabethan Revival turned-spindle work characteristic of the furniture popularly dubbed "Jenny Lind" in the United States.

The shops in which the Hill Country cabinetmakers worked were quite small, generally consisting of a room within a residence or a shed in its yard. Their tools were brought from Germany—they favored the distinctive horned German smoothing plane over the

MAP 5. Texas cabinet shops with an annual product exceeding $500 in value, 1850. County lines as in 1850. (Information from the manuscript census returns for Texas, schedule of products of industry, 1850.)

MAP 6. Texas cabinet shops with an annual product exceeding $500 in value, 1860. County lines as in 1860. (Information from the manuscript census returns for Texas, schedule of products of industry, 1860.)

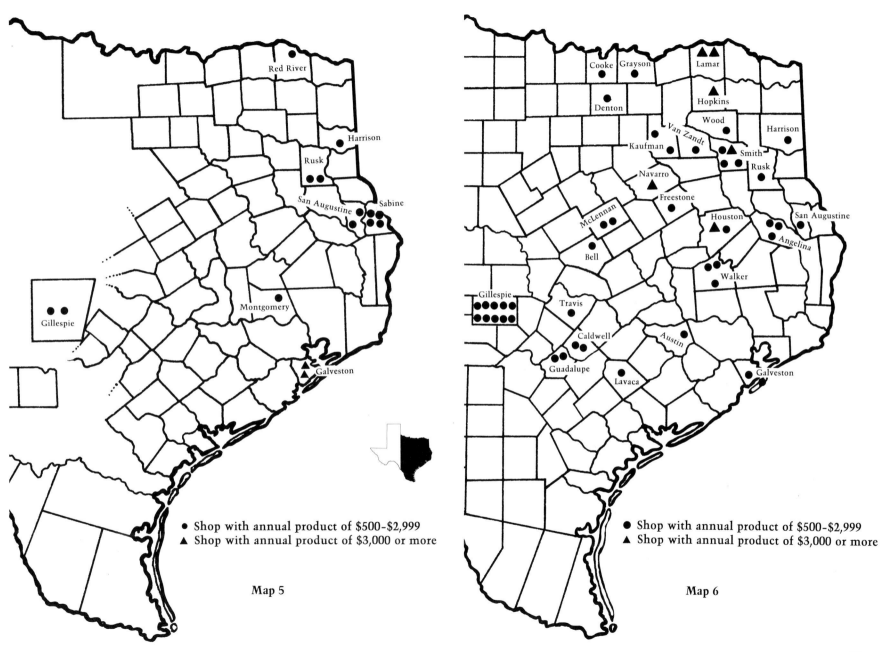

Red River

Harrison

Rusk

San Augustine   Sabine

Montgomery

Gillespie

Galveston

● Shop with annual product of $500–$2,999
▲ Shop with annual product of $3,000 or more

Map 5

Cooke Grayson   Lamar

Denton   Hopkins

Van Zandt   Wood   Harrison

Kaufman   Smith

Navarro   Rusk

Freestone

McLennan   Houston   San Augustine

Bell   Angelina

Walker

Gillespie   Travis

Caldwell   Austin

Guadalupe   Galveston

Lavaca

● Shop with annual product of $500–$2,999
▲ Shop with annual product of $3,000 or more

Map 6

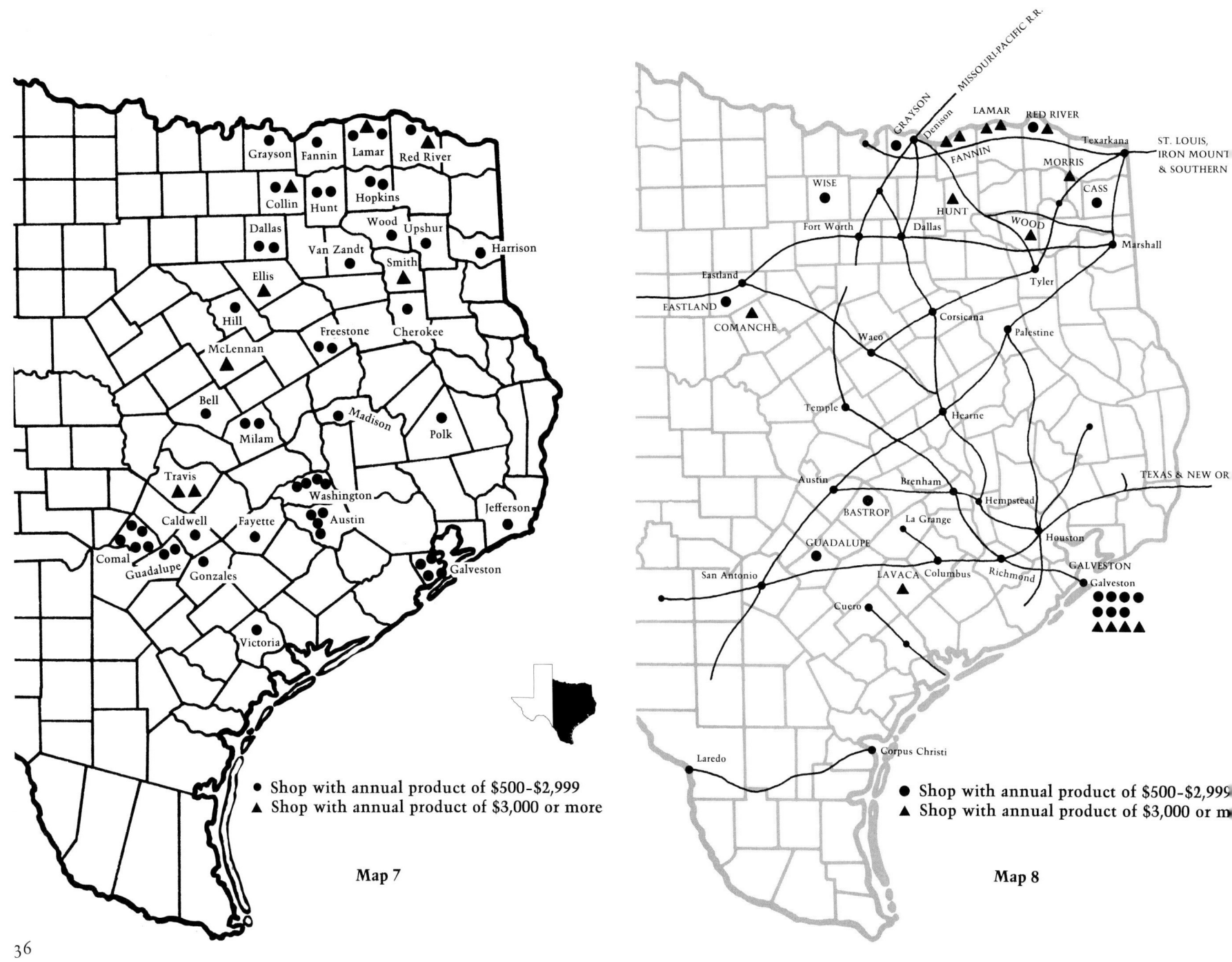

Map 7

Map 8

Shop with annual product of $500-$2,999

Shop with annual product of $3,000 or more

American or English varieties—or were made on the spot. Ferdinand "Sontag" Schulze of Fredericksburg (so called because he was a freethinker and treated Sunday as a normal working day) made his own carpenter's bench, using cypress instead of the usual iron for the dogs, and the large foot-treadle lathe built by Heinrich Scholl of New Braunfels is still preserved by his granddaughter, along with his other tools. For wood, the cabinetmakers relied on the alluvial hardwood forests of the Guadalupe and Pedernales bottoms, rich in cypress and walnut, or upon pine or imported woods obtained at Bastrop lumberyards.[84]

The Hill Country cabinetmakers flourished in the first years of their area's colonization, in the fifties and sixties, but by 1870 the number of shops in the region had declined dramatically. Imported factory-made furniture became available in San Antonio in the 1850's; Johann Jahn brought the first load of New York furniture to New Braunfels by wagon from Indianola in 1866. The railroads brought this furniture infinitely closer in the seventies, and the people of the Hill Country found it cheaper and more fashionable than the products of their local craftsmen. Johann Peter Tatsch's grandchildren remembered that his last years were saddened by the thought that his neighbors preferred glossily finished factory furniture to his own productions.[85]

So, in the long run, the same forces of industrialization that

MAP 7. Texas cabinet shops with an annual product exceeding $500 in value, 1870. County lines as in 1870. (Information from the manuscript census returns for Texas, schedule of products of industry, 1870.)

MAP 8. Texas cabinet shops with an annual product exceeding $500 in value and Texas railroads, 1880. County lines as in 1975. (Information from the manuscript census returns for Texas, schedule of products of industry, 1880, and A. B. Langermann, comp., *The Railroad System of Texas on September 1, 1881*.)

had helped push the Hill Country cabinetmakers out of Germany caught up with them in Texas, and, in spite of their isolation and the unique quality of their work, they met the same fate as cabinetmakers in the rest of the state. However, they left behind them the largest body of well-documented furniture in Texas. The Hill Country, like the Brazos-Colorado area, has been popular with collectors, but much of its most remarkable furniture still remains with the grandchildren and great-grandchildren of its makers and is used and cherished by them. This is, perhaps, the final characteristic that distinguishes the Hill Country from the other cabinetmaking regions: the fact that its isolation and the stability of its population have preserved so much of its furniture.

The story of Texas cabinetmaking, then, is the story of a double failure: the failure of a craft to sustain itself and the failure of an industry to grow up to replace it. As the iron bands of the railroad tied Texas to the rest of the Union, it became her destiny to export cattle, cotton, and oil rather than furniture. But the craft was not snuffed out quickly; old men in remote places continued to practice it well into the twentieth century, for their own pleasure or that of their neighbors. It is a shame that the *Index of American Design* surveyors, working in Texas in the 1940's, did not interview some of these men and record their techniques, rather than simply draw the objects they made; a few of the thousand men who made furniture in Texas in the middle years of the last century must have still been living then.

Today we have only their furniture and some of the written records they left behind them, by accident, in courthouses and census books. The records speak very softly and in fragments, but each piece of furniture shouts a clear, strong truth about the man who made it and the people who used it; a small truth, perhaps, but one that fills an empty place in the mosaic of our past.

S. OWELL, *Secretary.*
Bonham, Feb. 14th, 1855.　　(no.17..2ts)

SHANAHAN & BRIM'S

CHAIR AND CABINET SHOP.

THE UNDERSIGNED would announce to their friends and the public generally, that they are carrying on the Chair and Cabinet business on Main street, and having received a large supply of materials for their business including a large lot of Mahogany Veneering, are prepared to execute orders for the best class of furniture, such as

| BUREAUS, | TABLES, |
| LOUNGES, | SOFAS, |
| BEDSTEADS, Etc. |

All kinds of furniture manufactured in any other Cabinet shop in this country, will be manufactured in this shop. Those in the habit of going below to procure furniture, can be supplied with as good in this shop, as they can procure below.

They will manufacture all kinds of CHAIRS, and other articles in that line of business.

Having several hands in the establishment, orders for COFFINS, either in the neighborhood or from a distance, will be filled with dispatch.

☞ All work warranted.

J. B. SHANAHAN,
T. J. BRIM.

Clarksville, March 3d, 1855.　　(n17-12-tf

Furniture of the Frontier: The Surviving Evidence

The processes of natural selection by which some pieces of furniture survive their makers and original users are of great importance to anyone trying to draw conclusions from that furniture today. The richest source for the examples of furniture pictured in this chapter was the descendants of cabinetmakers who had kept and treasured pieces made by a grandfather or a great-grandfather, generally for his own or his family's use. These pieces were probably made with more care than those that were part of the craftsman's regular commercial output and are atypical in that sense, but they remain the best material source for our knowledge about Texas furniture. Most of the work shown here by William Arhelger, Franz Stautzenberger, Christofer Friderich Carl Steinhagen, Heinrich Scholl, Johann Peter Tatsch, Johann Michael Jahn, and Johann Martin Loeffler falls into this category. Visits with these men's descendants were always pleasurable occasions, confirming their judgment that a craftsman worthy of notice had been part of their family and our own hopes that some of his work and even, on several occasions, some of his tools and papers had survived. The high point in this line of search was the discovery of all of Heinrich Scholl's tools, including his nine-foot-long horse-powered lathe, still installed in a shop behind the house he lived in a century ago in New Braunfels and still being used by his grandson.

In some cases, Texas furniture was preserved by institutions with their origins in the nineteenth century, rather than by families. Several fine cabinets made by local craftsmen for county courthouses are still being used by county clerks, and at least one (8.4) has found its way into a private collection. An Austin-made wardrobe (2.16) in the Governor's Mansion has evidently been there since the beginning of the Civil War, and a grained secretary (7.16) that held the library of a frontier schoolteacher was preserved for years in the basement of rural Clifton College, to which the teacher left his books. However, furniture preserved in this way tends to be of a specialized nature and, again, probably atypical. The Texas Centennial of 1936 generated a great interest in "frontier relics," and a few good examples of locally made everyday furniture found their way into museums and county historical collections, where they found some shelter from the ravages of annual housecleaning and postwar family moves. A number of these examples are shown in this chapter.

Texans are a notoriously mobile people. The great population movement from the country to the city during the last twenty years and the accompanying necessities of apartment and housing-development living have undoubtedly destroyed much common locally made furniture. However, there are still a few cultural pockets in the state, especially in the Hill Country and the lower Brazos-Colorado region and to a lesser extent in parts of East Texas, where people have lived in the same house, or at least in the same community, for four or five generations. Some of the best examples of locally made, though frequently anonymous, furniture have come from these areas. The two fine beds made by Johann Umland (1.1 and 1.2) belonged to the great-grandchildren of two of Umland's customers, and one of them is still being used in Chappell Hill, the town in which Umland worked.

Furniture like this which can be traced to both a maker and an original purchaser is extremely important to the social historian as well as the decorative-arts specialist. During the past fifteen years several large collections of Texas furniture have been formed by private collectors who, with the aid of dealers, have drawn heavily upon furniture from these cultural pockets. Much of this furniture is anonymous but has a long tradition of use in a particular family or community and thus is still a valuable social document. Its usefulness as such is always lessened by an unclear provenance and by attempts at restoration which frequently and unfortunately include the removal of original paint. A good deal of furniture from private collections is represented in this chapter; and, in spite of its shortcomings as a body of historical evidence, it probably gives a clear picture of the ordinary furniture of the nineteenth-century Texan.

However, there is always a gap between the reality of the past and its surviving material evidence, and we hope that readers will examine these photographs with the thought in mind that they show only what remains, not what was.

1. Beds, Cribs, and Cradles

Beds of every variety were made and used in Texas, ranging from the primitive "Georgia horse," an arrangement of poles built into the side of a log cabin, to elegant four-posters with testers. The fashion for high-post beds, essentially an eighteenth-century furniture form, prevailed in the South long after they became passé in the North, and high-post beds were made in Texas until well into the 1870's. In the coastal areas they provided a convenient framework from which to hang mosquito netting. However, Texas cabinetmakers also produced beds in the fashionable styles of the mid-nineteenth century. The spindle turnings described by furniture dealers as "Elizabethan" were a favored form of decoration, and the low and graceful "Grecian" or "French" bed was also popular.

The word *bed* was reserved by nineteenth-century Texans for bedding: mattresses, feather beds, bolsters, and sheets; the piece of furniture was a *bedstead.* Bedding, especially feather beds, was quite valuable; while locally made bedsteads usually sold for between eight and fifteen dollars in the fifties and sixties, feather beds were valued at twenty-five or thirty dollars. The basic piece of bedding was the shuck mattress, a bag of ticking filled with shredded corn shucks and laid on the criss-crossed ropes that held the bedsteads together, or on slats. Over this went the feather bed and then the sheets and counterpane. Feather beds were often quite large: a Fayette County inventory taken in 1843 lists four feather beds weighing, respectively, forty, fifty-three, forty-nine, and thirty-two pounds. Bedsprings and spring mattresses do not seem to have come into general use until after the Civil War, although a patent for wire bedsprings was taken out by William Merriweather, a New Braunfels miller, in 1854, and bedsprings were manufactured in the North in the late fifties.[1]

Beds were frequently unmade and the bedding aired during the day; some household manuals recommended that this be done every day. For daytime reclining, a piece of furniture called a "lounge" or "day bed" was used; these are treated in section 5.

OBJECT: Bed

MAKER: Johann Umland

DATE: 1861

MATERIALS: Primary, walnut; secondary, pine

MEASUREMENTS: H. 93 1/4", W. 61 1/2", L. 84"

HISTORY: Made in Chappell Hill by Johann Umland for
Terrell J. Jackson in 1861 and descended in his family
to the present owner

OWNER: Anonymous loan to Winedale Museum, Round Top

PHOTOGRAPHER: Harvey Patteson

Among the surviving high-post beds made in Texas, this one by
Johann Umland, who worked in Washington County from 1854
until 1880, is undoubtedly the most impressive. Its general outline,
the massive plain posts, and the bold molded cornice of the tester
reflect the late neoclassical Restauration style. Crowning the foot
and head are richly carved crests of Gothic quatrefoils flanked by
bold anthemion ornamentation. The latter motif is repeated in the
side rails, while leafy rococo scrolls and diapered reserves ornament
the panels of the headboard. This overlay of ornament of various
styles is typical of the later phases of the Biedermeier style in Germany. Fine moldings are utilized on the feet, the rails, and the tops
of the posts. While the rococo decorations of the headboard and the
Grecian ornaments of the side rails are nailed on, the carved crests
are secured with pegs. The panels framed into the headboard are
characteristically beveled on the backside.

In sophistication of design and detail this bed represents a
height not generally achieved by Texas craftsmen. According to
family tradition, it is one of three made by Umland in 1861, for
Terrell Jackson, a Washington County planter.

Detail—headboard

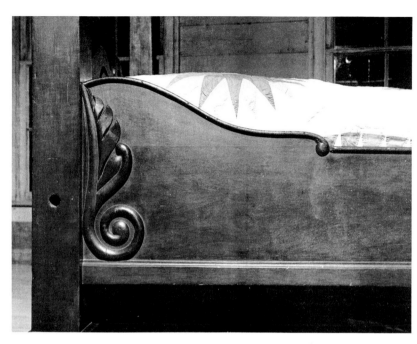

Detail—side rail

OBJECT: Bed

MAKER: Johann Umland

DATE: 1859

MATERIAL: Walnut

MEASUREMENTS: H. 86 3/4", W. 60 1/4", L. 83 3/4"

HISTORY: Made by Johann Umland for James Henry Thompson and descended in his family to the present owner, his great-grandson

OWNERS: Mr. and Mrs. Nath Winfield, Chappell Hill

PHOTOGRAPHER: Jim Bones

This second example of Umland's work shows the same fine craftsmanship and attention to detail found on 1.1, made two years later. The headboard is ornamented with a section of bobbin-turned spindle, indicating Umland's familiarity with the Elizabethan Revival style (see 1.8). The original owner was a planter who came to Chappell Hill from Lowndes County, Mississippi, in 1859 and commissioned Umland to make his house furniture upon arrival.

Detail—headboard

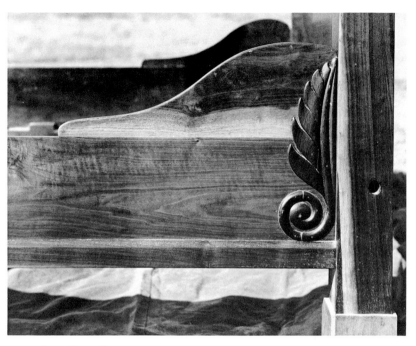

Detail—side rail

OBJECT: Bed

MAKER: Christofer Friderich Carl Steinhagen

DATE: 1850

MATERIAL: Pine

MEASUREMENTS: H. 78 1/2″, W. 64 1/4″, L. 84″

HISTORY: Made by C. F. C. Steinhagen of Anderson for his family and descended through his daughter, Etha Steinhagen Brown, and her descendants to the present owner

OWNER: Mrs. Mike Kelley, Pasadena

PHOTOGRAPHER: Harvey Patteson

The very distinctive carving of this four-post bed marks it as the work of Christofer Friderich Carl Steinhagen. The leaf-carved posts are remarkably similar to the pilasters of a signed wardrobe (2.32), and the leaf carving on the foot and head boards appears in some variation on nearly every one of his pieces. Large acorn finials repeat the central drop of Steinhagen's drum table now at Winedale (6.25). Slightly beveled panels are set into the headboard.

OBJECT: Bed

MAKER: Heinrich Jansen

DATE: 1860

MATERIAL: Walnut

MEASUREMENTS: H. 84", W. 58 1/2", L. 81"

HISTORY: The gift of the maker's grandson and his wife,
Mr. and Mrs. Philip Gupton, to Varner-Hogg State Park

OWNER: Varner-Hogg State Park, West Columbia

PHOTOGRAPHER: Jim Bones

The most interesting feature of this routine four-post bed is its
Renaissance Revival headboard with decorative cutout. In design
it is nearly the negative of the scrolled Grecian cresting on another
Jansen example (1.5). The bobbin turnings at the top of the posts
are recent additions, as are the hexagonal wooden bed bolt covers.

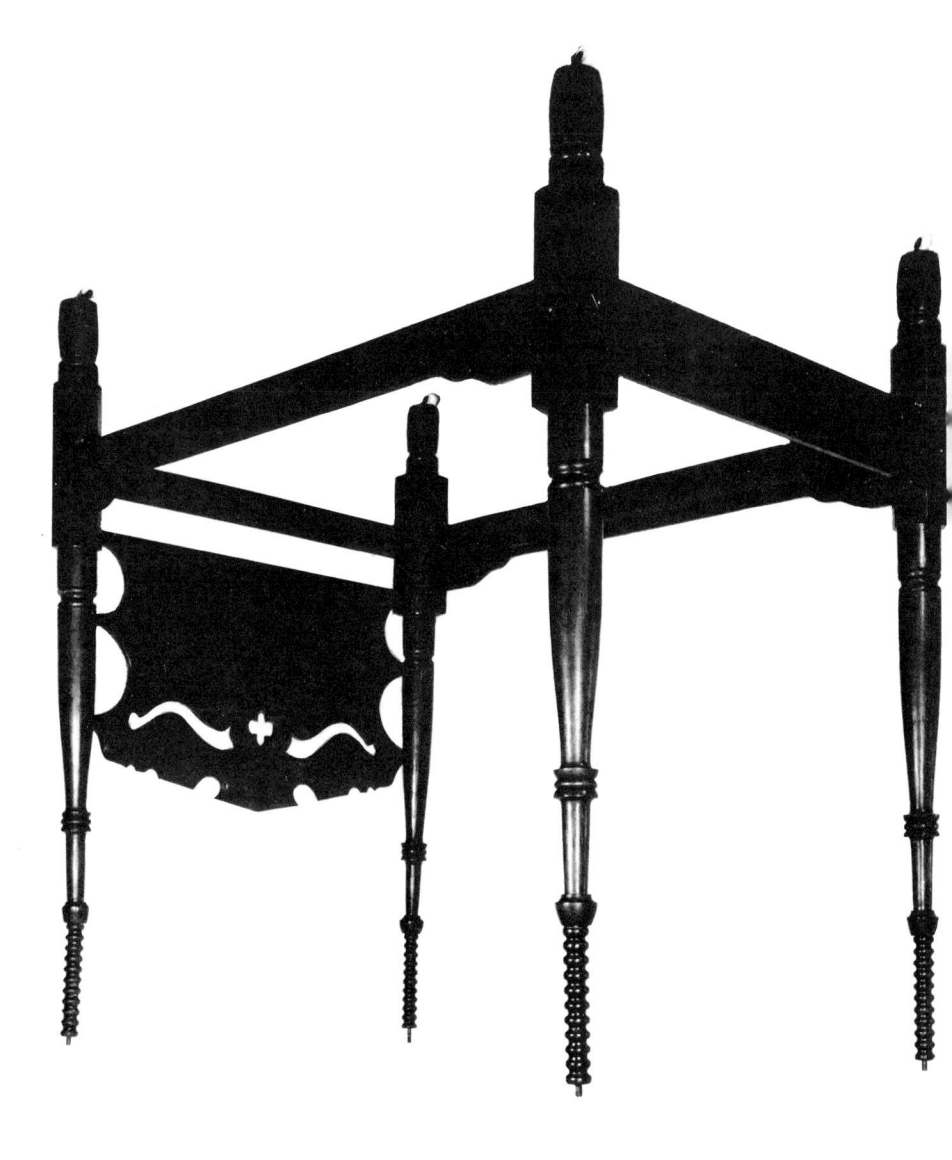

OBJECT: Bed

MAKER: Heinrich Jansen

DATE: 1870

MATERIAL: Cedar

MEASUREMENTS: H. 56″, W. 50 1/4″, L. 82″

HISTORY: Made at West Columbia and descended in the family of
the maker to the present owner, his great-granddaughter

OWNER: Mrs. C. C. Hart, West Columbia

PHOTOGRAPHER: Jim Bones

This attractive bed mixes early panel-and-frame construction with
nineteenth-century classical taste. The rounded corners of the
footboard manifest awareness of Rococo Revival design. Beveled
panels are let into the head and foot boards. The head posts were
originally squared off at the tops. The most remarkable feature
about this bed is its bold scrolled Grecian crest. Related in design
to the example at Varner-Hogg State Park (1.4), the crest combines
a central palmette and rosettes with flanking acroterialike scrolls
much in the manner of contemporary Texas-German wardrobes.
The bed is made entirely out of cedar.

Detail—headboard

OBJECT: Bed

MAKER: Unknown

DATE: 1850

MATERIAL: Pine

MEASUREMENTS: H. 59″, W. 58″, L. 80″

HISTORY: Collected by the owners in New Braunfels

OWNERS: Mr. and Mrs. Andrew Z. Thompson, San Antonio

PHOTOGRAPHER: Harvey Patteson

While a cursory examination would suggest that this bed is rather ordinary Renaissance Revival in style, a closer look reveals an extremely imaginative vigorous outline on the headboard which, combined with the scalloped footboard and boldly beveled panels framed into the headboard, suggests a Texas-German maker. It is true that the applied ornament does follow Renaissance Revival ideas, but even here the design is not typical. The bed is made of pine, and the care with which the craftsman has utilized the grain within the panels suggests that it probably was never intended to be painted.

OBJECT: Bed

MAKER: Johann Peter Tatsch

DATE: 1860–1870

MATERIALS: Cherry and walnut

MEASUREMENTS: H. 48", W. 50 1/2", L. 82"

HISTORY: Made in Fredericksburg and descended to the present owner through her mother, Sophie Tatsch Klingelhoefer, the maker's daughter

OWNER: Mrs. Lyne Lewis Harper, Fredericksburg

PHOTOGRAPHER: Harvey Patteson

Johann Peter Tatsch was trained in Germany as a turner, and it is not surprising that this small bed, made for himself, relies primarily on turned ornament. The bobbins along the crest reflect Elizabethan Revival taste. Elongate vases flanked by multiple rings in the posts are not unlike the treatment of the colonnettes on his family wardrobe (2.28). Here the posts are made of cherry, the remainder of walnut. The top third of each post is removable; and, according to family legend, Tatsch intended to add long sections to make high posts. The side rails are replacements.

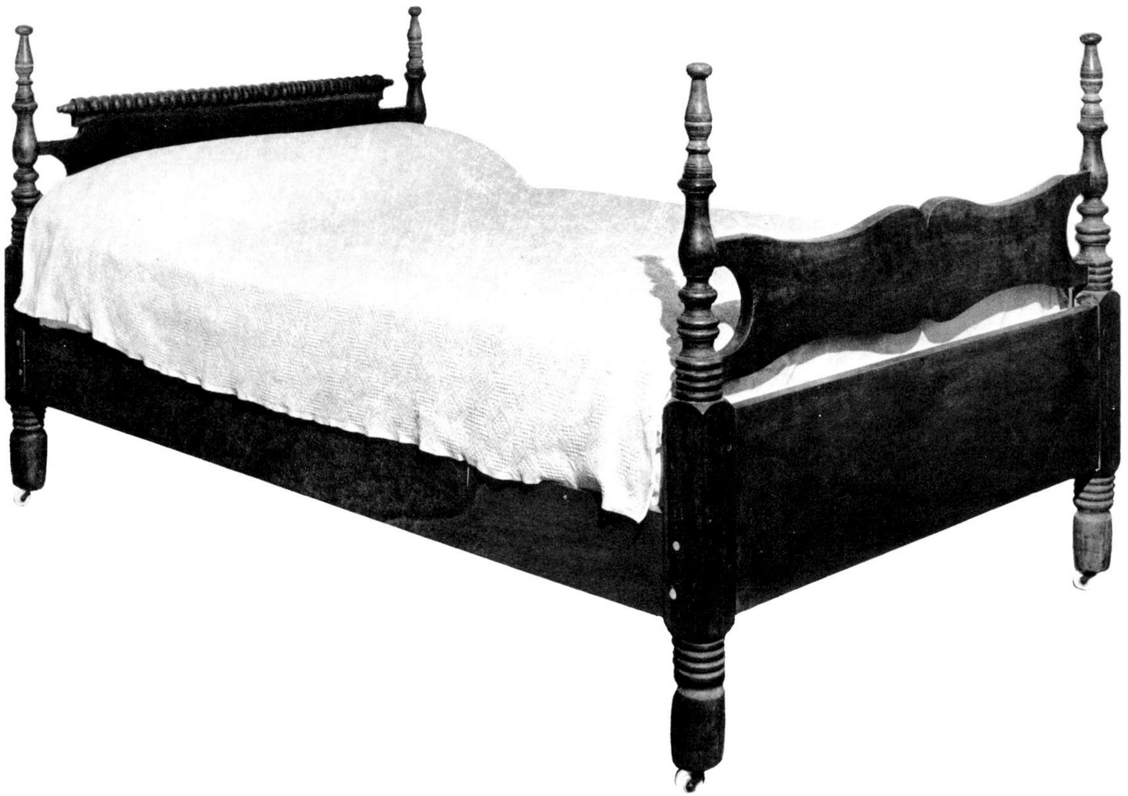

OBJECT: **Bed**

MAKER: William Arhelger

DATE: 1865

MATERIALS: Primary, bois d'arc and walnut; secondary, pine

MEASUREMENTS: H. 48 13/16″, W. 49 9/16″, L. 76 3/4″

HISTORY: Made in Fredericksburg and descended in the maker's family to his grandson, the present owner

OWNER: Mr. Crockett Riley, Fredericksburg

PHOTOGRAPHER: Harvey Patteson

Spool-turned beds of the Elizabethan Revival were occasionally dubbed "Jenny Lind," being in fashion during the height of her popularity in America. This Texas-German example was made by Fredericksburg wheelwright William Arhelger for his own family. He curiously has mixed walnut, used for the spindles and finials, with lighter bois d'arc for the rest of the members. Traces of dark paint, either black or green, over the bois d'arc suggest that this bed originally had a rather different appearance. It is held together with wooden pegs rather than bed bolts.

OBJECT: Bed
MAKER: Unknown
DATE: 1870
MATERIAL: Pine
MEASUREMENTS: H. 45 3/4″, W. 52 1/2″, L. 81″
HISTORY: Collected by the owner in Shelby
OWNER: Mrs. Wendell Steward, Houston
PHOTOGRAPHER: Ewing Waterhouse

This simple bed with spindles is made with interesting details. The head and foot boards taper both in height and in thickness in steps toward the posts. The side rails and posts are marked with corresponding Roman numerals to assure proper assemblage. The turned spindles of this bed stylistically reflect the Elizabethan Revival.

OBJECT: Bed
MAKER: Unknown
DATE: 1860
MATERIAL: Pine
MEASUREMENTS: H. 26″, W. 51 1/8″, L. 74 1/2″
HISTORY: Collected by the owner in Fayette County
OWNER: Mrs. George Hill, Fredericksburg
PHOTOGRAPHER: Harvey Patteson

Utilization of cedar pegs rather than bed bolts and a Fayette County history suggest that this low post bed is a Texas-German example. The posts are attractively turned, and the foot and head boards are naïvely ornamented in vaguely Renaissance style.

OBJECT: Bed

MAKER: Henry Kuenemann

DATE: 1870

MATERIAL: Pine

MEASUREMENTS: H. 35 7/8″, W. 37 5/16″, L. 79 1/8″

HISTORY: Made for a family in the Palo Alto community, Gillespie County

OWNER: Mrs. George Hill, Fredericksburg

PHOTOGRAPHER: Harvey Patteson

This attractive little bed is typically Germanic in its square posts with shaped tops. A further German touch is the spritely scrolled profile of the head and foot boards. The bed is held together with iron bed bolts. The side rails appear to be replacements.

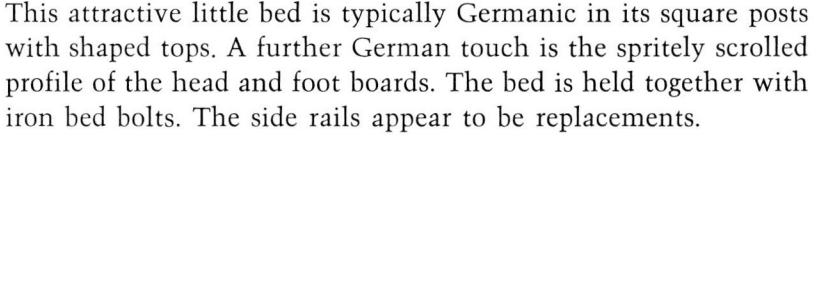

OBJECT: Bed

MAKER: Jacob Brodbeck

DATE: 1860

MATERIAL: Pine

MEASUREMENTS: H. 36 1/2″, W. 32 7/8″, L. 77 1/2″

HISTORY: Made by Jacob Brodbeck of Luckenbach for his son and purchased from him by the present owner; illustrated in the "Index of American Design, Data Report Sheets, Texas" (Tex-Fu-29), University of Texas at Austin Winedale Museum, Round Top; *Antiques* 53 (1948):450; Ralph and Terry Kovel, *American Country Furniture 1780–1875*, p. 11

OWNER: Miss Jean Pinckney, Austin

PHOTOGRAPHER: Harvey Patteson

The scrolled crests of the head and foot boards almost make this little bed look winged. The maker here has attractively turned the posts and spindles and, in an extra touch, molded the arched segment of the headboard.

OBJECT: **Bed**

MAKER: Fritz Kuehn

DATE: 1890

MATERIAL: Walnut

MEASUREMENTS: H. 42″, W. 39 1/2″, L. 73 1/2″

HISTORY: Made by Fritz Kuehn, an Austin County farmer and carpenter who lived near Bleiblerville, for his family; descended in his family to the present owner

OWNER: Mr. Newton Peschel, New Ulm

PHOTOGRAPHER: Harvey Patteson

Although the turned spindles here suggest an awareness of Elizabethan Revival taste, the square posts and curved lines of the foot and head boards place this example firmly in the traditional Germanic mode. Molding around the bottom edge of the rails is an attractive feature. The bed is held together with bed bolts. This is a good example of rural furniture made by an amateur for his own household.

OBJECT: Bed
MAKER: Unknown
DATE: 1860–1880
MATERIAL: Pine
MEASUREMENTS: H. 35 7/8″, W. 31 1/4″, L. 77 7/8″
HISTORY: Purchased by the owners in San Antonio
OWNERS: Mr. and Mrs. Marshall Steves, San Antonio
PHOTOGRAPHER: Harvey Patteson

Turned spindles in the Elizabethan taste are here combined with a typically Germanic scalloped crest. The posts are attractively shaped at the top, lightening them visually, and below is the faint suggestion of a Biedermeier curve to the legs. The rails, pegged into the foot and head boards, are replacements.

OBJECT: Bed

MAKER: Attributed to Friedrich Wilhelm Tietze

DATE: 1860

MATERIAL: Pine

MEASUREMENTS: H. 23 1/4″, W. 32 1/2″, L. 71 3/4″

HISTORY: Purchased by the owners from Mr. Ernest Tietze of
New Braunfels; possibly made by Friedrich Wilhelm Tietze,
who built his home in New Braunfels in 1854

OWNERS: Mr. and Mrs. W. H. Dillen, New Braunfels

PHOTOGRAPHER: Babette Fraser Warren

Typically Germanic square posts and shaped head and foot boards
are utilized here on this humble low-post bed. It is pegged together.
A strip screwed into the side rails supports the mattress.

OBJECT: Bed
MAKER: Unknown
DATE: 1850
MATERIAL: Walnut
MEASUREMENTS: H. 41 3/8", W. 51 1/4", L. 81 1/2"
HISTORY: Collected by the owner in New Braunfels
OWNER: Mr. Ted James, San Antonio
PHOTOGRAPHER: Harvey Patteson

During the First Empire a new type of bed was introduced into Europe. Based on antique prototypes, it was characterized by scrolled ends of equal height and was designed to be placed with one side against a wall. This sort of bed, which first became fashionable in America during the second decade of the nineteenth century, was known as a "Grecian" or "French" bedstead, the nomenclature alluding to the design origins. These beds were evidently popular for some time in Texas. William Chrysler, the Lavaca (now Port Lavaca) furniture dealer, listed "American bedsteads, French bedsteads, and cottage bedsteads" in an 1856 advertisement for furniture that he had imported from New York.[2] An 1861 inventory of the governor's house in Austin lists "1 french bed stead (cherry)" in the northwest room of the second floor, and in 1871 Isaac Crouch of McKinney was advertising that his stock included "French and Zouave Bedsteads of the latest styles."[3] The presence of an example of German origin in the Sophienberg Memorial Museum at New Braunfels suggests that some of this type may have been brought from Germany to Texas. Another example, today altered, has descended in the family of the New Braunfels cabinetmaker Heinrich Scholl and was made by him. The beautiful bed here was also made in New Braunfels. Handsome, deeply beveled panels are framed into the foot and head boards, while the scalloped skirt adds an unusual and attractive detail.

OBJECT: Bed

MAKER: Unknown

DATE: 1850

MATERIAL: Walnut

MEASUREMENTS: H. 40 5/8″, W. 50 3/4″, L. 79 11/16″

HISTORY: Formerly in the collection of Mr. and Mrs. W. H. Dillen, New Braunfels

OWNER: New Braunfels Conservation Society, New Braunfels

PHOTOGRAPHER: Harvey Patteson

This example is very similar to 1.16 but appears to be taller by virtue of its light side rail and long legs. The same sort of beveled panel is framed into the foot and head boards, but here on the reverse it assumes a slightly concave contour. In both beds the mattress is supported by slats.

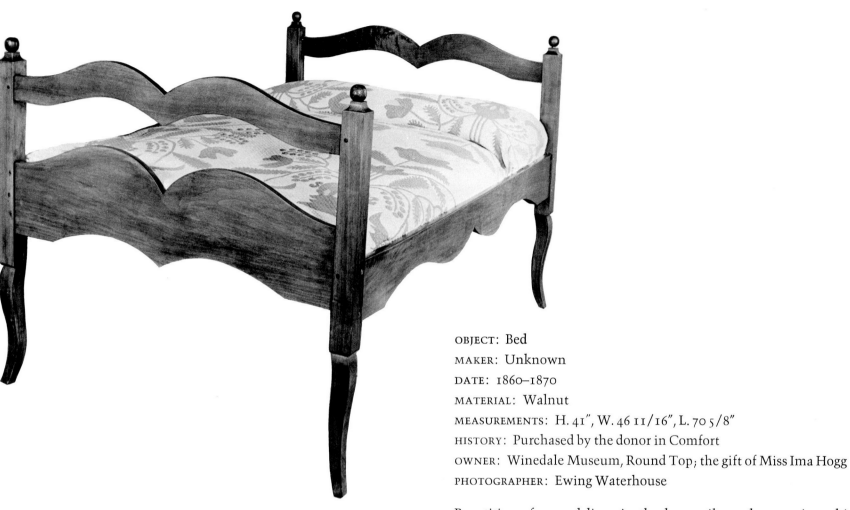

OBJECT: Bed

MAKER: Unknown

DATE: 1860–1870

MATERIAL: Walnut

MEASUREMENTS: H. 41″, W. 46 11/16″, L. 70 5/8″

HISTORY: Purchased by the donor in Comfort

OWNER: Winedale Museum, Round Top; the gift of Miss Ima Hogg

PHOTOGRAPHER: Ewing Waterhouse

Repetition of curved lines in the legs, rails, and stays gives this beautiful little bed an unusual degree of compositional unity. The square posts tapering to knobs are in the Germanic vernacular tradition, while the clean surfaces and curved legs reflect the Biedermeier taste. Finely figured walnut has been utilized. Mortise-and-tenon construction is employed, and wooden pegs rather than bed bolts hold the various members together. The little turned balls atop the posts are removable.

OBJECT: Bed
MAKER: Unknown
DATE: 1870
MATERIAL: Pine
MEASUREMENTS: H. 30 3/4″, W. 45 1/4″, L. 80 1/4″
HISTORY: Purchased by the owners in Fayette County
OWNERS: Mr. and Mrs. Robin Elverson, Houston
PHOTOGRAPHER: Ewing Waterhouse

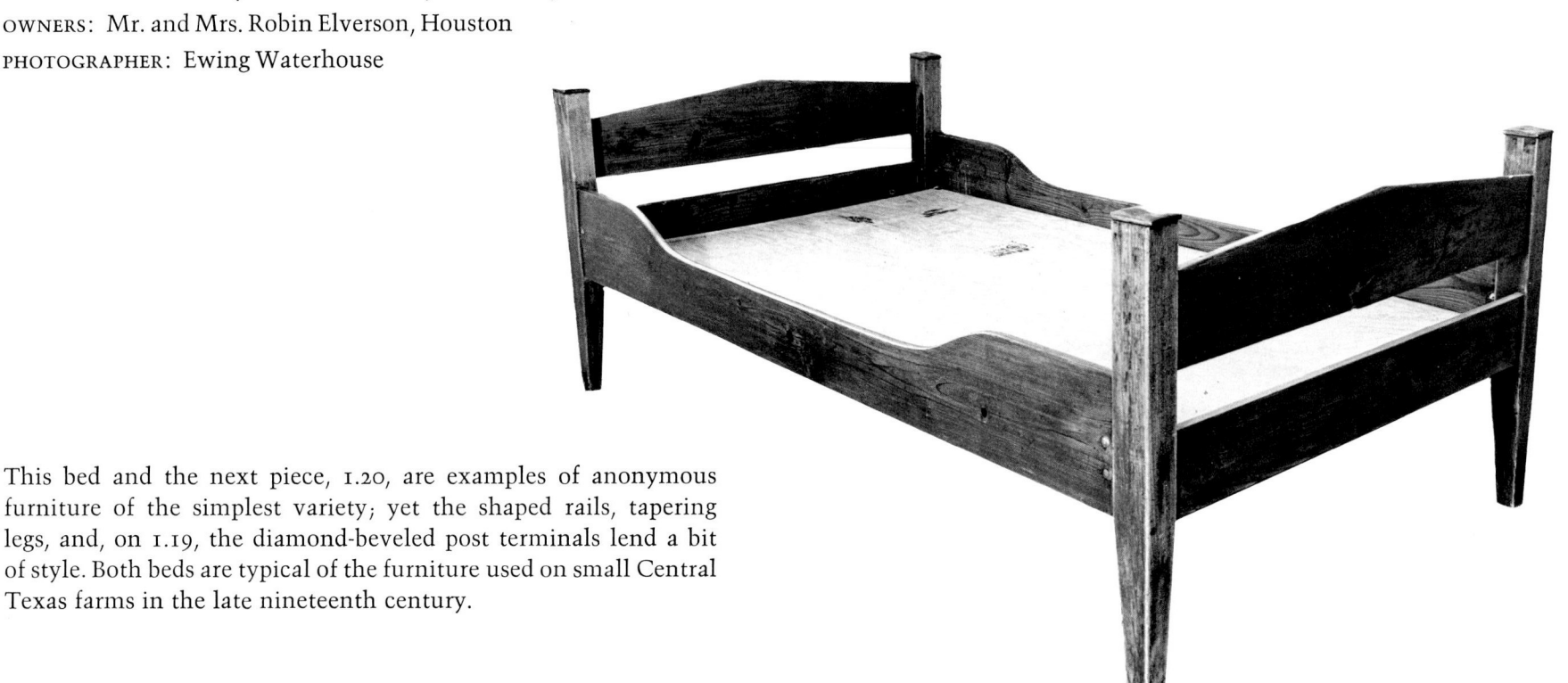

This bed and the next piece, 1.20, are examples of anonymous furniture of the simplest variety; yet the shaped rails, tapering legs, and, on 1.19, the diamond-beveled post terminals lend a bit of style. Both beds are typical of the furniture used on small Central Texas farms in the late nineteenth century.

OBJECT: Bed
MAKER: Unknown
DATE: 1870
MATERIAL: Pine
MEASUREMENTS: H. 40 5/8", W. 49 7/8", L. 78 1/4"
HISTORY: Purchased by the owners in Fayette County
OWNERS: Mr. and Mrs. Robin Elverson, Houston
PHOTOGRAPHER: Ewing Waterhouse

Winged head and foot boards and square posts give a most Germanic flavor to this example. The sharp tapering of the legs is both unusual and attractive.

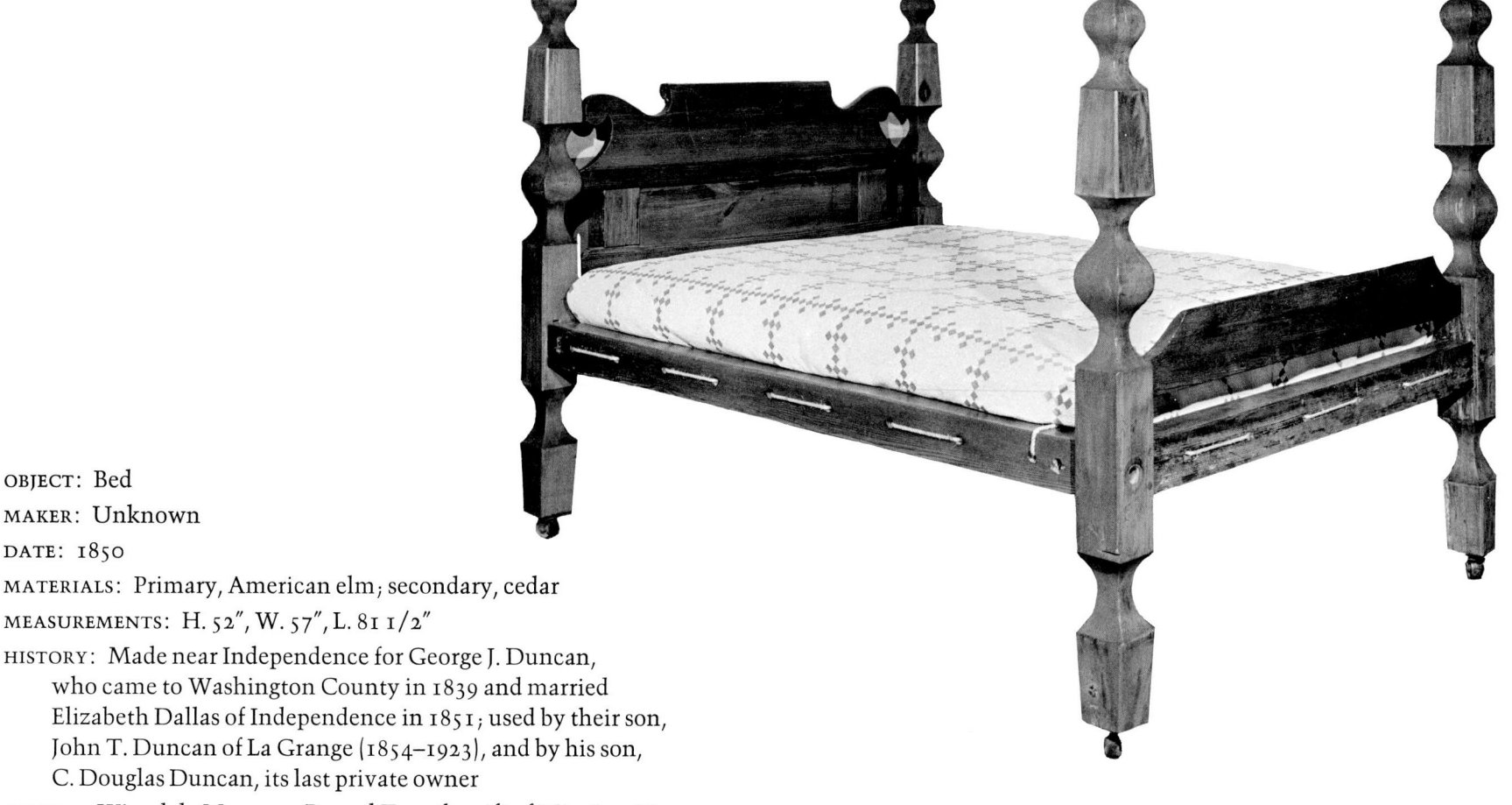

OBJECT: Bed

MAKER: Unknown

DATE: 1850

MATERIALS: Primary, American elm; secondary, cedar

MEASUREMENTS: H. 52″, W. 57″, L. 81 1/2″

HISTORY: Made near Independence for George J. Duncan,
who came to Washington County in 1839 and married
Elizabeth Dallas of Independence in 1851; used by their son,
John T. Duncan of La Grange (1854–1923), and by his son,
C. Douglas Duncan, its last private owner

OWNER: Winedale Museum, Round Top; the gift of Miss Ima Hogg

PHOTOGRAPHER: Harvey Patteson

The flat surfaces on the massive posts of this bed suggest that the
maker did not possess a lathe yet desired to approximate the variety of shape found in turned ornament. An unusual feature is the
presence of rope to support the mattress rather than the more
typical slats. A beveled panel of cedar is framed into the headboard.

OBJECT: Crib

MAKER: Unknown

DATE: 1870

MATERIAL: Walnut

MEASUREMENTS: H. 26 15/16", W. 20 7/8", L. 38 3/8"

HISTORY: Purchased by the owner in New Braunfels

OWNER: Mr. Ted James, San Antonio

PHOTOGRAPHER: Harvey Patteson

The scalloped foot and head boards combined with square, finial-topped posts are in the German vernacular tradition, while the introduction of spindles and tapered legs lends a nineteenth-century note. The crib is made of nicely figured walnut and is pegged together; the bedding was supported by slats.

OBJECT: Crib

MAKER: William Arhelger

DATE: 1870

MATERIALS: Primary, walnut; secondary, oak

MEASUREMENTS: H. 33 3/4", W. 30", L. 46 7/8"

HISTORY: Made in Fredericksburg and descended in the maker's family to his grandson, the present owner

OWNER: Mr. Crockett Riley; on loan to the Pioneer Museum, Fredericksburg

PHOTOGRAPHER: Harvey Patteson

Distinctive reverse-curved legs break the flowing, classical, klismos-inspired line on this unusual child's bed. In this very personal interpretation, the maker, William Arhelger, has mortised flat vase-shaped banisters (rather than turned spindles) into the rails and incorporated a handlelike treatment at the upper extremity of either end. Molding at the upper edge of the rails and applied buttons at the swirl of the stiles are attractive details. This example, along with two tables (6.28 and 6.37) and a bed (1.8), all made by Arhelger, has descended in his family.

1.23

1.24

OBJECT: Cradle

MAKER: Unknown

DATE: Unknown

MATERIAL: Walnut

MEASUREMENTS: H. 23 3/4", W. 20 1/4", L. 39 1/4"

HISTORY: The cradle has a history of ownership in Gonzales, and there is little reason to suspect that it was not made there.

OWNER: Mrs. J. B. Wells, Gonzales

PHOTOGRAPHER: Harvey Patteson

In general form this example relates to a more elaborate crib made in New Braunfels (1.22). It is pegged together except for the rockers, which are secured by screws. The present plywood bottom replaces slats.

1.25

OBJECT: Cradle

MAKER: Unknown

DATE: 1870

MATERIAL: Pine

MEASUREMENTS: H. 27 11/16", W. 21 1/8", L. 39 1/16"

HISTORY: Descended in the family of Charles Henry Nimitz, who settled in Fredericksburg in 1846

OWNER: Pioneer Museum, Fredericksburg

PHOTOGRAPHER: Harvey Patteson

The form of joined cradle found in seventeenth-century England, Holland, and Germany has been preserved almost intact in this late-nineteenth-century Fredericksburg example. Similar cradles were made in Pennsylvania by German settlers during the eighteenth century, and apparently the type survived as a vernacular expression in Germany well into the nineteenth century. The introduction of spindles, replacing framed panels, is the only concession to Victorian taste. The raked square posts with knob finials, scalloped head and foot boards, and elaborately shaped wide rockers deeply scrolled at each end are traditional features of this form.

OBJECT: Cradle

MAKER: Johann Peter Tatsch

DATE: 1870

MATERIAL: Pine

MEASUREMENTS: H. 10″, W. 9 1/2″, L. 13 1/2″

HISTORY: Made in Fredericksburg and descended in the maker's family to his granddaughter

OWNER: Mrs. Lyne Lewis Harper, Fredericksburg

PHOTOGRAPHER: Harvey Patteson

This miniature conforms to the Germanic type with its square tapering posts, knob finials, scrolled crests, and large shaped rockers. It is simply pegged together except for the bottom, which is secured by screws.

2. Wardrobes

The wardrobe, or armoire, as it was sometimes elegantly called, was an essential piece of furniture in nineteenth-century Texas homes because of the absence of closets. It was one of the most expensive pieces of furniture in the cabinetmaker's inventory, selling for about thirty-five dollars at mid-century. Since they were frequently used in upstairs rooms, most wardrobes could be disassembled for ease in moving up and down stairs, although a few massive Texas examples do not break down.

Among Texas Germans, the wardrobe was called a *Kleiderschrank*, and a number of wardrobes made by German cabinetmakers exhibit features which tie them directly to German folk furniture of the eighteenth century: heavy, framed construction; thick, beveled panels and drawer bottoms; and the existence of a central foot. German cabinetmakers seemed to lavish more detail on wardrobes than did their Anglo counterparts; several finely decorated German examples are pictured here.

Possibly because they offer a broader expanse of protected surfaces than other pieces of furniture, makers and owners have written pencil inscriptions, pasted tax receipts, and tacked calendars inside Texas wardrobes. Sometimes the inscription consists only of a name; whether it is the maker's or the owner's is often unclear. Others are extensively autobiographical; one, inside a

Schrank made at Winedale, reads, "This wardrobe was made by Dr. Jacob Graul after a long illness, during which his dear son lost his life, September 26, 1872."

OBJECT: Wardrobe

MAKER: Unknown

DATE: 1860

MATERIAL: Pine

MEASUREMENTS: H. 77 3/4″, W. 57 3/4″, D. 23 7/8″

HISTORY: Written in pencil inside the door is the inscription "C. Welgehausen 1860 / Crab Apple / Gillespie County Texas." This undoubtedly indicates that the piece belonged to Conrad Welgehausen, a farmer who settled in the Crab Apple community north of Fredericksburg. The date may be a wedding date.

OWNER: Pioneer Museum, Fredericksburg

PHOTOGRAPHER: Harvey Patteson

A seemingly simple piece, this handsome wardrobe embodies many of the characteristics that give Texas-German furniture its distinctive appeal. The bold molded cornice and short cabriole feet are in the Biedermeier taste. Two large raised panels are set into the single framed door, which hangs on Continental *fiche* type hinges. The back of the carcase is framed with similar raised panels, while the large dovetailed drawer has a beveled bottom.

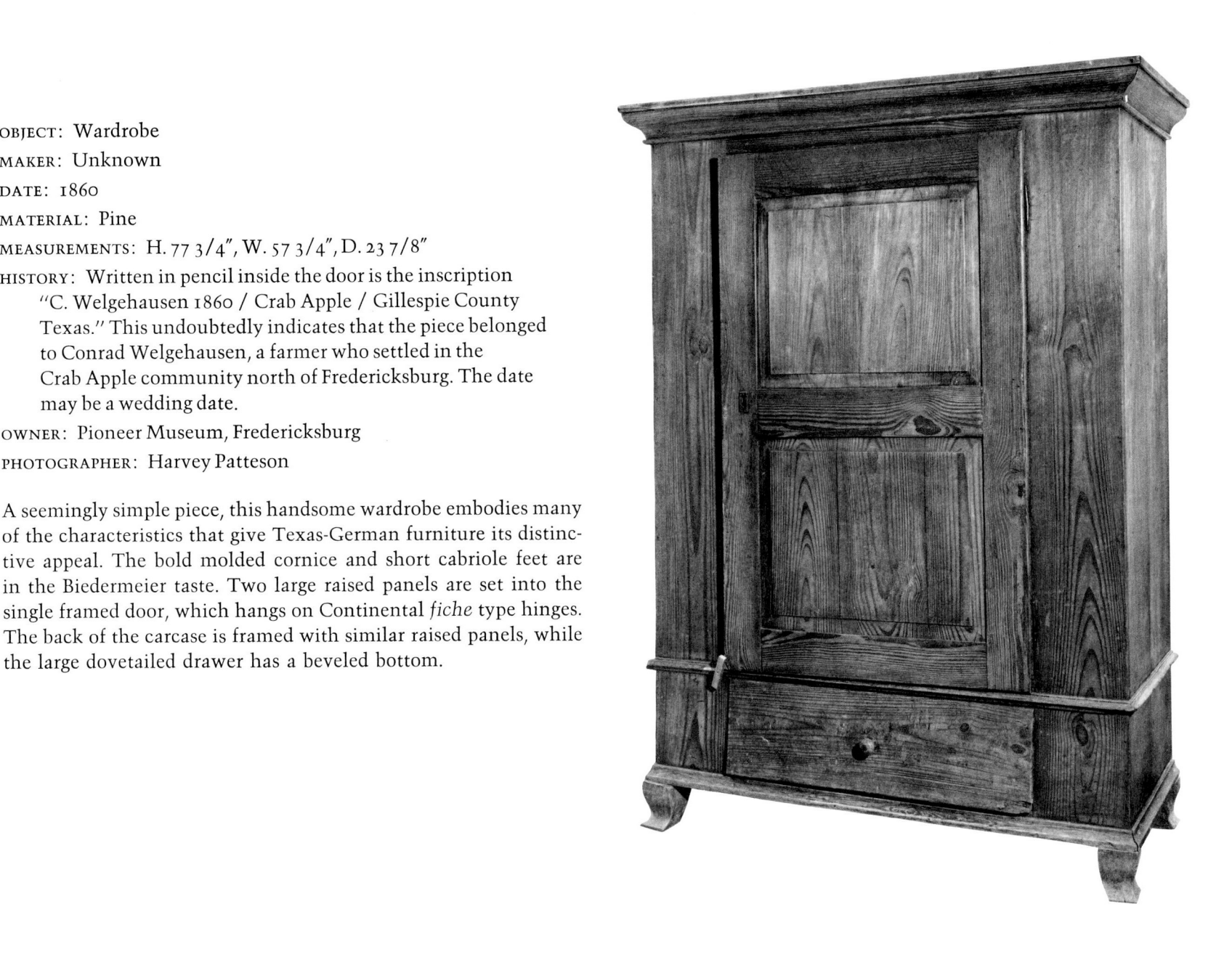

OBJECT: Wardrobe

MAKER: Jacob Schneider

DATE: 1860

MATERIAL: Pine

MEASUREMENTS: H. 77 1/2″, W. 59 9/16″, D. 22″

HISTORY: Made in Fredericksburg and descended in the maker's family to the present owners

OWNERS: Mr. and Mrs. Elgin Kuhlmann, Fredericksburg

PHOTOGRAPHER: Harvey Patteson

A simple two-door wardrobe or *Schrank* of framed and pegged construction, this example has fine beveled panels on the inside of the doors and sides of the carcase. The door panels of unpainted pine are each made of two figured boards held by a wooden butterfly splice on the inside. The grain is carefully matched to make an attractive pattern. Below, the bracket feet are dovetailed. Inside is a shelf and carved wooden pegs. The left-hand door is secured by a hand-carved wooden lock. The maker, Jacob Schneider, was a commercial cabinetmaker in Fredericksburg.

OBJECT: Wardrobe

MAKER: Attributed to Henry Sens

DATE: 1850

MATERIAL: Pine

MEASUREMENTS: H. 79 1/4″, W. 46″, D. 23″

HISTORY: Built for the Sens family homestead near Cat Spring, according to the present owners

OWNERS: Mr. and Mrs. Andrew Z. Thompson, San Antonio

PHOTOGRAPHER: Harvey Patteson

This small two-door wardrobe with one long drawer below is made of characteristically framed and pegged construction with beveled panels set into the frame.

OBJECT: Wardrobe

MAKER: Unknown

DATE: 1850

MATERIAL: Cedar

MEASUREMENTS: H. 79 1/4″, W. 52 1/4″, D. 22 1/4″

HISTORY: Made in Kirby, according to the present owners

OWNERS: Mr. and Mrs. Andrew Z. Thompson, San Antonio

PHOTOGRAPHER: Harvey Patteson

Made of cedar, this large two-door wardrobe with one drawer below is broken into a three-part composition of base, midsection, and cornice through the application of half-round moldings above and below the central section. Chamfered corners on the front of the carcase and a scalloped skirt are attractive features. The interior case has the usual beveled panels.

OBJECT: Wardrobe

MAKER: Unknown

DATE: Unknown

MATERIAL: Pine

MEASUREMENTS: H. 80 5/8″, W. 46 1/2″, D. 18 1/4″

HISTORY: Collected by the owner in Medina County

OWNER: Mr. Robert Quill Johnson, Castroville

PHOTOGRAPHER: Harvey Patteson

The example here is a small wardrobe with bold cavetto cornice in the late classical taste. A single door with pegged frame is fitted with four vertical panels, an unusual feature. These panels are beveled on the inside. Apparently this piece was never intended to have feet. The crudely installed escutcheon is modern.

OBJECT: Wardrobe

MAKER: Unknown

DATE: Ca. 1870

MATERIAL: Pine

MEASUREMENTS: H. 75″, W. 41 3/8″, D. 21 1/8″

HISTORY: Collected by the owner in Gillespie County

OWNER: Mrs. J. Hardin Perry, Fredericksburg

PHOTOGRAPHER: Harvey Patteson

This one-door wardrobe is a delightful little piece with spritely Grecian crest and nicely shaped dovetailed bracket feet. This latter feature recalls eighteenth-century design, while the crest or crown is in the Biedermeier taste. The door consists of one huge panel beveled on the reverse, set into a pegged frame. In the lower section an applied molding suggests a blind drawer, a feature utilized on occasion in Fredericksburg pieces. The surface bears traces of its original dark reddish stain.

OBJECT: Wardrobe

MAKER: Unknown

DATE: 1870

MATERIALS: Primary, cedar; secondary, pine

MEASUREMENTS: H. 86″, W. 58 1/4″, D. 23 5/8″

HISTORY: Ownership traced to Fritz Wendland (1847–1916),
a farmer in the Winedale area; descended in his family until
it came into the hands of the present owner

OWNER: Winedale Museum, Round Top; the gift of Miss Ima Hogg

PHOTOGRAPHER: Ewing Waterhouse

The short curved legs and elaborate crest lend extra charm to this cedar wardrobe. The carcase is pegged together and can be disassembled for ease of movement. As the Germanic nature of the exterior would suggest, the door panels are beveled, as are the bottoms of the dovetailed drawers below. Inside are wooden hangers.

OBJECT: Wardrobe

MAKER: Unknown

DATE: Unknown

MATERIAL: Pine

MEASUREMENTS: H. 88 1/2″, W. 62 7/16″, D. 22 3/8″

HISTORY: Ownership traced to 1893, when it belonged to
Wilhelm Merz of Wesley

OWNER: Mrs. Wendell Steward, Houston

PHOTOGRAPHER: Ewing Waterhouse

Juxtapositioned S curves in the crest, skirt, and door panels create attractive visual accents on the surface of this otherwise severely rectangular example. The combination of Gothic detail on the doors with the overall clean classical lines is typical of nineteenth-century Biedermeier taste, while the central foot of the skirt is a survivor of eighteenth-century German wardrobe design. Beveled panels appear, framed into the doors and sides as well as the back, where no less than four are utilized. The dovetailed drawers with beveled bottoms are secured by peg locks that drop down from the section above.

OBJECT: Wardrobe

MAKER: Uncertain (see 2.10)

DATE: 1870

MATERIAL: Cypress

MEASUREMENTS: H. 90 1/16″, W. 60 3/8″, D. 19 7/8″

HISTORY: Collected from a farmhouse near Lacoste

OWNER: Winedale Museum, Round Top; the gift of Miss Ima Hogg

PHOTOGRAPHER: Harvey Patteson

Here the elegant two-door wardrobe combines elements of the Gothic and Restauration styles in the late Biedermeier taste. Applied spandrels on the doors make complicated Gothic arches that are repeated at either side of the skirt below. The bold molded cornice is composed of several sections. Beveled and raised panels are set into the doors, and the bottom of the single interior drawer on the left is also beveled. On the right are two rows of hand-carved hooks, five in front, nine behind. The back of the carcase is made of five hand-planed vertical boards with beaded edges.

OBJECT: Wardrobe

MAKER: Uncertain (see below)

DATE: 1870

MATERIAL: Cypress

MEASUREMENTS: H. 84 1/2″, W. 58 1/8″, D. 20″

HISTORY: Ownership has been traced to Andreas Haby (1827–1888), a pioneer settler of Castroville. According to his daughter, the wardrobe was made by a carpenter named Bachmann who was building an addition to the Haby home.

OWNER: Mr. Robert Quill Johnson, Castroville

PHOTOGRAPHER: Harvey Patteson

This example is virtually identical to 2.9, with the same features throughout. It differs in size, being slightly smaller, and in the absence of an interior drawer. It is probable that they were made by the same craftsman.

OBJECT: Wardrobe

MAKER: Unknown

DATE: Unknown

MATERIAL: Pine

MEASUREMENTS: H. 85 1/4″, W. 59″, D. 23″

HISTORY: Collected by the owners in Castroville

OWNERS: Mr. and Mrs. Marshall Steves, San Antonio

PHOTOGRAPHER: Harvey Patteson

While this small pine example may not initially impress the viewer, its extreme simplicity, clean classical lines, and high quality of construction lend great distinction. On the interior, beautiful raised panels are set into the doors and sides, while the back is framed with three vertical beveled panels. The lower portions of the carcase and the cornice section are dovetailed, as are the bracket feet. Bone insets are utilized at the keyholes. The wardrobe is held together with wood pegs and can be disassembled. While they are not the same, a certain similarity of aspect relates this example visually to 2.9 and 2.10, where similarly raised panels are employed, suggesting the same provenance although not necessarily the same craftsman.

OBJECT: Wardrobe

MAKER: Unknown

DATE: 1875

MATERIALS: Primary, walnut; secondary, pine

MEASUREMENTS: H. 84 1/8", W. 53", D. 24 7/8"

HISTORY: Descended in the Keidel family of Fredericksburg

OWNER: Mrs. J. Hardin Perry, Fredericksburg

PHOTOGRAPHER: Harvey Patteson

A bold, simple, molded cornice and attached colonnettes at the front corners of the case are the major decorative features of this large walnut two-door wardrobe. While the former feature is in the Restauration style, the colonnettes suggest an awareness of Renaissance Revival taste. Concealed hinges and inset ivory escutcheons are attractive finishing details. This piece cannot be disassembled. The top is dovetailed onto the carcase, and the usual beveled panels appear on the backs of the doors and drawer bottoms. The cast-iron drawer pulls, probably purchased commercially, appear to be original. The interior has been altered for modern usage.

OBJECT: Wardrobe

MAKER: Unknown

DATE: Ca. 1860

MATERIALS: Primary, walnut; secondary, pine

MEASUREMENTS: H. 86", W. 72", D. 21"

HISTORY: Once belonged to Egmont Schramm of San Antonio

OWNER: Sophienburg Memorial Museum, New Braunfels

PHOTOGRAPHER: Babette Fraser Warren

A wardrobe of rather large and impressive proportions, this example is unusual for the utilization of three rather than two doors. Continental *fiche* type hinges and an ivory escutcheon (the brass one seems to be a replacement) are sophisticated details. Rounded corners, bold cornice, and shaped crest are in the Biedermeier taste. The scalloped skirt below echoes the lines of the crest. Raised panels are utilized on the inside of the doors and sides and the outside of the back.

OBJECT: Wardrobe

MAKER: Johann Michael Jahn

DATE: 1869

MATERIALS: Primary, walnut; secondary, pine

MEASUREMENTS: H. 91", W. 51", D. 23"

HISTORY: Made in New Braunfels and descended in the maker's family to his granddaughter

OWNER: Mrs. R. L. Biesele, Austin

PHOTOGRAPHER: Harvey Patteson

Made of attractively figured walnut, this large wardrobe by Johann Michael Jahn is perhaps the most sophisticated of New Braunfels examples. In the Biedermeier style with rounded cornice and Grecian crest, it is unusual for its quality of restrained elegance. The carved scrolled crest with central palmette is especially beautiful. The quality and style of the carving relate to that of a handsome rocking chair, also by Jahn, now on loan to the New Braunfels Conservation Society (4.2). Jahn has utilized raised panels on the drawer bottoms, on the inside of the doors, and on the sides of the case. The whole can be disassembled. The doors are made in such a manner that the central vertical section between them is actually attached to the left-hand door. The plain molding at the edge of the right-hand door appears to be a replacement. The white porcelain castors are original.

Detail—central cartouche

OBJECT: Wardrobe

MAKER: Franz Stautzenberger

DATE: 1861

MATERIALS: Primary, walnut; secondary, pine

MEASUREMENTS: H. 90 1/2", W. 75", D. 26 5/8"

HISTORY: Made at Clear Spring, Guadalupe County, by Stautzenberger for his niece, Magdalene, and her husband, Konrad Oelkers; part of a set (see 3.1, 5.11, and 6.43)

OWNER: Mrs. Hugo Biesele, New Braunfels

PHOTOGRAPHER: Babette Fraser Warren

Franz Stautzenberger's great wardrobe is a fascinating combination of eighteenth- and nineteenth-century design. The framed doors with fielded raised panels flanked by narrow vertical panels of the same design reflect the traditional eighteenth-century design, as do the panels at either end and the Continental *fiche* type hinges. Absence of a vertical dividing member between the doors follows nineteenth-century developments. The bracket feet, rounded corners, and three-rib horizontal moldings are all according to nineteenth-century taste. However, the charming little pierced gallery above, with acorn finials and central cartouche, seems to be a pure invention of Stautzenberger himself. An identical gallery was utilized on a chamber or dressing table by Stautzenberger (6.43). The central cartouche is carved with the initials K O and the date 1861; the background is carefully punched to create contrast.

On the interior there are four removable shelves to the left and five hand-carved hangers to the right. While the interior has flat rather than beveled panels, the back side of the framed carcase has beautiful raised panels like those of the exterior and doors. Beveled bottoms are utilized on the dovetailed drawers. Inlaid diamond-shaped bone key escutcheons lend a classical note. Below, wooden pulls replace the original bale type hardware.

OBJECT: Wardrobe

MAKER: Unknown

DATE: 1860

MATERIALS: Primary, walnut; secondary, cedar

MEASUREMENTS: H. 91 3/4", W. 80 3/4", D. 25"

HISTORY: Has a long history of usage in the Governor's Mansion in Austin and is very likely the "walnut wardrobe with mirror" listed in a November, 1861, inventory of the mansion "in the southwest room, second story"[4]

OWNER: Governor's Mansion, Austin

PHOTOGRAPHER: Harvey Patteson

An ambitious and complicated piece, this example combines a wardrobe with a dressing chest. The mirror section opens to reveal shelves behind, while on either side the long doors conceal space for hanging. The presence of beveled panels on the interior and thick, heavy dovetailed drawers with cedar sides and beveled cedar bottoms suggests a Texas provenance. The fact that the scalloped, vaguely Gothic arches are not exactly symmetrical evidences a limitation of ability that further suggests a local origin.

OBJECT: Wardrobe

MAKER: Attributed to John William August Kleine

DATE: 1870

MATERIALS: Primary, walnut; secondary, pine

MEASUREMENTS: H. 77 5/8", W. 62 2/3", D. 22 1/8"

HISTORY: Unknown

OWNER: Mrs. J. B. Wells, Gonzales

PHOTOGRAPHER: Harvey Patteson

Gothic arches add an unusual note of interest to this late classical two-door wardrobe. The doors extend all the way across the leading edge of the sides, as in 2.18. Thick, figured walnut panels are set into the doors. On the interior the panels, which are beveled on the bottoms and sides, conform to the Gothic arches at the top. The back and interior have been altered. The unusual hinge arrangement and a long history of local ownership suggest a Gonzales provenance.

OBJECT: Wardrobe

MAKER: John William August Kleine

DATE: 1870

MATERIALS: Primary, walnut; secondary, pine

MEASUREMENTS: H. 85 1/2″, W. 55 7/8″, D. 20 1/8″

HISTORY: Made for the maker's own use and descended to his daughter-in-law

OWNER: Mrs. Walter D. Kleine, Gonzales

PHOTOGRAPHER: Harvey Patteson

Elegant, clean lines distinguish this walnut wardrobe by the Gonzales cabinetmaker John William August Kleine. According to the products-of-industry schedule of the 1870 census return, Kleine made only three or four wardrobes in that year, his major output being bedsteads, tables, and coffins. He valued his wardrobes at between thirty-five and forty-seven dollars each, although this example, made for his own use, may be more finely made than his commercial products. An unusual and sophisticated feature that occurs on at least one other Gonzales area example (2.17) is the extension of the door edge all the way across the front, placing the hinges at the side and resulting in an unbroken sweeping frontal line. A rounded molding on the leading edge of the right door tapers at the bottom. The door frames are pegged together, with large single boards set in. These are beveled on the inside, as are the bottoms of the dovetailed drawers. The back of the carcase is framed with vertical beveled boards. Elegantly shaped bracket feet support the whole.

OBJECT: Wardrobe

MAKER: Attributed to Jacob Pfeil

DATE: 1865

MATERIAL: Pine

MEASUREMENTS: H. 88 3/4", W. 61", D. 25 1/2"

HISTORY: Made in New Braunfels and descended in the Pfeil family to the last private owner, Mrs. Robert Albes of New Braunfels

OWNER: San Antonio Museum Association, San Antonio

PHOTOGRAPHER: Harvey Patteson

Although it is likely that many pieces of Texas furniture were painted or in some manner grained to suggest a finer or more expensive material, few examples have survived with their original finish intact. This large, beautiful wardrobe has been painted dark reddish brown to simulate mahogany. Although apparently Gothic in style, with softly pointed arches, trefoils in the spandrels, and the suggestion of long quatrefoils in the rectangular panels below, the general shape has a classical origin, while the canted corners indicate a familiarity with the Renaissance Revival style. Inset shield-shaped bone escutcheons are a nice detail. This piece, which can be disassembled, is made with beveled panels on the interior. Dovetailing is utilized throughout the carcase. The drawers are secured with wooden peg locks which drop through the base of the upper section. On the back are traces of a painted inscription, J. PFEIL, in Roman capitals; whether Pfeil was the maker or the owner is not clear.

A small, naïve wardrobe of considerable charm, this example has been grained with painstaking effort. The spritely crest is not unlike that of the Pfeil piece (2.19), but the addition of leaves or feathers creates a more nervous profile which is almost a duplicate of that seen on a china cupboard collected in the same area (8.6). This quality of nervous line is echoed in the elaborately scalloped frame of the door panels. Below, the drawer section projects, a treatment seen on two other pieces with a Central Texas history (3.5 and 7.7). The usual beveled panels appear behind the doors and on the drawer bottom. Applied moldings terminating in small carved leaves at the corners (missing in this photograph) provide a slightly Renaissance Revival flavor to an otherwise Germanic piece.

OBJECT: Wardrobe
MAKER: Unknown
DATE: Unknown
MATERIAL: Pine
MEASUREMENTS: H. 89″, W. 42″, D. 21″
HISTORY: Collected near Wesley
OWNER: Winedale Museum, Round Top, the gift of Miss Ima Hogg
PHOTOGRAPHER: Harvey Patteson

OBJECT: Wardrobe

MAKER: Unknown

DATE: Unknown

MATERIAL: Pine

MEASUREMENTS: H. 81 7/8″, W. 52 1/8″, D. 17 1/4″

HISTORY: Made in Berlin, Washington County, according to the owner

OWNERS: Mrs. Charles L. Bybee and the late Mr. Bybee, Round Top

PHOTOGRAPHER: Harvey Patteson

The original splendor of this wardrobe is belied by its present appearance. Underneath its coat of drab, brown, peeling paint are evidences of rich graining much in the manner of 2.20. The simple overall design is enlivened by bold, unselfconscious scalloped curves in the skirt, doors, and crest. Typical construction techniques such as mortise and tenon and beveled panels framed into the back are utilized, but unbeveled boards are used in the doors. The present pulls are replacements.

A Germanic fondness for painted ornament manifests itself in a most unusual manner on this splendid grained wardrobe. The incredible brown-and-yellow door panels are rendered with such care that the resultant fantasy pattern more resembles microscopic views of wood cell structure than the exotic wood grain the artist sought to capture. Stippled, sponged, and painted graining in the skirt, drawer fronts, and bold cornice above unite the overall composition. In general outline the piece seems more closely related to *Schranks* of the eighteenth century than to those of its own era. Particularly interesting is the cutout, scalloped skirt with a "foot" in the center. This feature occurs on at least one other wardrobe (2.8) and a corner cupboard (8.11) and may be a regional characteristic.

OBJECT: Wardrobe

MAKER: Unknown, possibly decorated by Matthias Melchior

DATE: 1860

MATERIAL: Cedar

MEASUREMENTS: H. 76″, W. 64 1/2″, D. 22 15/16″

HISTORY: Has a history of ownership in the Tiemann family of Warrenton, Fayette County

OWNERS: Mrs. Charles L. Bybee and the late Mr. Bybee, Round Top

PHOTOGRAPHER: Harvey Patteson

OBJECT: Wardrobe

MAKER: Unknown

DATE: Unknown

MATERIAL: Pine

MEASUREMENTS: H. 85 3/8″, W. 63 3/4″, D. 23 1/4″

HISTORY: Collected by the owner in Seguin

OWNER: Mr. Walter Mathis, San Antonio

PHOTOGRAPHER: Harvey Patteson

This very architectural wardrobe, with plinth, pilasters, frieze, and cornice, is remarkably close to Pennsylvania-German *Schranks* made one hundred years earlier. However, its general proportions are considerably more attenuated and the details are much lighter than those of the eighteenth century, resulting in a rather vertical and comparatively skimpy composition. These features can be explained in part by the fact that this piece has been made in a vernacular style mutated from eighteenth-century prototypes and adapted to nineteenth-century proportions. The carcase, which can be disassembled, is put together with wooden pegs and mortise-and-tenon construction. The details, such as moldings, are applied. The capitals of the pilasters on either side are missing, but the remaining traces suggest that they were similar to the bases. On the interior, the panels set into the frames of the door, sides, and back are very thick, with bold beveled edges. The piece has been so thoroughly refinished that it is difficult to determine its original finish. However, it may have been stained to resemble walnut or perhaps grained like 2.24.

OBJECT: Wardrobe

MAKER: Unknown

DATE: Unknown

MATERIAL: Pine

MEASUREMENTS: H. 86 3/4", W. 61 7/8", D. 23 3/16"

HISTORY: Possibly made in Seguin

OWNERS: Mr. and Mrs. Marshall Steves, San Antonio

PHOTOGRAPHER: Harvey Patteson

The similarity between this wardrobe and 2.23 is indeed striking, and the likelihood that they were made in the same area is rather strong. However, minor differences in molding profiles and a slight simplification of design in this one suggest the possibility that another hand might be involved. The construction, framing, and large beveled panels are identical. A nice extra touch is the chamfered outer edge of the pilasters. The applied molding in the plinth section visually suggests drawers. Traces of yellow and brown paint indicate that this piece was at one point painted in imitation of grained wood.

OBJECT: Wardrobe

MAKER: Unknown

DATE: 1850

MATERIAL: Cedar

MEASUREMENTS: H. 92″, W. 54″, D. 25″

HISTORY: Probably made in Round Top; ownership traced to Leo Wagner (1805–1893), a native of Germany who immigrated to the Round Top area about 1850

OWNERS: Mrs. Charles L. Bybee and the late Mr. Bybee, Round Top

PHOTOGRAPHER: Harvey Patteson

This bold architectural wardrobe is one of the most handsome Texas examples. In general concept the design is very much in the spirit of the eighteenth century; only the neoclassical urn finials and crest indicate its nineteenth-century date. Superb raised and molded panels of a sort not generally utilized in the nineteenth century are set into the doors and sides. Applied colonnettes of elaborate turned design flank the doors, with the cornice and plinth breaking out to receive the colonnettes. These projecting surface planes give the piece a rather baroque character. The simple rectangular legs with molded feet relate to the work of Franz Stautzenberger (see his chest, 3.1) and are probably of eighteenth-century design origin as well. The piece is beautifully put together with pegs and mortised construction. Made of cedar, it is extraordinarily heavy; yet it does not disassemble for moving.

OBJECT: Wardrobe

MAKER: Unknown

DATE: 1850

MATERIAL: Cedar

MEASUREMENTS: H. 80 1/2″, W. 64″, D. 24″

HISTORY: Descended in the owner's family

OWNER: Mrs. Lorraine Kneip, Round Top

PHOTOGRAPHER: Jim Bones

Similarity of material, molded panels, and molded drawer fronts relates this wardrobe to 2.25. The design has been altered by placement of the colonnettes on canted corners and updated by the inclusion of curved legs. Bobbin turning at the base of the colonnettes and under the thin serpentine top suggests an awareness of the Elizabethan Revival style of the early Victorian era. Elements of the turned colonnettes here, especially juncture of the lower vase, repeat those on 2.25, lending credence to the belief that these two may be by the same as yet unidentified cabinetmaker. The crest is not attached to the wardrobe. An extremely similar piece is in the Winedale collection.

The raised panels of the doors combined with the horizontal grooving on the single drawer relate this piece closely to 2.26 and thus to 2.25. However, it is made of pine rather than cedar. A serpentine top also recalls 2.26. There are, however, features which suggest that this is a later wardrobe. Raised panels have been omitted from the sides; the central dividing member between the doors has not been included; and, while 2.26 has applied turned colonnettes at the corners, a single molded member appears here. However, the crowning corbel and the curved legs are nearly identical to those of 2.26. The piece is carefully constructed with mortise and tenon. The bottom is dovetailed to the carcase. Dovetails and a beveled bottom appear on the drawer.

OBJECT: **Wardrobe**

MAKER: Unknown

DATE: Unknown

MATERIAL: Pine

MEASUREMENTS: H. 74″, W. 51″, D. 18″

HISTORY: Unknown

OWNER: Mr. James L. Britton, Washington

PHOTOGRAPHER: Allen Mewbourn

OBJECT: Wardrobe

MAKER: Johann Peter Tatsch

DATE: 1860–1870

MATERIAL: Pine

MEASUREMENTS: H. 99 1/2", W. 60 1/2", D. 25 3/4"

HISTORY: Made in Fredericksburg by Johann Peter Tatsch for his own use and descended to the present owner through her mother, Sophie Tatsch Klingelhoefer, Tatsch's daughter

OWNER: Mrs. Lyne Lewis Harper, Fredericksburg

PHOTOGRAPHER: Harvey Patteson

This wardrobe is one of four closely related examples, all presumably the work of Johann Peter Tatsch. Its style is almost architectural, with a broad plinthlike base, columns on either side, entablature above, and a broken pediment at the top. The central lyre and the star-ornamented shield above it suggest traces of neoclassical taste, while the trapezoidal panels applied to the broken pediment evidence an awareness of Renaissance Revival designs.

Mortise-and-tenon construction is used throughout this piece. Beveled panels are screwed onto the frame on the interior of the doors and sides. The two large dovetailed drawers have beveled bottoms and are secured by peg locks, which drop from the interior above the drawers. The diamond-shaped inlaid ivory key escutcheons and porcelain pulls are original.

OBJECT: Wardrobe

MAKER: Johann Peter Tatsch

DATE: 1860–1870

MATERIAL: Pine

MEASUREMENTS: H. 83 5/8″, W. 61 11/16″, D. 25 1/2″

HISTORY: Collected by the owner in Fredericksburg

OWNER: Mrs. Schatzie Crouch, Fredericksburg

PHOTOGRAPHER: Harvey Patteson

Although upon initial appearance this example with its Renaissance Revival pediment or crown seems to be nearly identical to 2.28 and 2.30, its size, proportion, and general design are much more closely associated with those found in 2.31. Neoclassical ovals, utilized no less than five times here, are repeated in similar locations on 2.31. In profile the turned columns are very similar, as is the spacing of the two small drawers below. These, however, are dovetailed with beveled bottoms, like those in 2.28.

OBJECT: Wardrobe

MAKER: Johann Peter Tatsch

DATE: 1870

MATERIAL: Pine

MEASUREMENTS: H. 93″, W. 59 3/4″, D. 24 3/4″

HISTORY: Made by Tatsch as a wedding gift for his daughter
Elizabeth on the occasion of her marriage to Henry Kuenemann

OWNER: Mrs. George A. Hill, Fredericksburg

PHOTOGRAPHER: Harvey Patteson

While all of the Tatsch wardrobes are very similar, the turned columns of this example are virtually identical to those of the Tatsch family piece (2.28), and the same faceted panels appear at the base and capitals of each column. Small shield-shaped plinths on the drawers of 2.28 are repeated here on the drawers and above the frieze. Although most of the construction features are identical throughout, the drawer bottoms here are flat rather than beveled. The plain base is not original and possibly replaces some sort of scalloped skirt.

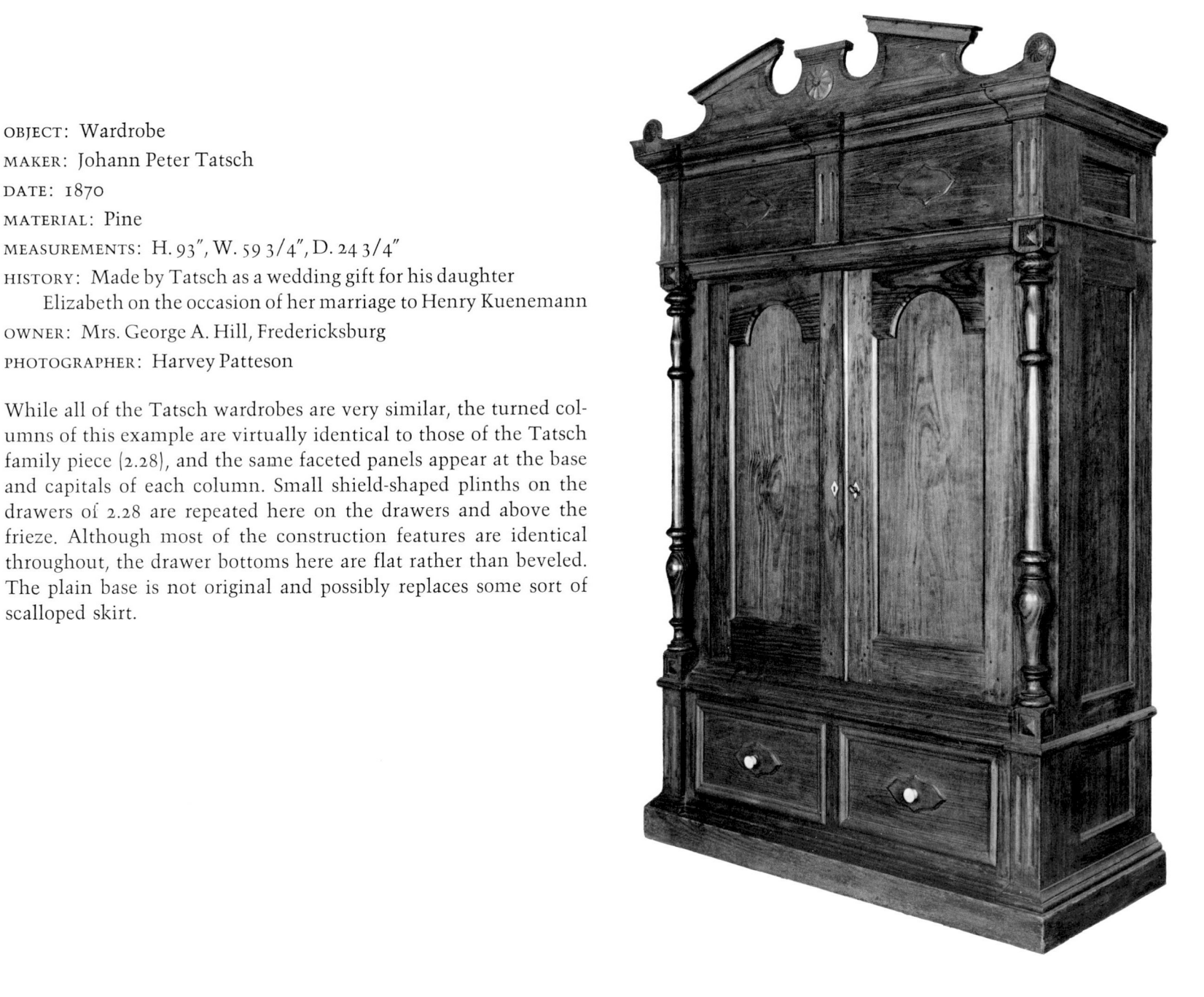

OBJECT: Wardrobe

MAKER: Attributed to Johann Peter Tatsch

DATE: 1860–1870

MATERIAL: Pine

MEASUREMENTS: H. 73″, W. 61 3/4″, D. 26 1/2″

HISTORY: Collected by the owner in Fredericksburg

OWNER: Mr. Albert Keidel, Fredericksburg

PHOTOGRAPHER: Harvey Patteson

"The twisted column," wrote Andrew Jackson Downing in 1850, "is a largely used feature of Elizabethan furniture."[5] Here handsome spiral-turned colonnettes have been incorporated in this architectural wardrobe. Pointed neoclassical ovals on the drawers, repeated above, relate this example to 2.29. The geometric cutout ornaments on the plinths below the colonnettes have a Gothic flavor. The skirt is vigorously scalloped in an attractive manner. Strangely, there is no evidence of this wardrobe's ever having had the distinctive Renaissance Revival crest that appears on the other three pieces. However, at the top of the back there is an unexplained trapezoidal projection pierced by a round hole, as if to receive a large hook for lifting. It is interesting to note that this wardrobe cannot be disassembled.

Beveled panels are screwed onto the doors and into the sides and framed vertically into the back. While the drawers are dovetailed, they have flat bottoms. When this wardrobe came into the possession of the present owner it was stained dark and grained to look like walnut. It stood on white porcelain castors.

OBJECT: Wardrobe

MAKER: Christofer Friderich Carl Steinhagen

DATE: 1878

MATERIAL: Walnut

MEASUREMENTS: H. 94″, W. 66 1/2″, D. 35″

HISTORY: Made in Anderson for the maker's family and descended
       in that family to the present owner, his great-granddaughter

OWNER: Mrs. Walter Holliday, Cleburne

PHOTOGRAPHER: Harvey Patteson

Clean geometric lines and a bold cornice place this wardrobe in
the Biedermeier taste. Stylized carved leaves on the pilasters relate
closely to the ornament found on other Steinhagen pieces. A
lengthy dialect pencil inscription inside reads "Christofer Friderich
Carl Steinhagen geborn 1814 / December 21 in Warckdorff bei
Wismar Mecklenburg Schwerin / Den Schran habe ich gemack
1878 Juni 12 [Christofer Friderich Carl Steinhagen born 1814 / December 21 in Warckdorff bei Wismar, Mecklenburg-Schwerin / I
made this wardrobe on June 12, 1878]." An interesting departure
from the maker's usual vocabulary of ornament is the well-carved
Rococo Revival crest incorporating floral scrolls and a pair of birds.

This example is made of beautifully figured walnut. It is very
similar to a pine wardrobe made by Steinhagen and dated May 19,
1861 (now in the possession of another Steinhagen descendant, Mrs.
Gene Burris of Beaumont), which has free-standing columns of bois
d'arc and paw feet rather than pilasters and bracket feet.

Detail—crest

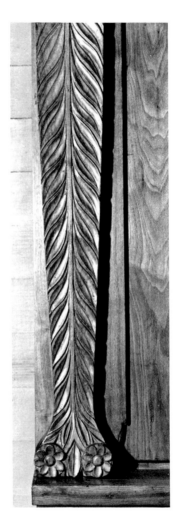

Detail—inscription

Detail—pilaster

OBJECT: **Wardrobe**

MAKER: **Unknown**

DATE: **Unknown**

MATERIAL: **Pine**

MEASUREMENTS: **H. 77″, W. 43″, D. 22″**

HISTORY: Collected by the owners in Washington County

OWNERS: Mr. and Mrs. Andrew Z. Thompson, San Antonio

PHOTOGRAPHER: Harvey Patteson

This apparently simple pine example captures the clean lines of the Biedermeier taste. A small triangular pediment lends a further classical note. Surprisingly, brass *fiche* type hinges are used. A beveled panel is framed into the door. It is very likely that this example originally had a grained surface which visually enriched it.

OBJECT: Wardrobe

MAKER: Unknown

DATE: Unknown

MATERIAL: Pine

MEASUREMENTS: H. 84 3/4″, W. 50 3/4″, D. 22 1/4″

HISTORY: Has a history of ownership in the Schuette family of New Ulm

OWNERS: Mr. and Mrs. Robin Elverson, Houston

PHOTOGRAPHER: Ewing Waterhouse

This classically inspired wardrobe is marvelously grained to look like walnut. Special emphasis has been placed on the thick beveled panels of the doors and sides by ornamenting them with scrolled graining. The single drawer is simply made, nailed together apparently out of material from a packing crate. On the bottom, one board reads "Galveston, Texas" in black paint, while another says "Halff Weise & C——."

OBJECT: Wardrobe

MAKER: Unknown

DATE: 1855

MATERIAL: Pine

MEASUREMENTS: H. 85″, W. 59 1/2″, D. 22 1/4″

HISTORY: According to the owner, this wardrobe belonged to
Robert F. Zapp (1818–1885), a Round Top merchant,
and was used in his home in Round Top.

OWNERS: Mrs. Charles L. Bybee and the late Mr. Bybee,
Round Top

PHOTOGRAPHER: Harvey Patteson

While the triangular pediment and angular lines of this large pine
wardrobe are in the Biedermeier style, the clean surfaces usually
associated with the style have here been broken up by sunken
panels in the base, frieze, and sides. The façade has been carefully
divided into three parts by means of ovolo moldings above and below the doors. Cavetto moldings unite the composition at top and
bottom. The piece is pegged together; on the interior, beveled panels
correspond to the sunken exterior surface panels, and similar pieces
are framed into the back. This wardrobe cannot be disassembled.

OBJECT: Wardrobe

MAKER: Henry Harms (1814–1897)

DATE: 1860

MATERIAL: Pine

MEASUREMENTS: H. 99 7/8", W. 65 1/4", D. 23 1/4"

HISTORY: Made for the maker's family's use in their home at Rutersville, Fayette County

OWNERS: Mrs. Charles L. Bybee and the late Mr. Bybee, Round Top

PHOTOGRAPHER: Harvey Patteson

While in general appearance this unusually large pine example has Biedermeier outlines, not unlike those of 2.37, there are several archaic features. Most apparent are the multiple, molded, fielded panels of the doors and sides, which visually break up the surface. The vertical division between the doors, a feature which disappears in the pure nineteenth-century form, is vestigially retained, attached to the right-hand door. The hand-carved pegs for hanging garments are visible in this picture, as are the mortises and tenons of the doors and the framed panels of the back. The pine surface has been painted dark brown to suggest a richer wood.

OBJECT: Wardrobe

MAKER: Unknown

DATE: Unknown

MATERIALS: Primary, walnut; secondary, pine

MEASUREMENTS: H. 87 1/2″, W. 64″, D. 22″

HISTORY: Collected in Frelsburg

OWNERS: Mrs. Charles L. Bybee and the late Mr. Bybee,
Round Top

PHOTOGRAPHER: Harvey Patteson

This handsome walnut wardrobe with deep plinth, rounded corners, finely detailed cornice, and classical triangular pediment is entirely in the Biedermeier style. An imaginatively scalloped skirt lends the only nonclassical touch. Seemingly out of harmony with the general sophistication of this example are the mundane white porcelain key escutcheons on the doors and similar escutcheons now missing from the drawers below; yet they appear to be original. The piece utilizes mortise-and-tenon joints throughout. Large panels, beveled on the reverse, are framed into the doors, and two similar panels are framed into the back of the carcase. The bottom of each dovetailed drawer is also beveled. The piece can be disassembled. On the interior are seven hand-carved swinging arms, or hangers, with seven hooks on each.

OBJECT: Wardrobe

MAKER: Attributed to Christian Afflerbach

DATE: 1870

MATERIAL: Pine

MEASUREMENTS: H. 77 1/4″, W. 69 7/8″, D. 24 3/4″

HISTORY: An 1878 Fayette County tax receipt glued to the interior of this wardrobe indicates that in that year it belonged to Louis Bartling, a farmer who lived near Fayetteville.

OWNER: Mrs. Wendell Steward, Houston

PHOTOGRAPHER: Ewing Waterhouse

Rectangular raised moldings interrupted by central circles indicate that the maker of this example was aware of the Renaissance Revival style. Andrew Jackson Downing illustrates a wardrobe with identically placed moldings and describes it and matching bedroom pieces as "excellent specimens of the modern Renaissance School of design."[6] While the surface ornament here may be in the mainstream of American furniture, the construction, which uses huge, thick beveled panels framed into the doors, sides, and back, is typically Germanic. Likewise, the drawers below have followed Texas-German patterns, having extremely thick dovetailed sides and beveled bottoms (see 2.39).

OBJECT: Wardrobe
MAKER: Christian Afflerbach
DATE: 1870
MATERIAL: Pine
MEASUREMENTS: H. 79 1/4″, W. 56″, D. 22″
HISTORY: This wardrobe was collected in the Round Top area and has been identified by a former owner as having been made by her grandfather, Christian Afflerbach (1840–1922). The initials X. A. are written on the back of the piece, and the name Annie Afflerbach is written on the inside of one door.
OWNER: Winedale Museum, Round Top
PHOTOGRAPHER: Harvey Patteson

Similarity of design and moldings strongly indicates that this example and 2.38 were made by the same hand. The design here has been slightly altered, omitting the Renaissance Revival moldings and the central dividing member between the doors. Otherwise, the construction is identical. Store-bought hardware and metal locks are substituted for the wooden knobs and peg locks of 2.38. Bracket feet and black paint outlining the moldings of the cornice and the edges of the inset panels and drawers are details here that very possibly existed originally on 2.38. On the interior are four handcarved swinging hangers with five pegs on each hanger.

3. Chests of Drawers

Chests of drawers, or "bureaus," as they were called by cabinet-makers and furniture dealers, seem to have been made in the Classical Revival, Renaissance Revival, and Restauration styles in Texas. One Houston cabinetmaker simplified this language by advertising that he made "Column bureaus, half column bureaus, [and] plain bureaus."[7] Although no examples have been located, a Clarksville cabinetmaker advertised in the fifties that he made bureaus with marble slabs.[8] The addition of a small two-drawer chest, and sometimes a mirror, converted a plain bureau into a "toilet bureau"; Wilcox and Company of La Grange advertised in 1859 that they made "bureaus with or without mirrors."[9] Some cabinetmakers made their own drawer pulls from wood; others used cast-iron pulls purchased from hardware dealers. At least one invented his own locks: in 1850 George Wode of Galveston took out a patent for "fastenings for bureau drawers."[10]

The bureau, along with the bedstead, wardrobe, and washstand, seems to have been a common piece of bedroom furniture and turns up with great regularity on inventories of mid-nineteenth-century Texas homes.

OBJECT: Chest of drawers

MAKER: Franz Stautzenberger

DATE: 1861

MATERIALS: Primary, walnut; secondary, pine

MEASUREMENTS: H. 41 3/4″, W. 44 1/2″, D. 24 3/4″

HISTORY: Part of a set made at Clear Spring for Konrad Oelkers and his wife, Magdalene, who was the maker's niece (see 2.15, 5.11, and 6.43)

OWNER: Mrs. Hugo Biesele, New Braunfels

PHOTOGRAPHER: Babette Fraser Warren

Geometric exactness and clean-cut surfaces have been incorporated by Franz Stautzenberger in his chest of drawers made for Magdalene and Konrad Oelkers. Included are subtle details of molding underneath the beveled top on the stiles and in a large square around the extremities of the combined drawer openings. The short square legs with applied block feet are not unlike the Marlborough treatment utilized in eighteenth-century Pennsylvania but in fact reflect early Biedermeier design. Only the cast-iron Rococo Revival hardware and key escutcheons reveal the mid-nineteenth-century date of the piece. Stautzenberger's chest is pegged together, the heavy, thick dovetailed drawers have beveled bottoms, and three vertical beveled panels are framed into the back.

OBJECT: Chest of drawers

MAKER: Unknown

DATE: 1860

MATERIALS: Primary, walnut; secondary, cedar and oak

MEASUREMENTS: H. 44″, W. 43 1/2″, D. 23 3/4″

HISTORY: Ownership traced to Joseph George Wagner, who immigrated from Silesia to Round Top in 1853 and purchased the Lewis farm at Winedale in 1882; in use at Winedale since that date

OWNER: Winedale Museum, Round Top; the gift of Miss Ima Hogg

PHOTOGRAPHER: Ewing Waterhouse

Rounded corners and clean surfaces relieved only by sunken panels are in the classical taste. Applied flat mitered moldings across the drawer fronts create sunken panels, which are further emphasized by the horizontal double molding between the drawer openings. Inlaid escutcheons, probably bone, which are now missing, would have added a bright visual accent.

The piece is put together with mortise and tenon. Large panels beveled on the inside are let into the sides of the carcase, and two similar panels appear in the back. Dovetails and beveled bottoms are incorporated into the extremely heavy drawers.

OBJECT: Chest of drawers

MAKER: Attributed to John Higgins

DATE: 1850

MATERIAL: Pine

MEASUREMENTS: H. 46", W. 51 5/8", D. 23 1/8"

HISTORY: Collected by the donor in Bastrop County

OWNER: Winedale Museum, Round Top; the gift of Miss Ima Hogg

PHOTOGRAPHER: Ewing Waterhouse

The architectural qualities of Empire case pieces are, in simplified form, evident here in this pine chest of drawers. Rudimentary pilasters support a deep, slightly projecting frieze into which is set one large drawer. Drawers of graduated size are placed between the pilasters below. The undulating front feet are almost a memory silhouette of Empire paw feet. Beveled panels appear on the interior of the back and sides, set into the pegged carcase. Similar panels have been utilized as the bottoms of skillfully dovetailed drawers.

OBJECT: Chest of drawers

MAKER: Attributed to Gerhard Eilert Kroeger

DATE: 1886

MATERIAL: Pine

MEASUREMENTS: H. 34 1/4″, W. 36 7/8″, D. 20″

HISTORY: According to family tradition, this chest was made in 1886 for Frederick Hillje of High Hill, by a man named Kroeger. The maker was possibly Gerhard Eilert Kroeger (1830–1896), a native of the Duchy of Oldenburg, who is buried in the High Hill Cemetery. The chest has descended in the Hillje family to the present owners.

OWNERS: Mr. and Mrs. Paul Herder, San Antonio

PHOTOGRAPHER: Harvey Patteson

This attractive little chest is in the same tradition as 3.2, with several minor variations. The two upper drawers have been visually united by an ogee molding which segregates them into one large, slightly recessed rectangle, while the lower, wider drawer laps over the drawer opening and also projects forward. This latter feature is echoed in the configuration of the skirt, and gentle S curves further break away from the rigid geometric planes of earlier examples. Bone inlays around the keyholes make a sharp visual contrast to the wood surface, which was originally stained or painted dark brown. The cabinetmaker has used beveled drawer bottoms and beveled backboards.

OBJECT: Chest of drawers

MAKER: Unknown

DATE: Ca. 1875

MATERIALS: Primary, walnut; secondary, pine

MEASUREMENTS: H. 40 5/8", W. 41 3/4", D. 21 9/16"

HISTORY: Collected by the owner in Fayette County

OWNER: Mr. Ted James, San Antonio

PHOTOGRAPHER: Harvey Patteson

While in general form this example differs very little from 3.2, the clean lines of the earlier style have begun to give way to the softly undulating curves often associated with the Restauration taste, as seen here in the upper and lower drawer fronts. Beautifully figured walnut has been used. In an interesting combination of techniques, the maker has carved the top drawer out of solid walnut but applied the projecting molding on the bottom drawer. The rounded front corners of the carcase are subtly tapered into a square profile at the bottom. The delightful vernacular curves and countercurves of the skirt echo the undulating surfaces above and visually unite the overall composition of this most satisfying piece. Although there seems to be an especially high quality of craftsmanship throughout, the dovetailed drawers do not have beveled bottoms. Flat boards secured with square nails are used here and on the back of the carcase, in an unusual departure from the norm.

OBJECT: Chest of drawers

MAKER: Attributed to Joseph W. Hannig

DATE: 1870–1880

MATERIAL: Walnut

MEASUREMENTS: H. 47 3/8″, W. 43 1/2″, D. 22 1/2″

HISTORY: Has a tradition of ownership by
    Mrs. Suzanna Dickenson Hannig, wife of the maker

OWNER: Winedale Museum, Round Top; the gift of Miss Ima Hogg

PHOTOGRAPHER: Harvey Patteson

Here the design of 3.5 has been further elaborated upon, with undulating surface across all the drawer fronts. The profile of the molded drawer fronts has been extended to the edge, resulting in an attractive serpentine line repeated in the curves of the fanciful skirt. The central section of the skirt breaks forward from the stiles, reflecting the projection of the drawers above, rather like that in 3.4. On the top, the attached smaller chest with a pair of drawers recalls the practice introduced in the early nineteenth century of fastening a looking glass with drawers to the top of a bureau (see 3.11). Here, of course, the looking glass has been omitted.

OBJECT: Chest of drawers

MAKER: Albert Giesecke

DATE: 1870

MATERIALS: Primary, walnut; secondary, pine

MEASUREMENTS: H. 32 1/8″, W. 43 7/8″, D. 20 11/16″

HISTORY: The maker, Albert Giesecke, was born in Germany and trained there as a surveyor. He migrated to Washington County, Texas, with his family in 1846. In 1866, he moved to Burnet County, where this chest was made, and engaged in sheep raising. He was not a commercial cabinetmaker but made this piece and others for his own use.

OWNERS: Mr. and Mrs. Andrew Z. Thompson, San Antonio

PHOTOGRAPHER: Harvey Patteson

Clean plain lines place this handsome chest in the classical German style. The feet set on the bias are a most unusual feature. Although this detail and the nicely molded stiles above are related to the treatment of a pine wardrobe (2.27), there are sufficient differences between the pieces to suggest that the similarities are only in concept and not as a result of their having come from the same craftsman or the same school. The thick top is attractively molded. Giesecke employed the typically Germanic mode of construction, framing two beveled panels into the back and using beveled bottoms on the three large dovetailed drawers. The large wooden pulls appear to be replacements.

OBJECT: Chest of drawers

MAKER: Unknown

DATE: Unknown

MATERIAL: Pine

MEASUREMENTS: H. 34 3/4", W. 41 1/2", D. 17"

HISTORY: Collected by the owner in Gillespie County

OWNER: Mrs. R. L. Patterson, San Antonio

PHOTOGRAPHER: Harvey Patteson

With the exception of great diamond-beveled projecting panels at each end, the design of this chest seems to be a throwback to eighteenth-century style, with its bold baroque moldings and rococo scalloping on the top drawer and skirt. Inside the top drawer, halfway toward the back, is an unusual compartment with a central arched pigeonhole flanked by two small drawers, much like a desk. The drawer bottoms of this example are not beveled, but their sides are dovetailed. The backboards, applied with nails, are beveled. Original bale type hardware has been replaced with the present pulls.

OBJECT: Chest of drawers

MAKER: Unknown

DATE: Unknown

MATERIALS: Primary, walnut; secondary, pine

MEASUREMENTS: H. 36 1/4″, W. 40 1/8″, D. 22 3/8″

HISTORY: Collected in Frelsburg

OWNERS: Mrs. Charles L. Bybee and the late Mr. Bybee,
Round Top

PHOTOGRAPHER: Harvey Patteson

Bold Renaissance Revival–style colonnettes relate the design of this sturdy little walnut chest to that of 3.10. The maker used handsomely grained walnut for the exposed areas of the carcase and pine for the backboards, which are secured with square nails, as well as for the dovetailed drawer sides and beveled drawer bottoms. While the wooden knobs are original, the smaller brass key escutcheons on the one large and two smaller drawers are replacements. The outline of a porcelain escutcheon, rather like that on 3.10, can be seen on the middle drawer.

OBJECT: Chest of drawers

MAKER: Unknown

DATE: Unknown

MATERIALS: Pine and walnut

MEASUREMENTS: H. 34 3/8″, W. 35 1/4″, D. 20 5/8″

HISTORY: Collected in Bellville

OWNERS: Mrs. Charles L. Bybee and the late Mr. Bybee, Round Top

PHOTOGRAPHER: Harvey Patteson

Rarely are two woods mixed in the manner that they are on this handsome chest, of which the drawer fronts are pine, the rest walnut. The two receding upper drawers are set within a beveled frame in a treatment similar to that of 3.4. The beautifully turned colonnettes attached to the corner in the Renaissance Revival mode recall the treatment of 3.9 and strongly resemble those on a wardrobe from Fredericksburg (2.12). In terms of construction, the expected dovetails and beveled drawer bottoms are present, and in addition three vertical beveled panels are framed into the back. The one remaining porcelain key escutcheon is original, and coloration of the wood at the location of the other two suggests that the drawer fronts may originally have been painted or grained.

OBJECT: Chest of drawers, with dressing glass

MAKER: Unknown

DATE: 1860

MATERIALS: Primary, walnut; secondary, pine

MEASUREMENTS: H. 70", W. 43 3/4", D. 18 3/8"

HISTORY: Has a history of usage in Gonzales

OWNER: Mrs. J. B. Wells, Gonzales

PHOTOGRAPHER: Harvey Patteson

Smooth, highly figured walnut surfaces, rounded corners, and ogee bracket feet place this example in the more simple classical phase of the Biedermeier style. Following nineteenth-century innovation, a small dressing chest with a looking glass held by lyre-shaped or dolphin-tail supporters has been built into the top of the bureau, creating what Houston cabinetmaker Marcus Williamson advertised as a "toilet bureau."[11] The cabinetmaker has made dovetailed drawers with rather thick sides and beveled bottoms. Although the carcase is pegged, the backboards, beveled around the edges, are nailed. The unusual brass hardware appears to be original.

OBJECT: Chest of drawers

MAKER: Unknown

DATE: 1860

MATERIALS: Primary, walnut; secondary, pine

MEASUREMENTS: H. 47 3/4″, W. 39 1/2″, D. 22 1/4″

HISTORY: Has a history of ownership in the Dublin family of Mount Selman, Cherokee County

OWNER: Winedale Museum, Round Top; the gift of Miss Ima Hogg

PHOTOGRAPHER: Harvey Patteson

Architectural pilasters of the earlier Empire (see 3.3) have here given way to the later scrolled ornament of the Restauration period. The overall composition remains basically the same, however, with a large heavy projecting drawer above and graduated drawers below. The two small drawers of the dressing chest above recall 3.11. Beveled panels are set into the sides and drawer bottoms.

OBJECT: Chest of drawers

MAKER: W. Richter

DATE: Ca. 1860

MATERIALS: Primary, cedar; secondary, pine

MEASUREMENTS: H. 46 1/2", W. 36 1/4", D. 19 3/4"

HISTORY: According to family tradition, made by W. Richter, a
Galveston cabinetmaker, for John Tod, a planter on
Clear Creek near Dickinson, Galveston County

OWNER: Miss Mary Tod, Houston

PHOTOGRAPHER: Harvey Patteson

This piece is one of the few surviving examples of the flourishing
Galveston furniture industry. It is especially important because of
the penciled inscription written on the interior behind the two
small drawers, "W. Richter & Comp. Moebel fabrik Galveston
[W. Richter & Co. Furniture Factory Galveston]." This shop undoubtedly had some association with D. Traugott Richter and L.
Richter, both Galveston cabinetmakers of the 1850's. In addition
to the penciled inscription, "J. G. Tod" and "John G. Tod" are
written in chalk on the back and under the small left-hand drawer.
Framed construction with beveled panels is used throughout; however, the two small drawers have flat bottoms which are framed
with nails.

OBJECT: Blanket chest
MAKER: Unknown
DATE: Unknown
MATERIALS: Primary, pine; secondary, cedar
MEASUREMENTS: H. 31 7/8", W. 42 15/16", D. 23 3/16"
HISTORY: Collected by the owners in New Braunfels
OWNERS: Mr. and Mrs. Marshall Steves, San Antonio
PHOTOGRAPHER: Harvey Patteson

A molded top and tapered feet relieve the stark simplicity of this chest. It is beautifully constructed, with sides, front, and back all let into the stiles. A beveled bottom and dovetails appear on the drawers. An attractive faded blue paint, probably original, covers the surface.

4. Chairs and Stools

The most common item in any nineteenth-century Texas house, from a slave cabin to the Governor's Mansion, was "the good old 'home-spun' chair," as a chairmaker at Washington called it in his advertisement.[12] The simple slat-back chair, with a seat of oak splints, laced rawhide strips, cowhide, or corn shucks, has been made in the Appalachian Mountains since the early part of the nineteenth century. Its form was carried over the South in the years before the Civil War by specialized craftsmen who called themselves "chairmakers" rather than cabinetmakers and who understood the technique of boiling wood for the curved slats and shaping them by placing them in pegged forms while wet. Chairmakers were sometimes itinerant craftsmen, traveling from community to community in the summer and returning to a shop in the winter to turn a new supply of stretchers; others had well-established "factories," equipped with water-powered or horse-powered lathes, which produced as many as a thousand chairs a year. Some chairmakers fit both descriptions; three generations of the Dorris family made chairs all the way from Tennessee to Texas before opening a shop in Lockhart.

More elegant chairs were made by cabinetmakers. These fell basically into two categories: "parlor chairs," or side chairs, and rocking chairs. The same technique was followed in making both: thin wooden templates were prepared for each part, and the parts were then sawed out, finished, and assembled. Most of the surviving examples of parlor chairs are of the klismos type, with caned or solid seats, and were made in sets. The rockers, which tended to be either of the "Voltaire" style or slat-backs, were used in bedrooms, sitting rooms, and porches; the parlor chairs were placed around the walls of more formal rooms and frequently doubled as dining-room chairs.

Special mention should be made of a type of chair made in the German areas of Texas. These chairs are the lineal descendants of an extremely old German folk furniture form, the *Brettstuhl*. Two examples of Texas-made *Brettstühle* are pictured (4.27 and 4.28), one from the Hill Country and one from Austin County, and several others are known.

OBJECT: Rocking chair

MAKER: Christofer Friderich Carl Steinhagen

DATE: 1870

MATERIALS: Primary, oak; secondary, pine

MEASUREMENTS: H. 40″, W. 23 1/2″, D. 35″

HISTORY: Made in Anderson for the maker's family and descended in that family to the last private owner

OWNER: Winedale Museum, Round Top; the gift of Miss Ima Hogg

PHOTOGRAPHERS: Ewing Waterhouse (chair); Jim Bones (template)

This open-arm rocking chair with contour back, scrolled arms terminating in acanthus leaves, and swans' heads in front conforms to a popular Restauration style form, the "Voltaire." The carving, in Steinhagen's distinctive style, repeats motifs, such as the acanthus leaves and swans' heads, that appear on two other pieces made to match this rocker (5.1 and 6.25). The oak frame is of mortise-and-tenon construction; the slip seat framed in pine has coil steel springs. The template for the arm rest has survived and is also in the Winedale collection.

Template

OBJECT: Rocking chair

MAKER: Attributed to Johann Michael Jahn

DATE: 1860–1870

MATERIALS: Primary, walnut; secondary, pine

MEASUREMENTS: H. 42 1/4″, W. 24 1/4″, D. 20 5/16″

HISTORY: Made in New Braunfels and descended in the maker's family to his grandson

OWNER: Lent by Paul Jahn of New Braunfels to the New Braunfels Conservation Society

PHOTOGRAPHER: Babette Fraser Warren

Sophistication of design and detail distinguishes this walnut Voltaire rocking chair. The subtle scroll at the knee and the molding at the junctures of the skirt with the front leg and arm are especially fine. The beautiful scrolled arm support echoes the leg below. The legs are pegged through the rockers, and the side rails of the set frame are let into the back rail. The caning is a replacement. The overall excellence of the piece suggests the hand of a first-rate craftsman—perhaps Johann Michael Jahn; ownership by a grandson of the cabinetmaker would seem to confirm this attribution.

OBJECTS: Rocking chair and footstool

MAKER: Heinrich Scholl

DATE: 1870

MATERIAL: Walnut

MEASUREMENTS: Chair, H. 44 1/2″, W. 22 1/8″, D. 20″;
   footstool, H. 8″, W. 10 7/16″, D. 14 7/8″

HISTORY: Made in New Braunfels; descended in the family of the
   maker to his great-granddaughter

OWNERS: Dr. and Mrs. O. A. Stratemann, New Braunfels

PHOTOGRAPHERS: Babette Fraser Warren (chair and stool);
   Harvey Patteson (templates)

A Voltaire rocking chair of a rather more usual design and with
a pegged frame, this piece survives with its original little footstool.
Of particular interest, however, is the existence of the original templates from which the parts of this chair were made. The maker,
Heinrich Scholl, was a house carpenter, a sash and door maker, and
a cabinetmaker, and he apparently must have made or intended to
make enough of these rocking chairs to merit cutting the templates.

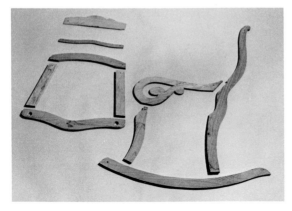

Templates

OBJECTS: Rocking chair and footstool

MAKER: Unknown

DATE: Unknown

MATERIAL: Walnut

MEASUREMENTS: Chair, H. 38 1/2", W. 21 1/2", D. 21 1/2"; footstool, H. 8 1/2", W. 15 1/2", D. 15 1/2"

HISTORY: Collected by the owner in New Braunfels

OWNER: Mr. Ted James, San Antonio

PHOTOGRAPHER: Harvey Patteson

Here is yet another variant on the Voltaire rocking chair; but, like the Steinhagen example, this one is upholstered rather than caned. Originally there were small upholstered pads pegged to the tops of the arms. The matching footstool with bold convex molded skirt echoing the chair's front seat rail shows the Biedermeier taste.

OBJECT: Rocking chair

MAKER: Johann Peter Tatsch

DATE: 1852–1870

MATERIAL: Walnut

MEASUREMENTS: H. 42″, W. 21 1/2″, D. 18 1/2″

HISTORY: Has a long history of ownership in Fredericksburg

OWNER: On loan to Pioneer Museum, Fredericksburg

PHOTOGRAPHER: Harvey Patteson

This banister-back rocking chair is vernacular in style in that many of its details are survivals of early eighteenth-century design. Both the boldly turned front arms and arm supports and the tentative vase-and-ring front stretchers (whose outline is repeated in the banisters) are elements found in chairs made at least a century and a half earlier, and as such they must have come down to the maker by means of traditional chair forms repeated generation after generation. The little wings which are attached to the serpentine crest rail by means of dovetails are particularly Germanic. In the Texas tradition, the seat is covered with cowhide. The similarity between this and 4.6, which has descended in the family of Johann Peter Tatsch, assigns this example to that craftsman.

OBJECT: Rocking chair

MAKER: Johann Peter Tatsch

DATE: 1852–1870

MATERIAL: Walnut

MEASUREMENTS: H. 39 3/4″, W. 21 1/2″, D. 18 3/4″

HISTORY: Made in Fredericksburg and descended in the maker's family to his granddaughter, the present owner

OWNER: Mrs. Lyne Lewis Harper, Fredericksburg

PHOTOGRAPHER: Harvey Patteson

Finely turned arms, arm supports, front stretchers, and banisters lend a degree of excellence here belied by the present rough appearance, a result of the chair's having sat outside for many years. The bamboolike turnings of the banisters are reminiscent of early-nineteenth-century design. The chair is made of walnut and carefully put together by pegged construction. The unfinished ends of the crest suggest that perhaps Tatsch originally intended to attach wings.

OBJECT: Rocking chair

MAKER: Unknown

DATE: 1870

MATERIAL: Walnut

MEASUREMENTS: H. 41 1/4″, W. 21 1/8″, D. 17 3/4″

HISTORY: Collected by the owner in Gillespie County

OWNER: Mrs. Schatzie Crouch, Fredericksburg

PHOTOGRAPHER: Harvey Patteson

While in general outline this example is related to 4.3, the vase-and-ring banisters as well as the front stretchers reflect the vernacular style represented in 4.5 and 4.6. Several not readily apparent yet sophisticated details are the beautifully scrolled arm terminals, the molded front seat rail, and the chamfered front legs. The frame is pegged together, but the rockers are secured with screws. The slip seat is held up with slats.

OBJECT: Rocking chair

MAKER: Attributed to Conrad Schueddemagen

DATE: 1855

MATERIAL: Hickory

MEASUREMENTS: H. 41 1/4", W. 19 1/2", D. 17 1/2"

HISTORY: Ownership has been traced to Leo Wagner (1805–1893), a native of Germany who migrated to Round Top about 1850. Mrs. Alma Schueddemagen Kellersberger of Leander has an identical chair which she attributes to her great-grandfather, Conrad Schueddemagen.

OWNERS: Mrs. Charles L. Bybee and the late Mr. Bybee, Round Top

PHOTOGRAPHER: Harvey Patteson

A gentle S curve in the back of this rocking chair faintly echoes the sinuous outlines of such high-style pieces as Johann Michael Jahn's great chair (4.2). The carved rail in the silhouette of a tablet flanked by anthemion further recalls the classical style. The remaining elements of this example are virtually styleless. The members have been pegged together and the arms mortised through the stiles. On the reverse of the seat, recessed to receive a cushion, is a raised panel. The whole has been painted a dark brown.

OBJECT: Rocking chair

MAKER: Unknown

DATE: Unknown

MATERIAL: Hickory

MEASUREMENTS: H. 39 1/2″, W. 18 3/4″, D. 14 7/8″

HISTORY: Collected in Round Top

OWNERS: Mrs. Charles L. Bybee and the late Mr. Bybee,
Round Top

PHOTOGRAPHER: Harvey Patteson

Although vernacular in style and crude in execution, this chair
has considerable charm. The high, slightly contoured back with
wide tablet recalls some Pennsylvania rockers. The maker has carefully mortised the arm supports through the arm, the arms through
the stiles; all the other members are mortised as well. The front
seat rail and hide bottom are modern replacements. Traces of original red paint are to be found in various places.

OBJECT: Rocking chair

MAKER: Unknown

DATE: Unknown

MATERIAL: Hickory

MEASUREMENTS: H. 38 7/8″, W. 22″, D. 16 1/2″

HISTORY: Collected by the donor near Rutersville

OWNER: Winedale Museum, Round Top; the gift of
　　　Miss Ima Hogg

PHOTOGRAPHER: Jim Bones

Although this example is a slat-back rocking chair of the ubiquitous vernacular type, several features make it distinctive. The slats, four rather than three, are attractively notched; the arm supports are nicely turned. With the exception of the seat rail, which is mortised, the members are nailed together.

OBJECT: Rocking chair

MAKER: Unknown

DATE: Unknown

MATERIAL: Pine

MEASUREMENTS: H. 35 1/2", W. 19 3/8", D. 17 1/8"

HISTORY: Collected by the owners in Houston; probably made in East Texas

OWNERS: Mr. and Mrs. Robin Elverson, Houston

PHOTOGRAPHER: Ewing Waterhouse

This slat-back rocking chair has generally heavier proportions than the norm, and its arm supports extend to the upper stretcher, a strengthening feature necessitated by the fact that the supports are not an extension of the front legs. This arrangement occurs in some chairs of Louisiana origin.[13] Attractively turned finials and arm supports are added notes of interest. The chair is painted blue.

OBJECT: Rocking chair

MAKER: Unknown

DATE: Unknown

MATERIAL: Hickory

MEASUREMENTS: H. 37 1/4″, W. 20″, D. 16 1/2″

HISTORY: Unknown

OWNERS: Mrs. Charles L. Bybee and the late Mr. Bybee,
    Round Top

PHOTOGRAPHER: Harvey Patteson

Although somewhat crude in workmanship, this chair with its complementary curves of rocker, arms, and back is visually rather pleasing. The maker has curved and bent a single piece of hickory to make the front leg and arm. The shaped back is curved. The four slats of the back are pegged, and the stretcher between the rockers is mortised. Screws are utilized to secure the arms to the stiles and the legs to the rockers. This example is remarkably similar to a more angular armchair made in Louisiana.[14]

OBJECT: Chair

MAKER: Johann Peter Tatsch

DATE: 1860–1880

MATERIALS: Pine and hickory

MEASUREMENTS: H. 30 1/2″, W. 21″, D. 17 1/8″

HISTORY: Made in Fredericksburg and descended in the family of the maker to his granddaughter, the present owner

OWNER: Mrs. Lyne Lewis Harper, Fredericksburg

PHOTOGRAPHER: Harvey Patteson

This chair is one of several that have descended in the family of the maker. In design they conform to the utilitarian firehouse or captain's chairs popular in the second half of the nineteenth century. The shallow, bamboolike turning of the front stretchers relates to the turnings on other Tatsch examples (4.5 and 4.6).

OBJECT: Armchair

MAKER: Schweer Schweers

DATE: 1870

MATERIAL: Pecan

MEASUREMENTS: H. 42 5/8″, W. 23 1/2″, D. 17 3/4″

HISTORY: This is one of a number of similar chairs made by
  Schweer Schweers at Quihi, Medina County, in the 1870's and
  1880's. According to his great-grandson, C. F. Schweers of
  Hondo, Schweers was not a commercial cabinetmaker but
  spent his declining years making these chairs as gifts for his
  children and neighbors. This chair was included in *The Index
  of American Design* and is pictured in Ralph and Terry Kovel's
  American Country Furniture 1780–1875, p. 101.

OWNER: Mr. Robert Quill Johnson, Castroville

PHOTOGRAPHER: Harvey Patteson

Notched finials and tapering arm supports lend a surprising degree
of elegance to this rather rough and crude armchair. It varies from
the slat-back norm, being carved rather than turned. It is entirely
pegged together. A pair of matching side chairs also exist (see 4.32).

OBJECT: Side chair

MAKER: Johann Michael Jahn

DATE: 1870

MATERIAL: Walnut

MEASUREMENTS: H. 33 1/2", W. 18", D. 16"

HISTORY: One of a pair belonging to the maker's granddaughter; part of a set of twelve made in New Braunfels for her father's dining room; illustrated in *Antiques* 75 (1959):462

OWNER: Mrs. R. L. Biesele, Austin

PHOTOGRAPHER: Harvey Patteson

This beautiful scroll-back side chair with swept rails, curved stiles, and curved front legs is the most sophisticated Texas example known to date. Based on the Grecian klismos, this chair relates more closely to English examples than to the New Braunfels Biedermeier taste. The skillfully carved cross splat of scrolled "Grecian" design is considerably more elaborate than the norm of New Braunfels chairs. Rather finely figured walnut has been utilized. The frame, to which the caning is attached, is pegged to the seat rails.

OBJECT: Side chair

MAKER: Johann Michael Jahn

DATE: 1870

MATERIAL: Walnut

MEASUREMENTS: H. 33 7/8″, W. 18 1/8″, D. 16 3/8″

HISTORY: Made in New Braunfels and descended in the family of
the maker to the last private owner, Ben Jahn of
New Braunfels

OWNER: Winedale Museum, Round Top; the gift of Miss Ima Hogg

PHOTOGRAPHER: Harvey Patteson

This chair is virtually identical to 4.15, differing only in minor
variations of dimension. Such variance could result from its being
handmade or could possibly mean that the chair in question belongs to another set.

OBJECT: Side chair
MAKER: Unknown
DATE: 1860–1870
MATERIAL: Walnut
MEASUREMENTS: H. 32 1/4", W. 17 5/8", D. 16 1/4"
HISTORY: Collected by the owner in New Braunfels
OWNER: Mr. Ted James, San Antonio
PHOTOGRAPHER: Harvey Patteson

Although the maker of this klismos type attempted to achieve the graceful sweep of the Grecian prototype, as seen in 4.15 and 4.16, his ambition surpassed his ability to handle this difficult design. As a result, this chair, with its exaggerated front legs and sweeping stiles, is almost a parody of the form. Nonetheless, the quality of crazy naïveté lends a note of charm.

OBJECT: Side chair

MAKER: Unknown

DATE: Unknown

MATERIAL: Walnut

MEASUREMENTS: H. 31 3/8″, W. 16 3/4″, D. 16 1/8″

HISTORY: Collected by the owner in New Braunfels

OWNER: Mr. Ted James, San Antonio

PHOTOGRAPHER: Harvey Patteson

The severely rectangular lines of this New Braunfels chair are here relieved by a serpentine rail and confirming seat above. The curved profile of the stay rail echoes the shape of the legs and seat rail, giving a continuity of composition in this distinguished example.

OBJECT: Side chair (one of a set of ten)

MAKER: Unknown

DATE: 1860

MATERIAL: Walnut

MEASUREMENTS: H. 32 3/8″, W. 16 1/4″, D. 16″

HISTORY: Once belonged to Sophie Schuenemann, the adopted daughter of Ernst Scherff, an early settler and prominent merchant in New Braunfels; collected by the present owner in New Braunfels

OWNER: Mr. Ted James, San Antonio

PHOTOGRAPHER: Harvey Patteson

One of an unusually large set of chairs, this example is particularly notable for the highly figured walnut utilized at the crest rail. In design, with square seat and curved front legs, it is representative of one type of New Braunfels chair.

OBJECT: Side chair

MAKER: Unknown

DATE: 1860

MATERIAL: Walnut

MEASUREMENTS: H. 31 3/4″, W. 17 5/8″, D. 15 1/2″

HISTORY: This is part of a set of chairs that once belonged to Mrs. Ernst Stein of New Braunfels, who inherited them from her grandparents, Mr. and Mrs. Ferdinand Nehls. Nehls was a teacher who immigrated from the Grand Duchy of Mecklenburg-Schwerin to New Braunfels about 1855. Another chair from this set is in the Winedale collection.

OWNER: Mr. Ted James, San Antonio

PHOTOGRAPHER: Harvey Patteson

This example is remarkably similar in design to 4.19, differing in having generally lighter proportions, especially in the stay rail, and a solid plank seat as opposed to the more expensive and complicated caning. Although the figure of the wood is not as fine as that of 4.19, in overall composition this chair is more beautiful.

OBJECT: Side chair (one of three)

MAKER: Unknown

DATE: Unknown

MATERIAL: Cherry

MEASUREMENTS: H. 33 1/8", W. 17 1/4", D. 15 5/8"

HISTORY: According to a story related to the present owner, these chairs were called the "Solms chairs" because they were used by Prince Carl von Solms-Braunfels, the founder of New Braunfels, while he was visiting a former owner's grandfather. Since Prince Carl left Texas in May, 1845, this story, if true, would make this chair the earliest known example of New Braunfels furniture.

OWNER: Mr. Ted James, San Antonio

PHOTOGRAPHER: Harvey Patteson

This chair and the three following examples represent a group of a rather more severe form made in New Braunfels. This form is characterized by a rectangular seat and straight front legs which, in all cases but 4.24, are slightly flared at the base. The double vase and central ball silhouette at the stay rail, used on 4.21, 4.22, and 4.23, was also employed by Jacob Schneider of Fredericksburg on 4.25. Although walnut appears to have been the usual material, this chair and 4.22 are made of cherry.

OBJECT: Side chair

MAKER: Unknown

DATE: Unknown

MATERIAL: Cherry

MEASUREMENTS: H. 33 15/16", W. 17 3/8", D. 15 3/8"

HISTORY: Collected by the owner in New Braunfels

OWNER: Mr. Ted James, San Antonio

PHOTOGRAPHER: Harvey Patteson

Extreme similarity in form and material between this chair and 4.21 suggests that possibly they were made by the same hand. However, a solid seat has been substituted here for the caning of 4.21. The unusual figure of the cherry wood has been skillfully employed by the maker, resulting in an attractive pattern of light accents across the seat and back.

OBJECT: Side chair

MAKER: Attributed to Johann Michael Jahn

DATE: 1860

MATERIAL: Walnut

MEASUREMENTS: H. 34 5/8", W. 18 1/2", D. 16 1/2"

HISTORY: Collected by the owners in New Braunfels

OWNERS: Mr. and Mrs. W. H. Dillen, New Braunfels

PHOTOGRAPHER: Babette Fraser Warren

While similar to 4.22, this chair is slightly larger and more graceful. The seat rail is pegged together, and the side rails are mortised through the stiles, as in 4.24 and 4.25.

OBJECT: Side chair (one of a pair)

MAKER: Heinrich Scholl

DATE: 1860–1870

MATERIAL: Walnut

MEASUREMENTS: H. 31 7/8″, W. 18 3/4″, D. 16 3/18″

HISTORY: Made in New Braunfels and descended in the maker's family to the present owners

OWNERS: Dr. and Mrs. O. A. Stratemann, New Braunfels

PHOTOGRAPHER: Babette Fraser Warren

Heinrich Scholl's cane-bottom chairs have remained in the possession of his descendants and are used today in the house built by him. Slightly lower and broader than the other New Braunfels examples, they lack the flared front leg often utilized on chairs of this rectangular type. Here Scholl has employed the simplest of stay rails. The seat rails are mortised through the stiles, while the cane seat is secured with large screws.

OBJECT: Side chair (one of six)

MAKER: Jacob Schneider

DATE: 1860–1870

MATERIAL: Walnut

MEASUREMENTS: H. 32 15/16", W. 17 1/8", D. 15 3/4"

HISTORY: Made in Fredericksburg and descended in the maker's family to his granddaughter, the present owner

OWNER: Mrs. Lewis Dolezal, Fredericksburg

PHOTOGRAPHER: Harvey Patteson

Closely related to the New Braunfels examples, this set of chairs by Jacob Schneider is the most sophisticated from the Fredericksburg area. Fashioned from attractive figured walnut, they follow the scrolled lines of the Grecian klismos prototype. Unlike any of the New Braunfels solid-seat examples, the seat here has been fitted between the seat rails, and the front conforms to the curvature of the rails. The side rails are mortised through the stiles. The rest of the frame is entirely pegged, with the exception of the large screws which secure the front leg to the rail. The set has descended in the family of the cabinetmaker. Also in their possession is the block of walnut from which the curved back stays were sawed.

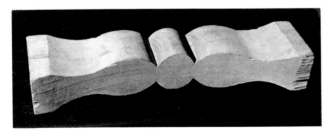

Walnut block from which back stays were sawed

OBJECT: Chair

MAKER: Unknown

DATE: Unknown

MATERIAL: Maple

MEASUREMENTS: H. 34 3/4″, W. 18 7/8″, D. 16 1/8″

HISTORY: Collected near Columbus

OWNER: New Braunfels Conservation Society, New Braunfels

PHOTOGRAPHER: Babette Fraser Warren

Stylistically this stocky side chair is almost vernacular, being a memory image of the Biedermeier style. The three vertical members of the back relate to the treatment of 4.28 and in a more general sense to the chair backs of Franz Stautzenberger's bench chest (5.11). The legs are slightly shaped to render them more fashionable, as are the stiles. An extra small detail is thumbnail molding around the edge of the seat. The deep skirt, mortised into the legs, is secured with pegs. While presently a light mellow brown, there is evidence that the surface once had a dark mahogany stain.

OBJECT: Side chair *(Brettstuhl)*

MAKER: Johann Martin Loeffler

DATE: 1855

MATERIAL: Pine

MEASUREMENTS: H. 31 3/4″, W. 18″, D. 14 1/4″

HISTORY: Made by Loeffler for the Wendel family in Fredericksburg

OWNER: On loan to the Pioneer Museum, Fredericksburg

PHOTOGRAPHER: Harvey Patteson

This chair, made in Fredericksburg by Johann Martin Loeffler, is a Germanic type of the simplest design, with a plank seat, rounded legs doweled through the seat, and a cutout plank back. Chairs of this sort, called *Brettstühle* in German, stem from late medieval forms and were common in Germany until the nineteenth century.[15] They appear in the areas of German settlement in America, notably eighteenth-century Pennsylvania but also North Carolina, where they are often called "Moravian." This example, made of pine, now rough and gray from exposure to weather, has a slightly bowed seat and front and charmingly notched sides on the back.

OBJECT: Side chair *(Brettstuhl)*

MAKER: Unknown

DATE: Unknown

MATERIAL: Pine

MEASUREMENTS: H. 33 1/2″, W. 17 7/8″, D. 14″

HISTORY: Collected near Cat Spring

OWNERS: Mrs. Charles L. Bybee and the late Mr. Bybee,
    Round Top

PHOTOGRAPHER: Harvey Patteson

While this chair is basically the same as 4.27 in construction, the maker here has attempted to lend sophistication to his chair by shaping the seat and giving it a framed rather than a plank back. The flared back and three banisters reflect an awareness of the Biedermeier taste. Braces running from front to back are dovetailed into the seat. The stiles continue down through the seat, and braces are secured with pegs.

OBJECT: Side chair *(Brettstuhl)*

MAKER: Unknown

DATE: 1845

MATERIAL: Oak

MEASUREMENTS: H. 33 5/8″, W. 17 3/4″, D. 16 1/8″

HISTORY: See below

OWNERS: Mrs. Charles L. Bybee and the late Mr. Bybee,
    Round Top

PHOTOGRAPHER: Harvey Patteson

This oak example was made in Germany and is clearly a prototype
for 4.27 and 4.28. According to the owner, this chair was made as
a going-away present for a family emigrating to Texas and was
disassembled and brought to America in a trunk. Immediately
noticeable differences from Texas-made 4.27 are the molded seat
and elaborately cutout, carved, and ornamented back. The legs are
not doweled through the seat but rather are set into seat braces.
The back is let through the seat and secured with pegs.

Simple slat-back vernacular chairs were ubiquitous throughout America in the first half of the nineteenth century. While in some areas the seats were covered with rush, in Texas cowhide, sometimes with hair, was most often utilized—hence the name "cow chairs." Descended from slat-back chairs of the late seventeenth and the eighteenth century, these vernacular versions are reduced in scale, in slats, and in turned ornament. Occasionally, on the better examples, there is some sort of turned finial at the top of the stile; from time to time the slats are shaped. Cow chairs appear to have been the products of specialized craftsmen who described themselves as "chairmakers" rather than of more skilled cabinetmakers; they were still being made in East Texas in the late 1950's. They found usage not only in humble households but also in grander settings, such as the Greek Revival Governor's Mansion, in Austin, where in 1861 no less than fourteen were scattered in bedrooms, the upper hall, servants' rooms, and the kitchen.[16] These examples from the Winedale collection are typical.

PHOTOGRAPHER: Ewing Waterhouse

OBJECT: Hide-bottom chair

MAKER: Unknown

DATE: Unknown

MATERIAL: Cherry

MEASUREMENTS: H. 34 1/2″, W. 18 5/8″, D. 15 3/4″

HISTORY: Collected by the owner in Fredericksburg

OWNER: Mr. Ted James, San Antonio

PHOTOGRAPHER: Harvey Patteson

This attractive hide-bottom side chair is unusual in that it is made of cherry rather than the customary hickory. The stiles are slightly raked and terminate in tiny button finials. The sharply tapered cone-shaped feet are typical of better examples.

OBJECT: Hide-bottom chair

MAKER: Bernhard Romberg

DATE: Ca. 1870

MATERIAL: Mulberry

MEASUREMENTS: H. 33 1/4″, W. 16 1/2″, D. 17″

HISTORY: Descended in the maker's family to the donor

OWNER: Winedale Museum, Round Top; the gift of
Miss Annie Romberg

PHOTOGRAPHER: Harvey Patteson

This little chair is unusual for a number of reasons. The maker
gave special attention to it, adding a decorative top slat, because
he made it as a wedding present for his brother, Julius Romberg,
and his bride. It was part of a set of six, made by Romberg at his
windmill-powered chair factory at Black Jack, Fayette County. The
factory was equipped with a sixty-foot windmill with canvas sails,
a landmark for miles, which operated a saw and lathe.

OBJECT: Side chair (one of a pair)

MAKER: Schweer Schweers

DATE: 1870

MATERIAL: Pecan

MEASUREMENTS: H. 31 1/4", W. 17 5/8", D. 15 1/2"

HISTORY: Collected by the owner at Quihi

OWNER: Mr. Robert Quill Johnson, Castroville

PHOTOGRAPHER: Harvey Patteson

This crude, basic chair, a variation on the usual turned variety, looks as if it were made with a draw knife. Nevertheless, the upward-tapering stiles, notched finials, and arched slats give it a charming sense of style. It matches an armchair, 4.14.

OBJECTS: Miniature side chair, table, and rocker

MAKER: Johann Peter Tatsch

DATE: 1852–1870

MATERIAL: Walnut

MEASUREMENTS: Side chair, H. 26", W. 14 7/8", D. 13";
table, H. 18 3/8", W. 21 1/2", L. 26 7/8";
rocking chair, H. 26 3/4", W. 13", D. 15"

HISTORY: These pieces were ordered from Tatsch by a
Fredericksburg customer who refused to pay for them on
completion. Tatsch gave them to his own daughter, from
whom they descended to the
present owner, his granddaughter.

OWNER: Mrs. Lyne Lewis Harper,
Fredericksburg

PHOTOGRAPHER: Harvey Patteson

These simple, yet charming pieces of walnut have descended in the family of Johann Peter Tatsch. Each piece is well put together with pegs and mortise-and-tenon joints. The attractively turned arms of the rocking chair are very similar to those on the full-sized examples by Tatsch (4.5 and 4.6), and the legs of the table assume the same general outline. The chair legs, rounded on the outer and rear sides, are flat on the two inner surfaces. Tatsch has nailed the drawer sides together rather than dovetailing them and has utilized a plain flat board for the drawer bottom.

OBJECT: Chair

MAKER: Unknown

DATE: 1850

MATERIAL: Gum

MEASUREMENTS: H. 31 1/2″, W. 15 1/2″, D. 12″

HISTORY: Made by a Norwegian workman living on the farm of Carl Questad near Norse, Bosque County, for Questad's use; descended in Questad's family to his granddaughter, Mrs. Sadie Hoel of Clifton

OWNER: Bosque Memorial Museum, Clifton

PHOTOGRAPHER: Harvey Patteson

This crude cowhide-bottomed chair is stylistically related to some of the finer Hill Country furniture (see 4.19, 4.20, and 4.25). It was undoubtedly copied from a remembered European example.

OBJECT: Footstool

MAKER: John William August Kleine

DATE: Ca. 1870

MATERIAL: Walnut

MEASUREMENTS: H. 7 7/8", W. 11 3/4", D. 15 3/4"

HISTORY: Made in Gonzales for the maker's own use and
descended in his family to the present owner

OWNER: Mrs. Walter D. Kleine, Gonzales

PHOTOGRAPHER: Harvey Patteson

A walnut frame and solid walnut top suggest that this footstool
may not always have been upholstered. The boldly curved legs
relate to those on the next example.

4.35

OBJECT: Footstool

MAKER: Unknown

DATE: Ca. 1850

MATERIAL: Walnut

MEASUREMENTS: H. 6 1/2", W. 15", D. 8 1/2"

HISTORY: Made by a cabinetmaker resident on the Charles Fordtran
farm near Industry, Austin County; part of the dowry of
Anna Portia Fordtran when she married Dr. Gregor McGregor
in 1861; descended in the McGregor family to the last
private owner

OWNER: Winedale Museum, Round Top; the gift of
Almeida McGregor Harris

PHOTOGRAPHER: Harvey Patteson

The bold S curve of the legs is repeated in the handhold cut through
the upper surface. Thin dovetails join the sides and ends of the
cyma-curved skirt. While the original usage of these stools is not
entirely clear, it is very likely that they were used with rocking
chairs.

4.36

5. Sofas, Settees, Benches, and Day Beds

Sofas do not appear to have been a common furniture form among Texas cabinetmakers, possibly because of the complexities of upholstering them. They are seldom mentioned in advertisements or on the products-of-industry schedules, although in the mid-fifties Frederick Law Olmsted reported seeing one "covered with cheap pink calico with a small vine pattern" in the sitting room of a New Braunfels hotel and another in his bedroom.[17]

Settees, on which thick mattresses stuffed with horsehair, Spanish moss, or corn shucks were laid, were more common and were frequently used in hallways or on porches, as were unupholstered wooden benches. The day bed, or lounge, is the most frequently encountered of all four forms; it was not only a seating device but was also used for daytime reclining and "dinner naps" and was properly a piece of bedroom or hall furniture.

OBJECT: Sofa

MAKER: Christofer Friderich Carl Steinhagen

DATE: 1860

MATERIALS: Primary, oak; secondary, pine

MEASUREMENTS: H. 42″, W. 84″, D. 25″

HISTORY: Made in Anderson and descended in the maker's family to the last private owners, his granddaughters

OWNER: Winedale Museum, Round Top; the gift of Miss Ima Hogg

PHOTOGRAPHER: Ewing Waterhouse

This sofa with its amazing fish across the back is an imaginative interpretation of the neoclassical form undoubtedly known to the maker in his native Germany. It is part of a highly decorative set of furniture made by C. F. C. Steinhagen for use in his own home at Anderson. The swans'-head arm terminals, a motif derived from the type of rocking chair often called "Voltaire," have been curiously adapted, perhaps to match the rocker made by Steinhagen and used with this sofa (see 4.1). Shallow-carved acanthus-leaf ornament in Steinhagen's readily recognizable style decorates the skirt. Although the front of the frame is pegged, the back, fitted with three flat recessed panels, is held on by screws. Oak slats beneath the frame support the steel coil springs, an improved upholstery technique that appeared about 1850.

OBJECT: Sofa

MAKER: Unknown

DATE: 1860

MATERIALS: Primary, mahogany; secondary, pine

MEASUREMENTS: H. 43 1/4″, W. 84 3/8″, D. 30″

HISTORY: Collected in New Braunfels

OWNER: New Braunfels Conservation Society, New Braunfels

PHOTOGRAPHER: Babette Fraser Warren

Upholstered sofas of Texas provenance are indeed rare. This example is transitional between the classical and Rococo Revival tastes. A serpentine back, outlined by a veneered mahogany astragal molding which is repeated in the scalloped skirt, heralds the first rococo phase of the Victorian era, while the scrolled arms and cornucopia feet are remnants of the neoclassical style. An unusual and rather Germanic note is seen in the applied diamond-beveled panels below the arms at either end of the skirt. The solid mahogany legs are mortised into the frame. Three vertical braces are utilized across the back. The slightly naïve quality of overall design, the construction techniques and ornament, and a long New Braunfels history suggest that this piece was made there.

OBJECT: Sofa

MAKER: Unknown

DATE: 1860

MATERIALS: Primary, walnut; secondary, pine

MEASUREMENTS: H. 37", W. 80", D. 27 1/8"

HISTORY: Collected by the owner in New Braunfels

OWNER: Mr. Ted James, San Antonio

PHOTOGRAPHER: Harvey Patteson

This handsome walnut upholstered example is considerably more Germanic in character than 5.2 and closely related to the more prevalent settees (see 5.4 and 5.8). In general outlines the neo-classical taste has been preserved in the scrolled arms and legs and the scalloped top. The ornamental top is one large piece of wood, as is each delicately curved front and scrolled leg. While the frame is pegged, the members of the back are secured with large screws.

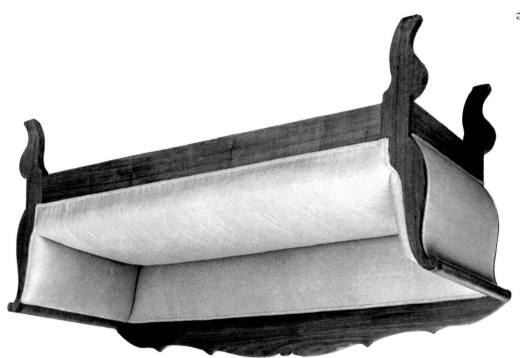

OBJECT: Settee

MAKER: Unknown

DATE: Unknown

MATERIAL: Oak

MEASUREMENTS: H. 36″, W. 77 3/4″, D. 25 7/8″

HISTORY: Has a history of ownership in the Wunderlich family
of Winedale, Fayette County

OWNERS: Mrs. Charles L. Bybee and the late Mr. Bybee,
Round Top

PHOTOGRAPHER: Harvey Patteson

Fine lines and attention to detail mark this oak settee as one of the most successful of its form. Particularly attractive are the delicately curved neoclassical arms and slender legs. Small details, such as the vaguely "Grecian" central ornament of the back and the molding above and below the banisters, lend an extra quality of finish. The simple parade of cutout double-vase-and-ball banisters is reminiscent of the treatment in stair rails of vernacular wooden architecture. The entire frame is pegged and mortised. Small iron braces strengthen the juncture of the top rail and arms at either side of the back. New webbing replaces the original rawhide strips which, nailed to the inside of the frame, supported the loose cushion.

OBJECT: Settee

MAKER: Unknown

DATE: Unknown

MATERIAL: Pine

MEASUREMENTS: H. 32 7/8″, W. 81 7/8″, D. 22 1/4″

HISTORY: Collected near Brenham

OWNERS: Mrs. Charles L. Bybee and the late Mr. Bybee,
Round Top

PHOTOGRAPHER: Harvey Patteson

One wide pine plank across the back places this settee in a stylistic category of its own. The gentle curve of the neoclassical arms is echoed in the lines of the back. At either end are simple baluster-shaped rails. Somewhat straight legs suggest a desire to conserve wood that is confirmed by the fact that those on the right-hand side are spliced. While the seat frame is of mortise-and-tenon construction, the back is attached to the arms with nails rather than screws, and the slats supporting the seat are secured with square nails. A central brace extending from front to back is nailed to the underside of the frame.

OBJECT: Settee

MAKER: Unknown

DATE: Unknown

MATERIAL: Pine

MEASUREMENTS: H. 32 7/8", W. 81 3/8", D. 22 3/8"

HISTORY: Collected in Washington County

OWNERS: Mrs. Charles L. Bybee and the late Mr. Bybee,
Round Top

PHOTOGRAPHER: Harvey Patteson

A simple porch settee with open rounded slats, this pine example
is related to 5.8 in its design. Its frame is mortised and pegged;
the back is secured with large screws. Originally it was painted
white.

This settee and 5.8 were made as a pair. This one was originally used outside on a porch or dog run. Open, rounded slats flush with the surface, rather than inset for a cushion as in 5.8, are used here. Extra details include the curve between the leg and arm at the juncture of the seat rail and the applied scrolled molding across the center of the back. The construction is the same as that of 5.6.

PHOTOGRAPHER: Harvey Patteson

OWNERS: Mr. and Mrs. Paul Herder, San Antonio
present owners

HISTORY: Made at Frelsburg, Colorado County, for Buller's kinsman, Frederick Hillje, Fayette County oil-mill operator, and descended in the Hillje family to the

MEASUREMENTS: H. 37″, W. 80″, D. 19″

MATERIAL: Pine

DATE: 1870

MAKER: Henry W. Buller

OBJECT: Settee

OBJECT: Settee

MAKER: Henry W. Buller

DATE: 1870

MATERIAL: Pine

MEASUREMENTS: H. 35 1/2″, W. 78 1/2″, D. 21 3/8″

HISTORY: Made at Frelsburg for Frederick Hillje and descended in his family to the present owners

OWNERS: Mr. and Mrs. Paul Herder, San Antonio

PHOTOGRAPHER: Harvey Patteson

This settee was one of the pair made for the Hillje family (see 5.7). In its simplicity of line it relates closely to 5.6. The seat, of flat slats nailed to the pegged frame, is inset to receive a cushion or pad, indicating usage in the interior of the Hillje house.

Heavy proportions and ponderous appearance belie the ultimate neoclassical designs from which this settee springs. Obviously the craftsman has remembered—yet misunderstood. The reverse curve of the legs and the repeated scallops of the back are extremely naive. Nonetheless, the piece is made with care. Rather nicely grained walnut has been used. A good molding runs along the top edge of the skirt and the lower edge of the arm rail. Screws are used to secure the back to the arms, a not unusual feature, and screws also hold the arm rail to the scrolled support. As if the maker was not sure about the screws, he has placed wooden pegs on either side. Pegs also secure the vertical supports to the back rail. Similar reverse-curved legs appear on a walnut crib (1.23) made by William Athelger, and their presence here may indicate his hand.

PHOTOGRAPHER: Harvey Patteson
OWNER: Mrs. Schatzie Crouch, Fredericksburg
HISTORY: Collected by the owner in Fredericksburg
MEASUREMENTS: H. 31 1/8″, W. 71 7/8″, D. 26 3/8″
MATERIAL: Walnut
DATE: 1870
MAKER: Unknown
OBJECT: Sofa

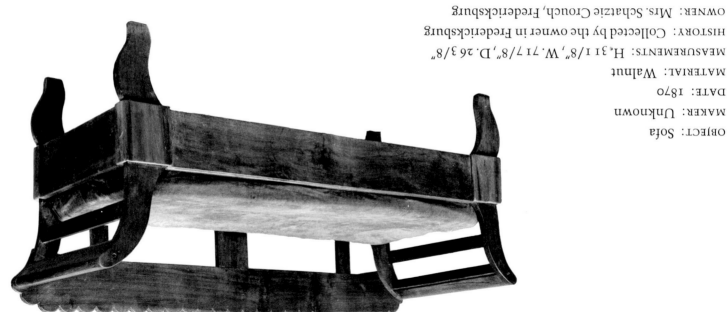

OBJECT: Settee

MAKER: Unknown

DATE: Unknown

MATERIAL: Pine

MEASUREMENTS: H. 31 7/8″, W. 82 1/4″, D. 22 3/4″

HISTORY: Collected near Serbin, Lee County

OWNERS: Mrs. Charles L. Bybee and the late Mr. Bybee, Round Top

PHOTOGRAPHER: Harvey Patteson

Despite heavy crude members, this settee or porch bench has been put together with mortise-and-tenon construction. In all likelihood it represents yet another interpretation of the Biedermeier classical form brought to Texas. There is an upholstered settee of virtually identical line — curved arms, straight legs, and scrolled back — in the Danish artist Wilhelm Bendz's painting *Interior, Amaliegade, Copenhagen, with the Artist's Brothers*, done about 1830.[18] Although the piece has been refinished, there is evidence of original dark red paint.

OBJECT: Bench and chest

MAKER: Franz Stautzenberger

DATE: 1861

MATERIALS: Primary, walnut and pine; secondary, pine

MEASUREMENTS: H. 37 1/2", W. 76", D. 23"

HISTORY: Part of a set of furniture made at Clear Spring
   by Stautzenberger for his niece, Magdalene Oelkers;
   descended in the Oelkers family to the present owner
   (see also 2.15, 3.1, and 6.43)

OWNER: Mrs. Hugo Biesele, New Braunfels

PHOTOGRAPHER: Babette Fraser Warren

This bench is an extraordinarily interesting form, without parallel in Anglo-American furniture. Although the family of the present owner has always called it a *Bank Kiste*, literally a bench-chest, very similar nineteenth-century examples in Baden and Württemberg are described as a *Bank Siedel* and a *Bank Sittel*.[19] In terms of design, the back is made of six severely rectangular chair backs with three-part splats of Egyptian design. Small side chairs of this sort were made in quantity in the Biedermeier period in Germany and Austria. The arms are of the simplest, almost vernacular, design. In terms of construction, the chest section is framed together with mortise and tenon; three small panels are let into the frame on the front, two larger ones on the sides; across the back is one huge plain plank. Each front corner post and the stile above are carved from one continuous piece. This leg construction is similar to that of a chest (3.1) also made by Stautzenberger. The arms are let into the stiles and secured with pegs at the arm support and at the juncture of the support with the seat. The seat of the bench, hinged at the rear, lifts to reveal the storage section below. It is secured at the front right by a handmade iron hook. Strangely, the panels of the chest section are neither raised nor beveled.

OBJECT: Bench and chest

MAKER: Unknown

DATE: Unknown

MATERIAL: Pine

MEASUREMENTS: H. 42 1/4″, W. 66 1/4″, D. 15 3/16″

HISTORY: According to the owners, may have been made for the Ursuline Convent in San Antonio

OWNERS: Mr. and Mrs. Marshall Steves, San Antonio

PHOTOGRAPHER: Harvey Patteson

Here a medieval Germanic form has survived to the mid-nine-teenth century. This bench chest relates in concept to Stautzen-berger's bench (5.11). It differs in that the back of the chest section is open, suggesting that this piece was built into a wall at its original location. Five raised panels (flat on the reverse) are framed into the back; one similar long horizontal panel (beveled on the reverse) is set into the skirt. The seat lifts to provide access to the chest section.

OBJECT: Bench

MAKER: Unknown

DATE: Unknown

MATERIAL: Walnut

MEASUREMENTS: H. 36 1/2″, W. 69 5/8″, D. 13 1/2″

HISTORY: Collected in the Round Top area

OWNERS: Mrs. Charles L. Bybee and the late Mr. Bybee, Round Top

PHOTOGRAPHER: Harvey Patteson

Austere and simple but pleasing design lends distinction to this little bench. The slightly curved arms, arm supports, and corresponding line of the stiles are fine details. The whole is put together with pegs; the spindles of the back are mortised into the frame. Originally painted, it has stood outside for years; the wood surface has now turned a mellow silvery gray.

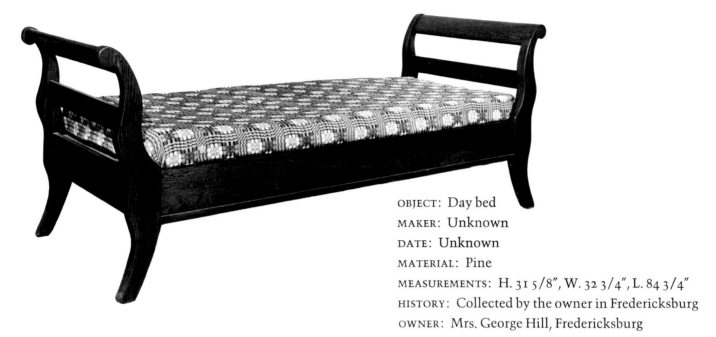

OBJECT: Day bed
MAKER: Unknown
DATE: Unknown
MATERIAL: Pine
MEASUREMENTS: H. 31 5/8", W. 32 3/4", L. 84 3/4"
HISTORY: Collected by the owner in Fredericksburg
OWNER: Mrs. George Hill, Fredericksburg
PHOTOGRAPHER: Harvey Patteson

Sweeping S curves of ancient Greek klismos chairs were adapted in the neoclassical period to long narrow couches, today often called Récamier sofas after the Gérard portrait of Madame Récamier seated on one. In America during the Empire period these were referred to as "French" or "Grecian" couches, and the form enjoyed continued popularity throughout the first half of the nineteenth century. The settlers in Texas imported a fondness for this form, and a number of examples survive, suggesting that it was one of the most prevalent types of seating equipment.

In this piece, the ends have a sharp double curve rather than the more historically correct smooth sweep seen in such examples as 5.17. The outward flare of the legs is considerably more pronounced here than is the norm. This day bed is carefully constructed with mortise-and-tenon construction; the end rail is mortised all the way through the legs. Molding on the side and stay rails is an extra finishing detail. Slats support the upholstered section.

OBJECT: Day bed and chest

MAKER: Unknown

DATE: 1870

MATERIAL: Pine

MEASUREMENTS: H. 29 3/4″, W. 25″, L. 77 13/16″

HISTORY: Collected by the owner near Castroville

OWNER: Mr. Robert Quill Johnson, Castroville

PHOTOGRAPHER: Harvey Patteson

This rather heavy model combines a chest for storage with a day bed and is thus related in concept to 5.11 and 5.12. The commodious storage area has resulted in a rather deep skirt, which visually creates a heavy appearance furthered by the stubby legs. The carcase is pegged together. The spindle stay rails can be freely turned in their sockets.

OBJECT: Day bed

MAKER: Unknown

DATE: 1860

MATERIAL: Pine

MEASUREMENTS: H. 30″, W. 26″, L. 91 9/16″

HISTORY: Collected in the Round Top area

OWNERS: Mrs. Charles L. Bybee and the late Mr. Bybee, Round Top

PHOTOGRAPHER: Harvey Patteson

The tentative, almost memory image and the scrolled klismos line combined with nailed construction suggest that this example is rather late. Nevertheless, the attractively shaped foot and head boards lend charm. The original slats have been replaced. Traces of dark red paint are evident.

OBJECT: Day bed

MAKER: Attributed to Charles Blank

DATE: 1870

MATERIALS: Primary, cedar; secondary, pine

MEASUREMENTS: H. 73 1/2″, W. 28 3/4″, L. 73 1/2″

HISTORY: Two of these beds have been collected in the
   Brenham area and are at Winedale, and several more are
   known to be in Brenham homes.

OWNER: Winedale Museum, Round Top; the gift of Miss Ima Hogg

PHOTOGRAPHER: Jim Bones

Scrolled Grecian detail is combined with turned members, suggesting the influence of the Elizabethan Revival taste. At one end a
small rectangular section supported on a ratchet can be raised to
various heights, indicating that this piece certainly was designed
for use in a recumbent position. Although it is made of cedar, the
surface is covered with a dark brown paint, perhaps to simulate
walnut.

OBJECT: Day bed

MAKER: Unknown

DATE: 1850

MATERIALS: Primary, pecan; secondary, pine

MEASUREMENTS: H. 33 1/2", W. 32 3/4", L. 83 3/4"

HISTORY: Collected by the owner at Rio Medina, Medina County

OWNER: Mr. Robert Quill Johnson, Castroville

PHOTOGRAPHER: Harvey Patteson

Straight legs, rather than curved, distinguish this day bed from the more usual Texas types. Slightly beveled panels are framed into the foot and head boards.

6. Tables and Stands

Tables and stands of all varieties were made by Texas cabinetmakers. Shops in Bastrop and Tyler in the fifties specifically advertised "Dining Tables, Common Tables, . . . Extension Tables," and "Centre, Dressing, Dining, and Folding Tables"; Gaines and Miller of Clarksville noted more generally that "they get up all kinds of tables."[20] Perhaps the most care was lavished on center tables, which were elegant pieces of parlor furniture with a certain symbolic value (Andrew Jackson Downing called them "the emblem of the family circle").[21] Certainly the center tables made by Christofer Friderich Carl Steinhagen, Heinrich Scholl, and William Arhelger were intended not only to occupy but also to dignify the owners' most formal rooms. Few dining tables of comparable quality have survived, although in the houses of wealthy Texans the dining room was also an important formal space. Small sewing tables and ladies' workstands abound, and the inscriptions on two of them indicate that they were an acceptable present for a bride or a fiancée. Of the more utilitarian table forms, washstands seem to have been the most common, with kitchen tables, frequently with drawers, a close second. Many sturdy nineteenth-century tables have been preserved on Texas farms by being relegated to the smokehouse and used as "butcher tables"—surfaces upon which to cut up meat and make sausage.

OBJECT: Extension table
MAKER: Unknown
DATE: 1860
MATERIALS: Primary, pine; secondary, oak (runners)
MEASUREMENTS: H. 29″, W. 29″, L. 62″ closed, 96″ extended
HISTORY: Collected in Schulenburg
OWNERS: Mrs. Charles L. Bybee and the late Mr. Bybee, Round Top
PHOTOGRAPHER: Harvey Patteson

Extension dining tables of varying design were newly introduced during the second third of the nineteenth century. Their availability in pre–Civil War Texas is indicated by an 1854 advertisement for John B. Burke and Company's La Vaca Furniture Warerooms in Lavaca (now Port Lavaca). Burke offered "dining tables; plain and extension; side, centre, sofa, card, dressing, work, toilet, and saloon, ditto."[22] While the extent of the actual usage of extension tables is not certain, the small number of known examples suggests that it was not wide. The table here is related to draw tables in that its extension leaf drops down to fit under the upper surface when in the closed position. Slightly bulbous turned legs are in the late Sheraton tradition. The white porcelain castors are original. A former owner remembers that at one time a black line about three inches wide was painted around the outer edge of the top as a guard against dirty elbows.

OBJECT: Extension table

MAKER: Unknown

DATE: 1860

MATERIAL: Walnut

MEASUREMENTS: H. 29 7/8″, W. 42 5/16″, L. 42″ closed,
    162″ extended

HISTORY: Purchased by the owner in New Braunfels

OWNER: Mr. Ted James, San Antonio

PHOTOGRAPHER: Harvey Patteson

Although related in concept to 6.1, this extension table is considerably more sophisticated in design, material, and mechanism. The
curved skirt is made of laminated walnut which has been veneered.
A pair of central legs drop down to support the five two-foot leaves,
which when inserted result in an extremely long table. More delicate than those of 6.1, the turned legs here are nonetheless also
in the late Sheraton tradition.

Detail—central legs

OBJECT: Draw table

MAKER: Unknown

DATE: Unknown

MATERIAL: Pine

MEASUREMENTS: H. 28 7/8″, W. 35 1/8″, L. 35 1/8″ closed

HISTORY: Purchased by the owners in San Antonio

OWNERS: Mr. and Mrs. Marshall Steves, San Antonio

PHOTOGRAPHER: Harvey Patteson

Subsidiary leaves tilted on raking bearers draw out at either end of the main board, extending this table to nearly double its closed length. This ingenious space-saving arrangement, a survival of seventeenth-century design, is found in examples from the San Antonio–New Braunfels area as well as further east in Fayette and Austin counties. Shaped tapered legs are in the Biedermeier taste. The sides are let into the legs. The iron castors are original.

OBJECT: Draw table

MAKER: Attributed to Johann Michael Jahn

DATE: 1860

MATERIALS: Primary, walnut; secondary, pine

MEASUREMENTS: H. 29 7/8″, W. 35 3/4″, L. 53 7/8″ closed

HISTORY: Purchased by the owners in New Braunfels
    and identified by Jahn's grandson as his work

OWNERS: Mr. and Mrs. W. H. Dillen, New Braunfels

PHOTOGRAPHER: Babette Fraser Warren

This table extends in the same manner as 6.3. Made of walnut, it
is considerably more refined, however, with its molded edges and
clean rectangular lines. A single drawer at the end is made in the
eighteenth-century manner with the molded front projecting over
the opening. In the usual Texas-German mode, a beveled bottom
appears on the dovetailed drawer. The white porcelain castors are
original.

OBJECT: Table
MAKER: Unknown
DATE: Unknown
MATERIAL: Pine
MEASUREMENTS: H. 27″, W. 37 1/2″, L. 56″
HISTORY: Collected near Seguin
OWNERS: Mr. and Mrs. Robin Elverson, Houston
PHOTOGRAPHER: Ewing Waterhouse

In design this rectangular stretcher table is representative of a very early, at least seventeenth-century, type. Mortise-and-tenon construction is utilized throughout, with the exception of the three-board top, held by three lateral braces which are screwed on. The stretchers show considerable wear.

OBJECT: Table

MAKER: Unknown

DATE: 1873

MATERIAL: Pine

MEASUREMENTS: H. 30 1/4″, W. 28 3/4″, L. 27 1/2″

HISTORY: According to the inscription, given as a wedding gift
to Hulda Franke, October 25, 1873; collected in
the Round Top area

OWNERS: Mrs. Charles L. Bybee and the late Mr. Bybee,
Round Top

PHOTOGRAPHER: Harvey Patteson

Although made of pine, this table, with its rounded corners, flared
legs, and concealed drawer, all Biedermeier in origin, is indeed
stylish. It is entirely pegged together; the legs and sides are marked
with Roman numerals, apparently to aid in assembling it. The
front third of the dovetailed drawer is divided into three small
compartments, the partitions of which are dovetailed into the
drawer sides. The bottom is beveled. Under the top is a pencil inscription reading "Züm Hochzeits Geschenk für Hulda Franke 25
October 1873 [for a wedding gift for Hulda Franke, October 25,
1873]."

OBJECT: Table

MAKER: Unknown

DATE: 1860

MATERIAL: Pine

MEASUREMENTS: H. 30″, W. 23 3/4″, L. 26″

HISTORY: Collected in Brenham;
     presumably has a Washington County origin

OWNER: The Bayou Bend Collection, The Museum
     of Fine Arts, Houston

PHOTOGRAPHER: Edward A. Bourdon

A small, simple table with typical flared Biedermeier legs, this example was one of the first pieces of Texas-German furniture collected by the Houston philanthropist, Miss Ima Hogg. Originally without a knob, the drawer was concealed in the skirt; a cutout semicircular handhold under the edge provides purchase for opening. Also typical of Texas-German construction techniques is the utilization of mortise-and-tenon construction in the skirt, a beveled drawer bottom, and dovetails on the drawer sides. The table has been stained dark brown to suggest some richer material, possibly walnut.

OBJECT: Table

MAKER: Unknown

DATE: Unknown

MATERIALS: Primary, cedar and walnut; secondary, pine

MEASUREMENTS: H. 29″, W. 22 1/8″, L. 23 7/8″

HISTORY: Collected in the Round Top area

OWNERS: Mrs. Charles L. Bybee and the late Mr. Bybee, Round Top

PHOTOGRAPHER: Harvey Patteson

This table, while very similar to 6.7, is notable for its slender Biedermeier legs and the rounded corners of the molded top. The brass knob appears to be original. Typical construction details are utilized throughout. A dark stain masks the mixture of primary woods.

6.8

OBJECT: Table

MAKER: Attributed to Carl Johann Rudolph Schiege

DATE: 1860

MATERIALS: Primary, cedar (top) and walnut (legs); secondary, pine

MEASUREMENTS: H. 29″, W. 15 1/4″, L. 23 3/4″

HISTORY: According to the last private owner, made by a Round Top cabinetmaker in 1860 for her grandfather, Matthias Melchior; attributed to Schiege because he is the only commercial cabinetmaker listed in Round Top in the 1860 census

OWNER: Winedale Museum, Round Top; the gift of Miss Helen Kuehne

PHOTOGRAPHER: Jim Bones

Closely related in form to 6.7 and 6.8, this table, like 6.7, originally had a concealed drawer. A projecting lower lip provided a handle. The top front edge of the drawer is curiously shaped into a semicircular molding.

6.10

6.9

OBJECT: Writing table

MAKER: Unknown

DATE: 1850–1860

MATERIALS: Primary, walnut; secondary, pine

MEASUREMENTS: H. 30", W. 26 1/8", L. 40 5/16"

HISTORY: Collected by the owner in New Braunfels

OWNER: Mr. Ted James, San Antonio

PHOTOGRAPHER: Harvey Patteson

Elegant simplicity of line and a high quality of craftsmanship mark this piece as one of the finest examples of Texas-German furniture. Delicate tapering legs, flared at the bottom, are in the Biedermeier taste. The molded top, which overhangs the front and sides, is flush with the skirt at the back; the single dovetailed drawer with beveled bottom is divided into four sections, three of equal size in front and one long section behind. These features suggest that this handsome table was intended to stand next to a wall and perhaps to be used as a writing desk. The table is put together with mortise-and-tenon joints. The one-board top is pegged onto two cleats let into the skirt running from front to back.

Although the maker of this piece is not known, his finesse in terms of design and construction techniques suggests a man of high talent.

OBJECT: Table

MAKER: Unknown

DATE: Unknown

MATERIALS: Primary, walnut (legs) and pecan (top and frame); secondary, pine

MEASUREMENTS: H. 30 1/16", W. 26 7/8", L. 41 7/8"

HISTORY: Collected by the owner in Boerne and presumed to have been made there

OWNER: Mrs. R. L. Patterson, San Antonio

PHOTOGRAPHER: Harvey Patteson

A lipped drawer front breaks the flat surfaces of this piece. Related to some New Braunfels examples (see 6.17), the table is carefully constructed with mortised skirt and legs, dovetailed drawer, and beveled drawer bottom. Even the drawer runners are mortised into the skirt; yet the top is secured with four large screws.

OBJECT: Table

MAKER: Unknown

DATE: Unknown

MATERIALS: Primary, walnut; secondary, pine

MEASUREMENTS: H. 31", W. 25 1/2", L. 42 3/4"

HISTORY: Collected by the owner in New Braunfels

OWNER: Mr. Walter Mathis, San Antonio

PHOTOGRAPHER: Harvey Patteson

Dark stains and an unexpected taper at the feet of this table suggest that at one time it stood in water-filled ceramic insect traps. Although considerably larger, it is related stylistically to 6.17. The top is held by a brace at either end of the underside, and this in turn is pegged into the frame. The small flush drawer with original pull is dovetailed and has a beveled bottom.

6.11

6.12

OBJECT: Table

MAKER: Dominique Neff

DATE: 1870

MATERIAL: Pine

MEASUREMENTS: H. 30″, W. 47 1/8″

HISTORY: Ownership traced to Jacob Habe (1825–1899) of Castroville

OWNER: Mr. Robert Quill Johnson, Castroville

PHOTOGRAPHER: Harvey Patteson

Although on initial appearance this table does not appear very complicated, there are several construction features that are surprisingly sophisticated. The removable top, made of five boards rabbeted together, is strengthened on the underside by two cleats which are dovetailed into it. The cleats themselves are notched to fit over the skirt. Chamfering on the legs is an attractive finishing detail.

OBJECT: Table

MAKER: Dominique Neff

DATE: 1860

MATERIALS: Primary, pine; secondary, oak

MEASUREMENTS: H. 29 5/8", W. 33 7/16", L. 65 1/4"

HISTORY: Ownership traced to Andreas Haby (1827–1888), a pioneer settler of Castroville

OWNER: Mr. Robert Quill Johnson, Castroville

PHOTOGRAPHER: Harvey Patteson

Certain construction features relate this large table to a smaller round table by the same maker (6.13). The top, made of several boards, is rabbeted together and braced underneath by a big dovetailed cleat. Large removable pegs through the cleats secure the top to the skirt. Mortise and tenon join the skirt and legs. Commodious drawers of different sizes suggest that the table probably was intended for kitchen use. Beveled drawer bottoms and dovetailed sides are employed.

OBJECT: Table

MAKER: Unknown

DATE: 1890

MATERIALS: Primary, walnut; secondary, pine

MEASUREMENTS: H. 30 1/2″, W. 33 1/2″, L. 59 1/4″

HISTORY: Ownership traced to Joseph Slacik (1866–1945), a Czech farmer who lived near Bleiblerville

OWNER: Winedale Museum, Round Top; the gift of Richard Schill

PHOTOGRAPHER: Ewing Waterhouse

Although this is basically a rather simple and utilitarian example, there has been some concession to style in the handsomely beveled drawer fronts. The drawers themselves are dovetailed in the front, nailed in the back, and have flat bottoms. The frame is pegged.

OBJECT: Table

MAKER: Unknown

DATE: Unknown

MATERIAL: Pine

MEASUREMENTS: H. 28 5/8″, W. 32″, L. 38″

HISTORY: Collected in New Ulm

OWNERS: Mr. and Mrs. Robin Elverson, Houston

PHOTOGRAPHER: Ewing Waterhouse

Although the skirt is mortised into the legs and the drawer runners mortised into the skirt, this example has a drawer nailed together rather than dovetailed and a drawer bottom that is flat rather than beveled. These features suggest that the table may be a late example. The top has a rather wide overhang. The tentative quality of the curved Biedermeier legs may be the result of their being shortened slightly. The top has two concentric circles, 12 3/4 inches and 11 3/4 inches in diameter, crudely inscribed in the center, perhaps as a game board of some sort.

OBJECT: Table

MAKER: Unknown

DATE: Unknown

MATERIALS: Primary, walnut; secondary, pine

MEASUREMENTS: H. 28 13/16″, W. 16 1/8″, L. 29 1/2″

HISTORY: Collected by the owner in New Braunfels

OWNER: Mr. Ted James, San Antonio

PHOTOGRAPHER: Harvey Patteson

The Biedermeier taste for neat, trim, clean lines is especially evident here. A single long drawer fits flush with the skirt and stiles; the table has tall tapering legs and is crisply sharp in contour. Rounded corners on the top and at the upper inner extremity of the legs subtly relieve the rectangular quality of the table. Mortise-and-tenon construction, dovetails, and a beveled drawer bottom all appear.

6.17

OBJECT: Table

MAKER: Unknown

DATE: 1870

MATERIALS: Primary, walnut and pecan; secondary, pine

MEASUREMENTS: H. 30 5/8″, W. 19 7/8″, L. 25 1/2″

HISTORY: According to a former owner, made in the Round Top area

OWNER: Winedale Museum, Round Top; the gift of Miss Elsie Urbantke

PHOTOGRAPHER: Jim Bones

Similar clarity of line relates this table stylistically to 6.17. However, the inclusion of two shallow drawers here is rather unusual. The maker has utilized mortise-and-tenon construction and incorporated the typical beveled bottoms on the dovetailed drawers. The carved wood pulls are original. Ink stains in the top drawer indicate that the table was once used as a writing desk.

6.18

OBJECT: Table

MAKER: See below

DATE: 1860

MATERIAL: Pine

MEASUREMENTS: H. 29 1/4″, W. 23″, L. 26 1/2″

HISTORY: This table has a history of ownership in the Pochmann family of Round Top and may have been made by Round Top organ builder Traugott Wantke (1808–1870) or by his son-in-law, Zollstin Pochmann (d. 1862).

OWNERS: Mrs. Charles L. Bybee and the late Mr. Bybee, Round Top

PHOTOGRAPHER: Harvey Patteson

This small, useful pine table has several unusual features. The drawer is fitted with a lock. On the interior the thick drawer sides are rounded on the upper edge, and an extremely thick board is used for the beveled bottom. Although presently stripped to its bare wood surfaces, the table was undoubtedly stained originally.

6.19

OBJECT: Washstand

MAKER: Unknown

DATE: 1860

MATERIALS: Pine (top) and pecan (legs)

MEASUREMENTS: H. 29 1/4″, W. 21 1/2″, L. 27″

HISTORY: Collected in the Brenham area

OWNER: Winedale Inn, Round Top; the gift of Miss Ima Hogg

PHOTOGRAPHER: Jim Bones

Although small stands or tables are fairly common, this example is the only Biedermeier-style washstand known to us. This general type was referred to as an "open washstand," as opposed to an "enclosed stand."[23] The skirt is mortised, but the molding around the upper section is applied.

6.20

OBJECT: Table
MAKER: Unknown
DATE: Unknown
MATERIALS: Primary, walnut; secondary, pine
MEASUREMENTS: H. 31 3/8", W. 21 1/2", L. 24"
HISTORY: Has a long history of ownership in Gonzales
OWNER: Mrs. J. B. Wells, Gonzales
PHOTOGRAPHER: Harvey Patteson

Tapering legs and an overlapping drawer front are attractive details on this small, utilitarian table. The frame is mortised to the legs and the top is held with pegs. The square, hand-carved drawer pull is original. Typical dovetails and beveled bottom appear on the inside of the drawer.

6.21

OBJECT: Table
MAKER: Unknown
DATE: Unknown
MATERIALS: Primary, walnut; secondary, pine
MEASUREMENTS: H. 25 1/4", W. 15 3/8", L. 27 1/2"
HISTORY: Collected by the owner in Gruene
OWNER: Mr. Ted James, San Antonio
PHOTOGRAPHER: Harvey Patteson

This small table is characterized by an overall stocky, stolid appearance, despite a slight taper to its legs. The single large deep drawer, with overlapping front, nearly covers the entire skirt. Surprisingly, although the drawer is dovetailed, it has a flat, rather than beveled, bottom. The skirt is mortised into the legs. A carved acorn-shaped pull seems to be original.

6.22

OBJECT: Table

MAKER: Unknown

DATE: Unknown

MATERIALS: Pine and oak

MEASUREMENTS: H. 30″, W. 30 7/8″, L. 47 5/8″

HISTORY: Collected in Fayette County

OWNERS: Mrs. Charles L. Bybee and the late Mr. Bybee,
   Round Top

PHOTOGRAPHER: Harvey Patteson

This table, while sturdy and utilitarian, nevertheless has a great deal of style. It stands on attractively shaped Biedermeier legs. The top is secured by pegs, which are driven through the skirt into cleats running from front to back at either end of the interior. On the inside of the drawer, compartmentalizing members are let into the drawer sides. The usual dovetails and beveled bottom are also used.

OBJECT: Center table

MAKER: Unknown

DATE: 1860

MATERIALS: Primary, walnut; secondary, pine

MEASUREMENTS: H. 29 1/4″, W. 39 1/4″

HISTORY: Collected by the owner in New Braunfels

OWNER: Mr. Ted James, San Antonio

PHOTOGRAPHER: Harvey Patteson

Large, round, pedestal-based center tables became an important part of interior design during the Empire period. A fondness for this form was apparently transmitted to Texas, for a good number of the tables survive. Although in its original conception this sort of table was intended to be placed in the center of a parlor, the Biedermeier fashion often utilized it as a tea table near a sofa.[24] This practice may have been followed in Texas-German homes. Indeed several tables (6.29, 6.30, 6.31), much like eighteenth-century English and American pedestal tea tables, have tops that can be tilted to conserve space when not in use.

This large, handsome example is supported by a bold, hand-carved pedestal. Three scrolled legs, virtually silhouettes of the animal paw- and leaf-carved legs of Empire furniture, are supported on original white porcelain castors. The large central acorn-shaped drop extends nearly to the floor, saved from contact by the elevation of the castors. The top is solid walnut; the skirt is constructed of laminated pine with walnut veneer. At the top of the pedestal, a large beveled block is screwed to the underside of the top, and screws through the skirt secure the top.

OBJECT: Drum table

MAKER: Christofer Friderich Carl Steinhagen

DATE: 1860–1875

MATERIALS: Primary, oak and pine; secondary, pine

MEASUREMENTS: H. 30 3/4″, W. 39 5/8″

HISTORY: Made in Anderson and descended in the maker's family to his granddaughters, the last private owners

OWNER: Winedale Museum, Round Top; the gift of Miss Ima Hogg

PHOTOGRAPHER: Ewing Waterhouse

Made to match a number of other pieces (1.3, 2.32, 4.1, and 5.1), C. F. C. Steinhagen's table is elaborately ornamented with the shallow acanthus-leaf carving that appears on several of his wardrobes (see 2.32), on the posts of one bed (1.3), and on an open-armed rocking chair (4.1). The central acorn drop is similar to the finials on 1.3. The carved animal legs may have been remembered by the cabinetmaker from Empire examples. They more closely resemble the *pied-de-biche* of eighteenth-century furniture. The four drawers are dovetailed, with pine sides and flat bottoms made of rough circular sawed wood. The bottoms are nailed to the sides.

Detail—top

OBJECT: Center table

MAKER: Heinrich Scholl

DATE: 1854

MATERIALS: Primary, walnut; secondary, pine

MEASUREMENTS: H. 30 1/2", W. 46 1/2"

HISTORY: According to family tradition, Heinrich Scholl made this table for his bride in 1854. After her death in 1863, he remarried, and at that time he added the ornamental skirt. This may be one of several inlaid tables made by Scholl, as his obituary in the *Neu-Braunfelser Zeitung* reads, "There is not one . . . who can build an inlaid table as skillfully as Heinrich Scholl."[25] This table has descended in the maker's family to his granddaughter, the present owner.

OWNERS: Dr. and Mrs. O. A. Stratemann, New Braunfels

PHOTOGRAPHERS: Harvey Patteson (table); Babette Fraser Warren (detail)

In general appearance this piece relates closely to 6.24, although the silhouette of the legs is similar to those used by Steinhagen on his center table, 6.25. The utilization of four rather than three legs is an unusual feature, one that lends awkwardness to this otherwise handsome example. The top is attractively decorated with inlaid ornament: a central eight-pointed mariner's star and a circular sawtooth border. Two medial braces screwed to the underside of the top are mortised into a large block at the top of the pedestal. The skirt, sawed out of solid pine, is rabbeted together; the fluted ornament is nailed onto it.

OBJECT: Tea or center table

MAKER: Unknown

DATE: 1855–1865

MATERIAL: Walnut

MEASUREMENTS: H. 28 11/16", W. 35 7/8"

HISTORY: Formerly belonged to the Blumberg family in
New Braunfels

OWNER: Mr. Ted James, San Antonio

PHOTOGRAPHER: Harvey Patteson

Generally light proportions give grace to this small center or tea
table. Particularly pleasing is the delicately turned pedestal. Elaborately scrolled legs reflect an awareness of Renaissance Revival
designs, perhaps known to the maker through factory-produced
examples. The top, made of four pieces of walnut, has two large
cleats attached to the underside. A rectangular block joins top to
pedestal.

OBJECT: Center table

MAKER: William Arhelger

DATE: 1870

MATERIALS: Primary, walnut; secondary, pine

MEASUREMENTS: H. 29 3/4″, W. 36″

HISTORY: Made in Fredericksburg and descended in the family of the maker to the present owner, his grandson

OWNER: Mr. Crockett Riley, Fredericksburg

PHOTOGRAPHER: Harvey Patteson

The underlying classical taste of the Biedermeier style has been utilized in an unusual manner in this table. The normal pedestal form is embellished with a pair of lyre supports, so that the end result is not unlike the arrangement of central pillar and supports utilized on contemporary forms in the Renaissance Revival style.[26] Carved honeysuckle or anthemion ornaments the top of each leg, and the vase-shaped pedestal is decorated with slightly swirled reeding. Below, the drop is deeply fluted. At the base of each lyre is a carved rosette. The lyre supports are mortised into the pedestal and held to the top by screws. Arhelger has used four legs rather than the usual three, and these are also mortised into the pedestal. Made entirely of walnut, except for a large octagonal pine block which secures the top to the pedestal, this table was originally stained a dark brown.

OBJECT: Center or tea table

MAKER: Unknown

DATE: 1870

MATERIALS: Primary, walnut; secondary, pine

MEASUREMENTS: H. 30 1/2", W. 36 1/2"

HISTORY: Collected in Fayetteville and thought to have been made there

OWNERS: Mrs. Charles L. Bybee and the late Mr. Bybee, Round Top

PHOTOGRAPHER: Harvey Patteson

An urn-shaped pedestal above complicated ring turnings and spritely scrolled legs are distinguishing features of this tilt-top table. The three-piece top, held together by two large cleats, has a shallow skirt secured to it by screws. The legs are glued to the hexagonal base.

OBJECT: Center or tea table

MAKER: Unknown

DATE: 1875

MATERIALS: Primary, walnut; secondary, pine

MEASUREMENTS: H. 29 3/8″, W. 45″

HISTORY: Was the property of Baron Otfried Hans von Meusebach (John O. Meusebach), the founder of Fredericksburg, and was in his home at Loyal Valley

OWNER: Pioneer Museum, Fredericksburg

PHOTOGRAPHER: Harvey Patteson

This large tilt-top table is rather similar in design to 6.27, particularly in the shape of the legs. However, the pedestal is somewhat thicker and is made of three vertical pieces glued together and turned. The multiple-plank top is held by a pair of cleats. The maker ingeniously devised a rectangular wooden pin which slides through two brackets into the pedestal and keeps the top from tilting.

OBJECT: Center or tea table

MAKER: Conrad Schueddemagen

DATE: Ca. 1860

MATERIALS: Walnut and pine

MEASUREMENTS: H. 30", W. 47 3/4"

HISTORY: Made by Conrad Schueddemagen in Round Top
about 1860 and descended in his family to the last private
owner, his great-granddaughter

OWNER: Winedale Museum, Round Top; the gift of
Miss Ima Hogg

PHOTOGRAPHER: Harvey Patteson

This is an exceptionally large example. The pine top, which can
be tilted, is made of several boards held together underneath by
butterfly joints. The hefty legs are let into the pedestal. Traces of
red lead paint, perhaps an undercoat for graining, appear on the
pedestal. The fact that both pine and walnut are used further
suggests that the surface was covered in some manner.

OBJECT: Center or tea table

MAKER: Unknown

DATE: 1860–1880

MATERIAL: Pine

MEASUREMENTS: H. 31″, W. 33″

HISTORY: According to the owners, made in New Ulm

OWNERS: Mr. and Mrs. Andrew Z. Thompson, San Antonio

PHOTOGRAPHER: Harvey Patteson

This is a pine example of simplified design attractively turned at the base of the vase-shaped pedestal. Undoubtedly this piece was originally painted or stained.

OBJECT: Stand

MAKER: Unknown

DATE: 1860–1870

MATERIALS: Mesquite and pine

MEASUREMENTS: H. 30 1/2", W. 24 1/4"

HISTORY: Collected near Muldoon, Fayette County

OWNERS: Mrs. Charles L. Bybee and the late Mr. Bybee, Round Top

PHOTOGRAPHER: Harvey Patteson

Perhaps the maker of this piece did not have a lathe, for here the pedestal has been rendered in the simplest form, a sawed hexagonal stem. The simple curved legs are let into the stem, while the top is braced and secured to the pedestal with one rough board. Mesquite has been used for the lower section, pine for the round top.

OBJECT: Stand

MAKER: Heinrich Scholl

DATE: 1880

MATERIALS: Primary, walnut, maple, and cedar; secondary, pine

MEASUREMENTS: H. 30 1/8", W. 18"

HISTORY: According to a family tradition, made in New Braunfels as a gift for Scholl's son; descended in the maker's family to the present owners

OWNERS: Dr. and Mrs. O. A. Stratemann, New Braunfels

PHOTOGRAPHER: Babette Fraser Warren

This pretty little stand with inlaid ornament and fluted skirt recalls Scholl's large center table (6.26). Again the craftsman has employed four legs rather than the usual three, and again they are mortised into the pedestal. Within the inlaid sawtooth circle of the top, Scholl has placed an eight-pointed mariner's star surrounded by highly figured walnut. The fluted ornament of the octagonal skirt is applied.

6.33

6.35

6.34

OBJECT: Stand

MAKER: Heinrich Scholl

DATE: 1870

MATERIAL: Walnut

MEASUREMENTS: H. 31 1/2", W. 17"

HISTORY: Made in New Braunfels and descended in the
  maker's family to the present owners

OWNERS: Dr. and Mrs. O. A. Stratemann, New Braunfels

PHOTOGRAPHER: Harvey Patteson

Although it is considerably more simple in concept than 6.34, this
attractive stand relates rather closely stylistically to that example.
Indeed, in profile, the turned pedestal, while larger, is nearly identical. Utilizing the more customary three rather than four legs,
Scholl has placed them at an acute angle, finishing them off with
spritely hooflike terminals.

OBJECT: Stand

MAKER: Christofer Friderich Carl Steinhagen

DATE: 1860

MATERIALS: Walnut and oak

MEASUREMENTS: H. 29 3/4″, W. 16 3/4″

HISTORY: Made in Anderson and descended in the maker's family to the last private owners, his granddaughters

OWNER: Winedale Museum, Round Top; the gift of Miss Ima Hogg

PHOTOGRAPHER: Jim Bones

This small stand is one of several of very similar design made by Steinhagen for his home in Anderson. The form has been simplified to such an extent that it seems a faint echo of his handsome drum table (6.25), with which it was undoubtedly used. While the turned stem is oak, the top is walnut, as are the legs—which have the same curious animal shape as those on the drum table and are mortised into the base.

OBJECT: Sewing table

MAKER: William Arhelger

DATE: 1863

MATERIALS: Primary, walnut; secondary, pine

MEASUREMENTS: H. 26 1/4″, W. 13 15/16″, L. 16 1/16″

HISTORY: Made by Arhelger while he was an apprentice in Boerne, as a gift for his fiancée, Katharina A. Gruen, whose name he carved in the top; descended in their family to the present owner, their granddaughter

OWNER: Mrs. Erwin Jordan, Fredericksburg

PHOTOGRAPHER: Harvey Patteson

Boldly curved legs set into the turned pedestal are reminiscent of those utilized by Arhelger on his fanciful center table (6.28). Ornamental trim of an unidentified light wood has been pegged to the corners and bottom edge of the upper section, as well as the lip of the single drawer. Inside, the dovetailed drawer has been compartmentalized, with the dividing members let into the drawer sides. The flat drawer bottom is pegged to the sides. Scratched above Katharina's name is the date 1863, an inscription which may have been added at a later time.

OBJECT: Sewing table

MAKER: Johann Michael Jahn

DATE: 1850–1860

MATERIALS: Primary, walnut; secondary, pine

MEASUREMENTS: H. 30 1/2", W. 16 7/8", L. 20 5/8"

HISTORY: Made in New Braunfels and descended in the family
of the maker to his granddaughter, the present owner

OWNER: Mrs. R. L. Biesele, Austin

PHOTOGRAPHER: Harvey Patteson

This attractive little sewing table is a fine example both of Jahn's sense of design and of his capability as a craftsman. In typical late Biedermeier mode, classical elements, such as the slender vase-shaped pedestal and torus-molded sides, are combined with the complicated interlaced scrolls of the Rococo Revival. The inlaid brass shield-shaped escutcheon lends a further classical note.

A double molding around the top edge, repeated singly below, visually lightens the upper part of the composition. The table, finished on all four sides, was meant to stand free. On the interior the dovetailed drawer is compartmentalized into nine sections of various sizes, the divisions being let into the drawer sides. The drawer bottom is beveled. A large beveled pine block, which is screwed to the top, connects the pedestal to the upper section.

OBJECT: Sewing table

MAKER: Unknown

DATE: 1860

MATERIALS: Primary, pine (top) and walnut; secondary, pine

MEASUREMENTS: H. 31″, W. 22 7/16″, L. 23 1/8″

HISTORY: Collected by the owner in Fayette County

OWNER: Mrs. Wendell Steward, Houston

PHOTOGRAPHER: Ewing Waterhouse

Although this example is less ambitious than the work tables made by Jahn, it is nonetheless an extremely attractive piece, with its clean lines and canted corners. The dovetailed drawer has a typical beveled bottom and is divided into six compartments of varying size. The dividers are let into the drawer sides.

OBJECT: Sewing table

MAKER: John William August Kleine

DATE: 1866

MATERIALS: Primary, mahogany; secondary, pine, rosewood, and pecan

MEASUREMENTS: H. 31″, W. 23 1/4″, L. 24 1/2″

HISTORY: Made in Gonzales by Kleine for his wife immediately after his return from the Civil War and descended to his daughter-in-law, the present owner

OWNER: Mrs. Walter D. Kleine, Gonzales

PHOTOGRAPHER: Harvey Patteson

Detail—top

While the basic form here is classical (particularly such details as the lyre-shaped supports), Gothic touches like the crockets within the lyres and the pointed arches of the skirt, combined with the late Restauration wavy moldings under each drawer, are indicative of the eclectic mixture of design popular after the Civil War. Kleine completed the table with elaborate Germanic inlaid ornament on the top and factory-manufactured hardware. Similar intricate inlay appears on other furniture made by Kleine. While the drawers are of dovetailed construction, Kleine has used flat rather than beveled drawer bottoms.

OBJECT: Sofa table

MAKER: Unknown

DATE: 1860

MATERIALS: Primary, walnut; secondary, pine

MEASUREMENTS: H. 30 3/8", W. 30", L. 43" closed, 62 1/2" open

HISTORY: Ownership traced to Joseph George Wagner, who immigrated from Silesia to Round Top in 1853 and purchased property in Winedale in 1882; descended in the Wagner family to the last private owner

OWNER: Winedale Museum, Round Top; the gift of Miss Ima Hogg

PHOTOGRAPHER: Ewing Waterhouse

The sofa table, introduced as a new furniture form about 1800, is characteristically rectangular and has small drop leaves or flaps at either end. As the name suggests, its intended use was in front of a sofa. An expensive and rarefied form, sofa tables of American origin are not common. On this example, four tapering and flared legs in characteristic Biedermeier design are attractively rounded at the outer edge. The single drawer is typically without any pulls. A nice extra detail is the cock beading around the drawer opening. Two lateral runners at either end draw out to support each drop leaf. The skirt is mortised into the legs; the drawer is dovetailed front and back and finished with a beveled bottom.

OBJECT: Sofa table

MAKER: Engelbert Krauskopf

DATE: 1860

MATERIALS: Primary, walnut; secondary, pine

MEASUREMENTS: H. 30 7/8″, W. 33 1/2″, L. 23″ closed, 60 3/4″ open

HISTORY: Made in Fredericksburg and descended in the maker's family to the present owner

OWNER: Mrs. Schatzie Crouch, Fredericksburg

PHOTOGRAPHER: Harvey Patteson

Austere plain surfaces distinguish this cheval-base sofa table. The lyres and Restauration-style scrolled legs are of classical origins, while the handsomely turned stretcher with lotus blossoms flanking a ringed ball reflects the leitmotif of Egyptian influence that runs through the Empire style. The stretcher is mortised into the lyres, which themselves are mortised into the frame of the upper section. Concealed in the skirt is a single long drawer with dovetailed sides and the typical Germanic beveled bottom.

OBJECT: Chamber or dressing table

MAKER: Franz Stautzenberger

DATE: 1861

MATERIALS: Primary, walnut; secondary, pine

MEASUREMENTS: H. 28 7/8″, W. 21″, L. 29 1/8″

HISTORY: Part of a set of furniture made at Clear Spring for the maker's niece, Magdalene Oelkers, and her husband, Konrad (see 2.15, 3.1, and 5.11)

OWNER: Mrs. Hugo Biesele, New Braunfels

PHOTOGRAPHER: Babette Fraser Warren

Simplicity of appearance masks the underlying sophistication of this small chamber or dressing table. The piece is beautifully constructed, the skirt and shelf being mortised into the legs and the top dovetailed to the skirt. The dovetailed drawer with beveled bottom is unusual in that the front laps over the drawer opening, a feature recalling eighteenth-century practices. However, the clean, unadorned surfaces and sharp edges, particularly in the legs, manifest the Biedermeier taste. Around the shelf, Stautzenberger has utilized the same attractive pierced gallery as on his great wardrobe (2.15).

OBJECT: Checker table

MAKER: Unknown

DATE: 1870

MATERIALS: Primary, walnut; secondary, pine

MEASUREMENTS: H. 30 15/16″, W. 21 3/4″, L. 37 1/4″

HISTORY: According to the owner, has a history of ownership in the Tengg family, early settlers and prominent merchants in San Antonio

OWNER: Mr. Ted James, San Antonio

PHOTOGRAPHER: Harvey Patteson

This unusual table reflects the social usage of nineteenth-century Texas, when checkers and dominoes were popular forms of entertainment. Made of walnut, it originally had a leather checkerboard applied to the top. Turned legs are in the late Sheraton tradition. In the skirt is a small felt-lined drawer which is nailed together and has a flat bottom.

7. Desks

A good desk, or secretary, was the most expensive item in the Texas cabinetmaker's inventory, retailing in the 1850's for about forty-five dollars. In private homes the desk was the sanctuary of the male head of the household; its locked drawers contained the family's deed records, notes, mortgages, and sometimes a bottle of medicinal whiskey or a pistol carefully wrapped in oiled rags. It was generally located in the parlor or in a central hallway. In German homes one room was designated as the *Gutestube*, a combination parlor and guest bedroom; it contained the best bed, the best (and sometimes only) lamp, and a desk, or secretary, at which important farm business—the sale or purchase of land, for instance—was ceremonially concluded. In humbler homes a *Wandtisch*, a shelf that folded down from the wall, was substituted for a desk and was surmounted by a wall-mounted document box.

Other desks had special uses: schoolmasters' desks with hinged tops that could be banged for attention; store desks with tall, narrow compartments for ledgers. Like wardrobes, desks provided a variety of surfaces for inscriptions. Two pictured here have cabinetmakers' labels; nearly all have enigmatic penciled memoranda in the drawers and on the insides of the doors—numbers, dates, weather notations, addresses. The interior decoration of the next to last example shown here is unique; we have seen nothing else like it in Texas.

OBJECT: Schoolmaster's desk

MAKER: Unknown

DATE: Unknown

MATERIAL: Pine

MEASUREMENTS: H. 35 1/4″, W. 53 1/4″, D. 34 1/8″

HISTORY: Used for many years at San Geronimo School
near Rio Medina

OWNER: Mr. Robert Quill Johnson, Castroville

PHOTOGRAPHER: Harvey Patteson

Although this schoolmaster's desk is of rather crude design and construction, beveled panels are framed into the pegged doors. The upper section rests on the pedestals below and is not permanently attached.

OBJECT: Desk

MAKER: Eduard Steves

DATE: 1858

MATERIALS: Cypress and walnut

MEASUREMENTS: H. 38 1/16″, W. 34″, D. 22 1/16″

HISTORY: Made at Cypress Creek; descended in the maker's
family to the present owners

OWNERS: Mr. and Mrs. Marshall Steves, San Antonio

PHOTOGRAPHER: Harvey Patteson

While furniture was often made by craftsmen for their own use, rarely did these men sign or otherwise label their work. This example made by Eduard Steves, progenitor of the eminent San Antonio family, bears the inscription, "Ed Steves / Cypress Creek / made out of his own / cut Cypress trees / and made by himself / 1858." Although the general appearance is simple, attractive details, such as the thumbnail molding around the upper edge, ovolo molding at the skirt, and tapered legs which become round at the bottom, combined with the classical crest, work together to make this a pleasing piece. The skirt is mortised into the walnut legs. The disparity of color between the cypress top and the walnut legs was apparently corrected by a dark stain.

OBJECT: Desk and bookcase

MAKER: Unknown

DATE: 1860

MATERIAL: Pine

MEASUREMENTS: H. 77 13/16", W. 36 15/16", D. 32 3/8"

HISTORY: Has a history of ownership in the Schuette family of New Ulm

OWNERS: Mr. and Mrs. Robin Elverson, Houston

PHOTOGRAPHER: Ewing Waterhouse

This simple, almost vernacular, desk and bookcase retains traces of the Biedermeier style in its rectangular lines and shaped crest. Of interest is the construction of the skirt and sides, which are rabbeted into the stiles of the bookcase section. Under the hinged writing surface, two vertical boards, dovetailed front and back, divide the area into three compartments. Made of pine, the desk is carefully painted to look like walnut.

OBJECT: Desk

MAKER: Unknown

DATE: Unknown

MATERIALS: Walnut, pine, and cedar

MEASUREMENTS: H. 63″, W. 52 3/8″, D. 30 3/8″

HISTORY: Collected in Brenham

OWNERS: Mrs. Charles L. Bybee and the late Mr. Bybee, Round Top

PHOTOGRAPHER: Harvey Patteson

This clumsy desk has just enough naïve detail, such as the applied leaf-and-acorn ornament and ogee spandrels on the cupboard doors and the pointed arch, to make it appealing. A hole in the central open compartment served as a chimney for the heat and smoke of an oil lamp. The frame is pegged together; the drawers are crudely dovetailed. The vaguely Grecian crest may be a replacement or a later addition.

OBJECT: Desk

MAKER: Unknown

DATE: Unknown

MATERIALS: Primary, walnut; secondary, pine

MEASUREMENTS: H. 67 1/2″, W. 43 3/4″, D. 33″

HISTORY: Collected near Industry

OWNERS: Mrs. Charles L. Bybee and the late Mr. Bybee,
Round Top

PHOTOGRAPHER: Harvey Patteson

This slant-top desk represents a common nineteenth-century American type. However, the decorative ogee molding around the door panel, not unlike the treatment of eighteenth-century Pennsylvania spice or valuables chests, suggests a Texas and Germanic provenance (compare 7.8). The large drawer is dovetailed with a beveled bottom, and a beveled walnut panel is framed into the cupboard door.

OBJECT: Desk

MAKER: Attributed to Henry W. Buller

DATE: Ca. 1870

MATERIALS: Primary, walnut; secondary, pine

MEASUREMENTS: H. 71 1/2″, W. 34 1/2″, D. 24 3/4″

HISTORY: This desk was used by Dr. Bernard Fehrenkamp (1855–1928) at Frelsburg and was in his home until acquired by the present owner. Dr. Fehrenkamp's mother was a relative of the cabinetmaker Henry W. Buller, and it is on this basis and a comparison of the palmette with that on a known Buller piece (7.7) that the attribution is made.

OWNERS: Mrs. Charles L. Bybee and the late Mr. Bybee, Round Top

PHOTOGRAPHER: Harvey Patteson

This example is related in concept to 7.5 but differs in the upper section, which is completely open and expanded to provide more storage for ledgers and papers. This desk is considerably smaller and visually more graceful than 7.5. A scrolled crest with a vestigial central palmette or anthemion identical to that on 7.7 lends a classical note, while the curves and countercurves at the base of the upper shell echo the lines in the crest above. Beveled panels are framed into the back and used as bottoms on the nicely dovetailed drawers. The upper bookcase section is removable from the desk.

OBJECT: Desk and bookcase

MAKER: Henry W. Buller

DATE: 1875

MATERIALS: Walnut and pine

MEASUREMENTS: H. 99″, W. 52″, D. 22 1/2″ closed

HISTORY: Made for Buller's kinsman Frederick Hillje, a prominent Fayette County oil-mill operator, and descended in his family to the present owners

OWNERS: Mr. and Mrs. Paul Herder, San Antonio

PHOTOGRAPHER: Harvey Patteson

In its original configuration, this example was rather similar to 7.12; that is to say, it consisted of a drawer section with a slant top above. The bookcase, made of pine, was a slightly later addition. Most distinctive is the manner in which the bottom drawer breaks forward from the façade. Bold moldings mark the horizontal divisions of the composition, while chamfered corners add a finishing touch to the lower section. An extremely simplified carved anthemion lends a Grecian touch to the scrolled crest. In the lower section, the drawers have beveled bottoms, and beveled panels are framed into the back. Plain boards form the back of the upper section. An interesting feature is the fact that the top edges of the drawer sides are molded. Bone is inlaid around the keyholes.

OBJECT: Desk and bookcase

MAKER: Eugen Benno Ebensberger

DATE: 1870

MATERIALS: Primary, walnut; secondary, yellow pine

MEASUREMENTS: H. 80 3/4", W. 52 13/16", D. 31 3/16"

HISTORY: Used in the office of Ferdinand Jacob Lindheimer (1801–1879), botanist and editor of the *Neu-Braunfelser Zeitung*

OWNER: New Braunfels Conservation Society, New Braunfels

PHOTOGRAPHER: Babette Fraser Warren

Labeled or similarly documented pieces of Texas furniture are indeed rare. This desk bears the legend: "E. EBENSBERGER / MANUFACTURER & DEALER IN / FURNITURE / MOLDINGS PICTURE / FRAMES & COFFINS ON HAND AND MADE / TO ORDER / ALSO LUMBER FOR SALE / NEW BRAUNFELS TEXAS." This stenciled advertisement, found under the drawers on each side, tells us a great deal about the scope of business of the maker. Also included in the advertisement are pictures of a balloon-back side chair and a coffin. The whole is contained within a scrolled cartouche.

This desk's turned legs with lotus capitals are in the Sheraton tradition, while the sharp, clean lines and scrolled cornice with central anthemion reflect the later classical taste of Biedermeier Germany. Ogee-molded frames on the doors repeat the motif of the lower central section and are reminiscent of the treatment seen in 7.5. Surprisingly, the exterior excellence is superior to the internal construction of this example. While the sides are crudely dovetailed and the drawer bottoms are beveled, the backboards of the bookcase section are secured with nails rather than framed.

OBJECT: Desk

MAKER: Adolph Kempen

DATE: Ca. 1875

MATERIALS: Primary, mahogany; secondary, pine, maple, walnut, and cherry

MEASUREMENTS: H. 58 7/8", W. 40 3/4", D. 26 1/2"

HISTORY: Won at an Austin charity raffle by the present owner's father

OWNER: Mr. Ernest von Rosenberg, Austin

PHOTOGRAPHER: Harvey Patteson

If this remarkable desk did not bear the label of an Austin cabinet-maker it would be difficult to ascribe a Texas provenance to such a sophisticated piece. Kempen in fact states on his label that he makes furniture to order. His desk manifests the eclectic mixture of revived styles that so frequently occurred in the Victorian era. While the piece, with its cabriole legs, scrolled brackets, and leaf carving, is generally in the rococo mode, the cupboard area incorporates elements of Renaissance Revival design in its arched central section with stylized anthemion crest and strap-work corbels which support the frieze. Incised ornament throughout the piece also has Renaissance Revival origins. Kempen has included Gothic motifs in the door panels. Rich, figured mahogany is used throughout. Particularly effective is the crotch pattern of the solid beveled panels set into the cupboard doors. On the writing surface, an inlaid star of maple and cherry is surrounded by burled walnut veneer. The finely dovetailed drawers with veneered mahogany fronts have beveled bottoms. Kempen's label is pasted on the bottom of a small compartment with lift top, hidden behind the frieze of the cupboard section.

Detail — writing surface

OBJECT: Desk

MAKER: Henry Harms (1814–1897)

DATE: 1860

MATERIAL: Pine

MEASUREMENTS: H. 41 1/4", W. 38", D. 20 3/8" closed

HISTORY: Made for the maker's family's use in their home at Rutersville, Fayette County

OWNERS: Mrs. Charles L. Bybee and the late Mr. Bybee, Round Top

PHOTOGRAPHER: Harvey Patteson

Raised panels on the doors and lid combined with small inset brackets at the block feet give an eighteenth-century flavor to this example. The interior is severely plain, with small pigeonholes. Beveled panels appear on the interior of the doors, but the flat backboards are nailed rather than framed. The sides of the carcase itself are dovetailed top and bottom. A dark brown paint, probably original, covers the surface.

OBJECT: Desk and bookcase

MAKER: Unknown

DATE: 1870

MATERIAL: Pine

MEASUREMENTS: H. 86 1/4", W. 43", D. 21 1/4" closed

HISTORY: Collected by the present owner in La Grange

OWNER: Mrs. Wendell Steward, Houston

PHOTOGRAPHER: Ewing Waterhouse

Scalloped lines on the skirt and at each side of the juncture of the bookcase with the desk section visually unite the composition and lend distinction to this example. The vertical molding flanking the large drawers is another attractive feature. Two small slides pull out to support the open writing surface. A light contrasting wood is inlaid in a diamond shape around the keyholes. Brown porcelain hardware is used throughout. The construction includes beveled panels, dovetailed drawers, and interestingly dovetailed bracket feet.

OBJECT: Desk

MAKER: Unknown

DATE: Ca. 1860

MATERIALS: Primary, walnut; secondary, pine

MEASUREMENTS: H. 52 3/4″, W. 39 1/4″, D. 21 1/2″ closed, 42″ open

HISTORY: Ownership has been traced to Carl Linstaedter
(1834–1919), a Washington County landowner who lived
near Latium. His grandson believes the desk was
made in Brenham.

OWNER: The Bayou Bend Collection, The Museum of Fine Arts,
Houston

PHOTOGRAPHER: Allen Mewbourn

The middle-class German Biedermeier taste preferred simplified
classical Empire forms, often in conjunction with frivolous, seemingly incongruous scrolled ornament. While the severe rectilinear
quality of the exterior of this piece is pure early Biedermeier, the
Doric columns supporting an arched frieze and the projecting
molded front of the lower drawer remain close to Empire prototypes. However, the fanciful gallery pegged into the top hints at a
rather personal statement which is revealed in the unusual design
of the interior when the slant top is open. There a graduated tier
of small drawers flanks a large, open central compartment. Compartments such as this derive from French desks of the early nineteenth century. An elaborate cutout molding extends across the
top, and its design is echoed by the scrolled moldings flanking the
tiers just below. Ropelike inlay ornaments the drawer fronts. What
appears to be three small drawers across the upper section is in
fact one long rectangular one.

OBJECT: Desk and bookcase

MAKER: Charles Blank

DATE: 1880

MATERIALS: Walnut and pine

MEASUREMENTS: H. 66", W. 37 1/4", D. 24 1/4" (desk),
21 1/4" (bookcase)

HISTORY: Collected by the donor in Chappell Hill

OWNER: Winedale Museum, Round Top; the gift of Miss Ima Hogg

PHOTOGRAPHER: Harvey Patteson

The bookcase section of this desk is of walnut and is inscribed in ink on the top, "Charles Blank, Brenham / Jan'y 20, 1880." Blank was a prominent Brenham cabinetmaker of the sixties and seventies. The base is pine and contains a pull-out writing desk with a hinged lid in the drawer, which is dovetailed and has a beveled bottom.

Detail—writing surface

OBJECT: Desk and bookcase

MAKER: Attributed to Frederick Eduard Usener

DATE: Ca. 1875

MATERIALS: Primary, walnut; secondary, poplar and pine

MEASUREMENTS: H. 84″, W. 44 1/16″, D. 20 1/2″ closed

HISTORY: Used by the maker, an early settler of Houston, in his business office during the late 1870's

OWNER: Museum of American Architecture and Decorative Art, Houston Baptist College; the gift of Mrs. Dorothy E. Tishman

PHOTOGRAPHER: Harvey Patteson

Elements of the Renaissance Revival style are reflected here in the applied panels and turned ornament of the lower section. Although dovetails were used throughout the drawer construction and one drawer has a beveled bottom, flat, mill-sawed lumber was used for the remaining drawer bottoms and the panels at the sides of the desk section, indicating the piece's urban origin.

OBJECT: Desk and bookcase

MAKER: Unknown

DATE: Unknown

MATERIALS: Primary, walnut; secondary, cedar

MEASUREMENTS: H. 78″, W. 44 1/2″, D. 20 1/16″ closed

HISTORY: Collected by the present owner in Brenham

OWNER: Mrs. John R. Estill, Houston

PHOTOGRAPHER: Harvey Patteson

Crisp, clean lines exemplify the Texas-German interpretation of the late classical Biedermeier style, as seen in this small desk and bookcase. The paneled section of the bookcase lowers to provide a commodious writing surface. Two half-round strips on the leading edge insure that books or papers will not slide from the slanted leaf. Beveled panels are incorporated into all doors and drawer bottoms.

OBJECT: Desk and bookcase

MAKER: Jacob Olson

DATE: Ca. 1880

MATERIAL: Pine

MEASUREMENTS: H. 77 1/2″, W. 37 1/4″, D. 16 1/2″ closed

HISTORY: Made near Clifton and given by the maker to Clifton
Junior College in 1937; later given by the college to
Bosque Memorial Museum

OWNER: Bosque Memorial Museum, Clifton

PHOTOGRAPHER: Harvey Patteson

This rather commonplace pine desk is elevated to the ranks of the unique by the remarkable decoration applied to it by the maker. Olson was a member of the Norwegian community at Norse, in Bosque County, and was a farmer, teacher, antiquarian, collector, and part-time cabinetmaker. He worked portraits of himself and his friend John Burow into the graining applied to the interior of the doors. The date 1884 is written in pencil on the bottom of one of the drawers, all of which are beveled and dovetailed.

Detail—left door   *Detail—right door*

OBJECT: Desk and bookcase

MAKER: Unknown

DATE: Ca. 1850

MATERIALS: Primary, walnut; secondary, cedar and cherry

MEASUREMENTS: H. 102 3/4", W. 70 1/4", D. 21 1/4" closed

HISTORY: Has a history of ownership in an Austin family

OWNER: Harris County Heritage Society, Houston

PHOTOGRAPHER: Harvey Patteson

This monumental desk and bookcase has an Austin history, and it is likely that it was made there. Stylistically, it relates to a large walnut wardrobe also thought to have an Austin provenance (2.16). The fine bold cavetto cornice, rounded corners, and ogee feet are in the best Restauration mode. The four-part composition of the lower section is unusual. Beveled boards are framed vertically into the back, and the drawers are dovetailed. A secret compartment concealed in the cornice section is opened from above.

8. Cupboards

The term *cupboard* includes a variety of case furniture forms, all fitted with doors and storing and sometimes displaying small objects. The corner cupboard, originally designed to conserve space, was an important form in Texas and was usually fitted with glass-paneled doors in order to display china in a dining room. Corner cupboards were often made from walnut or even mahogany, and one example pictured here (8.1) retains the original mirrors set at the back of the upper compartment to enhance the viewers' impression of its contents. Among the Germans this piece was known as an *Eckschrank*; Anglo cabinetmakers usually advertised them as "corner china-presses." There were also rectangular china presses. Other cupboards, with solid doors, held linen and were used in hallways or bedrooms; at least one pictured here (8.4) was built especially to hold courthouse documents. Rough, simple cupboards of pine were built for kitchen use, primarily for the storage of kitchen utensils.

An imaginatively shaped crest and skirt lend a charmingly vernacular tone to this otherwise rather suave cupboard. Richly
grained walnut veneers ornament the façade. Applied diamonds
accent the door fronts, and the inlaid bone escutcheons above and
below echo that motif. In construction the maker has used raised
panels on the cupboard doors and the bottoms of two small interior drawers of the upper section. Mirrors set into the back of the
glazed portion are old and may possibly be original. This cupboard
is one of the earliest identified examples of Texas cabinetmaking.

OBJECT: Corner cupboard

MAKER: Unknown

DATE: Unknown

MATERIALS: Primary, walnut veneer on pine and cedar;
secondary, pine

MEASUREMENTS: H. 88 3/4", W. 41 3/4", D. 29"

HISTORY: Collected by the owner near Bastrop in the 1920's;
included in the *Index of American Design* and pictured in
Antiques 53 (1948):450 and in Ralph and Terry Kovel's
American Country Furniture 1780–1875, p. 161

OWNER: Miss Jean Pinckney, Austin

PHOTOGRAPHER: Harvey Patteson

OBJECT: Cupboard

MAKER: Unknown

DATE: 1870

MATERIAL: Pine

MEASUREMENTS: H. 76 1/4″, W. 40 1/8″, D. 22 3/4″

HISTORY: Collected by the owner in Round Top about 1960

OWNER: Mrs. Wendell Steward, Houston

PHOTOGRAPHER: Ewing Waterhouse

This chest of drawers with enclosed cupboard above is an unusual form, and its original usage is uncertain. Stylistically, the molded, canted corners with scrolled corbels reflect Renaissance Revival design. However, the treatment of the crest seems to be unique. This example manifests typical Germanic drawer construction with dovetails and beveled bottoms.

OBJECT: China cupboard

MAKER: Unknown

DATE: 1860

MATERIALS: Primary, walnut; secondary, pine

MEASUREMENTS: H. 87 1/8", W. 48 1/16", D. 14 13/16"

HISTORY: Collected by the owner in New Braunfels

OWNER: Mr. Ted James, San Antonio

PHOTOGRAPHER: Harvey Patteson

The classical taste is reflected by the rounded corners and plain surfaces of this tall cupboard. Bold Restauration-style curves appear in the cornice and are repeated in the ogee bracket feet. The cupboard is constructed in the German manner, with two large raised panels framed vertically into the back of the carcase; similar panels are utilized on the inside of the doors. The doors themselves are carefully hinged at the sides to maintain the cleanness of line. On the interior, the walnut shelves can be adjusted by means of ratchets.

OBJECT: Cupboard

MAKER: Unknown

DATE: Ca. 1860

MATERIAL: Pine

MEASUREMENTS: H. 91 1/16″, W. 77 7/8″, D. 24 1/2″

HISTORY: Made for the Gillespie County Courthouse

OWNER: Mrs. J. Hardin Perry, Fredericksburg

PHOTOGRAPHER: Harvey Patteson

This huge cupboard shows little evidence of its nineteenth-century origins except for the diamond-shaped inlaid bone key escutcheons. The bold molded cornice, raised panels in the doors, bracket feet, and scalloped skirt all stem from eighteenth-century fashion. The frame is pegged together with mortise and tenon; the upper surface of the lower section is dovetailed to the sides. Behind the lower doors are long shelves, probably for the storage of bound books, while the area above is divided into small five-inch-square compartments undoubtedly used for storing documents.

OBJECT: China cupboard

MAKER: Unknown

DATE: Ca. 1840

MATERIAL: Pine

MEASUREMENTS: H. 88 1/8″, W. 73 7/8″, D. 16 1/2″

HISTORY: Ownership traced to François Guilbeau (d. 1845),
an early San Antonio merchant

OWNER: Mr. Ted James, San Antonio

PHOTOGRAPHER: Harvey Patteson

In general design this two-part china cupboard relates to 8.4. In detail the tripartite door arrangement and glazed upper section differ. The carcase is similarly pegged, and the upper surface of the lower section is dovetailed to the sides. However, there are no raised or beveled panels. The utilization of two vertical panels in each of the doors below is not unlike domestic millwork of the mid-nineteenth century. The vertical boards between the panels echo the three central muntins of the glazed sections, unifying the overall composition. At the base, the maker has boldly scalloped the skirt, nearly creating a central foot, following the precedent of eighteenth-century German wardrobes. The piece shows traces of having at one time been painted white.

OBJECT: China cupboard

MAKER: Unknown

DATE: 1880

MATERIAL: Pine

MEASUREMENTS: H. 83″, W. 38 1/4″, D. 15 1/4″

HISTORY: Collected near Wesley, in Washington County

OWNER: Winedale Museum, Round Top; the gift of Miss Ima Hogg

PHOTOGRAPHER: Harvey Patteson

The absence of dovetails and beveled panels suggests that this little cupboard is a late example. The design combines Renaissance Revival features, such as canted corners and colonnettes, with a Greek-inspired scrolled crest attractively ornamented with stylized leaves or feathers. This feature relates visually to the treatment of a small, grained wardrobe, also at Winedale (2.20). Although the doors of the upper section are now glazed, the possibility exists that they originally were closed with wire or tin.

OBJECT: China cupboard

MAKER: Attributed to William Etzel

DATE: 1860

MATERIAL: Cedar

MEASUREMENTS: H. 81 1/2″, W. 46″, D. 18″

HISTORY: Descended in the Etzel family; may have been made by William Etzel, a native of the Duchy of Nassau who was living at Round Top as early as 1844

OWNER: Winedale Museum, Round Top; the gift of Miss Ima Hogg

PHOTOGRAPHER: Ewing Waterhouse

This cupboard is a less sophisticated version of 8.3, with similar rounded corners and molded cornice. The clean surfaces are broken by the molding at the base, the multiple fielded panels, and the hinge placement. The cedar carcase is pegged together; narrow cedar boards cover the back. As in 8.8, the rounded corners of the cornice and molding below are set in with glue.

OBJECT: Cupboard

MAKER: Unknown

DATE: 1870

MATERIALS: Primary, walnut; secondary, pine

MEASUREMENTS: H. 75 3/4″, W. 47 1/4″, D. 19″

HISTORY: This cupboard was collected in Weimar and was presumably made in the Fayette County area. When found, it was being used as a kitchen safe. The upper halves of all four door panels had been cut out and replaced with screen wire, but the lower halves were intact.

OWNER: Winedale Museum, Round Top; the gift of Miss Ima Hogg

PHOTOGRAPHER: Ewing Waterhouse

A vernacular piece with no little charm, this example is notable for its imaginative crest, triple arched doors, and Biedermeier feet. The case is pegged together and the top dovetailed to the sides, but the simple pine backboards are nailed. Bold ovolo moldings outline the crude drawers, which are dovetailed front and back. Surprisingly, each drawer bottom consists of three rough boards secured with nails. The walnut panels of the doors are replacements.

OBJECT: Cupboard

MAKER: Unknown

DATE: 1880–1890

MATERIAL: Pine

MEASUREMENTS: H. 61″, W. 32 7/8″, D. 15″

HISTORY: Used at Saint Mary's University in San Antonio, according to the owner

OWNER: Mr. Robert Quill Johnson, Castroville

PHOTOGRAPHER: Harvey Patteson

Applied turned ornament around the cornice lends a vaguely Gothic style to this otherwise vernacular piece. A pegged carcase and beveled panels inside the doors are indicative of careful construction techniques often associated with German craftsmen. Yet the back is made of ordinary beaded tongue-and-groove boards. On the interior, small vertical dividers are dovetailed to horizontal shelves. Traces of white paint remain.

OBJECT: Cupboard

MAKER: Unknown

DATE: Unknown

MATERIAL: Pine

MEASUREMENTS: H. 70 7/8", W. 32", D. 24 5/8"

HISTORY: Collected by the owner in Medina County

OWNER: Mr. Robert Quill Johnson, Castroville

PHOTOGRAPHER: Harvey Patteson

Undoubtedly intended for kitchen use, this small cupboard has a distinct charm. While on initial appearance it would appear to date from the eighteenth century, the tall thin proportions of the panels framed into the back, sides, and doors of the lower section indicate its nineteenth-century origin. All these panels are beveled on the reverse, as are the small multiple ones of the doors above. Extremely thick boards form the shaped bracket feet. This cupboard appears to have always been painted and is now a dark red.

OBJECT: Corner cupboard

MAKER: Unknown

DATE: 1855

MATERIAL: Pine

MEASUREMENTS: H. 86″, W. 54″, D. 28″

HISTORY: Collected near Bleiblerville

OWNERS: Mrs. Charles L. Bybee and the late Mr. Bybee, Round Top

PHOTOGRAPHER: Harvey Patteson

The triangular pediment adds a note of classicism to this large corner cupboard. Made of pine and stained a dark brown, it exhibits many details of construction typical of Texas furniture. Raised panels are framed into the doors below as well as the sides and back of the carcase; the one small, dovetailed drawer has a beveled bottom. In the upper section, openings which visually correspond to the panels below are framed with astragal moldings. There is no evidence of wire or tin being utilized here. It is possible that removable cheesecloth was employed. The beautifully scalloped skirt nearly forms a central foot not unlike those occasionally appearing on some wardrobes (see 2.22).

OBJECT: Corner cupboard

MAKER: Unknown

DATE: 1860

MATERIALS: Primary, walnut; secondary, pine

MEASUREMENTS: H. 80 1/8″, W. 36 5/8″, D. 25 3/8″

HISTORY: Collected by the present owner in New Braunfels

OWNER: Mr. Ted James, San Antonio

PHOTOGRAPHER: Harvey Patteson

Plain, angular lines contrast sharply with the curves and counter-curves in the open central section of this attractive cupboard. While its angularity is completely in the Biedermeier mode, the utilization of curves recalls eighteenth-century taste. The piece is skillfully constructed with mortise and tenon, concealed hinges, and beveled panels on the doors. The pine backboards are dovetailed top and bottom. At one point the upper and lower sections were made into two separate cupboards; they were subsequently reunited and the top doweled into the bottom.

OBJECT: Corner cupboard

MAKER: Attributed to Johann Michael Jahn

DATE: 1860

MATERIALS: Primary, mahogany veneer on pine; secondary, pine

MEASUREMENTS: H. 60 1/4″, W. 37 1/2″, D. 25 1/2″

HISTORY: Ownership traced to Joseph Klein, Jahn's brother-in-law

OWNER: Mr. Ted James, San Antonio

PHOTOGRAPHER: Babette Fraser Warren

Unlike most pieces of Texas-German furniture, this beautiful bow-front cupboard with its clean-cut surfaces and block feet is completely in the classical Biedermeier taste. Magnificently grained mahogany has been skillfully veneered across the façade of the pine carcase. On the interior are four shelves above a single drawer which conforms to the shape of the cupboard. Each of the shelves is notched at the right to permit the door to open. The drawer is dovetailed at the front and along the sides where they turn to converge at the back. Surprisingly, the drawer has a flat rather than a beveled bottom, but this may result from the fact that it runs on a central rail or guide. Four large raised panels are framed into the back sides.

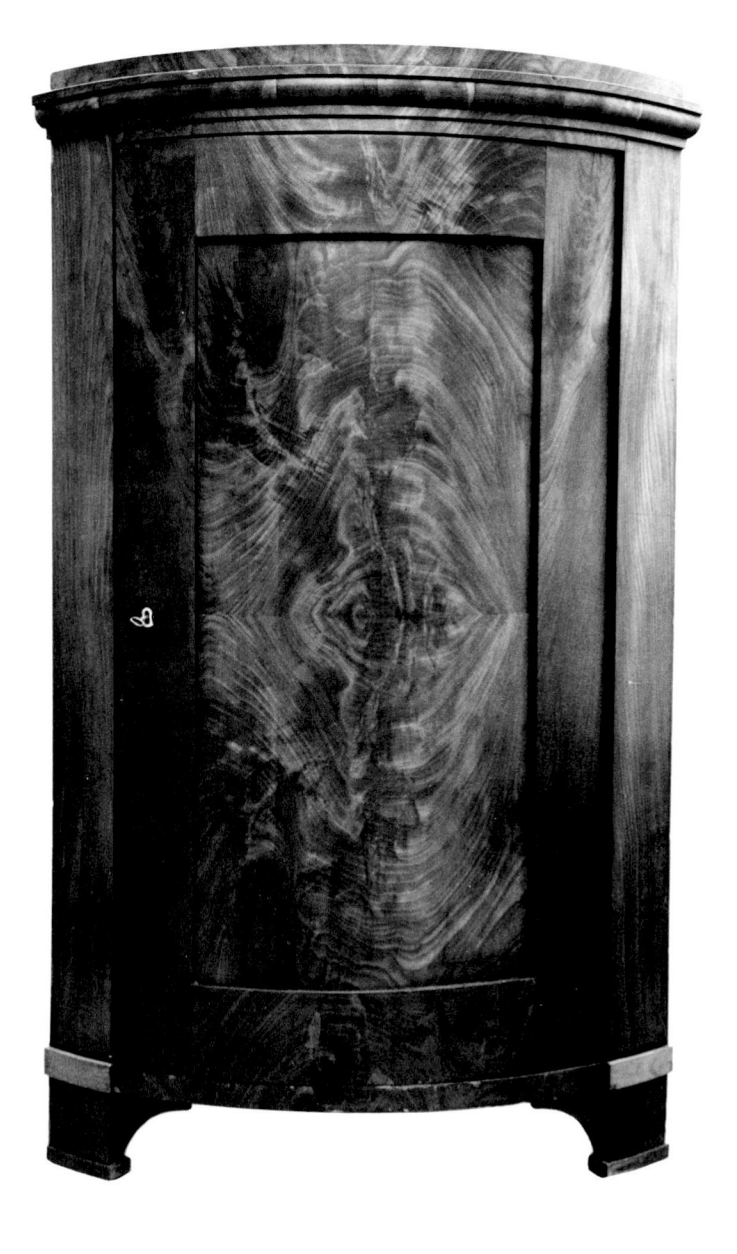

OBJECT: Corner cupboard

MAKER: Unknown

DATE: Unknown

MATERIALS: Primary, walnut; secondary, pine

MEASUREMENTS: H. 85 1/4", W. 50 1/4", D. 26"

HISTORY: Found in Industry, in the Schramm family home, which was built in the mid-1850's

OWNERS: Mr. and Mrs. Robin Elverson, Houston

PHOTOGRAPHER: Harvey Patteson

While the general aspect of this beautiful walnut cupboard does not differ greatly from examples made in the late eighteenth century or early nineteenth century in the Southern United States, its presence until 1972 on the second floor of an old German house in Austin County and the lavish use of walnut in the exceedingly thick beveled panels framed into the doors below strongly indicate a Texas-German provenance. Beveled boards are nailed to the back. The interior is painted an attractive light blue.

OBJECT: China cupboard

MAKER: Gunarius Shefstead

DATE: Ca. 1880

MATERIAL: Pine

MEASUREMENTS: H. 73″, W. 33 3/4″, D. 20 1/4″

HISTORY: Descended in the family of the maker to his granddaughter, Mrs. E. V. Henry of Clifton, who donated it to the Bosque Memorial Museum

OWNER: Bosque Memorial Museum, Clifton

PHOTOGRAPHER: Harvey Patteson

Gunarius Shefstead, a carpenter, was a member of the Norwegian colony at Norse and was responsible for the interior work at Our Savior's Lutheran Church there. He used a strip of the same decorative ornament that is found on the church's pulpit below the cornice of his china cupboard, which exhibits nailed, rather than framed, construction. The skirt is a replacement. This is one of the few surviving examples of furniture made in Texas by Norwegian craftsmen (see also 7.16).

9. Safes

The American food safe is probably a lineal descendant of the seventeenth-century hutch, a small hanging cupboard with ornamentally perforated doors. The safe, whose perforated doors permitted air circulation while keeping out insects, was a ubiquitous piece of furniture in nineteenth-century Texas homes. It was used for the storage of meat, especially cooked meat, and baked goods (hence the term "pie safe") and was normally placed in the kitchen or on the kitchen porch.

The use of punched tin panels in the doors gave rise to the term "tin safe"; G. W. Hagy of Bastrop advertised that he made tin safes, and the term is also used on a bill of furniture sold in Waco in 1860. Wire panels were also used; a Fayette County inventory taken in 1843 lists a "wire safe," and in 1870 two Texas cabinetmakers listed brass wire among the materials they used on the products-of-industry schedules. Occasionally cheesecloth was used on the door panels, especially if the safe was used to set pans of fresh milk in while the cream separated. Safes with this modification were sometimes called "milk safes."

In the fifties and sixties the average price for a safe seems to have been about fifteen dollars. They were utilitarian pieces of furniture and were generally made of pine, although a few walnut examples exist.

OBJECT: Safe

MAKER: Paul Maureaux

DATE: 1860

MATERIALS: Primary, walnut; secondary, pine

MEASUREMENTS: H. 74", W. 43 3/8", D. 21"

HISTORY: Found in San Antonio in the early 1930's by Miss Jean Pinckney; identified as Maureaux's work by his son, who said his father had replaced the walnut upper door panels with cheesecloth in order to use the piece as a milk safe

OWNER: Winedale Museum, Round Top; the gift of Miss Jean Pinckney

PHOTOGRAPHER: Harvey Patteson

Bobbin-turned ornament in the Elizabethan Revival style updates an otherwise classical cupboard. The walnut side panels and glass were installed by the present owner. This example does not have the usual beveled panels and drawer bottoms.

OBJECT: Safe

MAKER: Possibly Johann Michael Jahn

DATE: 1880

MATERIALS: Primary, walnut; secondary, pine

MEASUREMENTS: H. 73 3/4", W. 39 7/8", D. 17 3/4"

HISTORY: Collected by the owner in New Braunfels

OWNER: Mr. Walter Mathis, San Antonio

PHOTOGRAPHER: Harvey Patteson

The generally simple design and crude construction of this piece would not attract sufficient attention to merit consideration here if it were not for the painted inscription on the back. The piece is representative of the late, factory-produced work of Johann Michael Jahn, or possibly even of work factory-produced elsewhere and shipped to Jahn for sale in his furniture store. Rough-sawed flat boards are used on the bottom of the dovetailed drawer. Thin, machine-cut raised panels are used inside the door and on the backside. The entire piece is screwed together rather than mortised. Although there originally was screen or tin in the upper section, it has been replaced with glass.

OBJECT: Safe

MAKER: John William August Kleine

DATE: 1868

MATERIALS: Primary, walnut; secondary, pine

MEASUREMENTS: H. 74 1/8", W. 46 7/8", D. 20 5/8"

HISTORY: Made in Gonzales and descended in the maker's family to his daughter-in-law

OWNER: Mrs. Walter D. Kleine, Gonzales

PHOTOGRAPHER: Harvey Patteson

Although J. W. A. Kleine's handsome safe was intended for use in the kitchen, he nevertheless used walnut rather than a lesser material. Perhaps the wood was purchased from a Mr. Fentress of Prairie Lea, some twenty-five miles away from Gonzales, for Kleine carefully recorded in his notebook:

> D. M. Fentress
> Prairie Lea
> will furnish any lumber
> needed, especially walnut[27]

This safe certainly is not the only one made by Kleine, for he further mentions, in the same source, safe doors described as "5 feet high, 3 feet 5 inches wide."[28] Here he has used a crisp rectangular composition crowned with a bold cavetto cornice. Varying from the norm of the safe with a single shallow drawer and lower cupboard, Kleine has included a pair of deep drawers. These are dovetailed and have the expected beveled bottoms. Similar beveled panels appear on the inside of the doors and the sides of the carcase, and two beveled panels are framed into the back in the same manner as in Kleine's wardrobe (2.18). The original screening and the ovolo molding which secured it are now missing.

OBJECT: Safe
MAKER: Unknown
DATE: Unknown
MATERIAL: Pine
MEASUREMENTS: H. 73 3/4", W. 43 1/4", D. 18 1/2"
HISTORY: Collected by the owner in San Antonio
OWNER: Mr. Walter Mathis, San Antonio
PHOTOGRAPHER: Harvey Patteson

This example is a pine safe with cupboard section below, of the simplest design, ornamented solely with molding at the top and bottom, above plain bracket feet. Beveled panels are set into the doors and sides, and on the back three vertical beveled panels are used. The screen has been renewed.

OBJECT: Safe
MAKER: Unknown
DATE: Unknown
MATERIAL: Pine
MEASUREMENTS: H. 74 1/8″, W. 47 1/2″, D. 19 1/4″
HISTORY: Ownership traced to Franz Wurzbach of Rio Medina
OWNER: Mr. Robert Quill Johnson, Castroville
PHOTOGRAPHER: Harvey Patteson

This safe from the Castroville neighborhood is not unlike the Fredericksburg examples (9.7 and 9.8) in overall composition, being raised upon legs and having a pair of drawers below. Here the details have been simplified, resulting in an almost styleless piece. Beveled panels appear inside the doors and at the interior sides, but the back has simple planks. The bottom of one leg, the right rear, has rotted away.

cloth replaces the original tin or screen at the openings.

The whole is pegged together, and the usual dovetailed, beveled drawer construction is utilized. Modern heavily textured

visual accent in the center of the composition.

beaded. A diamond-shaped escutcheon, now missing, made a bright case have been chamfered and the edge of the right-hand door horizontally delineate the various parts. The corners of the car-

The maker has taken care in his details, utilizing fine moldings to adding verticality suggest awareness of nineteenth-century taste.

form. Only the tapering legs raising the overall composition and baroque quality and eighteenth-century style to this utilitarian

Handsome raised panels framed into the sides and doors give a bold

PHOTOGRAPHER: Harvey Patteson

OWNER: Mrs. Schatzie Crouch, Fredericksburg

HISTORY: Collected by the owner in Fredericksburg

MEASUREMENTS: H. 75 3/4″, W. 51 5/8″, D. 21 3/8″

MATERIAL: Pine

DATE: Unknown

MAKER: Unknown

OBJECT: Safe

OBJECT: Safe
MAKER: Unknown
DATE: Unknown
MATERIAL: Pine
MEASUREMENTS: H. 73 1/4″, W. 65 7/8″, D. 21″
HISTORY: Collected by the owner in Fredericksburg
OWNER: Mrs. Schatzie Crouch, Fredericksburg
PHOTOGRAPHER: Harvey Patteson

While in basic components—partly open, partly paneled doors, ornamental side panels, and the pair of drawers below—this safe is similar to 9.6, its stubby legs, large panels, and broad proportions give it a very different aspect. The carcase is similarly mortised, and the expected beveled drawer bottoms appear. However, simple planks form the back. The unusual inward curve of the legs is not unlike that seen on a local sofa (5.9) and a crib by William Arhelger (1.23). This feature may be either a characteristic of Arhelger's work or a Fredericksburg-area regional characteristic. As in 9.6, modern fabric closes the openings.

OBJECT: Safe

MAKER: Unknown

DATE: 1860

MATERIAL: Pine

MEASUREMENTS: H. 81 13/16″, W. 52 7/8″, D. 19 3/4″

HISTORY: Has a long history of use in Fredericksburg and was presumably made there

OWNER: Pioneer Museum, Fredericksburg

PHOTOGRAPHER: Harvey Patteson

This tall pine safe is perhaps the most stylish of extant Texas examples. A shallow triangular pediment above lends a classical note which seems at variance stylistically with the complicated raised-diamond-ornament panels of the doors and the sunken molded panels on the sides. The latter motif is visually echoed by the applied molding on the drawer fronts. What seems quite complicated has been skillfully blended together in this distinctive safe, with a pleasing result. Raised panels are framed into the back and interior sides, and beveled panels form the bottom of the dovetailed drawers. The crest is attached by large screws. A thin red stain has recently been washed across the surface. In the doors is the original hand-blown glass.

OBJECT: Safe

MAKER: Unknown

DATE: 1880

MATERIAL: Pine

MEASUREMENTS: H. 83 3/16", W. 45 1/8", D. 19 1/2"

HISTORY: Collected by the donor in East Texas

OWNER: Winedale Museum, Round Top; the gift of Miss Ima Hogg

PHOTOGRAPHER: Ewing Waterhouse

A scalloped crest and punched tin work lend a decorative air to this otherwise rather severely utilitarian safe. In composition—a food-storage section above, one long shallow drawer, and a cupboard below—the example here conforms to the norm. The piece is rather well put together, with mortise-and-tenon construction. Two vertical beveled panels are framed into the back, while similar beveled panels appear on the interior doors and sides. The single drawer has been dovetailed front and back and has a beveled bottom. Screws secure the spritely crest. A recent coat of silver paint covers what may be the original punched tin work.

OBJECT: Safe
MAKER: Unknown
DATE: 1860
MATERIAL: Pine
MEASUREMENTS: H. 83 9/16″, W. 54 1/2″, D. 22 1/4″
HISTORY: Ownership traced to Andreas Haby of Castroville
OWNER: Mr. Robert Quill Johnson, Castroville
PHOTOGRAPHER: Harvey Patteson

A fine molded cornice lends distinction to this otherwise rather plain safe. However, moldings around the bottom edge of the upper section and at the edge of the doors, now missing, originally created a somewhat more finished appearance; and feet, now absent, added to the vertical proportions. Small dovetailed drawers have wide lips which project over the drawer opening, as in a table from the same household (6.14). Dovetail construction is used in the drawers and also in securing the sides of the upper section. Beveled panels are framed into the lower doors, and similar treatment appears on the drawer bottoms.

OBJECT: Safe

MAKER: Unknown

DATE: Unknown

MATERIALS: Primary, cedar; secondary, pine

MEASUREMENTS: H. 75 3/8″, W. 68 1/4″, D. 26 3/8″

HISTORY: Collected near Manheim

OWNERS: Mrs. Charles L. Bybee and the late Mr. Bybee, Round Top

PHOTOGRAPHER: Harvey Patteson

Many uncommon features are incorporated into this unusual safe. Despite being raised on curved Biedermeier legs, the piece visually has a horizontal rather than vertical impact. Apparently it was used as a room divider, with the result that there is a door in the back as well as the two in front. Cheesecloth rather than wire or tin closed the open areas, and accordingly the end panels can be removed to facilitate changing the cloth. The attractive curved legs are a continuation of the stiles. Mortise-and-tenon construction is used throughout. Ovoid bone key escutcheons add a further Biedermeier note.

OBJECT: Safe

MAKER: Unknown

DATE: Unknown

MATERIAL: Pine

MEASUREMENTS: H. 79 3/8″, W. 52 3/16″, D. 23 1/4″

HISTORY: Collected by the owners in New Ulm

OWNERS: Mr. and Mrs. Robin Elverson, Houston

PHOTOGRAPHER: Harvey Patteson

This attractive safe is remarkable for its superb graining in imitation of highly figured woods. Particular care has been exercised on the cornice, frieze, and door panels. Rather more vertical than most examples, this safe stands on slender, tapering legs and is crowned with a fine molded cornice. Raised panels are set into the lower section of the doors. Beveled boards are nailed vertically onto the back.

OBJECT: Cheese safe

MAKER: Unknown

DATE: Unknown

MATERIAL: Pine

MEASUREMENTS: H. 30 9/16″, W. 23 1/4″, D. 27 7/8″

HISTORY: Collected by the owner in Medina County

OWNER: Mr. Robert Quill Johnson, Castroville

PHOTOGRAPHER: Harvey Patteson

This strictly utilitarian form of small safe was designed to hang free from the ceiling, from which it could be lowered as needed. The frame is pegged together, but the central shelf is nailed to the supporting struts. A small cavetto molding ornaments the top. Three wrought-iron hooks are present, under the top, under the shelf, and at the top. A similar example is in a private San Antonio collection.

JAMES CHAMBERS.
CABINET MAKER.

RESPECTFULLY informs the citizens of Matagorda, and vicinity, that he is fully prepared to manufacture and repair every description of work in his line, in as neat and substantial a manner as can be done elsewhere. His charges will always be found moderate, and his work will be executed with promptitude.

Daguerreotype.

In connection with his shop, he has a Daguerreotype room conveniently fitted up, will an apparatus of the latest i~ he will always be found ~ ~. shadow ere the substan~ who may require it.
Matagorda. Dec. 21. ~

Western Milita~
BLUE LICK S~

A CERTIFICATE OF had at this offic~ youth, who is desirou~ shall be entitled. witho~ for tuition. to all the ~

On Hand Again!

—o—

I HAVE OPENED BUSINESS IN MY Shop, and will do work as before, such as Furniture of all kinds, Coffins, &c., and repair Cotton Gins.

In returning thanks to my old customers for past favors, I solicit their patronage again, with as many new ones as may need my work.

TERMS Positively Cash, Cloth, Meat, Salt, Flour, Lumber, or something that I can use in my Shop. for my family.

Shop at the old stand, where the Printing Office is located and business carried on.

I am prepared to do all kinds of Turnery. Call and see me—I can fix you up in a trade if you want my work. Necessity drives me to my terms, as I was broke up in the army.

W. J. FOSTER,
Crockett, Texas.

A Checklist of Texas Cabinetmakers

The checklist that follows contains information about 874 men who practiced the trade of cabinetmaking in Texas before 1875. The basic source for the list was the manuscript census returns (MCR) for the schedules of slave and free population (schedules 1 and 2) and of products of industry (schedule 5) of the United States censuses of 1850, 1860, and 1870 for every county in Texas. This source was supplemented by a reading of advertisements in every Texas newspaper printed before 1875 to be found in the newspaper collection of the University of Texas at Austin, the largest Texas newspaper collection in the state.

The manuscript census returns are the completed forms used by the census enumerator in taking the census from house to house. Those for the schedule of free population are organized by dwelling house and contain the names, ages, birthplaces, and occupations of all members of the household. The products-of-industry schedules include all manufacturers whose annual product exceeded a value of five hundred dollars. Depending on the census year, they may also contain information concerning the number of employees in a particular shop, the amount of wages paid, the type of motive power used, the number and type of machines in the shop, the amount and kinds of raw material used, and the value and nature of the shop's annual product. Obviously, these documents are valuable sources for the study of any craft.

This list includes the name of every person in Texas who told the census taker that he was a cabinetmaker or chairmaker. These entries are in the following form: name; date of census; age; birthplace; occupation; place of residence. When a cabinetmaker appears on two successive census returns or on all three, his age at the time of the earliest return is given. Where supplementary information has been found on a cabinetmaker in the products-of-industry schedule, this has been included in the entry, along with information from newspapers and other sources, which are noted in the entry and included in the bibliography. Occasionally, a cabinet shop will appear on the products-of-industry schedule when the owner is not listed on the population schedule as a cabinetmaker. He may be there under some other profession, such as "mechanic," "carpenter," or "businessman," or he may simply have been omitted through error. In these latter cases, the entry appears under the name of the manufacturer or shop as it is given on the products-of-industry schedule, with the census date but without the other information given for men listed on the population schedule.

Men who made furniture were not always listed in the census as cabinetmakers; they sometimes told the census enumerator that they were carpenters or woodworkers or even farmers. In these cases they have been included here if another source shows that they made furniture for a living. In addition, a large number of men who were professional Texas cabinetmakers were not included in the census because they were not in Texas during a census year. The names of many of these, taken from newspaper advertisements, county histories, and county records, have been listed here; their entries do not include census information. Undoubtedly, many other cabinetmakers, whose names did not appear on the census or in the other sources that we examined, have been omitted.

The manuscript census returns are, of course, handwritten, and there is considerable room for error in reading the names on them. The difficulties arise not so much from the enumerators' handwriting as from their tendency to spell phonetically the names that were unfamiliar to them; thus "Stroehschneider" becomes "Straw Snider"; "Riemenschnider," "Reamschnerder"; "Roemer," "Raymer"; and so on. Occasionally they simply gave up. One Austin County resident is simply written down as "Hans, a German." In cases where it has been possible to check a questionable spelling against another source, preferably the cabinetmaker's own spelling of his name, this has been done and corrections made where appropriate. Otherwise, some of the obvious errors have been corrected, and the remaining spellings have been left standing.

In using this checklist, the reader or researcher must keep in mind that some of the boundaries of Texas counties have been shifted and that new counties have been created from old ones. A Hempstead cabinetmaker who lived in Austin County in 1870 would have found himself in Waller County in 1875; and a man who made furniture at Comfort would have been listed on the Kerr County census in 1860 and the Kendall County census in 1870.

It is our hope that the publication of this checklist will stimulate local and regional studies of Texas cabinetmakers. Texas furniture studies, including this one, have been heavily weighted toward the Brazos-Colorado region and the Hill Country, areas that have combined a stable population with a ready access to collectors. Few examples of furniture from Galveston, Austin, the Piney Woods, and the Blackland Prairie have been pictured here because few have been discovered so far. Local historians, using the information on this list as a basis for further research in their own communities, should eventually be able to fill some of these gaps. In order to coordinate these efforts, the Winedale Museum has established a permanent survey of Texas cabinetmakers, in which it invites all interested researchers to participate.

ABEL, A. MCR 1860; age 25; b. Germany; cabinet work; Bellville, Austin County.

ABERNATHY, HENRY. MCR 1870; age 46; b. North Carolina; cabinet-maker; Starville, Smith County.

ACKERMAN, ———. *See* Grainger and Ackerman.

ADDINGTON, JOSHUA. MCR 1850, 1870; age 34 in 1850; b. Tennessee; cabinet workman; Upshur County in 1850. In 1870, Addington was living in Dallas, where he had a furniture business employing two hands to produce furniture valued at $1,800 and to do $400 worth of repair work. He was one of two cabinetmakers in Dallas County in that year whose annual product exceeded $500.

AFFLERBACH, CHRISTIAN. Afflerbach was born in Germany in 1840 and was trained there as a cabinetmaker. According to a descendant, Warren C. Meitzen, he migrated to the United States in 1866 and settled first in Philadelphia, where he worked as a cabinetmaker. He came to Fayette County in 1877 and lived at Round Top, where he farmed and made furniture. He died in 1922 and is buried in Florida Chapel Cemetery, Round Top. (Interview with Warren C. Meitzen, Houston, February 10, 1973; Fayette County Deed Records, book 4, p. 330.) For examples of his work, see 2.38 and 2.39.

AHRENS, J.F.W. MCR 1860, 1870; age 42 in 1860; b. Holstein; cabinet-maker; Galveston, Galveston County. J. F. W. Ahrens may be the Johann Friedrich Ahrens who immigrated to Galveston from the Kingdom of Hanover on board the *Hamilton* in 1845 (Chester William Geue and Ethel Hander Geue, *A New Land Beckoned*, p. 76). He was definitely in Galveston in 1849, for the *Galveston Weekly News* of July 16, 1849, carried his advertisement: "Cabinet Making and Repairing. The subscribers furniture manufactory to be found on the corner of Post Office and 22nd Streets, directly opposite Mr. Lurcher's Grocery. He is prepared to execute, at short notice, all orders for making, repairing, or cleaning any kind of furniture that may be wanted. He keeps on hand a supply of Cedar, Black Walnut, Magnolia, Mahogany, etc. ready seasoned and prepared for use. His prices will be found very low, and the style of work may be seen by giving him a call. Ahrens." A. Delono's *Galveston Directory 1856–7* carries substantially the same advertisement but gives Ahrens's ad-

dress as "Market Street, between 24th and 25th Streets." By 1860 Ahrens was Galveston's leading cabinetmaker, with a shop employing two hands and using 8,000 feet of lumber to produce 24 desks valued at $960, 18 bookcases valued at $540, and 48 tables valued at $192. Ahrens was still in business in Galveston in 1870.

ALBERTHAL, JOHN A. MCR 1870; age 37; b. Prussia; joiner; Gillespie County.

ALEXANDER, D.C. Alexander was a partner in the San Antonio cabinetmaking firm of Bender and Alexander from 1855 to 1860. *See* Bender, Thomas.

ALLDRIGE, JOHN D. MCR 1870; age 38; b. Mississippi; chair manufacturer; Cameron, Milam County.

ALLEN, D.H. MCR 1870; age 24; b. Arkansas; cabinet manufacturer; Paris, Lamar County.

ALLEN, G.W. Allen advertised in the *Brenham Enquirer*, July 16, 1858: "Cabinet Making. The undersigned having purchased the cabinet shop formerly belonging to Mr. Hoffman in Brenham, would inform his friends and the public that he is prepared to fill orders in the FURNITURE line. He hopes to merit and receive a share of public patronage by strict attention to business. His work shall not be surpassed in durability and neatness by any in the country. Work warranted to be well made, and of the best material the county affords. Orders for coffins filled in the shortest possible time, and on reasonable terms. He would ask those wishing to buy furniture, to call at his shop near Connor's Hotel, and examine his work and prices, as he is determined to make his prices low for cash, or to solvent men on time. Cash notes and lumber taken for exchange for furniture. G. W. Allen, Brenham, Jan. 9, 1857." Allen evidently left Brenham before 1860, as he is not on the Washington County census for that year.

ALSUP, JOHN. MCR 1850; age 25; b. Alabama; chairmaker; Upshur County.

ALSUP, JOHN. MCR 1850; age 21; b. Alabama; chairmaker; Upshur County. This John Alsup was recorded by the census marshal four days after the previous John Alsup; perhaps they were cousins.

ALVIS, WILLIAM C. MCR 1850; age 38; b. Tennessee; cabinetmaker;

Shelby County.

ANDERSON, ASA. MCR 1860; age 21; b. Mississippi; cabinet workman; Fairfield, Freestone County.

ANDERSON, E.A. MCR 1860; age 40; b. Tennessee; cabinetmaker; Montgomery County.

ANDERSON, H.B. H. B. and Joseph Anderson were in partnership with William Chrysler in San Antonio in 1867. *See* Chrysler, William.

ANDERSON, JACK. MCR 1860; age 18; b. Missouri; cabinet apprentice; Fairfield, Freestone County.

ANDERSON, JOHN A. MCR 1860; age 77; b. Anderson District, South Carolina; cabinet workman; Texana, Jackson County.

ANDERSON, JOSEPH. *See* Chrysler, William.

ANDERSON, WILLIAM H. MCR 1860, 1870; age 28 in 1860; b. Virginia; cabinetmaker; Waco, McLennan County. In 1860, William H. Anderson had a cabinet shop in Waco employing two hands and using 1,000 feet of pine lumber and 4,000 feet of walnut lumber, valued at $235, to produce 6 wardrobes valued at $210; 24 safes valued at $480; and other articles valued at $700. By 1870, he was the state's largest furniture manufacturer, with a shop employing six hands and using $3,300 worth of mahogany, walnut, and other woods to produce 5,000 pieces of furniture valued at $11,000. In the *Waco Daily Advance* for June 8, 1872, Anderson advertised that he made wooden coffins to order and sold metallic coffins, window glass, doors, blinds, and sashes at his furniture store. The 1876 Waco city directory lists Wm. Anderson as a merchant on the city square; an 1882 directory lists him as a dealer in coffins, furniture, and merchandise on South Third Street (Roger Conger, Waco, March 10, 1973, to LT).

ANDERSON, WILLIAM W. MCR 1870; age 28; b. Mississippi; cabinetmaker; Waxahachie, Ellis County.

ANSELIN, JULIUS. MCR 1860; age 30; b. France; cabinetmaker; Colorado County. Anselin was in partnership with a man named Miller in Columbus in March, 1858, when they announced "to the good citizens of Columbus and vicinity that they are now prepared to attend to all calls in their line of business. They have a one-horse power turning lathe in operation, and will be ready to manufacture bedsteads, bed posts, and all sorts of Fancy Turning work. Bureaus, Dressing and Wash Stands, Wardrobes, Tables, Etc. manufactured in the best style of workmanship" (*Colorado Citizen,* March 20, 1858). Anselin applied for United States citizenship in Columbus on May 21, 1858, and received it on October 30, 1860. His sponsors were Cleveland Windrow and William J. Darden (Colorado County District Court Minutes, vol. C-2, p. 201).

ARHELGER, WILLIAM. MCR 1870; age 32; b. Nassau; wheelwright; Gillespie County. Arhelger was born at Ritterhausen, Dillenburg, Nassau, on April 6, 1838. He came to Texas with his parents, Jacob and Elisabeth Arhelger, on board the *Herschel* in 1845. The Arhelgers were among the founders of Fredericksburg. As a young man, William was apprenticed to Henry Wendler at Boerne to learn the trades of cabinetmaker and wheelwright. During his apprenticeship he became engaged to Katharina A. Gruen, for whom he made an inlaid table (6.37). They were married on May 14, 1865. Arhelger operated a wheelwright and cabinetmaking shop on North Adams Street in Fredericksburg, where he built wagons, hacks, and buggies and repaired farm implements as well as made furniture. (Gillespie County Historical Society, *Pioneers in God's Hills,* pp. 3–4.) For examples of his work, see 1.8, 1.23, 6.28, and 6.37.

ARNOLD, L.N. MCR 1860; age 40; b. Tennessee; cabinet workman; Hillsboro, Hill County.

ARNOLD, LEWIS. MCR 1850; age 30; b. South Carolina; cabinetmaker; Hunt County.

ASHNARTH, JAMES. MCR 1860; age 38; b. New York; cabinet work; Paris, Lamar County.

ASHNARTH, ORMAN. MCR 1860; age 36; b. New York; cabinet work; Paris, Lamar County.

ASHWORTH, JAMES. MCR 1870; age 50; b. Kentucky; cabinetmaker; Paris, Lamar County.

ASKEW, T.J. MCR 1860; age 24; b. Georgia; cabinetmaker; Paris, Lamar County.

AUGUST, WILLIAM. MCR 1860; age 30; b. Baden; cabinetmaker; Gonzales, Gonzales County.

BABCOCK, WILLET. MCR 1860, 1870; age 34 in 1860; b. New York; cabinetmaker; Paris, Lamar County. Babcock was one of the men who made Paris a center of furniture manufacture; he was a craftsman who became a successful entrepreneur and died a wealthy man. He was born in Ithaca, New York, October 6, 1828 (according to his tombstone), and came to Paris sometime before 1860. In that year, he and A. A. Walker had a large shop on South Main Street in Paris, opposite R. B. Francis's livery stable, which employed six hands and used 35,000 feet of lumber valued at $1,250 to produce 500 pieces of furniture valued at $6,000—the largest output of furniture in the state in that year. In 1863, Babcock bought the two-story Masonic Hall on the corner of Main and Kauffman streets and operated a furniture factory on its first floor until his death in 1881; the second floor housed another of his enterprises, the Babcock Opera House (A. W. Neville, *The History of Lamar County*, p. 104; Mrs. James Baird, Paris, March 12, 1970, to LT). In 1870 he reported to the census marshal that his factory had one machine powered by two horses and employed twelve male hands and three females. He used 77,000 feet of lumber to make $7,900 worth of furniture, described on the census return as "400 bedsteads, etc." His factory was second only to that of William H. Anderson in Waco in terms of value of product. By 1875 he had installed steam power and advertised that he was "now turning out some of the finest, cheapest, and best work in the Furniture line ever seen in this section, and as the business increases, prices are lowered in proportion . . . having no rents to pay and running hands who have been with me for years I am enabled to SELL AT LOWER PRICES than ever was known here before . . . WHOLESALE BILLS & ORDERS FROM THE COUNTRY will receive special and prompt attention" (*Paris Weekly Press*, September 3, 1875; also in the *North Texan*, May 6, 1876). Like many cabinetmakers, Babcock was also in the undertaking business. He used his profits to purchase a number of city lots in Paris and several large farms in Lamar County (Lamar County Deed Records). He died on August 27, 1881, and his monument is one of the most imposing in the Paris cemetery.

BAKER, JOSEPH T. MCR 1850; age 23; b. New York; cabinetmaker; San Augustine County.

BALL, JOHN. MCR 1860; age 33; b. Belgium; cabinetmaker; Houston, Harris County.

BALLARD, JOSH. MCR 1860. In 1860, Ballard was operating a chair and wheel shop in Canton, Van Zandt County. He used hickory and ash lumber valued at $150 to produce 1,248 chairs and 200 wheels with a combined value of $1,000, according to the 1860 products-of-industry schedule for Van Zandt County. The value seems low and may be an error, as the average price of a chair in 1860 was between $1.00 and $1.25. Ballard does not appear on the population schedule for 1860.

BAMES, FREDERICK. MCR 1870; age 41; b. Prussia; cabinetmaker; Indianola, Calhoun County.

BARBETT, WILLIAM. MCR 1860; age 40; b. Tennessee; cabinetmaker; Honey Grove, Fannin County.

BARCLAY, HUGH. MCR 1850; age 61; b. Pennsylvania; cabinetmaker; Hopkins County.

BARNES, JOSEPH. MCR 1860; age 13; b. Tennessee; apprentice cabinetmaker; Paris, Lamar County.

BARRY, JEAN. MCR 1850; age 53; b. France; cabinetmaker; Liberty County.

BARTHOLEMEW, A. MCR 1860; age 41; b. Saxony; cabinetmaker; Seguin, Guadalupe County.

BARTLETT, GEORGE. MCR 1850, 1860, 1870; age 45 in 1850; b. England; cabinetmaker; Sabine County. In 1850, Sabine County was one of the leading furniture-producing counties in Texas, and Bartlett was one of four cabinetmakers there with a product valued at more than $500 annually. His shop employed two hands and used 3,000 feet of lumber, including walnut valued at $90 and pine valued at $25, to produce $600 worth of furniture. He was still working in Sabine County in 1870.

BARTON, JAMES A. Barton and his partner, Newton Powell, took over Henry Bushfield's established shop in the cabinetmaking center of Clarksville, Red River County, in 1861 and inserted the following advertisement in the *Standard*, July 13, 1861: "CABINET MAKING, IN ALL ITS BRANCHES! THE SHOP heretofore carried on in Clarksville by Henry Bushfield will be kept up, and a large stock of all kinds of Cabinet Ware, and Chairs of various patterns, will be manufactured and kept on hand by the undersigned, who have increased their facilities for the business, including steam machinery. Prompt attention will be given, as heretofore, to the preparation of coffins and attendance at burials. A Hearse always ready." The firm evidently did not survive the Civil War.

BATHKE, WILLIAM. MCR 1850; age 26; b. Germany; cabinetmaker; Harris County.

BATTERS, CARL. MCR 1850; age 27; b. Germany; cabinetmaker; Bexar County.

BAUHOFF, FERDINAND. MCR 1870; age 31; b. Bohemia; cabinetmaker; Bastrop, Bastrop County.

BAYLEY, J.T. MCR 1850; age 23; b. Tennessee; cabinetmaker; Harrison County.

BEARD, WILLIAM H. MCR 1870; age 50; b. Alabama; cabinetmaker; Kaufman, Kaufman County. In 1870, Beard reported to the census marshal that his shop had been in operation for four months during the previous year and had used $100 worth of lumber to produce bedsteads valued at $80, safes valued at $160, and tables valued at $20.

BEAUMONT, JOHN A. MCR 1850, 1860; age 42 in 1850; b. Pennsylvania; cabinetmaker; Jefferson County. On the 1860 census return, Beaumont was listed as living at Grigsby's Bluff, Jefferson County.

BECK, CHARLES. Charles Beck is listed by W. Richardson and Co., *Galveston Directory for 1866–7*, as a cabinetmaker with a shop on the north side of Market Street, between Church and Post Office streets. The *Galveston Directory for 1868–9* (by idem) gives his business address as 227 22nd Street and his residence as 70 East Mechanic Street. John H. Heller's *Galveston City Directory 1872* lists him as a "cabinetmaker at Joseph Sauters, 122 and 124 Tremont Street." Sauter was a leading Galveston furniture dealer.

BECK, E., AND C. MILLER. *See* Beck, Ernest.

BECK, ERNEST. MCR 1870. Ernest Beck is listed in W. Richardson and Co.'s *Galveston Directory for 1868–9* as a cabinetmaker at 208 Tremont Street. In 1870, he and C. Miller were partners in a Galveston shop that used 3,000 feet of lumber valued at $120, 500 feet of walnut valued at $50, and various other materials valued at $75 to produce 20 desks worth $300, 10 wardrobes worth $375, and 20 safes worth $500 and to do $500 worth of repairs.

BECK, JACOB, JR. MCR 1870; age 29; b. Indiana; cabinetmaker; Kaufman, Kaufman County.

BEEL, JEREMIAH. MCR 1870; age 47; b. Ohio; cabinetmaker; Denton, Denton County.

BEEMAN, ALONZO. MCR 1860; age 60; b. Vermont; cabinetmaker; Belton, Bell County. Alonzo Beeman came to Bell County in 1852 and settled on Stampede Creek. In 1860 he had a chairmaking shop with hand-powered machinery which used 3,000 feet of lumber valued at $120 to produce 1,000 chairs valued at $1,500. He had one employee, D. McNall, who lived in his household and earned $35 a month. Beeman later added water-powered machinery, according to Bell County historian George W. Tyler, who remembered him as "an educated and accomplished man" who was an outspoken Unionist and defended the Union in a public debate at Aiken in February, 1861. He was physically attacked by some of the crowd but was defended by his Secessionist neighbors. In September, 1863, the Bell County Commissioners' Court appointed him superintendent of commissary for Beat 1 and charged him with overseeing the distribution of food and clothing to soldiers' families. He was a charter member of Belton Lodge No. 166, A.F. and A.M. (George W. Tyler, *The History of Bell County*, pp. 158, 199, 230, 241, 381.)

BEEMAN, J.J. MCR 1870; age 54; b. Indiana; cabinetmaker; Dallas, Dallas County.

BEITS, F. MCR 1860; age 31; b. Germany; cabinetmaker; Galveston, Galveston County.

BELL, BAXTER M. MCR 1860; age 36; b. Tennessee; cabinetmaker; McKinney, Collin County.

BELL, J.W. MCR 1850; age 22; b. Tennessee; cabinetmaker; Limestone County.

BELL, WATSON W. MCR 1860; age 34; b. Connecticut; cabinetmaker; Sulphur Springs, Hopkins County. Watson W. Bell was an early user of steam power. In 1860 he advertised that he "would respectfully call the attention of the public to his STEAM SHOP, situated in the west part of the town of Sulphur Springs, west of Roger's Hotel and north of the steam mill. Having machinery, he is prepared to do such work as Sash, Door, Blind, and HOUSE FURNITURE cheaper than any other establishment in the country. He will make to order any of the above articles on short notice, and keep large quantity of FURNITURE on hand. He is also prepared to do any kind of PAINTING, HOUSE, SIGN, & ORNAMENTAL. As there is a Hub Morticer in the shop, he will keep on hand HUBS, and will fill all orders in that line. Carriage and Wagon Makers would do well to avail themselves of this opportunity" (*Independent Monitor,* December 1, 1860).

BENDER, THOMAS. Bender advertised in the San Antonio *Western Texan* of February 16, 1854, that he had opened a "Furniture Ware-Room on Commerce or Main Street, one door west of Rose & McCarthy's, where he intends keeping on hand a general assortment of furniture...he is also prepared to Manufacture and Repair any article of furniture that may be ordered or entrusted to his care." On July 13 of that same year he advertised in the *San Antonio Ledger* that "he has received and is now receiving a large assortment of CHAIRS, which he offers for sale, together with his general assortment of HOUSEHOLD FURNITURE, consisting of plain and ornamental sofas, Bureaus of a variety of styles, Dinner and Center tables, Office, Common, and Parlor Chairs, Secretaries, Wardrobes, Writing Desks, Footstools, Bedsteads, Etc. Country dealers and the public generally are invited to call." That he was not merely a dealer but also a maker of furniture, however, is indicated by an advertisement in Spanish in the short-lived newspaper *El Bejareño,* in which he describes himself and his partner, D. C. Alexander, as retail and wholesale merchants for all kinds of furniture: "Muebles a proposito para el mercado de Mejico, hechos de manera que puedan empacarse sin riesgo en Bultos frequenos [pequeños] [furniture made to order for the Mexican market, made so that it can be packed without risk in small bundles]" (*El Bejareño,* February 17, 1855). Bender dissolved his partnership with Alexander on March 1, 1860 (*San Antonio Ledger and Texan,* March 10, 1860).

BENNEWITZ, THEODORE. MCR 1860; age 39; b. Germany; cabinetmaker; Hempstead, Austin County. Bennewitz was in Austin County (now Waller County) as early as August 18, 1859, when he bought two acres of land on the J. Nichols League from F. W. Brandes; he was still there on November 3, 1866, when he purchased five more acres on the same league from Brandes. (Waller County Deed Records, vol. A, pp. 19, 22.)

BERG, JOHN. John Berg, cabinetmaker, is listed as living on Broadway between 21st and 22nd streets in the *Galveston Directory for 1859–1860.*

BERGENSIER, ANTON. MCR 1860; age 25; b. Prussia; cabinetmaker; San Antonio, Bexar County.

BEVEL, AARON. MCR 1870; age 54; b. Tennessee; chairmaker; Charleston, Hopkins County.

BIGHAM, W.M.C. MCR 1860; age 45; b. Tennessee; cabinetmaker; Red Oak, Ellis County.

BILGER, WILLIAM. MCR 1870; age 31; b. Württemberg; cabinetmaker; Jefferson, Marion County. The name is also spelled Belger. His brother, H. H. Bilger, was a wagon builder in Jefferson.

BILLBERRY, ESAW. MCR 1870; age 18; b. Illinois; chairmaker; Gainesville, Cooke County.

BILLBERRY, JOHN. MCR 1870; age 45; b. Tennessee; chairmaker; Gainesville, Cooke County.

BILLIGMAN, F. The *Galveston Directory for 1868–9,* by W. Richardson and Co., lists F. Billigman as a cabinetmaker with a residence on Avenue K between 12th and 13th streets.

BIUINS, J.G.W. MCR 1860; age 53; b. Tennessee; cabinetmaker; Canton, Van Zandt County.

BJERKE, P.M. MCR 1860; age 33; b. Norway; cabinetmaker; Bonham, Fannin County.

BLACK, I.C. MCR 1860; age 32; b. Tennessee; cabinetmaker; Dangerfield, Titus County.

BLACKWELL, JEREMIAH. MCR 1860; age 48; b. Mississippi; chairmaker; Pruitt's Tan Yard, Anderson County.

BLAKE, GEORGE W. MCR 1850, 1860, 1870; age 32 in 1850; b. New Hampshire; cabinetmaker; San Augustine County in 1850; Jasper, Jasper County, in 1860 and 1870. In 1850, Blake had a cabinet shop in San Augustine which employed two male hands and used walnut, pine, and gum lumber valued at $200 to produce $600 worth of cabinet furniture and $200 worth of other articles. This was one of two shops in San Augustine that produced more than $500 worth of furniture that year. (The other was that of J. George Woldert.)

BLAND, E.T. MCR 1870; age 15; b. Texas; apprentice cabinetmaker; Paris, Lamar County.

BLANK, CHARLES. MCR 1860, 1870; age 43 in 1860; b. Prussia; cabinetmaker; Brenham, Washington County. Blank was living in Brenham as early as July 5, 1858, when he became a United States citizen (Washington County Probate Records, vol. D, p. 317). At that time he had been in the United States for five years. In 1870, his one-man cabinet shop used 2,000 feet of lumber worth $60 to produce furniture worth $105 in three months of operation. He was still working in Brenham in January, 1880, when he signed and dated a secretary (7.13) now in the Winedale collection. A distinctive style of day bed with an adjustable back, of which several examples are known (see 5.17), has been attributed to him by a descendant.

BLASCHKE, RUDOLPH. MCR 1870; age 36; b. Austria; carpenter; Cat Spring, Austin County. In 1870, Blaschke had a cabinet shop in Cat Spring which used lumber valued at $150 to manufacture 20 tables valued at $200 and 10 cabinets valued at $400.

BLENNERHASSETT, T. SPOTSWOOD. Blennerhassett advertised in the Clarksville *Standard*, February 5, 1853, that he was operating a "bedstead, chair, and cabinet factory" in Bonham, Fannin County, and "wanted to employ one or two Regular bred Cabinet Makers. None other need apply, as I will not offer to the Public the work of Suckers or Cobblers at the Trade. Having in connexion with the above, a Horse Power Lathe, Turning in wood or Iron, can be done at short notice: Also the repairing of Gins, Thrashing, or Reaping and Cutting Machines, Horse Powers, &c. &c.: Also the placing or setting up of Cylinder or Flue Boilers, on the latest and best plan for draught, and Safety; and with horizontal, perpindicular or Vibrating Cylinders, for Mill purposes &c. &c."

BLYTHE, F.M. MCR 1860; age 39; b. Tennessee; cabinetmaker; Washington, Washington County.

BOOKER, CHARLES. MCR 1870; age 39; b. Maine; cabinetmaker; Milam, Sabine County.

BOSTICK, THOMAS M. MCR 1860; age 25; b. Missouri; cabinetmaker; Travis County. Bostick was working in Austin in January, 1854, when he dated an advertisement that was still running in October, 1856: "Cabinet Making: The subscriber would respectfully inform the citizens of Travis County, that he is prepared to execute any work in this line of business, as promptly and cheaply as it can be done in the place. He invites the public to call and examine his work and prices.

Shop on Congress Avenue, three doors below F. T. Duffau's Drug Store. Thos. M. Bostick. Austin, Jan. 28, 1854" (*Tri-Weekly Times*, October 3, 1856). In October, 1857, under the heading "Excelsior Furniture Rooms," he advertised that he had reopened his furniture rooms on Congress Avenue, opposite the old Treasury Department and one door above John's Paint Shop (*Southern Intelligencer*, October 14, 1857). In January, 1858, he entered into a short-lived partnership with J. W. England and opened a new shop on Pecan Street, in Peck's Store House, where he and England kept "a fine new hearse" and made and repaired furniture (ibid., January 20, 1858). However, the partnership was dissolved in April of that same year, and Bostick announced that he would continue the business at the same location by himself (ibid., April 21, 1858).

BOUCHER, HENRY. MCR 1850; age 22; b. Germany; cabinetmaker; Galveston, Galveston County.

BOWERS, J.E. MCR 1860; age 18; b. Tennessee; cabinetmaker; Crockett, Houston County.

BOYNTON, G.S. An advertisement in the *Corsicana Observer*, August 2, 1867, indicates that Boynton was a mill employee who made furniture to order: "All persons desirous of purchasing good walnut furniture will leave their order at C. P. Kerr's store, or by application to G. S. Boynton at Ingram's mill. Fine bedsteads made on the shortest notice in patterns to suit purchasers."

BOZE, T.B. MCR 1860; age 34; b. Virginia; cabinetmaker; Kaufman, Kaufman County.

BRACKNEY AND COLLINS. A firm operating under this name advertised in the Clarksville *Northern Standard*, July 3, 1847, that the partners had "opened a Cabinet Shop in the town of Paris, Lamar County, a short distance from the public square, where they will keep a supply of cabinet furniture on hand. They are prepared to fill any order that they may be favored with, in good style. Persons wishing to furnish houses would do well to give them a call before purchasing elsewhere, as they pledge themselves to do as good work as can be had in this country, at moderate charges. Coffins furnished at the shortest notice, and general attention at burials, if required. Paris, July 3, 1847." In 1850 their shop was located on the corner of South Main and Kaufman streets (A. W. Neville, *The History of Lamar County,* p. 65). The 1860 census lists a J. T. Collins, who may have been one of the partners in this firm; *see* Collins, J. T. Brackney may have been the John Brackney of Clarksville who sold a city lot to Charles Durfee in 1858; *see* Durfee, Charles.

BRADBURRY, W.H. MCR 1870; age 39; b. Georgia; cabinetmaker; Marshall, Harrison County.

BRADFORD, WILLIAM. MCR 1860; age 34; b. Missouri; cabinetmaker; Sherman, Grayson County.

BRAMLETTE, GILBERT. MCR 1870; age 33; b. Kentucky; cabinet manufacturer; Paris, Lamar County.

BRANAN, J. In December, 1853, J. Branan advertised "that he has located in Washington, where he is manufacturing the good old 'home-spun' chair, which for strength and durability are equal to any. His shop is on Ferry Street, a few doors below Rucher's Drug Store" (*Texas Ranger and Lone Star,* December 15, 1853).

BRANDT, HEINRICH CHRISTIAN. MCR 1860, 1870; age 22 in 1860; b. Germany; cabinetmaker; Chappell Hill, Washington County. Brandt was born in the Principality of Schaunberg-Lippe, where his father was a teacher. He served a four-year apprenticeship to a *schreiner* (joiner) in Bückeburg and received his journeyman's certificate on March 15, 1856. He immediately came to Texas and stayed for a time with an uncle in Industry before moving to Chappell Hill, where he attended Soule University for a short time. He worked as a cabinetmaker and building contractor in Chappell Hill until 1874, when he opened a general merchandise store. He served as an alderman in Chappell Hill in 1876 and 1877. He was a Mason and a Methodist and rebuilt the Methodist Church in Chappell Hill after it was destroyed in the 1900 storm. During the Civil War he served in Waul's Legion, was captured at Vicksburg, and was held prisoner in Indianapolis until the end of the war. A set of his carpenter's planes and a chair made by him are at the Chappell Hill Historical Society Museum. (Nath Winfield, Chappell Hill, June 13, 1972, to LT; Frank W. Johnson, *History of Texas and Texans, 1799–1884,* IV, 1628–1631.)

BRAUTIGAM, PETER E. MCR 1870; age 43; b. Prussia; cabinetmaker; Galveston, Galveston County. John H. Heller's *Galveston City Directory 1872* lists Brautigam as living at 312 East Avenue I and does not list a separate shop address for him.

BREITLING, J.W. MCR 1860; age 38; b. Germany; cabinetmaker; Galveston, Galveston County. In 1870, Breitling won a $5 prize for exhibiting the best bureau at the first Texas State Fair in Galveston (*Galveston Daily News,* May 27, 1870).

BREM, JOHN M. MCR 1860; age 41; b. North Carolina; cabinetmaker; Seguin, Guadalupe County. John M. Brem was in Seguin as early as July 15, 1853, when he purchased four city lots there from W. C. Baxter (Guadalupe County Deed Records, vol. D, p. 811). In March, 1858, he announced "to the citizens of Seguin and vicinity that he is now prepared to attend to all calls in his line of business. He has a one-horse power turning lathe in operation and is now ready to manufacture Bedsteds, Bed posts, and all kinds of fancy work. Bureaus, Wardrobes, Dressing and Washstands, Center and Dining tables, Chairs, etc., at moderate prices say: Cottage bedsteds, $10; Plain ditto, $8; Chairs, $1.50; Coffins, trimmed and lined, $25.00, and all other work in proportion. Terms cash" (*Seguin Mercury,* March 3, 1858). In 1860, Brem's shop employed two hands and horse power and used 4,000 feet of lumber valued at $120 to produce 1,500 chairs valued at $2,250 and other items valued at $300 and was one of two shops in Seguin whose annual product exceeded $500.

BREM, JOHN W. John W. Brem of Clarksville, Red River County, advertised in an ad dated March 18, 1857, and still running on September 5, 1857, that he had located five miles east of Clarksville and in addition to continuing his old business of "Repairing Carriages, Making Bureaus, Bedsteads, Tables, Chairs, etc.," he was "now prepared to manufacture... SPIKE THRASHERS & SIDE THRASHERS. The latter is a new invention, highly commended by competent judges" (*Standard,* September 5, 1857). Brem seems to have been a partner in the firm of G. B. Brem and Company, which bought and sold a number of town lots in Clarksville during the Civil War and was dissolved on May 16, 1867 (Red River County Deed Records, vol. N, pp. 428, 631).

BRIESH, SEBASTIAN. MCR 1860; age 30; b. Poland; carpenter; Bexar County. According to a descendant, Briesh came to San Antonio before the Civil War and made millwork and furniture, including day beds, trunks, tables, doors, and coffins. He died during a cholera epidemic on November 2, 1866. (Shirley Insall Collin, San Antonio, August 8, 1973, to LT.)

BRIGENDINE, W.L. MCR 1860; age 39; b. Virginia; cabinetmaker; Austin, Travis County.

BRIGGS, STEPHEN. MCR 1860; age 45; b. Virginia; master cabinetmaker; Stuart Creek, Denton County.

BRIM, T.J. Brim was a partner in J. B. Shanahan's Clarksville cabinet shop in 1855. *See* Shanahan, James B.

BRINKMANN, OTTO. MCR 1870. Brinkmann was born August 15, 1832, in Hoexter, Westphalia. He served an apprenticeship to a cabinetmaker in Germany before coming to Texas in 1852. He lived at Hortontown, Comal County, until 1858, when he moved to Comfort. He worked in both Comfort and San Antonio as a house carpenter and built the Ernst Altgelt home on King William Street in San Antonio. In 1870 his shop in Comfort produced 12 doors valued at $130, 18 windows valued at $130, 2 tables valued at $14, 1 safe valued at $30, 1,000 feet of flooring valued at $40, repairing valued at $100, and other work valued at $50. From 1871 to 1880 he operated a mercantile business in Comfort with Christoph Flach; from 1880 until his death in 1915 he managed the Comfort branch of the Ed Steves and Son lumber yard. (Guido Ransleben, *A Hundred Years of Comfort in Texas: A Centennial History*, pp. 184–186.)

BRITTAIN, HENRY. MCR 1860; age 37; b. England; carpenter; Corpus Christi, Nueces County. On January 2, 1858, Brittain advertised in the *Nueces Valley* that he had "opened a jobbing shop in Mrs. Bryant's concrete building, and is now prepared to do all kinds of jobbing, such as making and repairing bedsteads, tables, chairs, building fences, etc."

BROCK, JAMES R. MCR 1860; age 52; b. North Carolina; cabinetmaker; Canton, Van Zandt County.

BROOKAW, J.P. MCR 1850; age 25; b. New Jersey; cabinetmaker; Galveston, Galveston County. *See also* Journey, Henry.

BROUGHTON, JOHN. MCR 1870; age 20; b. Mississippi; chairmaker; McKinney, Collin County.

BROUGHTON, LEROY. MCR 1870; age 26; b. Mississippi; chairmaker; McKinney, Collin County.

BROWN, ANDERSON. MCR 1870; age 21; b. Tennessee; chairmaker; Denton, Denton County.

BROWN, EDWIN E. MCR 1870; age 29; b. Maine; cabinetmaker; Galveston, Galveston County.

BROWN, MARTIN J. MCR 1850, 1860, 1870; age 39 in 1850; b. Pennsylvania; cabinetmaker; Sabine County. In 1850, Martin J. Brown was one of four cabinetmakers in Sabine County who had a shop using hand power to produce at least $500 worth of furniture annually. He used 2,000 feet of wood valued at $50 to produce furniture valued at $500. He was still living in Sabine County in 1870.

BROWN, TAYLOR. In 1859, Taylor Brown and John Harrop were partners in a cabinet shop in Henderson, Rusk County. They advertised that their work was "of the latest style and good workmanship" and added that "with attention added to our experience, ability, and facility of manufacturing all articles in the above line, we fear no competition" (*Southern Beacon*, May 21, 1859). We have no other information about either man.

BROWN, W.W. W. W. Brown is listed as a cabinetmaker employed by William F. Howe in John H. Heller's *Galveston City Directory 1872.*

BROWNING, JOHN. MCR 1870; age 40; b. Alabama; cabinetmaker; Garden Valley, Smith County.

BUCH, CHARLES. MCR 1870; age 25; b. Württemberg; cabinetmaker; Galveston, Galveston County.

BUCKHANAN, CALVIN. MCR 1870; age 48; b. South Carolina; farmer and cabinetmaker; Henderson, Rusk County.

BUERGER, BARTHOLEMEW. MCR 1860, 1870; age 36 in 1860; b. Prussia; cabinetmaker; Seguin, Guadalupe County. Buerger was in Seguin as early as March 26, 1853, when he purchased a town lot from A. B. Moore (Guadalupe County Deed Records, vol. D, p. 121). In 1860 his cabinet shop in Seguin used hand power and 2,000 feet of plank valued at $110 and 800 feet of "scantling" valued at $50 to produce $1,000 worth of furniture. It was one of two shops in Seguin whose annual product exceeded $500. In 1870, Buerger was still in Seguin, but the value of his annual product had declined to $700.

BUESCHER, GOTTFRIED. MCR 1870; age 33; b. Prussia; cabinet- and chairmaker; Industry, Austin County. Buescher was in Austin County as early as February 7, 1859, when he purchased a parcel of land at New Ulm from Charles Goethe (Austin County Deed Records, vol. A, p. 169). In 1870 he had a cabinet shop at New Ulm which used hand power and employed two men to produce furniture valued at $1,000 and 300 chairs valued at $500. He was still active in August of 1876, when he entered into a contract with August Mueller and Leopold Darrazin to build, for $550, a carousel with "twenty wooden horses and two buggies" (Austin County Civil Dockets, docket 24).

BULLER, HENRY W. MCR 1860; age 39; b. Prussia; carpenter; Plum Grove, Fayette County. Buller was born in Germany in 1823. He moved to Colorado County in 1874. In April, 1875, he purchased sixteen acres of land two miles north of Frelsburg, on which he operated his cabinet shop. He was married to Anna Maria Hillje and died on June 20, 1903. (Colorado County Deed Records, vol. L, p. 14; Colorado County Death Certificates.) For examples of his work, see 5.7, 5.8, 7.6, and 7.7.

BUMGARTNER, F.W.A. MCR 1850, 1860; age 30 in 1850; b. Germany; cabinetmaker; Grimes County.

BUNGE, WILLIAM. MCR 1850; age 34; b. Germany; cabinetmaker; Austin County.

BUNTZEL, FREDERICK. MCR 1860, 1870; age 34 in 1860; b. Prussia; carpenter; Austin County. Buntzel and his family migrated to Texas from Prussia in 1854 and settled in the Cat Spring neighborhood of Austin County (Cat Spring Agricultural Society, *The Cat Spring Story*, p. 28). In 1870, he had a shop at Cat Spring, using hand power and $175 worth of lumber to produce 15 cabinets valued at $600 and 4 desks valued at $100.

BURKS, ALBERT. MCR 1870; age 37; b. Tennessee; cabinetmaker; Pennington, Trinity County.

BURNAM, HENRY T. MCR 1850; age 33; b. Tennessee; cabinetmaker; Smith County.

BURNES, WILLIAM. MCR 1870; age 34; b. Alabama; cabinetmaker; Plano, Collin County.

BURNS, R.S.J. MCR 1860; age 27; b. Tennessee; cabinetmaker; Linden, Cass County.

BURRESS, A.D. MCR 1850; age 42; b. Kentucky; engineer; Marshall, Harrison County. In June, 1849, Burress was operating a sawmill and wagon factory at Marshall, Harrison County, which produced furniture as a sideline. In August of that year he invited "the public to call at the Subscriber's Wagon and Carriage Manufactory, which he has recently erected at his steam mill, one mile and a fourth northwest from the town of Marshall. He is prepared with as good materials as the country affords for making to order, and repairing wagons, carriages, and vehicles of every description, at short notice. Connected with the above establishment he also has a blacksmith shop in which he is prepared to execute every description of work without delay. Also a cabinet shop and warehouse in which can be found at all times a general assortment of household furniture, made of good materials, and neatly finished" (*Texas Republican,* August 10, 1849). The next year Burress reported to the census marshal that his mill employed four hands and used 3,000 feet of lumber valued at $500, 20 gallons of oil, $100 worth of paints and colors, and 32 gallons of varnish to produce $4,500 worth of wagons, carriages, bedsteads, bureaus, and chairs.

BURROUS, DAVIS. MCR 1870; age 45; b. Indiana; cabinetmaker; Fairfield, Freestone County.

BURROWS, D.L. MCR 1860; age 43; b. Indiana; cabinetmaker; Springfield, Limestone County.

BURTLE, ANDREW. MCR 1860; age 34; b. Kentucky; cabinetmaker; Dallas, Dallas County.

BUSHFIELD, HENRY. Bushfield and his partner, Jasper Longe, purchased the Clarksville cabinet shop of William C. Gaines in August, 1860 (*Standard*, September 22, 1860). In December of that year, Bushfield announced that he had bought Longe's interest in the shop and that he "would continue the manufacture of cabinet work in all its branches, including Bureaus, Tables, Bedsteads, Chairs, etc. . . . He has a hearse, and will answer promptly to all calls for coffins, and attentions at Burials" (ibid., December 22, 1860).

BUSHMEIER, CHARLES. MCR 1870; age 28; b. Baden; cabinetmaker; Bastrop, Bastrop County.

BUSKMEYER, CHARLES. MCR 1870; age 28; b. Germany; works in a cabinet shop; Brenham, Washington County.

BYRD, WILLIAM E. MCR 1850; age 35; b. Mississippi; cabinetmaker; San Augustine County.

CADE AND ROBIN. The 1870 products-of-industry schedule for Canton, Van Zandt County, lists the firm of Cade and Robin, a two-man shop that used $400 worth of wood to make $1,200 worth of furniture.

CAGHILL, MICHAEL. MCR 1870; age 56; b. Ireland; cabinetmaker; Galveston, Galveston County.

CAMER, C. MCR 1860; age 24; b. Germany; cabinet work; Georgetown, Williamson County.

CAMPBELL, NAPOLEON. MCR 1860; age 45; b. Kentucky; cabinetmaker; Carthage, Panola County.

CANNADY, JAMES. MCR 1870; age 21; b. Alabama; cabinetmaker; Farmersville, Collin County.

CANTWELL, M. MCR 1860; age 26; b. Iowa; cabinetmaker; Bonham, Fannin County.

CARBACK, G.A. MCR 1870; age 32; b. Prussia; cabinetmaker; Bryan, Brazos County.

CARR, H.C. MCR 1860; age 25; b. Illinois; cabinetmaker; Stephenville, Erath County.

CARTER, JAMES. MCR 1850; age 32; b. North Carolina; cabinetmaker; Dallas County.

CASTON, G.W. MCR 1860; age 40; b. Alabama; cabinetmaker; Gay Hill, Washington County.

CAWOOD, MOSES. MCR 1860; age 84; b. Virginia; cabinet workman; Winnsborough Wood, Titus County.

CHAFER, I.E. MCR 1860; age 20; b. Ohio; cabinetmaker; Harrisburg, Harris County.

CHAMBERS, JAMES T. MCR 1850, 1860; age 29 in 1850; b. South Carolina; cabinetmaker; Matagorda, Matagorda County. Chambers practiced a dual profession in Matagorda. On July 21, 1851, he ran an advertisement in the *Colorado Tribune,* informing "the citizens of Matagorda, and vicinity, that he is fully prepared to manufacture and repair every description of work in his line, in as neat and substantial a manner as can be done elsewhere. His charges will always be found moderate, and his work will be executed with promptitude . . . In connection with his shop, he has a Daguerreotype room conveniently fitted up, with an apparatus of the latest improvements, where he will always be found ready to preserve the 'shadow ere the substance fade' of all who may require it." He was still in business as a cabinetmaker in Matagorda in 1860.

CHAMPION, ROBERT G. MCR 1860, 1870; age 45 in 1860; b. South Carolina; cabinetmaker in 1860; cabinet workman in 1870; Livingston, Polk County, in 1860; Athens, Henderson County, in 1870.

CHEATUM, SAMUEL. MCR 1860; age 70; b. Virginia; cabinet workman; Tarrant, Hopkins County.

CHOATE, M.L. MCR 1860; age 65; b. Prussia; cabinetmaker; Livingston, Polk County.

CHRYSLER, WILLIAM. Chrysler was both a manufacturer and an importer of furniture at Lavaca (now Port Lavaca) in the late 1850's. In a September, 1856, advertisement he described himself as a "manufacturer and dealer in all kinds of cabinet furniture" and listed thirty-seven categories of furniture that he had imported from New York, adding that goods would be "carefully packed for transportation at the shortest notice" (*Lavaca Herald,* September 13, 1856). An April, 1857, advertisement identified him as "Manufacturer and Dealer in all kinds of cabinet furniture, bedsteads, mattresses, etc.," and went on to say that he was currently importing window sash, wagons, and plows (*Lavaca Herald,* April 3, 1857). He was still in business in Lavaca in January, 1859 (*Gonzales Inquirer,* January 15, 1859; *Goliad Messenger,* March 31, 1860). In July, 1867, he was a partner with Joseph Anderson and H. B. Anderson in the firm of Chrysler, Anderson and Company, "Manufacturers and Dealers in all Kinds of Cabinet Furniture and House Furnishing Goods," in San Antonio; the firm also bought wool and hides (*San Antonio Express,* July 1, 1867).

CHUTE, JAMES. In June, 1845, James Chute of Red River County advertised that he did "White and Blacksmithing, Gunsmithing, Cabinet Work, Wagonmaking, Etc. The undersigned has re-established himself, at his old business, at Atwoods 6 miles east of Clarksville, and will do any work in the above named branches, he will also make spinning wheels and Chairs. As usual, he can be paid without difficulty, in such articles as the County affords" (*Northern Standard,* June 14, 1845).

CLANSEN, RICHARD H. MCR 1860, 1870; age 27 in 1860; b. Virginia; cabinetmaker; Linden, Cass County.

CLARK, JOHN. MCR 1860; age 80; b. New Hampshire; chairmaker; Gonzales, Gonzales County.

CLAWSON, J. MCR 1870; age 30; b. Arkansas; cabinetworker; Belton, Bell County.

CLEAVER, HENRY P. MCR 1870; age 30; b. Alabama; cabinetworker; Rusk, Cherokee County.

COLLINS, J.T. MCR 1860; age 35; b. Alabama; master carpenter; Paris, Lamar County. Collins may have been a partner in the firm of Brackney and Collins.

CONROW, ANDREW J. MCR 1860; age 30; b. New Jersey; cabinetmaker; Waco, McLennan County. Conrow and William H. Anderson were the two most important cabinetmakers in Waco before the Civil War. Conrow was in Waco as early as March, 1854, when he bought city lot 14, block 4, from Caleb M. Huby (McLennan County Deed Records, vol. C, p. 114). In November, 1858, he advertised that he was "at the sign of the Sash and Blind" and was "prepared with well-seasoned lumber, and all other necessary materials, to make skillfully and promptly . . . window sash and venitian and pannel window shutters; pannel doors, safes, wardrobes, wash stands, candle stands, beaureaus, etc." (*Southern Democrat*, November 18, 1858). In that same year Conrow bought the patent rights to manufacture and sell Isaac Buck's improved churn in McLennan County (McLennan County Deed Records, vol. H, pp. 660–661). In 1859, he purchased lots 4, 5, 6, and 7 in block 10 in Waco (ibid., vol. I, p. 36). The next year he reported to the census marshal that his shop employed seven men and used hand and horse power, 10,000 feet of pine, 3,558 feet of walnut, 400 pounds of lead, and 40 gallons of oil and turpentine to produce $848 worth of sash and doors, $261 worth of blinds, and $2,642 worth of furniture. A sampling of this furniture is included in a list of goods sold on credit by Conrow to George W. Miller in 1860: "1 wardrobe, $18.00; 1 enclosed wash stand, $7.50; 1 open wash stand, $2.50; 1 panel end lounge, $8.00; 1 tin safe, $12.00; 1 folding leaf dining table, $6.00; 1 bedstead, $6.00," as well as several counters and showcases (ibid., vol. J, p. 61). In January, 1861, a judgment for $350.00 against Conrow

on a note due to the firm of Lewis and Killough was handed down in county court (ibid., p. 552), but he was still in business in August, 1861, when he advertised that he made window sashes in four sizes, repaired and manufactured "any article in the furniture line," and made coffins (*South-West Quarter Sheet*, August 22, 1861).

COOPER, JAMES. MCR 1870; age 38; b. Hungary; cabinet workman; Honey Grove, Fannin County.

COOPER, WILLIAM B.L. MCR 1870; age 40; b. Maryland; cabinetmaker; Brenham, Washington County.

COX, JOHN. MCR 1850; age 23; b. Indiana; cabinetmaker; Gonzales, Gonzales County. In July, 1853, Cox advertised that he "would respectfully inform his friends and the public in general, that he keeps constantly on hand every variety of family furniture, which he imports direct from New York, comprising in part Bedsteads, Armoirs, Tables, Chairs, Safes, Washstands, &c., which he will dispose of on liberal terms. I have also an excellent horse power TURNING LATHE, and all wood turning executed to order and at the shortest notice. Also, coffins executed to order" (*Gonzales Inquirer*, July 2, 1853).

COX, JOHN. MCR 1860; age 27; b. Tennessee; chairmaker; Millwood, Collin County.

CRACKER, W.B. MCR 1860; age 37; b. Indiana; cabinetmaker; Orangeville, Fannin County.

CRAIG, JOHN A. MCR 1860; age 33; b. Indiana; cabinet workman; Tarrant, Hopkins County.

CRAIG, THOMAS A. MCR 1860; age 30; b. Illinois; cabinet workman; Tarrant, Hopkins County.

CRAWFORD, W.B. MCR 1860; age 36; b. Ohio; cabinetmaker; Muskite, Navarro County. In 1860 Crawford was a partner in the firm of Crawford and Porter, which had a shop in Corsicana that employed five hands and used a 2 1/2-horsepower steam engine and 2,000 feet of plank valued at $600 to produce furniture valued at $4,000. This was the third-largest cabinet shop in the state in that year.

CRAWFORD AND PORTER. *See* Crawford, W. B.

CREAGER, FRANK A.W. MCR 1860; age 24; b. Maryland; cabinetmaker; Huntsville, Walker County. In 1860, Creager and his partner, Hugh H. Hopkins, had a cabinet shop on Cedar Street in Huntsville which used

5,800 feet of lumber to produce furniture valued at $1,600. In April, 1861, Hopkins sold his interest in the business to Creager for $100 (Walker County Deed Records, vol. F, p. 27). In 1868, Creager and his partner, George Fearhake, doing business as Frank Creager and Company, bought a small steam engine for their shop, which manufactured window sashes and coffins as well as furniture (John W. Baldwin, "An Early History of Walker County" [M.A. thesis, Sam Houston State Teachers College, 1957], p. 65). Creager was still in Huntsville in January, 1874, when he sold a half interest in a herd of horses (Walker County Deed Records, vol. G, p. 474).

CREISLER, WILLIAM. Creisler is listed in John H. Heller's *Galveston City Directory 1872* as a cabinetmaker employed by William W. Patch at 264 Tremont Street and living at that same address.

CRENWELGE, CHRISTIAN. MCR 1860; age 26; b. Germany; cabinetmaker; Gillespie County. A pine food safe attributed to Crenwelge was in the American Heritage Museum, Fredericksburg, in 1973.

CROLLY, HARMON. MCR 1860; age 20; b. Saxony; cabinetmaker; San Antonio, Bexar County.

CRONE, C.S. MCR 1860; age 39; b. Ohio; cabinetmaker; Tyler, Smith County. The products-of-industry schedule of the 1860 census return gives Crone's name as S. C. Crone. In that year his shop used horse power and 8,000 feet of pine and 4,000 feet of oak to produce 30 bedsteads valued at $240, 3 safes valued at $30, 60 chairs valued at $60, and wardrobes, bureaus, etc., valued at $300. He was one of four cabinetmakers in Smith County that year whose furniture product exceeded $500 in value.

CROUCH, ISAAC. MCR 1870; age 35; b. Kentucky; cabinetmaker; McKinney, Collin County. Isaac Crouch was in McKinney as early as April, 1866, when he and his partner, Lewis Wetsel, purchased a town lot from another cabinetmaker, Philip Hocker (Collin County Deed Records, vol. I, p. 484). In 1870, Crouch and Wetsel were major Texas cabinetmakers, with a three-man shop that produced $7,000 worth of furniture that year. In April, 1871, Crouch, describing himself as a "manufacturer and dealer in furniture . . . west of the Public Square, at the old Cabinet Shop," advertised that he had on hand "the Largest and Best Lot of Furniture Ever in the Market, Consisting of BUREAUS,

SAFES, STANDTABLES, WASHSTANDS, LOUNGES, French and Zouave Bedsteads of the latest styles, and Bedsteads of all kinds. All Kinds of Furniture Made to Order" (*Weekly Enquirer*, April 15, 1871). The next month he was advertising for "a boy from 13 to 16 years of age, to work and learn the business of Cabinet Making" (ibid., May 20, 1871).

CROUCH AND WETSEL. *See* Crouch, Isaac.

CROW, JAMES. MCR 1860; age 33; b. Arkansas; farmer and chairmaker; Alvarado, Johnson County.

CROW, THOMAS. MCR 1850; age 45; b. Virginia; cabinetmaker; Rusk County.

CULBERTSON, THOMAS. MCR 1850; age 25; b. Alabama; cabinetmaker; Leon County.

CULLISON, JOHN J. MCR 1860, 1870; age 29 in 1860; b. Maryland; master cabinetmaker; Springfield, Limestone County, in 1860. By 1870 Cullison had moved to Fairfield, Freestone County, where he was operating a three-man cabinet shop that produced furniture valued at $1,000. It was one of two shops in Fairfield whose product exceeded $500 in value that year.

CUMMINS, J.C. MCR 1860; age 39; b. Tennessee; cabinetmaker; Buchanan, Johnson County.

CUTTICA, C. Cuttica, on Church Street between Tremont and 24th, Galveston, advertised in November, 1872, that he was a "cabinet maker and furniture repairer. Banking Houses, Offices, Stores, and Saloons fitted up in any style, with superior workmen" (*Galveston Daily News*, November 17, 1872).

DAHME, F. MCR 1860; age 37; b. Bremen; cabinetmaker; Indianola, Calhoun County.

DALE, WILLIAM. MCR 1870; age 50; b. Tennessee; cabinetmaker; Pilot Point, Denton County.

DANIEL, WILLIAM B. MCR 1860, 1870; age 37 in 1860; b. North Carolina; cabinetmaker; Columbus, Colorado County.

DANN, C.W. MCR 1860; age 41; b. Kentucky; cabinetmaker; Leonville, Coryell County. Dann was in business on Market Street in Galveston in November, 1854, when he advertised that he was "prepared to manufacture all kinds of Cabinet Work, of Mahogany, Walnut, Cedar, &c., of the best style and finish, and made in the most substantial manner at moderate prices; Also, all kinds of repairing in the cabinet line, polishing, &c." (*Civilian and Gazette,* November 21, 1854).

DARBY, W.R. MCR 1860; age 43; b. South Carolina; cabinetmaker; Montgomery, Montgomery County.

DAVENPORT, J.W. MCR 1860; age 25; b. South Carolina; carpenter; Quitman, Wood County. In 1860, Davenport had a cabinet shop at Quitman employing two hands and using 6,000 feet of pine and walnut lumber valued at $300 to produce cabinet work valued at $1,000.

DAVIDSON, A. MCR 1850; age 35; b. Georgia; cabinetmaker; Titus County.

DAVIDSON, ALLEN. MCR 1860; age 74; b. Virginia; chairmaker; La-Fayette, Upshur County.

DAVIS, JESSE. MCR 1860; age 48; b. South Carolina; cabinetmaker; Papalote, Bee County.

DAVIS, SAM. MCR 1870; age 39; b. Georgia; cabinetmaker; Mount Pleasant, Titus County.

DAVIS, WILLIAM F. MCR 1860; age 29; b. South Carolina; cabinetmaker; Lexington, Burleson County.

DAVISS, H.P. MCR 1860; age 26; b. Alabama; master cabinetmaker; Fairfield, Freestone County. In 1860, Daviss had a shop in Fairfield which employed 2 1/2 hands (either two hands and an apprentice or two full-time hands and one part-time hand) and used 10,000 feet of lumber valued at $300 and $400 worth of varnish and locks to make furniture and window sash valued at $2,400. An article in the Corsicana *Navarro Express,* January 14, 1860, throws some light on Daviss's business methods: "The Cash System: Mr. H. P. Daviss, cabinet maker, Fairfield, in advertising his business in the *Pioneer,* gets off the following good thing: 'Whenever mechanics shall have purged themselves of the credit system, they will, in a great degree, assist in overthrowing mercantile credit—a system which enables rogues and drones to live uselessly and often fare sumptuously at the cost of honest, industrious people. Whenever "pay down" shall be the general rule in buying goods, their average cost to consumers shall be reduced at least ten per cent. And why should those who pay bear a tax of ten per cent on their earning, for the benefit of those who never pay? Tell us why?'"

DAY, WILLIAM. MCR 1860; age 30; b. Georgia; cabinetmaker; Waco, McLennan County.

DEAN, GREENWOOD W. MCR 1870; age 25; b. Texas; cabinetmaker; Madisonville, Madison County. In 1870, Greenwood Dean had a cabinet shop in Madisonville which used materials valued at $100 to produce furniture valued at $500.

DEAN, JOB A. MCR 1850; age 25; b. Kentucky; cabinetmaker; Rusk County. In 1850, Job Dean had a shop which used 2,000 feet of sawed lumber valued at $200 to produce "a variety of bedsteads and other furniture."

DE LEON, V. In 1872, V. De Leon of Austin advertised that he was a "manufacturer of bureaus, washstands, wardrobes, tables, chairs, bedsteads, lounges, etc., wholesale and retail. Dealers will find it to their interest to examine my prices before sending North. Coffins and Picture frames made to order with dispatch, scroll sawing and wood turning" (S. A. Gray and W. D. Moore, *Mercantile and General City Directory of Austin, Texas, 1872–73*).

DENSON, MATTHEW. MCR 1860; age 50; b. Alabama; carpenter; Tyler, Smith County. On August 1, 1861, Denson advertised in the *Tyler Reporter* that his "cabinet shop (at Josephus Taylor's) is situated seven and a half miles north of Tyler, where I make all kinds of FURNITURE and sell it cheaper than anybody. Don't throw away your money, but come and buy cheap furniture from M. Denson."

DEWITT, C.W. MCR 1860; age 22; b. Ohio; cabinetmaker; Paris, Lamar County.

DEWITT, L.W. MCR 1860; age 24; b. Ohio; cabinetmaker; Paris, Lamar County.

DICKSON, J. MCR 1860; age 18; b. Missouri; cabinetmaker; Waxahachie, Ellis County.

DICKSON, LEVIN S. MCR 1860; age 43; b. Maryland; cabinetmaker; Waxahachie, Ellis County. The inventory of Levin S. Dickson's estate, made at his death in 1866, lists "1/2 acre of land and improvement; cabinet tools, benches, &c belonging to shop; household and kitchen furniture; 4 cows and yearlings" (Ellis County Record of Probate, vol. E, p. 490).

DICKSON, WILLIAM. MCR 1860; age 15; b. Missouri; cabinetmaker; Waxahachie, Ellis County.

DILLARD, HENRY H. MCR 1850; age 27; b. North Carolina; cabinet-maker; Walker County.

DILLARD, WILLIAM M. MCR 1850; age 34; b. North Carolina; cabinet-maker; Walker County.

DONIVAN, DANIEL. MCR 1870; age 27; b. England; cabinetmaker; Baytown, Harris County.

DONSIL, CHARLES. MCR 1860; age 38; b. Prussia; cabinetmaker; Gay Hill, Washington County.

DORRIS, ANDERSON. MCR 1860. Anderson Dorris, chairmaker, was born about 1818. He was working in Lockhart, Caldwell County, as early as November, 1852, when he and William T. Dorris purchased lot 2, block 27, in Lockhart from the estate of Jonathan Tanner (Caldwell County Deed Records, vol. C, p. 320). In 1856 he and his son, John E. Dorris, purchased 5 1/2 acres of land on the outskirts of Lockhart from the estate of Samuel Wilson (ibid., vol. F, p. 9). Three years later they sold this land to Hiram A. Dorris (ibid., p. 598), who failed to complete payment for it before his death in 1868, causing its return to Anderson Dorris (ibid., vol. G, p. 592). In 1860, Anderson and John E. Dorris were operating a chairmaking shop in Lockhart using hides and timbers valued at $135 to produce 450 chairs valued at $675. This shop was evidently on lots 2 and 3 of block 27 in Lockhart, at the northeast corner of Walnut and Main streets (ibid., vol. C, p. 105). In 1869, the "A. Dorris and Son Chair Manufactory" advertised: "The very best article of hide bottomed chairs manufactured and sold low for cash. Shuck bottomed chairs made to order at a small additional cost" (*Texas Plowboy*, October 30, 1869). The next year Dorris bought two more city lots in Lockhart, paying $300 for one and $100 for the other (Caldwell County Deed Records, vol. I, p. 59). He died in 1888, "an old man over seventy years old," leaving personal property valued at $350 and "a small house and lot in Lockhart" (Caldwell County Probate Minutes, vol. H, p. 144). See also Caldwell County Deed Records, vol. N, p. 565; vol. Q, p. 145; Caldwell County Probate Minutes, vol. H, pp. 70–74.

DORRIS, ELIAS. MCR 1850; age 28; b. Tennessee; cabinetmaker; Hunt County.

DORRIS, ELIAS. MCR 1870; age 32; b. Tennessee; chairmaker; La Grange, Fayette County.

DORRIS, HIRAM A. MCR 1850; age 17; b. Tennessee; cabinetmaker; Montgomery County. Hiram A. Dorris was working in Lockhart, Caldwell County, in October, 1859, when he purchased 5 1/2 acres of land from Anderson Dorris and John E. Dorris (Caldwell County Deed Records, vol. F, p. 598). He died in Lockhart in December, 1868, leaving a widow and children (Caldwell County Probate Minutes, vol. E, p. 32). *See also* Dorris, Anderson.

DORRIS, JOHN E. MCR 1860. John E. Dorris, son of Anderson Dorris, was born about 1837. He married Matilda J. Brown on March 24, 1859, and practiced the trade of chairmaker with his father in Lockhart, Caldwell County, in the 1860's. (Caldwell County Deed Records, vol. F, p. 568; Caldwell County Marriage Records, vol. C, p. 43.) *See also* Dorris, Anderson.

DORRIS, ROBERT. MCR 1870; age 33; b. Tennessee; chairmaker; Lockhart, Caldwell County.

DORRIS, STEPHEN J. MCR 1860. Stephen J. Dorris, chairmaker, was in Lockhart, Caldwell County, as early as August, 1858, when he purchased the *labor* of land (177 acres) originally granted to Elbert Hines from William T. Dorris for $275. In 1860 he had a chairmaking shop in Lockhart which used hides and timber valued at $160 to produce 600 chairs valued at $800. He married Jane C. Gilliland on July 19, 1864, and was still in Lockhart in February, 1871. (Caldwell County Deed Records, vol. G, p. 531; vol. M, p. 424; Caldwell County Marriage Records, vol. C, p. 107.)

DORRIS, WILLIAM T. MCR 1850, 1870; age 18 in 1850; b. Tennessee; cabinetmaker in 1850; carpenter in 1870; Montgomery County in 1850; Caldwell County in 1870. William T. Dorris moved to Lockhart, Caldwell County, as early as November, 1852, when he and Anderson Dorris purchased a city lot there. *See* Dorris, Anderson.

DOWNS, N.D. MCR 1860; age 42; b. Tennessee; cabinet worker; Bethany, Panola County.

DUFF, JAMES M. MCR 1870; age 39; b. Indiana; cabinetmaker; Waxahachie, Ellis County.

DUNCAN, F. LEMUEL. MCR 1870; age 50; b. Georgia; chairmaker; Douglass, Nacogdoches County. In 1860, Duncan had a cabinet shop in Rusk County which used horse power and lumber valued at $100 and paints and varnish valued at $100 to produce 96 bedsteads valued at $1,152, according to the MCR products-of-industry schedule; he is not listed on the population schedule for 1860.

DUPHRATE, JOHN. MCR 1870; age 35; b. England; cabinetmaker; Pinetree, Upshur County. In 1870, Duphrate had a one-man cabinet shop which used hand power and one lathe. He used walnut valued at $50, oak valued at $40, pine valued at $10, paint valued at $3, and varnish valued at $15 to produce 20 bedsteads valued at $400, 10 wardrobes valued at $150, 10 safes valued at $200, 10 chairs valued at $15, and 1 bureau valued at $25. It was the only cabinet shop in Upshur County whose product exceeded $500 in value that year.

DURFEE, CHARLES. MCR 1870; age 56; b. Ohio; cabinet workman; Clarksville, Red River County. Durfee must have been working in Clarksville before July, 1854, for in that month the firm of Hatley, Gaines, and Stephen announced that they were carrying on their cabinetmaking business at "the old stand of Charles Durfee" (*Standard*, July 22, 1854). On November 20, 1858, Durfee purchased lot 1 in block 7, Clarksville, from John Brackney, another cabinetmaker (Red River County Deed Records, vol. L, p. 511).

EARPS, C.A. MCR 1860; age 44; b. South Carolina; cabinet workman; Douglasville, Cass County.

EASON, ROBERT. MCR 1870; age 23; b. Georgia; cabinetmaker; Garden Valley, Smith County.

EASON, SEABORN. MCR 1860; age 29; b. Mississippi; chairmaker; Danville, Montgomery County.

EASTMAN, E.J. MCR 1860; age 54; b. New York; cabinetmaker; Travis, Austin County.

EAVES, JAMES. MCR 1870; age 58; b. Georgia; cabinetmaker; Dangerfield, Titus County.

EBENSBERGER, EUGEN BENNO. MCR 1870; age 28; b. Prussia; joiner; New Braunfels, Comal County. Eugen Ebensberger was a native of Santomischel, Posen, Prussia. He and his brother, Oscar Ebensberger, came to Texas in 1860; he married Katherine Sattler in New Braunfels on April 1, 1866. (Comal County Probate Records, vol. D, p. 303; Register, First German Protestant Church of New Braunfels [Family 3].)

On November 27, 1868, he advertised in the *Neu-Braunfelser Zeitung*: "Fertige Särge jeder Grösse sind fortwährend zu haben bei / Coffins of every size always on hand / Eug. Ebensberger." In 1870 he and his brother were operating a joinery which used $400 worth of timber to manufacture an annual product valued at $1,200; it was one of five cabinet shops in Comal County which produced more than $500 worth of furniture that year. His advertisements in the *Neu-Braunfelser Zeitung*, July 15, 1870, read: "Möbel Möbel! zu haben bei Eugen Ebensberger [furniture furniture! available from Eugen Ebensberger]." A desk made by Ebensberger for *Zeitung* editor Ferdinand Lindheimer (7.8) bears the stenciled advertisement: "E. EBENSBERGER / MANUFACTURER & DEALER IN / FURNITURE / MOLDINGS PICTURE / FRAMES & COFFINS ON HAND AND MADE / TO ORDER / ALSO LUMBER FOR SALE / NEW BRAUNFELS TEXAS."

EBENSBERGER, OSCAR. MCR 1870; age 25; b. Prussia; works in joinery; New Braunfels, Comal County. *See also* Ebensberger, Eugen Benno.

EBERHARD, BERNHARD. MCR 1860; age 57; b. Weimar; turner; New Braunfels, Comal County. In his petition for naturalization, Bernhard Eberhard stated that he had arrived in Texas in 1853 (Comal County District Court Minutes, vol. C, p. 127).

EBERHARD, EDWARD. MCR 1870; age 38; b. Prussia; turner; New Braunfels, Comal County. In 1870, Edward Eberhard had a turnery in New Braunfels which used $150 worth of timber to manufacture products valued at $600.

ECKHART, A. MCR 1860; age 51; b. Germany; cabinet work; Bellville, Austin County.

EDDY, WILLIAM. MCR 1860, 1870; age 49 in 1860; b. Tennessee; chairmaker; Marlin, Falls County, in 1860; Meridian, Bosque County, in 1870.

EDGARS, NICHOLAS. MCR 1850; age 65; b. Pennsylvania; cabinetmaker; Sabine County.

EDMISTON, CHARLES. MCR 1860; age 21; b. Tennessee; cabinetmaker; Independence, Washington County.

EDMONDSON, JOHN. John Edmondson was a partner with George M. Martin in the Houston cabinetmaking firm of Martin and Edmondson. The partnership was dissolved on October 20, 1839, and Edmondson advertised that "the turning and bedsteadmaking business will be continued by me at the old stand" (*Morning Star*, October 23, 1839). *See also* Martin, George M.

EDWARDS, THOMAS. MCR 1870; age 60; b. Kentucky; chairmaker; Denton, Denton County.

EITLE, WILLIAM H. MCR 1850; age 23; b. Tennessee; cabinetmaker; Bowie County.

ELKINS, A.M. MCR 1860; age 63; b. South Carolina; carpenter; Troup, Smith County. In 1860, Elkins and his partner, John Fields, had a wagon and cabinet shop in Canton, Smith County. Using hand power and 2,000 feet of pine valued at $50, 2,000 feet of oak valued at $100, and "other articles" valued at $200, they made 2 wagons valued at $100, 4 bedsteads valued at $40, and different kinds of furniture valued at $300 and did repairing valued at $200.

ELLISON, DANIEL W. MCR 1860; age 25; b. Alabama; cabinetmaker; Waverly, Walker County. Ellison died in Waverly in 1862. His inventory shows him to have owned a 120-acre farm, 30 cattle, 30 hogs, house furniture, 2 wagons, a buggy, mechanic tools, turning tools, and "a lot of gearing." The record of the administrator's sale of his tools lists "1 work bench and screw, 1 lot turning tools, 1 handsaw, 1 handsaw, 1 small handsaw, 1 crosscut saw; 1 hand axe; 1 iron square; 1 hammer and chisel; 1 bench screw and auger; 1 adze; 2 augers; match plains; 2 smoothing plains; 1 moulding and rabit plain; 2 fore plains; 2 jack plains; 2 drawing knives; 2 squares; 1 guage; 1 lot of chisels; bed castors; brace and bits; files." (Walker County Probate Minutes, vol. D, pp. 548, 581.)

ELVESS, C. MCR 1860; age 25; b. Germany; cabinetmaker; Galveston, Galveston County.

EMERY, J.R. Emery, "cabinetmaker and undertaker" in Lockhart, Caldwell County, advertised in the Lockhart *Rambler*, July 1, 1859, that he was "prepared to do all work in his line of business. Particular care is bestowed by him upon the construction of coffins, and he can furnish them, of all kinds, from the very cheapest to those of the most elaborate and costly description."

ENGEL, WILLIAM. MCR 1850; age 25; b. Germany; cabinetmaker; Colorado County.

ENGLAND, J.W. MCR 1860; age 33; b. Tennessee; cabinetmaker; Austin, Travis County. England was one of Austin's most prominent cabinetmakers in the late 1850's and early 1860's. In January, 1858, he and Thomas M. Bostick announced their partnership in a cabinetmaking shop (*Southern Intelligencer*, January 20, 1858; *see also* Bostick, Thomas M.). This partnership was dissolved in April, 1858 (ibid., April 21, 1858), and in October of that year England advertised that "the oldest establishment in the city is now opened again. In a short time we will be prepared to manufacture all kinds of furniture in a superior manner. None but the best workmen will be employed, and we confidentially [sic] expect a share of patronage. UNDERTAKING will be promptly and carefully attended to. We have a superior and new Hearse. Our terms will be reasonable. J. W. England & Co." (ibid., October 20, 1858). A year later, in October, 1859, he announced that he had formed a new partnership and that the "England and Woofter Furniture Emporium, Congress Avenue, opposite the Swenson Building . . . will keep constantly on hand an assortment of the various articles found in large establishments, which they will sell very low. None but the best workmen will be employed, and we confidently expect a share of patronage. Undertaking will be promptly and carefully attended to" (*Daily State Gazette and General Advertiser*, October 12, 1859). In February, 1860, England and Woofter advertised that they were "manufacturing all articles in their line of business and will keep on hand a supply of Northern made furniture. The best of mechanics will be employed, and we will endeavor to give satisfaction. And holding the appointment of Sexton, by the City Council, and the Superintendance of the burying grounds, we are prepared to do grave digging with neatness, and at all times" (*Southern Intelligencer*, February 1, 1860). England remained in business in Austin after the Civil War, and in July, 1865, he advertised that he had established himself "one door below Wm. Oliphant's Jewelry Establishment, on Pecan Street" (*Weekly Southern Intelligencer*, July 21, 1865). In that same month he formed a partnership with another cabinetmaker, Joseph W. Hannig (ibid., July 28, 1865), and in March, 1866, they advertised that they were "at the old stand of T. H. Tumey, on Pecan Street" (ibid., March 15, 1866). In June, 1868, Hannig ran an advertisement describing himself as "successor to England & Hannig" (*Daily Austin Republican*, June 1, 1868).

ENK, JACOB. MCR 1860; age 44; b. Prussia; joiner; New Braunfels, Comal County. In his petition for naturalization, Jacob Enk stated that he had arrived in Texas in 1851 (Comal County District Court Minutes, vol. B, p. 468).

ERNST, FREDERICK. MCR 1850; age 33; b. Germany; cabinetmaker; Galveston, Galveston County.

ERNST, GEORGE. MCR 1850; age 30; b. Germany; cabinetmaker; Comal County.

ETZEL, WILLIAM. MCR 1860; age 40; b. Nassau; farmer and carpenter; Round Top, Fayette County. Etzel was born at Wehrheim, Nassau, June 24, 1820. He was living in the Round Top neighborhood in July, 1844, when he was mentioned by Prince Carl von Solms-Braunfels as having been retained by Count Boos-Waldeck as the manager of Nassau plantation. He received fifty acres of land on the William Jack League from Count Boos-Waldeck for his services. He was trained in Germany as a cabinetmaker and practiced that trade in Texas; a cedar china cabinet made by him (8.7) is in the Winedale collection. He died September 15, 1889, and is buried in the Becker Cemetery near Winedale. (Chester William Geue and Ethel Hander Geue, *A New Land Beckoned*, p. 22.)

EVANS, W.W. MCR 1860, 1870; age 27 in 1860; b. Kentucky; cabinetmaker; Austin, Travis County. In May, 1866, Evans advertised that he had "opened at the old established stand of Jno. S. Spence, on Pecan Street, and am prepared to manufacture and repair furniture on reasonable terms. UNDERTAKING promptly attended to at satisfactory prices" (*Southern Intelligencer*, May 31, 1866). In June, 1868, he advertised that, in addition to manufacturing furniture, he made mattresses and did upholstering (*Daily Austin Republican*, June 11, 1868; also in the *Round Rock Sentinel*, January 19, 1870). In 1870 his two-man shop used 3,000 feet of lumber valued at $225 and 20 gallons of varnish valued at $30 to produce coffins and furniture valued at $3,000. He was still in business in Austin in July, 1871 (*Reformer*, July 22, 1871).

EVERS, CLEMENT. MCR 1870; age 35; b. Prussia; cabinetmaker; Galveston, Galveston County.

FAMBRO, JOHN. MCR 1850; age 40; b. Georgia; cabinetmaker; Rusk County.

FARR, J.B. MCR 1860; age 30; b. Ohio; cabinetmaker; Douglasville, Cass County.

FARRIS, J.J. MCR 1860; age 36; b. Tennessee; cabinetmaker; McKinney, Collin County.

FARRIS, W. MCR 1860; age 33; b. Tennessee; cabinetmaker; Montgomery, Montgomery County.

FARRISE, WILLIAM. MCR 1870; age 82; b. Kentucky; cabinetmaker; Sherman, Grayson County.

FEARHAKE, GEORGE. *See* Creager, Frank A. W.

FEHR, J.B. MCR 1860; age 51; b. Germany; master cabinetmaker; Bastrop, Bastrop County. J. B. Fehr was working in Bastrop as early as January, 1854, when he advertised that he had "opened a cabinet shop next door to Dr. Ploger's office on Main Street, where he can furnish anything in his line—such as Dining Tables, Common Tables, Wash Stands, Extension Tables, Bedsteads, Bureaus, Wardrobes, Safes, &c." (*Bastrop Advertiser*, May 27, 1854).

FEHR, WILLIAM. MCR 1870; age 27; b. Holstein; cabinetmaker; Bastrop, Bastrop County.

FELLOWS, R.G. MCR 1860; age 43; b. Alabama; cabinetmaker; Gatesville, Coryell County.

FELTS, JAMES. MCR 1870; age 50; b. South Carolina; cabinetmaker; Dallas, Dallas County.

FERGURSON, W.H. MCR 1870; age 44; b. Kentucky; cabinetmaker; San Marcos, Hays County.

FEST, SIMON. MCR 1870; age 20; b. Texas; apprentice joiner; New Braunfels, Comal County.

FIELDS, JOHN. MCR 1860; age 27; b. Tennessee; carpenter; Troup, Smith County. In 1860, Fields was in partnership with A. M. Elkins of Troup in a wagon and cabinet shop; *see* Elkins, A. M.

FILTON, CHARLES. MCR 1870; age 25; b. England; cabinetmaker; Galveston, Galveston County.

FISHER, DAVID W. MCR 1870; age 34; b. Tennessee; cabinetmaker; Denton, Denton County.

FISHER, PETER. MCR 1860; age 44; b. Kentucky; master cabinetmaker;

Little Elm, Denton County.

FISHER, WILLIAM G. MCR 1860, 1870; age 44 in 1860; b. Virginia; cabinet workman; Gainesville, Cooke County, in 1860; Quitman, Wood County, in 1870. In 1860, William G. Fisher was operating a three-man cabinet shop in Gainesville which used 8,000 feet of pine valued at $320 to produce 500 pieces of furniture valued at $850. In 1870 he had moved to Quitman, where he had a one-man shop equipped with a mortising machine, in which he used 2,000 feet of lumber valued at $200 to produce furniture valued at $600.

FITZGERALD, J.E. MCR 1870; age 49; b. Ireland; cabinetmaker; Galveston, Galveston County.

FLOEGE, KARL. MCR 1850; age 32; b. Germany; cabinetmaker; Comal County. Floege was born in 1819 in Hildesheim, in the Kingdom of Hanover. He arrived in Texas in April, 1846, and settled in New Braunfels. In 1860 he had a mercantile store on Main Plaza, and in 1872 he constructed a low-water bridge at the foot of San Antonio Street. He died in 1893 and is buried in Comal Cemetery, New Braunfels. (Comal County District Court Minutes, vol. A, p. 157; Oscar Haas, *History of New Braunfels and Comal County, Texas, 1844–1946*, p. 85.)

FLOYD, WILLIAM. MCR 1850; age 40; b. Tennessee; cabinetmaker; Shelby County.

FOSTER, JAMES. MCR 1870; age 59; b. Virginia; cabinetmaker; Mantua, Collin County. In 1870, James Foster had a one-man shop at Highland, Collin County, which used $1,000 worth of materials to produce $2,000 worth of furniture.

FOSTER, JOHN. MCR 1860; age 27; b. Tennessee; cabinetmaker; Crockett, Houston County. *See also* Foster, W. J.

FOSTER, JOSEPH. MCR 1860, 1870; age 52 in 1860; b. Virginia; cabinetmaker; Highland, Collin County.

FOSTER, W.J. MCR 1860, 1870; age 30 in 1860; b. Tennessee; cabinetmaker; Crockett, Houston County. In 1860, W. J. Foster had a three-man shop in Crockett which was equipped with a horse-powered lathe. He used 3,000 feet of sawed lumber valued at $675 to produce house furniture valued at $3,000 and coffins valued at $300 and to make gin repairs valued at $500. In November of that year, W. J. Foster "and Bro.," presumably John Foster, advertised that they "have on hand and will keep a good assortment of FURNITURE, Consisting in part of WARDROBES, BEDSTEADS, LOUNGES, SAFES, CRIBS, TABLES, and all kinds of household furniture. The ladies are particularly invited to call and examine our work. COFFINS made at the shortest notice in any style desired. To FARMERS: From years of experience we feel able to put any repairs needed upon gins, and guarantee satisfaction, if not damaged by unexperienced hands. All of the above we expect to do, make, and sell on as good terms as can be done in Texas. Shop near the corner of Rusk and Nacogdoches Roads" (*Crockett Printer*, November 14, 1860). Foster evidently suspended operations during the war, but in July, 1865, he advertised: "ON HAND AGAIN! I HAVE OPENED BUSINESS IN MY Shop, and will do work as before, such as Furniture of all kinds, Coffins, &c, and repair cotton gins. In returning thanks to my old customers for past favors, I solicit their patronage again, with as many new ones as may need my work. TERMS positively cash, cloth, meat, salt, flour, lumber, or something that I can use in my Shop or for my family. Shop at the old stand, where the Printing Office is located and business carried on. I am prepared to do all kinds of turnery. Call and see me—I can fix you up in a trade if you want my work. Necessity drives me to my terms, as I was broke up in the Army" (*Texas Weekly Quid Nunc*, July 25, 1865). He was successful in re-establishing his shop and was still working in Crockett in 1870.

FOWLER, JAMES. MCR 1850, 1860; age 44 in 1850; b. South Carolina; cabinetmaker; Nacogdoches County.

FRANCISCO, J.M. MCR 1860; age 22; b. Virginia; cabinetmaker; Morales de Lavaca, Jackson County.

FRANKLIN, EPHRAM. MCR 1860; age 35; b. unknown; chairmaker; Mantua, Collin County.

FRANKLIN, THOMAS. MCR 1870; age 28; b. Indiana; chairmaker; San Saba County.

FRICKE, ERNST. MCR 1850; age 24; b. Germany; cabinetmaker; Rusk County.

FRIEDRICH, WENZEL. MCR 1870; age 43; b. Bohemia; cabinetmaker; San Antonio, Bexar County. Friedrich was born at Gruenthal, Bohemia, on July 2, 1827. He immigrated to Texas in 1853 and established himself as a cabinetmaker in San Antonio. In the 1880's his firm became famous for the manufacture of furniture from animal horns. A selection of this furniture is in the Witte Memorial Museum, San Antonio, and is pictured by Cecilia Steinfeldt and Donald L. Stover, *Early Texas Furniture and Decorative Arts*, pp. 136–141.

FRIESE, FREDERICK. MCR 1870; age 28; b. Prussia; works in cabinet shop; Brenham, Washington County.

FRY, B.F. MCR 1850; age 37; b. North Carolina; cabinetmaker; Nacogdoches County.

FURGERSON, ALEX. MCR 1870; age 49; b. Tennessee; Denton, Denton County.

GAINER, WILLIAM H. MCR 1850; age 30; b. Alabama; cabinetmaker; Shelby County.

GAINES, WILLIAM C. Gaines was one of several prominent cabinetmakers working in Clarksville, Red River County, in the 1850's. He was there as early as December 18, 1852, when he and James H. Smith purchased a town lot from J. D. H. Epperson; on July 12, 1853, Smith sold his interest in the lot to Gaines (Red River County Deed Records, vol. J, pp. 41, 177). In July, 1854, the firm of Hatley, Gaines, and Stephen, "Cabinet makers and Undertakers," announced "to their friends and the public generally, that they are carrying on the Cabinet Making Business, at the old stand of Charles Durfee, on Main Street; and having received a large supply of materials for their business, including a fine lot of Mahogany and Rosewood, Veneering; are prepared to execute orders for the best class of furniture, such as Lounges, Tables, Bedsteads, Bureaus, &c. Having several hands in the establishment, orders for coffins, either in the neighborhood or from a distance, can be filled with despatch. They will endeavor to keep on hand a few polished Walnut Coffins at reduced prices" (*Standard*, July 22, 1854). In November, 1856, a fire, which started in the shop of his fellow craftsman James B. Shanahan, destroyed Gaines's shop, and he purchased lots 1–8 in block 70 as a new shop site (*Southern Intelligencer*, November 19, 1856; Red River County Deed Records, vol. K, p. 441). In February, 1858, he and his partner advertised that "Gaines and Miller, Cabinet Makers and Manufacturers of All Kinds of Chairs, offer for inspection at their shop on Locust Street, and will make to order, work of any desired style, of Fine or plain material. They make

Bureaus of all grades, with or without marble slabs, as preferred. They get up all kinds of tables, and a great variety of Chairs, Settees, and Bedsteads. An inspection of their ware-room is invited; and any work not on hand will be made to order, in any desired style, being prepared with the finest woods, and workmen competent to do all branches of work in their line. They will serve as undertakers, promptly and efficiently—are prepared to get up Coffins of polished mahogany or walnut, or cloth covered, in six to ten hours. They propose to furnish cabinet work of the best class, as cheap as it can be brought here, and all they ask of their fellow-citizens is to come and examine, compare quality and prices, and try them" (*Standard*, February 20, 1858). A news item in the same paper calls attention to the advertisement and says, "They are trying to do business on a larger scale than it has been heretofore done here, in their line" (ibid.). In April, 1860, Gaines ran an advertisement stating that "W. C. Gaines would respectfully announce to the public that he is at his old stand again, and prepared to do all kinds of work pertaining to his line. Will serve as an UNDERTAKER promptly and efficiently, and when called upon to serve in this line, will carry bodies in a Hearse, within three miles of town, free of charge; over that distance at moderate prices" (ibid., April 21, 1860). However, Gaines announced in September, 1860, that he had "sold his interest in the cabinet shop heretofore carried on by him in Clarksville" to Henry Bushfield and Jasper Longe (ibid., September 22, 1860).

GAMBEL, BENJAMIN. MCR 1870; age 18; b. Texas; cabinet workman; Honey Grove, Fannin County.

GANLEY, JAMES. MCR 1860; age 32; b. New York; cabinetmaker; Sherman, Grayson County.

GARDNER, EDWARD. MCR 1860; age 21; b. Indiana; cabinetmaker; Kaufman, Kaufman County.

GARDNER, JAMES W. MCR 1850; age 32; b. Virginia; cabinetmaker; Kaufman, Kaufman County.

GASTON, ELIAS. MCR 1870; age 42; b. Indiana; cabinetmaker and ship carpenter; Pennington, Trinity County.

GATES, W.E. MCR 1870; age 31; b. Georgia; cabinet workman; Cleburne, Johnson County.

GAULT, SAMUEL F. MCR 1860, 1870; age 48 in 1860; b. Kentucky; cabinetmaker; Sherman, Grayson County. Gault had a one-man cabinet shop in Sherman in 1860 which employed oxen as motive power and used 2,000 feet of lumber valued at $80 to produce 100 articles of furniture valued at $800. He also operated a carding machine (Graham Landrum, *An Illustrated History of Grayson County, Texas*, p. 138).

GENTMANN, FRIEDRICH. MCR 1860, 1870; age 36 in 1860; b. Hanover; cabinetmaker; Fredericksburg, Gillespie County. In 1860, Gentmann had a one-man shop in Fredericksburg which used timber valued at $300 to produce furniture valued at $900. This was one of ten cabinet shops in Fredericksburg which produced furniture valued at more than $500 in 1860.

GERLOFF, C.H.L. MCR 1870. In 1870, Gerloff had a one-man turning shop in Galveston, Galveston County, which used wood valued at $600 and bone and ivory valued at $100 to produce turning valued at $1,000 and billiard balls and "fancy articles" valued at $100.

GERON, JACK. MCR 1870; age 23; b. Mississippi; works in cabinet shop; Paris, Lamar County.

GILHULY, PATRICK. MCR 1860; age 61; b. Ireland; cabinetmaker; Nacogdoches, Nacogdoches County.

GILKIST, ALEXANDER. MCR 1850; age 36; b. Scotland; cabinetmaker; Rusk County.

GILLENWATERS, JOHN E. MCR 1870; age 29; b. Mississippi; cabinetmaker; Waxahachie, Ellis County.

GLASS, HENRY. MCR 1870; age 44; b. Pennsylvania; cabinetmaker; McKinney, Collin County.

GLASS, THOMAS. MCR 1870; age 22; b. Pennsylvania; cabinetmaker; McKinney, Collin County.

GLOVER, EDWARD C. MCR 1850; age 36; b. Virginia; cabinetmaker; Jefferson County.

GOHEEN, M.R. MCR 1850; age 43; b. New York; cabinetmaker; Grimes County.

GOHEEN, T.M. MCR 1850; age 45; b. Pennsylvania; cabinetmaker; Grimes County.

GOODALL, JOSEPH D. MCR 1850; age 30; b. New York; cabinetmaker; Gillespie County. Goodall was a member of the Mormon community founded at Zodiac, Gillespie County, by Lyman Wight in 1847. The community operated a water-powered saw mill, grist mill, and turning lathe on the Pedernales River, where in 1850 Goodall used timber and varnish valued at $100 to produce bedsteads, chairs, and tables valued at $892. (Don Biggers, *German Pioneers in Texas*, p. 94; Dick King, *Ghost Towns of Texas*, pp. 26–27.)

GOODE, D.J. MCR 1860; age 24; b. Pennsylvania; cabinetmaker; Waco, McLennan County.

GOODWIN, HENRY. MCR 1860; age 26; b. North Carolina; cabinetmaker; Marlin, Falls County.

GORSIDE, HUGH. MCR 1870; age 35; b. England; makes chairs; Decatur, Wise County.

GOSCH, FRED. MCR 1870; age 30; b. Germany; cabinetmaker; Galveston, Galveston County. John H. Heller's *Galveston City Directory 1872* lists Fred Gosch as living at 476 East Avenue H and being employed by B. R. Davis and Bro., 66 East Strand.

GOULD, J.M. J. M. Gould and L. M. Miner advertised as "Gould & Miner, Cabinet-Makers, Shop on Preston Street, Washington, Texas, Feb. 28, 1852" (*Lone Star*, October 23, 1852). Nothing more is known of either man.

GRAHAM, C.D. MCR 1870; age 45; b. New York; cabinetmaker; Marshall, Harrison County.

GRAHAM, JAMES. MCR 1860; age 61; b. Georgia; cabinetmaker; Lavaca (now Port Lavaca), Calhoun County.

GRAINGER AND ACKERMAN. This Houston firm advertised in August, 1846, as "Builders and Carriage Makers," saying that they "have removed from the south east corner of Market Square to their shop opposite the new Episcopal Church, where they intend to carry on the above branches of business, together with Cabinet Work and Turning. All orders from the country punctually attended to" (*Democratic Telegraph and Texas Register*, August 19, 1846). Nothing more is known of them.

GRANT, SAMUEL F. MCR 1860; age 46; b. Kentucky; cabinetmaker; Sherman, Grayson County.

GRAVES, W.P. MCR 1860; age 40; b. South Carolina; cabinetmaker; Woodland, Hopkins County.

GRAY, L.G. MCR 1860; age 33; b. Alabama; cabinet and wagonmaker; Big Rock, Van Zandt County.

GREEN, JAMES. MCR 1860; age 27; b. Missouri; cabinetmaker; Lancaster, Dallas County.

GREEN, JOHN. MCR 1860; age 63; b. Kentucky; cabinetmaker; Lancaster, Dallas County.

GREER, ROBERT. MCR 1870; age 37; b. Alabama; cabinetmaker; Garden Valley, Smith County.

GREER, WILLIAM. MCR 1870; age 58; b. Kentucky; cabinetmaker; Dallas, Dallas County.

GRIFFITH, L.A. L. A. Griffith and John W. Kincy of Houston advertised in February, 1846, to "respectfully inform the public that they have opened a shop on the west side of Market Square, in the building occupied by Mr. Schiermann as a Black Smith Shop, where they intend to manufacture all kinds of cabinet ware, and repair wagons, buggies, and ploughs in the most substantial manner, as their materials will be of the very best. Planters will find it to their interest to give them a call" (*Telegraph and Texas Register*, February 18, 1846).

GRIMES, JAMES. MCR 1860; age 46; b. Tennessee; cabinetmaker; Honey Grove, Fannin County.

GUILLAUME, ALEX. MCR 1870; age 63; b. France; cabinetmaker; Dallas, Dallas County.

GUINN, CHARLES. MCR 1860; age 39; b. Alabama; wheelwright; Angelina County. In 1860, Guinn was operating a one-man chair factory which used 20,000 feet of lumber valued at $150 to make $600 worth of chairs and other articles.

GURLEY, N.J. MCR 1860; age 40; b. Tennessee; cabinet workman; Elly, Titus County.

GURNEA, JOSEPH. MCR 1870; age 36; b. France; cabinetmaker; Harrisburg, Harris County.

GUTON, HENRY. MCR 1870; age 26; b. Tennessee; chairmaker; Clarksville, Red River County.

HAAS, JOHANN JOST. MCR 1860; age 49; b. Nassau; cabinetmaker; Comal County. Haas was born in Gusternkeim, Nassau, and came to Texas in November, 1845. During the Civil War he made his way to federally occupied New Orleans and joined the United States Army, serving in

Captain Adolf Zoeller's company, First Texas Cavalry. After the war he returned to Texas and practiced his trade at Blanco. (Comal County District Court Minutes, vol. B, p. 72; interview with Oscar Haas, New Braunfels, February 10, 1973.)

HADEN, J. MCR 1860; age 54; b. Kentucky; cabinetmaker; Weatherford, Parker County.

HAEMAN, WILLIAM. MCR 1850; age 40; b. Germany; cabinetmaker; Galveston, Galveston County.

HAGY, G.W. In May, 1854, G. W. Hagy of Bastrop advertised that, "having employed regular cabinet workmen, he will keep constantly on hand a good supply of EXTRA TIN SAFES, PLAIN WARD ROBES, TABLES, BEDSTEADS, LOUNGES, &C., &C. Undertaking particularly attended to. Coffins of all descriptions made at the shortest notice" (*Bastrop Advertiser*, May 27, 1854).

HALL, J.D. MCR 1860; age 34; b. North Carolina; cabinetmaker; Kaufman, Kaufman County. In 1860, Hall had a one-man cabinet shop in Kaufman which used 5,000 feet of lumber valued at $150 to produce 14 bedsteads valued at $140, 1 wardrobe valued at $20, 10 tables valued at $40, and other articles valued at $300. It was one of two shops in Kaufman that year which produced furniture valued at more than $500.

HALTOM, ———. *See* Whitehead, J. M.

HAMERLY, S.A. MCR 1860; age 44; b. Switzerland; cabinetmaker; Bonham, Fannin County.

HAMILTON, A.L. MCR 1850; age 30; b. Tennessee; cabinetmaker; Upshur County.

HAMILTON, JOHN. MCR 1870; age 31; b. Mississippi; cabinetmaker; Mount Pleasant, Titus County.

HAMILTON, MULBERRY. MCR 1870; age 52; b. Tennessee; cabinet workman; Mount Pleasant, Titus County.

HANCOCK, W.F. MCR 1870; age 46; b. Tennessee; cabinetmaker; Spring Hill, Navarro County.

HANDES, THEODORE. MCR 1850; age 28; b. Germany; cabinetmaker; Galveston, Galveston County.

HANKINS, JOSEPH. MCR 1860; age 36; b. Tennessee; cabinetmaker; Bright Star (now Sulphur Springs), Hopkins County.

HANNIG, JOSEPH W. MCR 1870; age 37; b. Prussia; dealer in furniture;

Austin, Travis County. Hannig was living in Lockhart, Caldwell County, in 1856, when he married Mrs. Suzanna Dickenson, one of the survivors of the Alamo and a woman eighteen years his senior. They kept a hotel in Lockhart before moving in the 1860's to Austin, where Hannig opened a cabinet shop across from the Missouri House, at the southeast corner of Brazos and Sixth streets. He subsequently joined Matthew Kreisle in a cabinet shop and undertaking business at two locations, 206 East Pecan and 803 Congress. (Mary Starr Barkley, *History of Travis County and Austin, 1839–1899*, p. 79.) In July, 1865, he entered into a partnership with J. W. England (*Weekly Southern Intelligencer*, July 28, 1865; *see also* England, J. W.), which evidently lasted until June, 1868, when he began advertising as "J. W. Hannig, successor to England & Hannig" (*Daily Austin Republican*, June 1, 1868). In 1869 he announced that he had "on hand, and will be receiving, the most complete variety of FURNITURE ever in this city, consisting in part of the following: WARDROBES, BUREAUS, BEDSTEADS, TABLES, CHAIRS, LOOKING GLASSES, MIRRORS, MATTRASSES, WILLOW WARE. etc. . . . Also does all kinds of work in the Cabinet Maker's line" (*Georgetown Watchman*, March 20, 1869). The next year, 1870, he reported that his three-man shop used 10,000 feet of lumber valued at $750, hardware valued at $2,000, velvet and trimming valued at $250, and sundries valued at $250 to produce coffins and furniture valued at $6,000, making it the fifth largest cabinet shop in Texas that year. In 1872 his business was on Pecan Street between Brazos and San Jacinto and his residence was on Pine between Neches and Red River. He died on January 7, 1890, and is buried in Oakwood Cemetery, Austin. (Barkley, *History*, p. 79; S. A. Gray and W. D. Moore, *Mercantile and General City Directory of Austin, Texas, 1872–73*, p. 56.) A chest of drawers attributed to Hannig (3.6) is in the Winedale collection.

HARDIN, A.D. MCR 1850; age 28; b. Tennessee; cabinetmaker; Fayette County. On October 30, 1852, Hardin paid $90 for nine acres of land known as the Mill Tract on Rocky Creek in the James Winn League, just east of the town of Round Top in Fayette County (Fayette County Deed Records, vol. F, p. 212). In April, 1855, he was elected justice of the peace for Beat Four, Fayette County (ibid., vol. I, p. 169). He and his wife sold their nine-acre tract to Andrew Gaither in May, 1857, for $600 (ibid., vol. M, p. 250).

HARDMEIER, CHARLES. MCR 1870; age 30; b. Switzerland; cabinetmaker; Brenham, Washington County.

HARDY, D.N. MCR 1860; age 56; b. Virginia; cabinetmaker; Clinton, DeWitt County.

HARIGEL, HEINRICH. MCR 1870; age 48; b. Prussia; cabinetmaker; La Grange, Fayette County. Harigel was born in Salzbrun, Prussia. At the age of fourteen he was apprenticed to a *schreiner* (joiner) in Waldenburg, where he remained until he received his master cabinetmaker's papers. He came to Texas in 1851 and established his shop in La Grange with the help of William Rabb, a local sawmill operator. Harigel became a prominent citizen, organizing a German volunteer fire company and serving as drillmaster of the Home Guard during the Civil War. In the late 1860's he began importing knocked-down furniture from Saint Louis and assembling it in his shop, and in 1870 he used 17 cases of knocked-down furniture, raw material valued at $1,710, and 2,000 feet of lumber valued at $90 to produce bedsteads, bureaus, chairs, tables, and other furniture valued at $2,700 altogether. His shop was on the southwest corner of Travis and Jefferson streets in La Grange. Harigel died on March 14, 1892. (Ben Harigel, *Leaflets from the Book of Life*, pp. 7–11.)

HARR, ———. *See* Walker and Harr.

HARRELL, ELISHA. MCR 1860; age 30; b. Missouri; cabinetmaker; Jasper, Jasper County.

HARRINGTON, A. MCR 1870; age 40; b. North Carolina; cabinetmaker; Sherman, Grayson County. In 1870, Harrington was operating a three-man cabinet shop that used hand power and 5,000 feet of lumber valued at $250, 20 pounds of paints valued at $6, oils, and 10 gallons of varnish valued at $40 to produce furniture valued at $1,500.

HARRIS, WILLIAM. MCR 1850, 1860, 1870; age 36 in 1850; b. England; cabinetmaker; Sabine Pass, Jefferson County. Harris made furniture in Sabine Pass for at least twenty years. In 1870 his one-man shop used 2,000 feet of lumber valued at $60 and 10 yards of brass wire valued at $20 to produce safes and tables valued at $500.

HARROP, JOHN. *See* Brown, Taylor.

HASTRIG, JACOB. MCR 1860; age 48; b. Nassau; cabinetmaker; Matagorda, Matagorda County.

HATLEY, GAINES, AND STEPHEN. *See* Gaines, William C.

HAYDIN, WILLIAM. MCR 1870; age 27; b. Illinois; cabinetmaker; Fort Worth, Tarrant County.

HEBERSON, JACOB. MCR 1870; age 56; b. Pennsylvania; cabinetmaker; Tyler, Smith County.

HEITMAN, ALBERT DIETRICH. Heitman was born October 26, 1812, in Bremen. After completing his apprenticeship to a cabinetmaker there he traveled through France and Germany as a journeyman and then worked for several years in Switzerland. In 1841 he immigrated to Galveston and worked there for a short time as a cabinetmaker; he then moved to Industry, Austin County, where he made furniture and coffins and built houses. He built a number of houses in the Zimmerscheidt Community (Colorado County), including the Leyendecker home, which is still standing. In 1847 he was working in La Grange. (William Trenckmann, *Austin County,* p. 83.)

HENDERSON, JAMES W. MCR 1860; age 57; b. unknown; cabinetmaker; Boonville, Brazos County.

HENDERSON, JOHN. MCR 1860; age 61; b. Tennessee; cabinetmaker; Waco, McLennan County.

HENDLY, DAVID. MCR 1850; age 48; b. Georgia; cabinetmaker; Hunt County.

HENDON, W.J. MCR 1860; age 24; b. Alabama; cabinet work; Rusk, Cherokee County.

HENDY, JOSHUA. MCR 1850; age 30; b. England; cabinetmaker; Houston, Harris County. Hendy was working in Houston as early as May, 1846, when he advertised as "J. Hendy, Cabinet maker, Main street, near the landing" (*Democratic Telegraph and Texas Register,* May 13, 1846).

HENERASKY, CHARLES. MCR 1870; age 36; b. Prussia; works in cabinet shop; Brenham, Washington County.

HENRY, FRED. MCR 1870; age 34; b. Württemberg; cabinetmaker; Jefferson, Marion County.

HENSHAW, JOHN. MCR 1850; age 55; b. England; cabinetmaker; Precinct 6, Cass County.

HERBERGER, ———. *See* Marshall and Herberger.

HERRINGTON, JOHN. MCR 1850; age 49; b. Illinois; cabinetmaker; Lamar County. Herrington was in Lamar County as early as July 5, 1841, when he received unconditional land certificate no. 26 from the Lamar County land commissioners. He was still living there in 1859, when he received a 320-acre grant on the basis of this certificate. (Lamar County Deed Records, vol. K, p. 230.)

HEWES, WILLIAM. MCR 1870; age 65; b. Tennessee; bottoms chairs; Houston, Harris County.

HICKS, JAMES F. MCR 1860; age 31; b. North Carolina; cabinetmaker; Sherman, Grayson County.

HICKS, THOMAS B. MCR 1860; age 27; b. North Carolina; cabinetmaker; Sherman, Grayson County.

HINES, J. MCR 1860; age 21; b. Georgia; cabinetmaker; Balch, Parker County.

HINES, JAMES. MCR 1870; age 29; b. South Carolina; cabinetmaker; McKinney, Collin County.

HINKLEY, HENRY E. MCR 1850; age 26; b. Maine; cabinetmaker; Brownsville, Cameron County.

HIRSCH, JACOB. MCR 1870; age 27; b. Hamburg; joiner; Fredericksburg, Gillespie County.

HOBBS, U.O. MCR 1870; age 24; b. Mississippi; chairmaker; Black Jack Springs, Fayette County.

HOCKER, PHILIP S. MCR 1860; age 27; b. Missouri; cabinetmaker; McKinney, Collin County. In August, 1860, Hocker and his partner, J. W. Kalfus, advertised that they "keep constantly on hand and make to order Bureaus, Wardrobes, Safes, Bedsteads, Lounges, Cribs, Tables of every variety, &c., &c. All articles manufactured by them are warranted equal to any made in this section of the state. They invite those in want of anything in their line to give them a call, and promise to use their best efforts to please. Orders for coffins promptly attended to" (*McKinney Messenger,* September 14, 1860). Hocker is included by J. Lee Stambaugh and Lillian J. Stambaugh, *A History of Collin County, Texas,* p. 39, in a list of men who made coffins in McKinney in the 1860's.

HOENSTER, ANTON. MCR 1870; age 23; b. Texas; joiner; Fredericksburg, Gillespie County.

HOFFMANN, WALDEMAR. MCR 1860; age 32; b. Prussia; cabinetmaker;

Sterling, Robertson County.

HOPKINS, HUGH H. MCR 1860; age 32; b. Alabama; cabinetmaker; Huntsville, Walker County. Hopkins was in Huntsville as early as February 5, 1856, when he purchased three town lots there (Walker County Deed Records, vol. E, p. 29). In 1860, he and his partner, Frank A. W. Creager, had a shop on Cedar Street in Huntsville (*see* Creager, Frank A. W.). Hopkins later had a shop in his home at 10th Street and Avenue M (*Huntsville Item*, March 6, 1941). He was still in Huntsville on October 3, 1868, when he accepted a certain amount of real and personal property in payment of a debt owed by M. D. Wynne (Walker County Deed Records, vol. K, p. 339).

HOPKINS AND CREAGER. *See* Creager, Frank A. W.

HOPPE, FRITZ. MCR 1870. Fritz Hoppe was a prominent Bastrop mill operator who manufactured chairs as a sideline. In 1870, he had an eight-horsepower steam saw and grist mill in connection with a cotton gin and used $400 worth of cedar and pine to make 100,000 shingles valued at $800 and 300 chairs valued at $275.

HORN, RANSOM. MCR 1850; age 21; b. Tennessee; ginwright; San Augustine County. In 1860, Horn and Brother, cabinetmakers and gunsmiths in San Augustine, San Augustine County, reported to the census marshal that their shop used horse power, 20,000 feet of lumber valued at $300, and 50 pounds of material valued at $50 to produce 250 pieces of cabinetwork valued at $2,500 and 6 guns valued at $1,800.

HORN, WILLIAM H. MCR 1860; age 24; b. Tennessee; cabinetmaker; Ladonia, Fannin County.

HORN AND BROTHER. *See* Horn, Ransom.

HORNICK, ANDREW. MCR 1860; age 43; b. Bavaria; cabinetmaker; El Paso, El Paso County.

HORTON, JOHN V. MCR 1860; age 43; b. New York; cabinet workman; Hagans Port, Titus County.

HOTON, WILLIAM L. MCR 1850; age 44; b. New York; cabinetmaker; Hopkins County.

HOWE, WILLIAM F. MCR 1870; age 23; b. Louisiana; cabinetmaker; Galveston, Galveston County. In 1870, Howe had a one-man cabinet and upholstery shop in Galveston, which used hand power, one moss-packing machine, and 1,000 pounds of moss valued at $40, 125 yards of haircloth valued at $185, 1,300 yards of ticking valued at $300, 5,000 feet of lumber valued at $150, and other materials valued at $150 to produce 150 mattresses valued at $700, 75 cots valued at $300, tables, desks, etc., valued at $1,025, and repairs and jobbing valued at $575. Howe patented a cane chair bottom and an improved mosquito-bar frame and was a frequent and imaginative advertiser in the *Galveston Daily News*, where he referred to his shop at 415 Church Street as "Fort Glue Pot." He was still in business in Galveston in February, 1876. Some examples of his short advertisements: "TOMORROW YE MAY DIE. Go and get one of WILL HOWE's MATTRESSES and GO OFF COMFORTABLY" (September 17, 1872). "YEP-YEP-WHOOP-AH! BIG CHIEF WILL HOWE, the hero of the Glue Pot, is still on the war path. He is scattering the forces of Gen. Furniture Debility like chaff before the whirl wind" (September 22, 1872). "The fashion—Get drunk, break a chair over your wife's head, sober up, and SEND THE PIECES TO WILL HOWE! GENTLEMEN, TRY IT!" (January 14, 1873). "If, (Unlike Them Austin Fellows) You Can't Lie Easy, Send for Will Howe to renovate your Mattresses" (January 28, 1873). "AS A REPAIRER OF FURNITURE He has no equal. History records no greater upholsterer. His MATTRESES are bully, and his name is Will Howe" (October 15, 1872).

HOWELL, JAMES. MCR 1870; age 41; b. Tennessee; cabinetmaker; Anderson County.

HUBER, AUGUST. MCR 1860; age 54; b. Germany; cabinetmaker; Travis, Austin County.

HUBY, H. SPENCER. MCR 1850, 1860; age 22 in 1850; b. New York; cabinetmaker; Milam County in 1850. In 1860, Huby was living in Hempstead, Austin County (now Waller County), where he had a two-man cabinet shop that used $800 worth of lumber to produce 75 bedsteads, etc., valued at $2,000.

HUCKABEE, JAMES. James Huckabee was in charge of the cabinet shop of Z. N. Morrel at Washington, Washington County, in May, 1838. *See* Morrel, Z. N.

HUFFMAN, JOHN A. MCR 1860; age 18; b. Illinois; cabinetmaker; Paris, Lamar County.

HUGHES, WILLIAM. MCR 1870; age 36; b. Pennsylvania; cabinetmaker; Rusk, Cherokee County. In 1870, Hughes and his partner, James A.

Stallings, had a two-man cabinet shop with a horse-powered lathe which used materials valued at $250 to produce $600 worth of furniture.

HUGHES AND STALLINGS. *See* Hughes, William.

HUNICK, J. MCR 1860; age 26; b. Prussia; cabinet workman; Austin, Travis County.

HUNTER, W.D. MCR 1870; age 38; b. Tennessee; cabinetmaker; Dallas, Dallas County.

HUNTER, WILLIAM D. MCR 1860; age 26; b. Missouri; chairmaker; Millwood, Collin County.

HUSTON, OBEDIAH. MCR 1860; age 28; b. Pennsylvania; cabinetmaker; Lavaca, Calhoun County.

HUTTO, PETER. MCR 1870; age 50; b. Georgia; chairmaker; Woodville, Tyler County.

INMAN, JACKSON. MCR 1860; age 34; b. Indiana; chairmaker; Cora, Comanche County.

IRVIN AND IRVIN. MCR 1850. A firm by this name was operating a cabinet factory in Montgomery, Montgomery County, in 1850. In that year they used 3,000 feet of lumber costing $60 and horse-powered equipment to produce furniture valued at $700.

IRWIN, T.J. MCR 1860; age 20; b. Tennessee; cabinetmaker; Black Jack Grove, Hopkins County.

IRWIN, THOMAS J. MCR 1860; age 20; b. Mississippi; cabinetmaker; Paris, Lamar County.

IRWIN, W.B. MCR 1860; age 28; b. Tennessee; cabinetmaker; Paris, Lamar County.

ISABEL, SAMUEL B. MCR 1850; age 21; b. Alabama; cabinetmaker; Jasper County.

JACKSON, THEOPHILUS. MCR 1870; age 50; b. Alabama; cabinet workman; Mount Pleasant, Titus County.

JAHN, CARL ANDREAS. *See* Jahn, Johann Michael.

JAHN, JOHANN MICHAEL. MCR 1860, 1870; age 44 in 1860; b. Pomerania; furniture maker; New Braunfels, Comal County. Jahn is probably the best-known of all Texas cabinetmakers. Although his work was not included in the *Index of American Design* survey carried on in Texas between 1939 and 1942, it has been known to collectors since

the mid-1940's. He was the subject of a short article by Pauline Pinckney in *Antiques* in 1959. Since that date many New Braunfels pieces have been attributed to him; some of these are undoubtedly from the hands of other New Braunfels cabinetmakers (*see particularly* Ebensberger, Eugen Benno; Eberhard, Edward; and Stroemer, Ludwig, all of whose annual production equaled or surpassed Jahn's in 1870). Jahn was born in Stralsund, Pomerania, in 1816. As a youth he was apprenticed to a cabinetmaker in Prague, and he later worked for six years in Switzerland. In 1844 he migrated to Texas, settling first at New Braunfels. Except for a few months in the mid-1840's when he worked in New Orleans, he remained in New Braunfels the rest of his life. He drew town lot number 177 when the original lots were distributed in 1845; he became a charter member of the German Protestant Church in 1846 and served as one of the first aldermen of New Braunfels when that city's charter was ratified in 1847. In 1850 he married a widow, Anna Bellmer. Jahn evidently made and sold furniture in New Braunfels from the date of his arrival. Although his name was omitted from the 1850 census, he appears on the 1860 returns as a "furniture maker." In 1866 he began supplementing his stock with factory-made furniture from New York, which he had shipped to Indianola and carried by wagon to New Braunfels. He also purchased knocked-down furniture from Joseph Peters, the Wm. Prufrock Co., H. W. Hanpeter, and the Conrades Chair Company in Saint Louis and the Sheboygan Chair Company in Sheboygan, Wisconsin. On November 27, 1868, he advertised in the *Neu-Braunfelser Zeitung:* "Fertige Möbel, bestehend in Commoden, Tischen, Stuhlen Sofas und Bettstellen u. sind bestanding zu haben bei J. Jahn [ready-made furniture, the best bureaus, tables, chairs, sofas, and bedsteads are always available from J. Jahn]." He was still manufacturing some furniture in 1870, when he and his son, Carl Andreas Jahn, were operating a "joinery" which used $100 worth of lumber to manufacture $600 worth of furniture. Examples of furniture from Jahn's shop exist marked with the initials *JJ* in a circle burned into the wood and with the legend *JJ / New Braunfels* or *Jahn* in black paint. Jahn died in 1883, but his son, Carl Andreas Jahn, and his grandchildren carried on his business until 1944. (*Memorial and Genealogical Record of Southwest*

Texas, s.v. "Johann Jahn"; *Neu-Braunfelser Zeitung,* November 5, 1908; Ruth Morgan, "The Crafts of Early Texas," *Southwest Review* [Winter 1945]:155–160; Pauline Pinckney, "Johann Michael Jahn, Texas Cabinetmaker," *Antiques* 75 [1959]:462–463; Oscar Haas, *History of New Braunfels and Comal County, Texas, 1844–1946,* pp. 50, 178, 273, 304; Cecilia Steinfeldt and Donald L. Stover, *Early Texas Furniture and Decorative Arts,* pp. 249–250; interview with Ben Jahn, New Braunfels, February 14, 1973.)

For examples of Jahn's work, see 2.14, 4.2, 4.15, 4.16, 4.23, 6.4, 6.38, 8.13, and 9.2. A sliding-catch carpenter's bench used in his shop is in the Winedale collection.

JAMES, ROBERT. MCR 1860; age 23; b. Kentucky; cabinetmaker; Sherman, Grayson County.

JAMES, THOMAS. MCR 1870; age 58; b. New York; chairmaker; Bryan, Brazos County.

JAMES, W.T. MCR 1860; age 31; b. Tennessee; cabinetmaker; Orange, Orange County.

JANSEN, HEINRICH. MCR 1860; age 41; b. Denmark; cabinetmaker; Columbia (now West Columbia), Brazoria County. Jansen was born April 2, 1819, in Copenhagen. About 1845 he married Maria Jurgensen and moved from Copenhagen to the Danish duchy of Schleswig, where he owned a carriage-building and blacksmithing shop. He and his wife left Schleswig during the 1849 revolution and came to Columbia, where he bought a homesite in March, 1852. For the rest of his life he followed the combined trades of carriagebuilder, blacksmith, and cabinetmaker in that town. He died on December 1, 1900. (Thurman M. Gupton, "Biography of Heinrich Jansen [1819–1900]," University of Texas at Austin Winedale Museum, Round Top.) For examples of his work, see 1.4 and 1.5.

JANUARY, SAMUEL. MCR 1860; age 58; b. Kentucky; cabinetmaker; Burnet, Burnet County.

JOHNSON, ALFRED. MCR 1850, 1860; age 37 in 1850; b. Wythe County, Virginia; cabinetmaker; Van Zandt County in 1850; Winnsborough Wood, Titus County, in 1860.

JOHNSON, GEORGE. MCR 1860; age 30; b. Canada; cabinet workman; Texana, Jackson County.

JOHNSON, J.H. *See* Johnson, W. C.

JOHNSON, JAMES W. MCR 1850, 1870; age 53 in 1850; b. Kentucky; cabinetmaker; Anderson County in 1850; Sumpter, Trinity County, in 1870.

JOHNSON, W. MCR 1860; age 24; b. Tennessee; cabinetmaker; Sherman, Grayson County.

JOHNSON, W.C. W. C. Johnson and J. H. Johnson, who also advertised as "Johnson and Son," worked in Belton, Bell County, in the early 1870's. It is not known which was the father and which the son. In February, 1872, they advertised as "manufacturers of chairs and cabinet workmen" and stated that they, "having located in Belton and erected a suitable building, are able to supply the demand for Chairs, and repairing in the line of cabinet work. Also, will furnish COFFINS on short notice, at any hour, day or night. A good hearse will be kept and orders filled with promptness. Having had an experience of 30 years, we feel confident of giving satisfaction" [*Belton Weekly Journal,* February 24, 1872]. In August, 1872, they advertised as "Cabinet Makers and Undertakers, East Street, Belton, Texas. Wardrobes, Bureaus, Bedsteads, Cupboards, Safes, Lounges, extension tables, breakfast tables, serving tables, baby cribs, trundle bedsteads, large arm rocking chairs, nursery rocking chairs, children's high table chairs and common chairs, all of which is custom work put up by us at our shop. We have a neat hearse and walnut and rosewood coffins ready made, or will make coffins to order" (ibid., August 3, 1872).

JONES, HIRAM P. MCR 1870; age 47; b. Georgia; cabinetmaker; Mount Pleasant, Titus County.

JONES, J.P. MCR 1860; age 23; b. Georgia; cabinetmaker; Linden, Cass County.

JONES, JAMES M. MCR 1860. James M. Jones, Angelina County chairmaker, had a one-man shop in 1860 that used 12,000 feet of timber valued at $80 to produce chairs and other articles valued at $600.

JONES, JOSEPH. MCR 1850; age 40; b. New Hampshire; cabinetmaker; Huntsville, Walker County. Joseph Jones of Huntsville died in 1851. He must have been a successful workman, as his inventory lists a good deal of real estate: three lots in Huntsville, one 8-acre lot near the male institute, and 140 acres six miles east of Huntsville. The document continues with "6 bee gums, 1 grindstone, 1 lot timber, 1 turning lathe and tools, 1 lot cabinet makers tools, benches, screws, &c., chair rounds and unfinished work, 1 new bedstead, 2 spinning wheels, 1 carpenters adze, 1 lot of glew, 1 varnish cannister and lot of bottels and bear oil, 1 lot of cherry lumber, 7 chair frames, workbench, mortise-machine, &c., 1 demijohn with oil and a part of a keg of white lead, 1 lot household furniture" (Walker County Probate Records, vol. A, pp. 463–464). The administrator's report of the sale of Jones's effects on January 10, 1852, gives more specific information about his tools:

lathe, 1.00	snead and blade, 1.05
bucksaw, .50	lot of screws, .50
3 planes, 3.00	set of chair rounds, 8.00
3 planes, 1.80	work bench, 4.50
3 planes, 1.30	glue kettle, .90
cased whetstone, 1.05	1 adze, .80
shelf of tools, 7.95	lot of glew, 1.50
3 saws, 3.45	lot of copal varnish, 2.60
drawing knife, square, keyhole saw, .50	5 bottles oil, 1.00
	keg of white lead, .50
3 squares and 8 chisels, 4.70	lot of cherry lumber, 2.00
2 shelf files etc., .40	1 workbench, 1.60
saw and 2 compasses, 2.05	1 mortising machine, 2.25
4 augers, 2.00	1 lot of plank, 9.25
brace and bits, 3.00	1 lot of 14 walnut plank, 1.00
5 plains and squares, 9.70	1 lot of thin plank
3 screws, 1.35	(ibid., pp. 478–479)

The *Texas Sentinel* for May 23, 1840, carries an advertisement that indicates that this Joseph Jones or another cabinetmaker by the same name was working in Bastrop, Bastrop County, at that time: "SPINNING WHEELS; CLOCK REELS, and chairs. The subscriber informs the public generally, that he keeps constantly on hand a supply of the above named articles. Orders will be promptly attended to. Joseph Jones, Bastrop, May 15, 1840." The presence of two spinning wheels on the inventory of property of Joseph Jones of Huntsville might indicate that these were the same person, but there is no other evidence to tie the two together.

JONES, R.D. MCR 1850; age 26; b. Ohio; cabinetmaker; Huntsville, Walker County.

JONES, WILLIAM A. MCR 1860; age 21; b. Tennessee; cabinetmaker; Comanche Peak, Johnson County (now Hood County).

JOURNEY, HENRY. MCR 1850; age 31; b. New York; carpenter; Galveston, Galveston County. Evidently Journey was primarily a building contractor, but the products-of-industry schedule of the 1850 census return lists his business as "undertaker, buildings, furniture, etc.," and records that he employed twenty men and used 800,000 feet of lumber worth $12,000 and horse power to produce "buildings, furniture, etc.," worth $30,000. Journey must have been one of the entrepreneurs who gave employment to the many cabinetmakers whom the Galveston city directories list as having no shops of their own. He is mentioned on the 1850 census return as living at a "livery stable and carpenter shop" whose residents also included eight German-born laborers, five German-born carpenters and a carpenter's apprentice, and a cabinetmaker, J. P. Brookaw.

KAISER, CHARLES. MCR 1850; age 25; b. Germany; cabinetmaker; New Braunfels, Comal County. Kaiser settled in San Antonio upon his arrival from Germany in the mid-1840's. He moved to New Braunfels in 1849 and worked there until 1855, when he moved his family to farm on the Guadalupe River about thirty miles west of New Braunfels. He was killed by Indians shortly afterward. ("Life History of Frank C. Kaiser, Old Texas Ranger," Haas Collection, New Braunfels.)

KALFUS, J.W. An 1860 advertisement in the *McKinney Messenger* gives J. W. Kalfus's name as a partner of Philip S. Hocker in a cabinet shop in McKinney, Collin County; *see* Hocker, Philip S. Nothing more is known of him.

KARGES, WILLIAM. MCR 1870; age 47; b. Prussia; cabinetmaker; La Grange, Fayette County.

KELTON, CHARLES. MCR 1860; age 19; b. Tennessee; cabinetmaker; Bastrop, Bastrop County.

KEMP, J.W. MCR 1860; age 35; b. South Carolina; cabinetmaker; Linden, Cass County.

KEMPEN, ADOLPH. MCR 1870; age 22; b. Germany; joiner; Austin, Travis County. In 1872, Kempen and Carl Theodor Sterzing were partners in the cabinetmaking firm of Kempen and Sterzing, on Congress Avenue between Pine and Cedar streets (S. A. Gray and W. D. Moore, *Mercantile and General City Directory of Austin, Texas, 1872–73*, p. 67). Kempen's label (see 7.9) reads: "A. Kempen, cabinetmaker. Picture frames, mouldings, wire cords, tassels and nails kept always on hand . . . Furniture made to order. Congress Avenue, next to Berryman's store, opposite Bengener's tin shop, Austin, Texas."

KENNEDY, PRIOR. MCR 1850; age 27; b. Tennessee; cabinetmaker; Milam County.

KENZEL, HENRY J. MCR 1860; age 22; b. Tennessee; cabinetmaker; Bonham, Fannin County.

KERBECK, G.A. MCR 1860; age 23; b. Prussia; cabinet workman; Anderson, Grimes County.

KERR, JOHN T. MCR 1870; age 26; b. Maryland; cabinetmaker; Fairfield, Freestone County.

KILLOUGH, WILLIAM. MCR 1870; age 29; b. Alabama; cabinetmaker; Rusk, Cherokee County.

KINCAID, A. MCR 1860; age 27; b. Tennessee; cabinetmaker; Bonham, Fannin County.

KINCY, JOHN W. *See* Griffith, L. A.

KIRCHNER, CHARLES. MCR 1870; age 59; b. Prussia; cabinetmaker; Clinton, DeWitt County.

KISTER, J. MCR 1860; age 32; b. Hanover; cabinetmaker; Indianola, Calhoun County.

KLAEDEN, CUNO J. MCR 1860, 1870; age 53 in 1860; b. Prussia; cabinetmaker; Brenham, Washington County. In his declaration of intent to become an American citizen, filed in Brenham in December, 1858, Klaeden stated that he had arrived in the United States in December, 1855 (Alphabetical Index of Naturalization Record, District Court, Washington County).

KLEINE, JOHN WILLIAM AUGUST. MCR 1860, 1870; age 39 in 1860; b. Prussia; cabinetmaker; Gonzales, Gonzales County. Kleine was born March 16, 1831, at Ziesar, near Brandenburg, Prussia. He left Germany by way of Bremen on September 27, 1853, and arrived in Gonzales that November. He practiced his trade in Gonzales until the spring of 1861, when he enrolled in Cook's Heavy Artillery. He served throughout the Civil War with the Confederate forces at Galveston and returned to Gonzales in 1865. In 1870 his one-man shop was equipped with one machine and used 5,000 feet of lumber valued at $250 to produce furniture valued at $1,786: 3 to 4 bureaus at $140, 12 to 15 tables at $96, 60 to 70 bedsteads at $660, 3 to 4 wardrobes at $140, and 50 to 60 coffins at $750. In 1875 he began importing factory-made furniture. He was a successful businessman and in 1877 he erected Kleine's Hall, a public theater and dance hall. Kleine died April 19, 1900. (*Memorial and Genealogical Record of Southwest Texas*, p. 395.)

Several pieces of Kleine's furniture are still in use in Gonzales homes, including that of his daughter-in-law (see 2.17, 2.18, 4.35, 6.40, and 9.3). A small notebook that he kept is in the hands of his descendants, and a set of molding planes that he used is in the Winedale collection.

KNAUER, GOTTLIEB. MCR 1850; age 58; b. Germany; cabinetmaker; San Antonio, Bexar County.

KOEHLER, HEINRICH. MCR 1870; age 47; b. Prussia; joiner; New Braunfels, Comal County.

KOSCHWITZ, CHARLES. MCR 1870; age 44; b. Prussia; cabinetmaker; Houston, Harris County.

KOSHEL, SAMUEL. MCR 1860; age 46; b. Prussia; carpenter; Columbia, Brazoria County. The *Texas Advertiser*, August 1, 1854, carries an advertisement reading: "Samuel Koshel. Cabinet maker, shop just above Mr. Lawrence Boarding House, Columbia, Texas."

KRAUS, PETER. MCR 1870; age 20; b. Nassau; apprentice to joiner; Fredericksburg, Gillespie County.

KRAUSKOPF, ENGELBERT. MCR 1850; age 32; b. Germany; cabinetmaker; Comanche Spring, Bexar County. Krauskopf was born August 21, 1820, in Bendorf, Prussian Rhine Province. He was trained in Germany as a cabinetmaker but gave up this profession to become a gunsmith, and it was for this latter skill that he was best known in Texas. He came to Texas in the spring of 1846, was an original settler of Fredericksburg, and was employed by the founder of that town, Baron O. Hans von Meusebach, as a hunter. In the late 1840's he and William Leilich were partners in a cabinet shop, and at least one table made by him is still in existence in Fredericksburg (see 6.42). He also operated a sawmill and a horse-powered cotton gin, but he soon turned to full-time gunsmithing, a profession he followed for the rest of his life. He died on July 11, 1881. (Gillespie County Historical Society, *Pioneers in God's Hills*, pp. 107–108.)

KREISLE, MATTHEW. *See* Hannig, Joseph W.

KROLL, HELMUT CONRAD. MCR 1850; age 37; b. Germany; cabinetmaker; Galveston, Galveston County. In 1850, Kroll was operating a two-man cabinet shop in Galveston which used 40,000 feet of plank valued at $1,200 to produce $3,000 worth of furniture, making him the second-largest producer of furniture in Texas in that year. By 1858 he was working in Chappell Hill, and on December 6 of that year he bought "5 setts castors and 2 gross screws" from Hiram Thompson and Sons, Chappell Hill merchants (Thompson, Hiram, and Sons, Business Ledger, Winfield Collection, Chappell Hill). On January 1, 1861, he sold his "upholster and cabinet Shop in the town of Chappell Hill with all tools and machinery incident thereto with the exception of the shop [building] and the land on which it stands with three mules, one hearse, one horse, wagon" to Charles Niederauer, another cabinetmaker (Washington County Deed Records, book S, p. 199). Eight days later he purchased a lot on the east side of Main Street from R. J. Swearingen, who sold it for "certain work executed for me by H. Kroll" (ibid., p. 200). In May, 1861, Kroll sold another lot in Chappell Hill to Niederauer (ibid., p. 201). By December 18, 1865, when he recorded another deed in Washington County, Kroll gave his residence as being in Fayette County (ibid., book V, p. 52).

KUNZ, JACOB. MCR 1870; age 18; b. Nassau; joiner; Fredericksburg, Gillespie County.

KUNZ, JOHANN ADAM. MCR 1860, 1870; age 39 in 1860; b. Nassau; cabinetmaker; Fredericksburg, Gillespie County. Johann Adam Kunz came to Texas on the *Sarah Ann* in 1845. By 1860 he had a one-man shop in Fredericksburg which used timber valued at $500 to produce furniture valued at $1,500; this was one of the largest of the ten cabinet shops recorded in Fredericksburg on the products-of-industry schedule that year. Kunz was a Roman Catholic and was one of the men who volunteered their labor to build St. Mary's Church in 1861. (Don Biggers, *German Pioneers in Texas*, p. 195.)

LANG, F. MCR 1860; age 40; b. Germany; furniture maker; Marshall, Harrison County.

LANG, P. WILLIAM. P. William Lang is the earliest Texas cabinetmaker to leave a printed record of his activities. The Houston *Telegraph and Texas Register* of December 2, 1837, carries his advertisement: "P. WILLIAM LANG, CABINET MAKER, TRAVIS STREET, HOUSTON. Every kind of cabinet Work done, and executed in the most fashionable style. Old furniture and musical instruments carefully repaired at the shortest notice and on reasonable terms. House carpentry also attended to. Dec. 1, 1837." The next summer his advertisement appeared again: "Cabinet and Sash Making. The subscriber is ready to do all kinds of cabinet work, as he has a splendid lot of Mahogany on hand, which makes him able to do all kinds of work in the most fashionable style. And he has at all times on hand a large and general assortment of window sashes with lights. And all those who may favor him with their custom may be assured that the work will be satisfactory, and price reasonable. P. W. LANG, Opposite the American Consul" (*Telegraph and Texas Register*, June 16, 1838).

LAWHORN, W.J. MCR 1860; age 20; b. Georgia; cabinetmaker; Paris, Lamar County.

LEACH, A.W. MCR 1850; age 33; b. Connecticut; cabinetmaker; Nueces County. In 1840, Leach was working in Austin in association with L. Vancleve. They advertised in February of that year that "they would inform their friends and the public in general that they have established the cabinet business, on Pecan Street, near the Brazos Hotel, where they will execute all orders in their line with neatness and despatch, and on reasonable terms" (*Texas Sentinel*, February 19, 1840). Since Austin was only seven months old at this time, they must be credited with being among the capital city's pioneer cabinetmakers.

LEE, ALEXANDER. MCR 1860, 1870; age 57 in 1860; b. Georgia; chairmaker; Homer, Angelina County, in 1860; Pennington, Trinity County, in 1870.

LEE, JOEL. In April, 1843, Joel Lee of Independence, Washington County, advertised his "Cabinet Manufactory," saying that he would "make to order any article in the above line. He has now, and will keep constantly on hand, a quantity of the best lumber. Orders from a distance promptly executed. Independence, September 24, 1842" (*Texian and Brazos Farmer*, April 15, 1843). Nothing more is known of him.

LEE, MARION. MCR 1860; age 22; b. Alabama; chairmaker; Homer, Angelina County.

LEGGETT, WILLIAM A. MCR 1850; age 40; b. Germany; cabinetmaker; Galveston, Galveston County.

LE GROS, E. Describing himself as "ARCHITECT, BUILDER, AND JOBBER," E. Le Gros of Indianola, Calhoun County, advertised in June, 1871, "soliciting the patronage of the citizens of Indianola. Plans furnished. Stores fitted up with taste and skill. Articles of portable furniture made to order. Everything in his line attended to with dispatch. Carpenter Shop, Main Street, next door but one above Post Office" (*Indianola Weekly Bulletin*, June 3, 1871). This is the only reference to "portable furniture" known in Texas cabinetmakers' advertisements; it reflects Indianola's position as a port of entry for immigrants coming to the interior of the state.

LEILICH, WILLIAM. MCR 1850, 1860, 1870; age 41 in 1850; b. Germany; cabinetmaker; Fredericksburg, Gillespie County. Leilich, a native of Neu Ruppin, Prussia, migrated to Texas on the *Garonne* in 1845 (Chester William Geue and Ethel Hander Geue, *A New Land Beckoned*, p. 119). He began his career in Texas as a partner of Engelbert Krauskopf, and by 1860 he was one of Fredericksburg's leading cabinetmakers, with a shop using "fancy timber" valued at $350 to produce furniture valued at $1,200. The census marshal's term *fancy timber* may mean that, like Johann Michael Jahn of New Braunfels, he imported mahogany and other exotic woods as well as using local walnut, cedar, pine, and cypress. If this is the case, he is the only Fredericksburg cabinetmaker that we know of who did so. A beautiful set of planes and marking gauges brought by Leilich from Germany are in the Pioneer Museum, Fredericksburg. Leilich was still working in Fredericksburg in 1870.

LEMONS, JAMES AUGUST. MCR 1850; age 29; b. Germany; cabinetmaker; New Braunfels, Comal County. Lemons was a charter founder of the city of New Braunfels and drew city lot number 264 when the town was laid out in April, 1845. He must have been a respected citizen, for in 1848 he was elected the second tax assessor-collector of

Comal County. (Oscar Haas, *History of New Braunfels and Comal County, Texas, 1844–1946*.) The Comal County Commissioners' Minutes for July 16, 1849, show that he was commissioned by the county to build a public ferryboat.

LEONARD, MALCOMB. MCR 1860; age 19; b. Alabama; apprentice cabinetmaker; Waco, McLennan County. Malcomb Leonard was the son of Thomas D. Leonard.

LEONARD, THOMAS D. MCR 1860; age 50; b. Tennessee; cabinetmaker; Waco, McLennan County.

LESTER, WILLIAM. MCR 1850; age 61; b. South Carolina; cabinetmaker; Rusk County.

LEWIS, JAMES. MCR 1870; age 32; b. Tennessee; cabinet workman; Douglasville, Davis County (now Cass County).

LINDSTEIN, A. MCR 1870; age 58; b. Prussia; cabinetmaker; Port Sullivan, Milam County. In 1870, Lindstein was operating a two-man shop with horse power which used 300 feet of walnut valued at $21, 1,500 feet of pine valued at $75, and 500 feet of other lumber valued at $30 to produce 20 bedsteads valued at $200, 25 tables valued at $175, 3 wardrobes valued at $105, and "other articles" valued at $200.

LIPTON, WILLIAM. MCR 1850; age 56; b. Maryland; cabinetmaker; Upshur County.

LLOYD, DAVID. MCR 1860; age 37; b. North Carolina; cabinetmaker; Bellville, Austin County.

LOCHERER, IZADORE. MCR 1870; age 61; b. Baden; cabinetmaker; Victoria, Victoria County. In 1870, Locherer had a one-man shop which used materials valued at $300 to produce furniture valued at $1,300.

LOCHIED, DANIEL. MCR 1850; age 36; b. Germany; cabinetmaker; Galveston, Galveston County. In 1850, Lochied was the largest producer of furniture in Texas. His three-man Galveston shop used 60,000 feet of plank valued at $1,500 to produce $4,000 worth of furniture. He does not appear on the 1860 census of Galveston County.

LOEFFLER, JOHANN MARTIN. MCR 1860, 1870; age 41 in 1860; b. Württemberg; cabinetmaker in 1860; joiner in 1870; Fredericksburg, Gillespie County. Johann Martin Loeffler came to Texas in 1854 and settled first in San Antonio. He moved to Fredericksburg in 1859 and opened his shop in one room of his house. In 1860 he used timber valued at $300 to produce furniture valued at $800. He died in 1892. (*Fredericksburg Standard*, July 20, 1955.) A chair made by Loeffler (4.27) is in the Pioneer Museum in Fredericksburg. Other examples of his work are owned by his descendants in Mason County.

LOEFFLER, PAUL. MCR 1870; age 23; b. Württemberg; joiner's apprentice; Fredericksburg, Gillespie County. Paul Loeffler was Johann Martin Loeffler's son.

LOGAN, DAVID. MCR 1870; age 48; b. Ireland; cabinetmaker; Galveston, Galveston County.

LOGAN, LOUIS. MCR 1870; age 53; b. Texas; cabinetmaker; Gatesville, Coryell County.

LONG, HENRY W. MCR 1860; age 55; b. South Carolina; cabinetmaker; McKinney, Collin County.

LONG, PETER B. MCR 1870; age 45; b. Indiana; cabinetmaker and preacher; Pilot Point, Denton County.

LONG, SAMUEL E. MCR 1860; age 20; b. North Carolina; cabinetmaker; McKinney, Collin County.

LONGE, JAMES. MCR 1870; age 21; b. Ohio; cabinetmaker; Red River County.

LONGE, JASPER. MCR 1870; age 52; b. Kentucky; cabinetmaker; Clarksville, Red River County. Jasper Longe was one of a group of cabinetmakers who made Clarksville a furniture manufacturing center from the 1840's into the mid-1870's; *see also* Brem, John W.; Chute, James; Gaines, William C.; Milke, August; Shanahan, James B. Our first record of him is in August, 1860, when, in partnership with Henry Bushfield, he purchased the cabinet shop of William C. Gaines (*Standard*, September 22, 1860). The partnership was short-lived, for on December 22, 1860, Bushfield announced in the *Standard* that he had purchased the entire interest in the firm and was now the sole owner; *see* Bushfield, Henry. We lose sight of Longe during the Civil War, but on February 21, 1866, he purchased lots 2, 3, 6, and 7 in block 67, Clarksville, for $250 from George Gordon (Red River County Deed Records, vol. O, p. 160). A year later he bought a tract of land 2 1/2 miles from town for $102 (ibid., vol. P, p. 216). On February 6, 1869, he entered into a partnership with Obadiah Stephens to manufacture "fencing, shingles, sash and blinds, planing lumber, and generally in-

cluded in the preparation of lumber for building purposes" (ibid., vol. Q, p. 16). The machinery for this enterprise was to be erected at "Stephens Steam Circular Saw Mill north of Clarksville" (ibid.), evidently at the site known as Stephensboro. In 1870 the census marshal described this partnership as "Stephens and Longe Furniture and Chair Factory" and reported that they had six male hands and used a twenty-horsepower steam engine and "stationary machinery" to produce 200 bedsteads valued at $2,000 and 1,000 chairs valued at $2,500. Red River County historian Pat B. Clark remembered that "in the 1870's...the people had household furniture manufactured at Stephensboro in carload lots" (*The History of Clarksville and Old Red River County*, p. 241). A cradle made by Longe was included in *The Index of American Design* (ed. Christensen) and is pictured by Ralph and Terry Kovel in *American Country Furniture 1780–1875*, p. 152, and by Cecilia Steinfeldt and Donald L. Stover in *Early Texas Furniture and Decorative Arts*, p. 135. It is now at the Witte Memorial Museum, San Antonio. Longe died October 25, 1883, and is buried at the Catholic Cemetery in Clarksville.

LOONEY, DAVID. MCR 1850; age 55; b. South Carolina; cabinetmaker; 8th Judicial District of Bowie County.

LOONEY, ROBERT. MCR 1850; age 21; b. Alabama; cabinetmaker; 8th Judicial District of Bowie County.

LOOPER, WILLIAM. MCR 1860; age 18; b. Pennsylvania; chairmaker; Duncans Woods, Orange County.

LUDULPH, FRANCIS. Francis Ludulph advertised in the Marshall *Texas Republican*, August 12, 1858: "TOWN MADE FURNITURE. FRANCIS LUDULPH begs to inform the citizens of Marshall and neighborhood, that he is prepared to make House and Office Furniture of all kinds, to order. A stock always kept on hand. Repairing, cleaning, and varnishing neatly executed, and all orders promptly attended to. February 16, 1856." Nothing more is known of him.

LUSKEAU, JOSEPH. MCR 1860; age 30; b. France; cabinetmaker; Bonham, Fannin County.

LYLES, JOHN. MCR 1870; age 44; b. Kentucky; cabinetmaker; Lockhart, Caldwell County. In 1870, Lyles's one-man shop in Lockhart was equipped with a horse-powered lathe and slitting saw and used 3,000 feet of walnut valued at $150 to produce 42 bedsteads valued at $504, 9 tables valued at $90, and 9 candlestands valued at $140.

LYNCH, JAMES. MCR 1860; age 22; b. Virginia; cabinetmaker; Honey Grove, Fannin County.

McALLISTER, SAMUEL WILLIAM. McAllister was born in Danville, Kentucky, on April 8, 1831. He moved to San Antonio in 1847 and became a prominent building contractor in that city. In the mid-1850's he also practiced cabinetmaking and advertised in the *San Antonio Herald*, November 22, 1856: "*WAR WITH ENGLAND!!* S. W. McAllister respectfully informs the citizens of San Antonio and surrounding country, that he has opened a CABINET SHOP at the corner of Alamo and Villita streets opposite the store of Victor Bracht, where he is prepared to make to order every description of PARLOR, DINING-ROOM, and CHAMBER FURNITURE, of the most fashionable styles and in the best workmanlike manner. Being himself a practical workman, he feels confident of being able to render satisfaction to all who may patronize him. Repairing, Polishing, Flowing, and Varnishing old Furniture promptly attended to. He hopes by giving strict attention to business, and by good workmanship and moderate charges, to merit and receive a liberal share of patronage. N.B.—Funeral calls promptly attended to at any hour, day or night." McAllister died May 18, 1893. (Frederick C. Chabot, *With the Makers of San Antonio*, p. 404.)

McART, ALBERT. MCR 1870. In 1870, McArt had a one-man cabinet shop in Greenville, Hunt County. He used 2,000 feet of lumber valued at $80, 300 nails valued at $30, 12 gross screws valued at $15, 24 butts (hinges) valued at $13, 12 sets of hinges valued at $50, and other materials valued at $50 to produce 300 chairs valued at $375, 50 tables valued at $250, 2 bureaus valued at $50, 3 safes valued at $30, 1 wardrobe valued at $25, 5 whatnots valued at $25, and other objects valued at $100.

McBRIDE, PATRICK H. MCR 1850; age 43; b. Kentucky; cabinetmaker; Shelby County.

McCARTEN, WILEY H. MCR 1860; age 28; b. Alabama; master cabinetmaker; Homer, Angelina County.

McCLANE, GEORGE. MCR 1870; age 40; b. Arkansas; cabinetmaker and sailor; Pennington, Trinity County.

McCLUNG, JOSHUA. MCR 1860. In 1860, McClung had a one-man cabinet shop at Mount Carmel, Smith County. He used horse power, 5,000 feet of pine valued at $100, and 4,000 feet of oak and ash valued at $100 to produce 30 bedsteads valued at $300, 6 bureaus valued at $120, 4 safes valued at $100, and 80 chairs valued at $100. Smith County historian Will Woldert, a cabinetmaker himself, remembered that, during the Civil War, McClung "established a chair factory about six miles north of Tyler. There he made chairs, using maple for posts, hickory for rungs, and oak for the backs; and put in what is called 'split bottoms' for seats, which were thin white oak or hickory split woven together. Sometimes the bottoms were formed of corn husks twisted into small rope form, then platted into seats... He used no glue at all in his work; the slat backs were held by wooden pins" (Will Woldert, Memoirs, p. 541, in possession of Smith County Historical Society, Tyler).

McCLURE, B.N. MCR 1860; age 23; b. Tennessee; cabinetmaker; Rockwall, Kaufman County.

McCUREY, WILLIAM. MCR 1870; age 55; b. Kentucky; chairmaker; Paris, Lamar County.

McDONALD, E.W. MCR 1870; age 28; b. Tennessee; cabinetmaker; Dallas, Dallas County.

McDONOUGH, T. *See* Stukes, William.

McGAN, G.O. MCR 1860; age 36; b. Virginia; cabinetmaker; Paris, Lamar County.

McGAN, WILLIAM M. MCR 1860; age 23; b. Tennessee; cabinetmaker; Paris, Lamar County.

McGARET, WILLIAM. MCR 1860; age 32; b. Tennessee; chairmaker; Belmont, Gonzales County.

McGOWAN, W.G. MCR 1860; age 33; b. Alabama; cabinetmaker; Clarksville, Red River County.

McGOWEN, G.R. McGowen, a Houston cabinetmaker, advertised in the Galveston *Civilian and Gazette*, January 30, 1854: "G. R. McGOWEN, manufacturer of ALL KINDS OF FURNITURE, McGowen's old stand, Main Street, Houston. Keeps constantly on hand a variety of fine Sofas, Bureaus, Mahogany, Cherry, Black Walnut, and common Tables; all kinds of Rocking and Parlor Chairs, Bedsteads, Mattresses, Washstands,

Wardrobes, &c., &c." Nothing more is known of him.

MACHEMEHL, MIKE. MCR 1860; age 41; b. Germany; cabinetmaker; Travis, Austin County.

McKILLOUGH, W.B. MCR 1860; age 23; b. Alabama; cabinet work; Rusk, Cherokee County.

McKINSEY, J.B. MCR 1850; age 24; b. Tennessee; cabinetmaker; Harrison County.

McMILLAN, J.A. MCR 1850; age 23; b. Tennessee; cabinetmaker; Harrison County.

McNALL, D. MCR 1860; age 27; b. North Carolina; employee cabinetmaker; Belton, Bell County. McNall is listed on the census as living in the household of cabinetmaker Alonzo Beeman.

McNEAMER, JOHN G. MCR 1860, 1870; age 32 in 1860; b. Tennessee; cabinetmaker; Belmont, Gonzales County. In 1870, McNeamer had a one-man shop in Belmont equipped with a horse-powered lathe and circular saw. He used 6,000 feet of lumber valued at $180 to produce 1 bureau valued at $30, 25 bedsteads valued at $250, 1 wardrobe valued at $40, and 6 tables valued at $60.

McQUIETEN, MARION. MCR 1870; age 46; b. Georgia; cabinetmaker; Pittsburg, Upshur County.

McREA, WILLIAM. MCR 1860; age 63; b. Scotland; cabinetmaker; Caldwell, Burleson County.

MANNER, CHRISTIAN. MCR 1870; age 24; b. Württemberg; cabinetmaker; Jefferson, Marion County.

MANNING, JAMES R. MCR 1870. In 1870, Manning had a cabinet shop in Bright Star (now Sulphur Springs), Hopkins County, which was equipped with a four-horsepower steam engine. He used 1,500 feet of lumber valued at $525 to produce "miscellaneous furniture" valued at $2,000.

MARSHALL, WILLIAM. MCR 1860; age 37; b. Maryland; chairmaker; Kickapoo, Anderson County.

MARSHALL AND HERBERGER. MCR 1870. The 1870 products-of-industry schedule for Hunt County includes the firm of Marshall and Herberger, in Greenville, which used 1,000 feet of wood valued at $115 to make $571 worth of furniture in one month of operation.

MARTIN, G.J. MCR 1860; age 35; b. South Carolina; chairmaker; Gilmer, Upshur County.

MARTIN, GEORGE M. George M. Martin was a partner with John Edmondson in a Houston cabinetmaking shop. Their advertisement in the Houston *Morning Star*, August 7, 1839, reads: "Turning & Cabinet Making. Bed-steads, Bureaus, tables, stands, sofas, book-cases, and furniture of almost every description, made to order with neatness and despatch. Also turning of every description in iron or wood, done to order. Also, repairing of furniture or chairs, done in the neatest manner, by MARTIN AND EDMONDSON, Corner of Market and Travis streets." The partnership was dissolved on October 20, 1839, and Edmondson continued the business alone (*Morning Star*, October 23, 1839).

MARTIN, OLIVER G. MCR 1850; age 28; b. Kentucky; cabinetmaker; Smith County.

MARTIN, WILLIAM M. MCR 1860; age 37; b. South Carolina; chairmaker; Huntsville, Walker County.

MASSANARI, JOSEPH. MCR 1870; age 57; b. Bavaria; cabinetmaker; Brenham, Washington County. In 1870 Massanari's one-man cabinet shop used 6,000 feet of lumber valued at $400 to make furniture valued at $1,446.

MAUREAUX, PAUL. MCR 1860; age 39; b. France; carpenter; San Antonio, Bexar County. Maureaux first came to San Antonio from France in 1852. He opened a carpenter's shop on West Commerce Street, near the corner of Navarro, and advertised in the *San Antonio Herald* of August 4, 1855, that he made sashes, doors, blinds, and frames there. According to an article written by his son and published in 1936, he located and purchased a grove of walnut trees two hundred miles southeast of San Antonio and had them cut and hauled to his shop. After curing the lumber he used it to make at least six four-poster beds ("Paul Maureaux, Early Texas Cabinetmaker," *Frontier Times* 13 [1936]:282–284). That he was definitely making furniture in 1859 is shown by an advertisement in the *Herald* for May 21 of that year, which reads: "CABINET WORK AND JOINER. P. Maureaux, well known to the citizens of San Antonio for the excellence of his work, which always speaks for itself, still continues to carry on at his old stand on Commerce Street, opposite Mr. Hummel's, where he does all kinds of cabinet and joiner's work; as also repairing and varnishing furniture etc. etc. Work done at reasonable prices." He was still making furniture in 1874, when he advertised in the *Herald* of September 18: "FURNITURE MADE AND REPAIRED. MR. PAUL MAUREAUX calls the attention of the public to his HOME-MADE FURNITURE, which can be inspected at his place of business, next door to Dr. Nette's." In the late 1870's, Maureaux owned a retail furniture store in San Antonio, according to his son's article. For an example of his work, see 9.1.

MAY, CHARLES. MCR 1860; age 54; b. Canada; cabinetmaker; Mount Enterprise, Rusk County.

MAY, HIRAM L. MCR 1860; age 24; b. Alabama; cabinetmaker; Mount Enterprise, Rusk County.

MERKELE, PETER. MCR 1850; age 39; b. Germany; cabinetmaker; New Braunfels, Comal County. Peter Merkele or Mergele came to Texas as one of Henry Castro's colonists but decided to settle in New Braunfels rather than in the Castroville area. He is listed on the 1860 census as a farmer; so he may have abandoned his trade by that year. He was still living in 1883, when he attended the funeral of another Castro colonist. (Oscar Haas, *History of New Braunfels and Comal County, Texas, 1844–1946*, p. 33.)

METZE, CHRISTOPH. MCR 1870; age 47; b. Prussia; joiner; New Braunfels, Comal County.

METZE, JOHANN. MCR 1870; age 34; b. Prussia; joiner; New Braunfels, Comal County.

MEYER, T. MCR 1860; age 43; b. Baden; cabinetmaker; Houston, Harris County.

MEYERS, DAVID. MCR 1860, 1870; age 40 in 1860; b. Prussia; cabinet workman; Cameron, Milam County. In 1870, David Meyers reported that he had a two-man cabinet shop with one "machine" that used $400 worth of wood to make furniture valued at $900 in five months of operation.

MEYERS, GEORGE. MCR 1870; age 35; b. Hesse; cabinetmaker; Clarksville, Red River County.

MEYERS, HENRY. MCR 1850; age 43; b. Germany; cabinetmaker; Sabine County. In 1850, Henry Meyers was operating a one-man cabinet shop in Sabine County which used 1,300 feet of lumber valued at $40 to produce $800 worth of furniture. It was the largest of four cabinet shops in Sabine County with an annual product of over $500 that year.

MILKE, AUGUST. MCR 1870; age 39; b. Prussia; cabinet workman; Clarksville, Red River County. In 1870, Milke had a shop which used lumber and paints valued at $400 to produce bureaus and bedsteads valued at $800. Milke reported to the census marshal that he employed two males and two females; this is one of the few examples noted in the census returns of women being employed in the cabinetmaking trade in Texas.

MILLER, C. *See* Beck, Ernest.

MILLER, CHARLES. MCR 1870; age 40; b. Prussia; cabinetmaker; Frelsburg, Colorado County.

MILLER, CHARLIE. MCR 1870. In 1870, Charlie Miller of Fairfield, Freestone County, had a two-man cabinet shop which produced $1,500 worth of furniture from $500 worth of materials.

MILLER, JEFF G. MCR 1860; age 29; b. Kentucky; cabinetmaker; Tidwell Creek, Hunt County.

MILLICAN, JOHN H. MCR 1860; age 41; b. Tennessee; chairmaker; South Sulphur, Hunt County.

MILLICAN, O.H. MCR 1860; age 50; b. Tennessee; cabinetmaker; Austin, Travis County.

MINER, L.M. *See* Gould, J. M.

MITE, JOHN. MCR 1860; age 50; b. Germany; cabinetmaker; Cunningham, Bastrop County.

MOCK, MOSES A. MCR 1870; age 52; b. North Carolina; cabinetmaker; Hillsboro, Hill County. In 1870, Mock had a one-man shop in Hillsboro which used materials valued at $1,000 to produce articles valued at $2,500. The census marshal noted that Mock "works by day or contract, materials furnished by others."

MOFFAT, GEORGE. MCR 1870; age 30; b. Scotland; cabinetmaker; Marshall, Harrison County. Moffat was born June 2, 1840, in Edinburgh, Scotland, came to the United States in 1865, and first settled in Utica, Indiana. He moved to Marshall in 1869 and opened a cabinet shop and furniture store on the south side of the town square. In 1870 he used lumber and varnish valued at $600 to produce chairs, coffins, and repairs valued at $1,200. He died November 10, 1885, but his family continued the retail furniture business for a number of years. (Harrison

County Conservation Society, *Heritage Sketch and Cook Book*, p. 120.)

MOHLER, JOSEPH. MCR 1870; age 39; b. Prussia; cabinetmaker; Winchester, Fayette County.

MONTGOMERY, THOMAS J. MCR 1870; age 47; b. South Carolina; cabinetmaker; Waxahachie, Ellis County. Montgomery was working in Waxahachie as early as May 20, 1863, when he purchased one acre of land from Lucie A. Phillips; he was still living there when he rendered the property for taxation on March 8, 1882 (Ellis County Deed Records, vol. F, p. 207; vol. 28, p. 549).

MOOG, FRANK. MCR 1850; age 25; b. Germany; cabinetmaker; Houston, Harris County.

MOORE, A.A. MCR 1870; age 52; b. Georgia; cabinetmaker; Corsicana, Navarro County.

MOORE, J.W. MCR 1870; age 50; b. Georgia; cabinetmaker; Corsicana, Navarro County.

MOORE, SAMUEL P. MCR 1850; age 25; b. Tennessee; cabinetmaker; Hunt County.

MORGAN, SAM. MCR 1850; age 30; b. Mississippi; cabinetmaker; Hunt County.

MORREL, Z.N. Morrel was born in South Carolina on January 17, 1803. He was ordained a Baptist minister in 1822 and migrated to Texas in 1836. On May 19, 1838, while operating a mercantile store at Washington, Morrel placed the following advertisement in the Houston *Telegraph and Texas Register*: "MANUFACTORY. To the Citizens of Washington and the surrounding country, the subscriber would just say he has established Two Turning Lathes running by horse power, where he will keep on hand a constant supply of bedsteads; chairs; tables of all descriptions, with preparation for turning house columns, and job turning of every description, under the direction of James Huckabee. All orders from a distance will be promptly attended to with neatness and despatch. A good Chair Maker can get employment by making application to the shop. Washington, May 17. Z. N. MORREL." Morrel moved from Washington to La Grange in 1839 and spent the next thirty-five years as an itinerant Baptist minister, traveling around central Texas. After the Civil War he migrated to British Honduras, but he returned to Texas to spend his declining years in Kyle, Hays County. His lengthy autobiography, *Flowers and Fruits from the Wilderness*, published in 1872, makes no mention of this cabinetmaking venture nor of any training that Morrel ever had as a cabinetmaker. It is possible that his role in the enterprise was strictly that of owner.

MORRIS, PASCAL. MCR 1860; age 17; b. Alabama; cabinet work; Rusk, Cherokee County.

MORTON, ASA W. MCR 1870; age 53; b. Kentucky; cabinetmaker; Dallas, Dallas County. In 1870, Morton had a one-man cabinet shop in Dallas which used $500 worth of lumber to produce furniture valued at $1,050.

MOSELY, JAMES. MCR 1850; age 52; b. Virginia; cabinetmaker; Tyler County.

MOSELY, JOSEPH E. MCR 1860; age 32; b. Virginia; cabinetmaker; Milam, Sabine County.

MOSSCROSS, LEANDER. MCR 1870; age 26; b. Massachusetts; chairmaker and turner; Hempstead, Austin County (now Waller County). In 1870, Mosscross had a shop in Hempstead equipped with a ten-horsepower steam engine and a planing machine, a mortising machine, a lathe, and two saws. He employed three men and in one month of operation had used 2,000 feet of timber and 30 hides to make 200 chairs valued at $275. His shop is the most highly mechanized to be found on the 1870 census returns.

MOWRAR, CRIS. MCR 1870; age 23; b. Württemberg; wood carver; Marshall, Harrison County.

MULLER, FIDEL. MCR 1850; age 44; b. Switzerland; cabinetmaker; Nacogdoches County.

MULLER, JOSEPH. MCR 1850, 1860; age 17 in 1850; b. Switzerland; cabinetmaker; Nacogdoches County.

MUNCRIEF, AUSTIN. MCR 1860; age 41; b. Georgia; cabinetmaker; Gilmer, Upshur County.

MURPHEY, A.N. MCR 1860; age 35; b. South Carolina; cabinetmaker; Burnet, Burnet County.

MURPHY, W.G. Murphy advertised in the *Seguin Journal and General Advertiser*, May 15, 1858, that he was "prepared to execute to order all articles in his line of business as a Cabinet Maker, of the best quality, on moderate terms, and at short notice. Burial Cases of every variety ranging from $20 to $30 plain and neat; unless per order a fine article is demanded, in which case prices will be according to quality. ALSO, All work in Carpentry and Joinery in all their branches. Now ON HAND, Bureaus, Fine Book Cases, Fine Bedsteads, and Safes. W. G. Murphy." Nothing else is known of Murphy.

MYER, JACOB. MCR 1850; age 24; b. Germany; cabinetmaker; Austin County.

MYERS, DAVID. Alternative spelling for Meyers, David.

NANCE, THOMAS. MCR 1870; age 37; b. Tennessee; cabinetmaker; Goliad, Goliad County.

NEAL, W.L. MCR 1860; age 23; b. Tennessee; cabinetmaker; Fairfield, Freestone County.

NEFF, DOMINIQUE. MCR 1860; age unknown; b. France; carpenter; Castroville, Medina County. Although listed on the census as a carpenter, Neff also made furniture in Castroville. For two examples of his work, see 6.13 and 6.14.

NELSON, MATT. MCR 1860; age 27; b. Alabama; cabinetmaker; Sulphur Bluff, Hopkins County.

NETTLES, WILLIAM. MCR 1850; age 40; b. South Carolina; cabinetmaker; Houston, Harris County.

NETTLES, WILLIAM. MCR 1870; age 65; b. Tennessee; cabinetmaker; Stafford, Fort Bend County.

NEUSE, LAURENCE. MCR 1850; age 29; b. unknown; cabinetmaker; Galveston, Galveston County. "L. Neuse, cabinetmaker" is listed in W. Richardson and Co.'s *Galveston Directory for 1866–7* as living on Post Office Street between 24th and 25th.

NICHOLS, THOMAS C. MCR 1860; age 45; b. Georgia; cabinet workman; Lone Star, Titus County.

NICK, FRANCIS. MCR 1850; age 33; b. Germany; cabinetmaker; Travis County.

NICKLESS, JACOB. MCR 1860; age 24; b. Mississippi; cabinetmaker; Nolan's River, Johnson County.

NIEBLING, CHARLES. MCR 1850; age 45; b. Germany; cabinetmaker; Galveston, Galveston County.

NIEDERAUER, CHARLES. Niederauer was born April 24, 1838. He was in Chappell Hill, Washington County, on October 12, 1860, when he petitioned Hubert Masonic Lodge No. 67 for admission, giving his occupation as a cabinet workman. On January 1, 1861, he purchased the "upholster and cabinet Shop in the town of Chappell Hill" which belonged to Helmut Conrad Kroll (Washington County Deed Records, book S, p. 199). On April 3, 1867, he sold all of his property in Chappell Hill to Joseph S. Simmons. At this time he was living in Fayette County. However, on September 1, 1884, he purchased land two miles north of Brenham in the Catherine Snodgrass survey. He died on January 4, 1929, and is buried in Prairie Lea Cemetery, Brenham. (Nath Winfield, Chappell Hill, October 17, 1973, to LT; Washington County Deed Records, book S, p. 199; book V, pp. 54–55; book 18, n.p.)

NITSCHKE, A. MCR 1860; age 38; b. Germany; cabinet work; Bellville, Austin County.

NITSCHKE, H.L. MCR 1860; age 46; b. Germany; carpenter; Austin, Travis County. On July 21, 1865, H. L. Nitschke and Company advertised in the *Weekly Southern Intelligencer* that they "have re-opened their shop on Congress Avenue, opposite E. Tillman's Confectionary, where they are prepared to make and repair MATTRASSES AND FURNITURE of all kinds. Pianos polished at short notice. Bed Furniture of all kinds made to order, including Bed Clothing. Old Furniture and Buggies repaired, and sold on commission. Gentlemen wanting offices furnished can be accomodated to their entire satisfaction."

NOBLE, J.R. MCR 1870; age 44; b. Alabama; chairmaker; San Augustine, San Augustine County.

NONERAK, ANDREW. MCR 1860; age 26; b. France; cabinetmaker; Bastrop, Bastrop County.

NONERAK, JOSEPH. MCR 1860; age 24; b. France; cabinetmaker; Bastrop, Bastrop County.

NORMAN, JOHN. MCR 1850; age 37; b. Tennessee; cabinet workman; Upshur County.

NORRIS, THOMAS. MCR 1870; age 54; b. Kentucky; cabinetmaker; Austin, Travis County.

NORTHCOT, W.G. MCR 1870; age 33; b. Georgia; cabinetmaker; Marshall, Harrison County.

NORTHCUT, J.W. MCR 1870; age 50; b. Virginia; cabinet workman; Quitman, Wood County.

NOTT, S.P. MCR 1860; age 36; b. Ohio; cabinetmaker; Sherman, Grayson County.

NUMZETON, JOHN. MCR 1860; age 40; b. Saxony; carver; San Antonio, Bexar County.

OCUNS, MICHAEL. MCR 1860; age 40; b. Baden; cabinetmaker; Bastrop, Bastrop County.

OFFIELD, JAMES. MCR 1860; age 46; b. Tennessee; cabinetmaker; Hillsboro, Hill County.

OLDEN, W. MCR 1860; age 25; b. Pennsylvania; cabinetmaker; Belton, Bell County.

OLIVER, JAMES R. MCR 1850; age 34; b. Georgia; cabinetmaker; Rusk County.

OLIVER, ROBERT J. MCR 1850; age 32; b. Georgia; cabinetmaker; Rusk County.

OPPIE, HARRY. MCR 1860; age 56; b. Germany; cabinetmaker; Bastrop, Bastrop County.

O'REILLY, EDWARD. MCR 1870; age 35; b. Ireland; cabinetmaker; Houston, Harris County. In 1870, O'Reilly and his partner, Alexander Travis, "upholsters and cabinetmakers," had a shop in Houston which used 2,000 feet of wood valued at $120, 6,000 pounds of moss and hair valued at $240, and other materials valued at $500 to produce 250 mattresses valued at $2,250 and do repairing valued at $2,000.

OUTLAW, JOHN C. MCR 1860; age 36; b. Tennessee; house carpenter; Huntsville, Walker County. In 1860, the firm of Outlaw and Talley, "undertakers and carpenters," employed three hands and used 7,000 feet of lumber valued at $140 to produce "coffins, furniture, and sundries" valued at $1,800.

OUTLAW AND TALLEY. *See* Outlaw, John C.

OVERSTREET, H.W. MCR 1860; age 32; b. Virginia; cabinetmaker; Paris, Lamar County. Overstreet, like Willet Babcock and James W. Rodgers, was one of the founders of the Paris furniture industry. In 1860 he and Rodgers had a five-man shop in downtown Paris which used 25,000 feet of wood valued at $800 to produce 400 pieces of furniture valued at $4,500, making it the second-largest cabinet shop in Texas that year, Willet Babcock's being the largest. On May 12, 1864, Overstreet sold his interest in the firm to his partner, James W. Rodgers (Lamar County

Deed Records, vol. O, p. 587), and nothing more is known of him.

OVERSTREET AND RODGERS. *See* Overstreet, H. W.

PACK, R. MCR 1860; age 49; b. Pennsylvania; cabinetmaker; Helena, Karnes County.

PAGE, JOSEPH. MCR 1870; age 32; b. North Carolina; cabinet workman; Clarksville, Red River County.

PAIRON, JOHN. MCR 1860; age 32; b. Sweden; cabinetmaker; San Antonio, Bexar County. John Pairon was working in San Antonio as early as July 22, 1856, when he advertised in the *San Antonio Reporter* that "he has opened a CARPENTER SHOP on Flores Street, opposite Mr. Jose Cassiano's house, where he is prepared to make to order all kinds of House Carpentering and Furniture work. Repairing, polishing and varnishing Pianofortes and other Furniture attended to with promptness, and on moderate terms. Being himself a practical workman, he hopes to merit a share of public patronage. San Antonio, Texas, July 22, 1856." By January, 1861, he had moved his shop to Indianola, and in the *Indianola Courier* of May 25, 1861, he advertised: "John Pairon, Cabinet Maker! Respectfully announces to the citizens of Indianola and vicinity that he will make new and repair old furniture to order. Shop on Main Street, at Mr. T. S. Coates's Furniture Store. Indianola, Jan. 26, 1861."

PALMER, JOSEPH F. MCR 1850; age 38; b. Connecticut; cabinetmaker; San Augustine, San Augustine County.

PANNEL, H.G. MCR 1860; age 48; b. Virginia; cabinetmaker; Houston, Harris County. Pannel was operating a furniture store in Houston on November 3, 1856, when he advertised in the *Tri-Weekly Telegraph* that he had "received and will continue to receive a full and complete assortment of FURNITURE of all kinds, styles, and qualities, for the supply of the city and Country trade. He has the most elegant sofas, lounges, divans, bedsteads, wardrobes, tables, chairs, and every variety of useful and ornamental furniture. The patronage of the planters is strictly solicited." Unfortunately, it is unclear from this advertisement whether Pannel's furniture was locally made or imported. Since he described himself as a "cabinetmaker" on the 1860 census, he probably made at least some of his merchandise himself.

PANNELL, REED FLINT. MCR 1870; age 24; b. Texas; cabinetmaker;

Houston, Harris County.

PANNIS, JOHN B. MCR 1870; age 28; b. Tennessee; cabinetmaker; Whitesboro, Grayson County.

PASCHAL, J. MCR 1860; age 62; b. North Carolina; cabinetmaker; Copper Hill, Parker County.

PATCH, WILLIAM W. MCR 1870; age 44; b. New York; cabinetmaker; Galveston, Galveston County. Although Patch was primarily an upholsterer, both his advertisements and his entry in the products-of-industry schedule of the 1870 census indicate that he also made furniture. He advertised in the June 9, 1867, issue of *Flake's Daily Bulletin* as "W. W. Patch & Co., cabinet makers, upholsterers, and general jobbing, Postoffice Street near the Postoffice. Furniture Repaired, Cleaned, and polished—Hair, Moss, and Spring Mattresses made to order—Store Work promptly attended to. Families can have their furniture repaired on their premises, if desired—saving drayage and risk of damage by moving." In 1870, he reported that his shop employed two men and used 1,200 pounds of moss valued at $50, 2 tons of hay valued at $30, 200 pounds of hair valued at $80, and 3,000 feet of timber valued at $120 to produce 50 mattresses valued at $200, 30 cots valued at $35, 10 desks valued at $200, 20 tables valued at $200, and repairing and jobbing valued at $1,000. An advertisement in the *Galveston Daily News,* November 20, 1872, gives the address of Patch's shop as "Tremont Street, between Church and Winnie," and says that he "has for sale superior Feather Beds, Bolsters and Pillows, also Cocoa Fiber Beds." In another *Galveston Daily News* advertisement on April 9, 1873, Patch describes himself as "Cabinet Maker and Upholsterer, Paper hanger and Glazier," and gives his address as 264 Tremont Street.

PATTEN, JOSEPH. MCR 1870; age 45; b. Illinois; works in furniture; Waco, McLennan County. It is unclear from this census entry whether Joseph Patten was a cabinetmaker or worked in a furniture store. He lived in the household of William H. Anderson, Waco cabinetmaker and furniture dealer.

PATTERSON, M. MCR 1860; age 21; b. Tennessee; chairmaker; Tidwell Creek, Hunt County.

PAULUS, FRIEDRICH. MCR 1870; age 22; b. Nassau; joiner; Fredericksburg, Gillespie County.

PEARSON, THOMAS J. MCR 1860; age 35; b. England; cabinetmaker; Stuart Creek, Denton County.

PEBIAN, THEODORE. MCR 1860; age 42; b. Ireland; cabinetmaker; Refugio, Refugio County.

PEERS, JOSEPH M. MCR 1860; age 48; b. Virginia; cabinetmaker; Carthage, Panola County.

PELOU, EDAORT. MCR 1860; age 48; b. France; cabinetmaker; Liberty, Liberty County. Pelou was working in Palestine, Anderson County, in September, 1856, according to a dated advertisement in the May 20, 1857, *Trinity Advocate:* "EDAORT PELOU, Cabinet Maker, takes this method of informing the public that he is now prepared to execute with neatness and dispatch Cabinet Work of all descriptions, Such as Centre-Tables, Bedsteads, Lounges, Stands, &c. He will also repair all kinds of musical instruments, except Brass. Having the advantage of a long experience in the best manufactories of Europe, he can promise all who patronize him full and entire satisfaction, and appeals to a just and liberal public for a share of patronage. Give him a call, on the South Side Public Square. Palestine, Sept. 3, 1856."

PENNY, CALEB. MCR 1860; age 57; b. North Carolina; chairmaker; Gilmer, Upshur County.

PERKINS, URIAH. MCR 1850; age 38; b. Kentucky; cabinetmaker; Smith County.

PETRI, JOHN. MCR 1860; age 50; b. Nassau; turner; Fredericksburg, Gillespie County. In 1860, Petri had a one-man turner's shop in Fredericksburg which used timber valued at $150 to produce "all kinds of furniture" valued at $600.

PHAT, THEODORE. MCR 1850; age 25; b. Germany; cabinetmaker; Austin County.

PHILLIPS, FRANCIS. MCR 1860, 1870; age 39 in 1860; b. Virginia; cabinetmaker; Rusk, Cherokee County, in 1860; Henderson, Rusk County, in 1870.

PICKENS, JOHN. MCR 1870; age 45; b. Mississippi; chairmaker; Seguin, Guadalupe County.

PLENCHOTT, C. MCR 1860; age 73; b. Germany; cabinetmaker; Galveston, Galveston County.

PLUNKETT, J.W. MCR 1860; age 28; b. Georgia; cabinetmaker; Paris,

Lamar County.

POINDEXTER, T.C. MCR 1860; age 44; b. Tennessee; cabinetmaker; Paris, Lamar County.

POINSARD, JULES. Poinsard came to Texas as a Castro colonist and purchased land in Medina County in 1847. He was living in San Antonio in 1850 and was probably the architect and building contractor for the Ursuline Convent there (Dorothy Steinbomer Kendall, *Gentilz: Artist of the Old Southwest*, p. 36; Willard B. Robinson, *Texas Public Buildings of the Nineteenth Century*, p. 180). He advertised in the San Antonio paper *El Bejareño*, February 17, 1855, as "JULES POINSARD, Calle de Soledad, Arquitecto, Carpintero y Ebnista, emprende toda clase de construciones de casas, &c., recibira tierras; certificados de tierras en parte o todo del pago de sus servicios. Habla la lengua Castellana [Jules Poinsard, Soledad Street, Architect, Carpenter, and Cabinetmaker, undertakes all kinds of housebuilding, etc.; he will accept land or land certificates in full or part payment for his services. He speaks the Castilian language]." He evidently migrated to Mexico at the end of the Civil War, for on March 7, 1865, he was issued a certificate by the Imperial Mexican Ministry of Foreign Affairs certifying that he was a French subject and was forty-six years old. The certificate is now in the collection of the San Antonio Conservation Society.

POLK, JESSE. MCR 1850; age 44; b. South Carolina; cabinetmaker; Hunt County.

PORTER, J.R. MCR 1860; age 31; b. Kentucky; cabinetmaker; Taos, Navarro County. In 1860, Porter was a partner in the firm of Crawford and Porter in Corsicana. *See* Crawford, W. B.

POSTON, JOHN F. MCR 1860; age 29; b. North Carolina; cabinet workman; Goudburgh, Titus County.

POWELL, HENRY. MCR 1870; age 75; b. Virginia; chairmaker; Victoria, Victoria County.

POWELL, NEWTON. Newton Powell was a partner of James A. Barton in a Clarksville, Red River County, cabinet shop in 1861. *See* Barton, James A.

POWERS, JACKSON. MCR 1870; age 56; b. North Carolina; chair bottomer; Jefferson, Marion County.

PREIBISCH, ADOLPH. MCR 1870; age 29; b. Bohemia; cabinetmaker; San Felipe, Austin County.

PRENZEL, ANTON. MCR 1860, 1870; age 35 in 1860; b. Germany (according to MCR 1860); cabinetmaker; Columbus, Colorado County, in 1860. In 1870, Prenzel was working in Bastrop, Bastrop County. At this time he gave his birthplace as Bohemia, which is probably correct.

PRICE, JOHN. MCR 1860; age 30; b. Missouri; cabinetmaker; Sherman, Grayson County.

PRIEST, E.T. MCR 1860; age 24; b. Mississippi; cabinetmaker; Bastrop, Bastrop County.

PROSCH, AUGUST F. MCR 1870; age 65; b. Holstein; cabinetmaker; Houston, Harris County.

PRUETT, WILLIAM. MCR 1860; age 36; b. Indiana; master cabinetmaker; Stuart Creek, Denton County.

RAATZ, JULIUS. According to a clipping from an unidentified and undated Austin newspaper in the Biographical File, Barker History Center, University of Texas at Austin, Julius Raatz was an Austin cabinetmaker who was born in Tempelburg, Prussia, September 28, 1832. He came to Texas in 1854, landing at Indianola and coming directly to Austin. He and two other cabinetmakers were associated with a retail store on Pecan Street, just opposite the present site of the Driskill Hotel. They sold furniture through the store on consignment. Raatz served in the Confederate army and was still living at 602 West 14th Street in Austin at the time the article was written, probably 1924.

RAINNAN, R.H. MCR 1870; age 55; b. Hesse-Cassel; cabinetmaker; Bryan, Brazos County.

RAINS, GEORGE W. Rains placed an advertisement in the Marshall (Harrison County) *Star State Patriot*, August 23, 1851: "CABINET SHOP. GEO. W. RAINS manufactures everything in the Cabinet Line, repairs all kinds of furniture with despatch, and requests all who may need bedsteads, safes, bureaus, tables, etc., to give him a call. Having experienced workmen constantly employed he hopes to merit a liberal share of patronage. Shop two squares north of Hudson & Hamlet. May 17, 1851."

RANKIN, JOHN. MCR 1870; age 33; b. Tennessee; cabinetmaker; San Augustine, San Augustine County.

RECTOR, F.B. MCR 1870; age 38; b. Virginia; cabinetmaker; Sherman, Grayson County.

REECE, THEOPHILUS. MCR 1870. In 1870 Theophilus Reece had a one-man cabinet and wagon shop at Livingston, Polk County, which used 500 feet of "wood for wagons and lumber" valued at $20 to produce "cabinetware and wagon repairing" valued at $600.

REIBENSTEIN, CARL. MCR 1850; age 28; b. Germany; cabinetmaker; Cat Spring, Austin County.

REID, CHARLETTIN. MCR 1870; age 24; b. Georgia; cabinetmaker; Mount Vernon, Titus County.

REVELL, THEODORE B. MCR 1860, 1870; age 27 in 1860; b. South Carolina; cabinetmaker; Ladonia, Fannin County, in 1860. By 1870 Revell had moved to Bonham, Fannin County, where he had a two-man cabinet shop which used materials valued at $300 to produce furniture valued at $800.

RHODES, ELISHA S. MCR 1850; age 45; b. North Carolina; cabinetmaker; Dallas, Dallas County.

RICE, "DAN." *See* Williamson, Bob.

RICHARDS, JOHN D. MCR 1850; age 40; b. Tennessee; cabinetmaker; Shelby County.

RICHARDSON, L.C. Richardson advertised in the *Crockett Printer* (Houston County), November 14, 1860: "WAGON MAKING AND CABINET WORK. L. C. RICHARDSON Begs leave to announce that his new building is completed, and he is now prepared to execute all orders for WAGON MAKING, repairing, all kinds of Cabinet Work neatly made or repaired. Orders in his line respectfully solicited. His shop is on the corner of Rusk and Nacogdoches streets."

RICHEY, B.L. MCR 1860; age 27; b. Indiana; cabinetmaker; Gamma, Parker County. B. L. Richey advertised in the Weatherford *Frontier News*, August 19, 1858: "B. L. Richey, Cabinet Maker & House Carpenter, Respectfully tenders his services to the citizens of Weatherford and vicinity. Work of all kinds in his line done at short notice, with neatness and dispatch and on reasonable terms."

RICHEY, BARNEY. MCR 1860; age 66; b. Indiana; cabinetmaker; Paris, Lamar County.

RICHEY, BROWN. MCR 1870; age 75; b. Kentucky; cabinet manufacturer; Paris, Lamar County.

RICHEY, WILLIAM. MCR 1860; age 61; b. Kentucky; cabinetmaker; Paris, Lamar County.

RICHTER, D. TRAUGOTT. MCR 1850; age 30; b. Germany; cabinetmaker; Galveston, Galveston County.

RICHTER, L. MCR 1860; age 48; b. Germany; cabinetmaker; Galveston, Galveston County.

RIEMENSCHNIDER, VALENTIN. MCR 1860, 1870; age 30 in 1860; b. Hanover; cabinetmaker; Hallettsville, Lavaca County. In 1860, Riemenschnider had a cabinet shop in Hallettsville which employed one male and one female and used 3,000 feet of walnut, pine, and other plank valued at $100 to produce 20 bedsteads, as well as bureaus, safes, and other articles, for a total value of $1,200. He was still working in Hallettsville in 1870. Riemenschnider's name is spelled *Remsnider, Reimsnider,* and *Reamenschnerder* on the census returns.

RIERSON, CHARLES N. MCR 1870; age 53; b. Norway; cabinetmaker; Kaufman, Kaufman County. Rierson was one of the original Norwegian settlers of Four Mile, Kaufman County (Martin F. Jenson, *History of Four Mile Settlement and Church, Established 1848,* pp. 22–23). In 1870 he had a one-man cabinet shop in Kaufman which, over a six-month period, used wood valued at $200 and produced bedsteads valued at $150, safes valued at $100, and tables valued at $50.

RIGGS, STEPHEN. MCR 1870; age 56; b. Virginia; cabinet workman; Athens, Henderson County.

ROBIN, ———. *See* Cade and Robin.

ROBINSON, W.A. MCR 1860; age 25; b. Alabama; cabinetmaker; Douglasville, Cass County.

ROBINSON, W.S. MCR 1860; age 33; b. Tennessee; cabinetmaker; Sherman, Grayson County.

ROCHAU, HENRY. Rochau was born in Erfurt, Saxony, April 9, 1833. He came to Texas in 1855 and settled at New Braunfels, where he operated a cabinet shop until 1857, when he moved west to Twin Sisters, Blanco County. At Twin Sisters he farmed and continued to practice his trade as a cabinetmaker, shouldering his tools and walking to farms where settlers desired work done. During the Civil War he served under the Unionist Captain Adolf Zoeller in the First Regiment of Texas Cavalry,

United States Army. (Oscar Haas, "Henry Rochau, Sr., My Maternal Grandfather's Civil War Story," Haas Collection, New Braunfels.)

RODGERS, JAMES W. MCR 1860, 1870; age 23 in 1860; b. Virginia; cabinetmaker; Paris, Lamar County. Rodgers was, along with Willet Babcock, one of the men who made Paris the furniture manufacturing capital of Texas. He came to Paris at the age of nineteen and opened a one-man shop just off the town square. By 1860 he was in partnership with H. W. Overstreet in a five-man shop which used wood valued at $800 to produce 400 pieces of furniture valued at $4,500—the second-largest cabinet shop in Texas. On May 12, 1864, Overstreet sold his interest in the business to Rodgers (Lamar County Deed Records, vol. O, p. 587). In 1870, Rodgers's shop was equipped with two machines and employed four men who used 70,000 feet of lumber valued at $700 to produce furniture valued at $2,600. In the Paris *North Texan,* May 6, 1876, Rodgers advertised that his "establishment is now stocked with every style of furniture to be found in any market, and the facilities at hand render its manufacture easy at a small cost, hence you may BUY AT HOME AND SAVE MONEY ... Wholesale bills filled at extremely low prices. Parties from adjoining counties should not fail to call and examine my stock and prices before purchasing." In the *North Texan* of September 6, 1879, Rodgers announced, "STEAM IN PARIS. J. W. RODGERS, BONHAM STREET, Keeps a full line of FURNITURE!! In connection with this establishment is a STEAM PLANING MILL, where work will be turned out promptly and satisfaction guaranteed." Rodgers died in 1891, but in 1894 the firm was reorganized as the Rodgers-Wade Furniture Company and continues in business in Paris today as the oldest furniture manufacturing company in the state ("Rodgers-Wade Furniture Company, Statement of Profit and Loss, 1921," Rodgers-Wade Company files, Paris).

ROEMER, HENRY. MCR 1860; age 28; b. Prussia; cabinetmaker; Brenham, Washington County. Roemer's name is spelled phonetically as *Raymer* on the census return.

ROGERS, J.C. MCR 1860; age 40; b. Tennessee; cabinetmaker; Tyler, Smith County. In 1860, J. C. Rogers was a partner in the firm of Rogers and Sheppard, which had a three-man cabinet shop in Tyler which used horse power and 15,000 feet of pine valued at $300 and 5,000 feet of oak valued at $100 to produce 75 bedsteads valued at $1,000, "bureaus, wardrobes, etc.," valued at $1,200, and "other furniture" valued at $800. Rogers and Sheppard advertised in the *Tyler Reporter,* August 1, 1861, as "Furniture Merchants and Cabinet Makers, North Broadway next door to Reporter Office," saying that they "continue to keep on hand a full assortment of furniture, consisting of Bureaus, Wardrobes, Lounges, Bookcases, Cupboards, Sofas, Bedsteads, Wash stands, Dining tables, Toilet tables, and every description of furniture usually found in the country. Connected with their establishment, they have in operation an extensive cabinet shop."

ROGERS AND SHEPPARD. *See* Rogers, J. C.

ROICE, B.L. MCR 1870; age 28; b. Kentucky; cabinetmaker; Bonham, Fannin County.

ROLAND, JOHN. MCR 1870; age 18; b. Tennessee; apprentice cabinetmaker; Paris, Lamar County.

ROMBERG, BERNHARD. Romberg was born in Boizenburg, Mecklenburg-Schwerin, in 1841. He came to Texas in 1847 with his parents, Johannes and Friederike Romberg, and grew up in the Black Jack settlement, near O'Quinn in southern Fayette County. During the Civil War he went to Mexico and Central America to avoid conscription, but he returned to Fayette County in 1867 and married Caroline Perlitz of La Grange. In the early seventies he operated a chair factory at Black Jack which produced rawhide-bottomed chairs of local mulberry wood (see 4.31). His saw and turning lathe were powered by a sixty-foot-high windmill with canvas sails. Romberg was an accomplished mechanic, an inventor, an amateur scientist, and an enthusiastic follower of Henry George's political theories. (Annie Romberg, *History of the Romberg Family,* pp. 5, 28, 31, 55.)

ROOKER, CALEB. MCR 1870; age 71; b. England; chairmaker; Bonham, Fannin County.

ROSE, STEPHEN. MCR 1870; age 61; b. Virginia; chairmaker; Gainesville, Cooke County.

ROSS, MARTIN W. MCR 1870; age 47; b. North Carolina; carpenter, cabinetmaker, and farmer; Gainesville, Cooke County.

ROUGET, LUIS. MCR 1870; age 35; b. Germany; cabinetmaker; Ladonia, Fannin County.

ROWLAND, M.S. MCR 1870; age 42; b. Kentucky; cabinetmaker; Buena-vista, Shelby County.

RUDOLPH, T.L. MCR 1860; age 22; b. Tennessee; cabinetmaker; McKinney, Collin County.

RUTERSTORF, JOHN. An advertisement in the Houston *Tri-Weekly Tele-graph,* October 13, 1858, reads: "JOHN RUTERSTORF, CITY SEXTON, Cabinet maker, and Carpenter. Shop, opposite the old Capitol, Houston, Texas." Nothing more is known of him.

SAMMONS, TENCH. MCR 1870; age 26; b. Alabama; cabinetmaker; Rusk, Cherokee County.

SANDERS, H.T. MCR 1860. In 1860, H. T. Sanders had a two-man cabinet shop in Beat 1 of Houston County which was equipped with a lathe and used 1,500 feet of sawed lumber valued at $30 and 5 cords of split lumber valued at $25 to produce 350 chairs valued at $400, 7 bedsteads valued at $77, 3 tables valued at $12, 4 coffins valued at $24, 10 spinning wheels valued at $50, and other work valued at $25.

SANDERS, WILLIAM. MCR 1870; age 41; b. Alabama; cabinet workman; Ladonia, Fannin County.

SANFORD, DANIEL. MCR 1870; age 33; b. Georgia; cabinetmaker; Garden Valley, Smith County.

SATERWHITE, WILLIAM. MCR 1860; age 28; b. Kentucky; furniture maker; McKinney, Collin County.

SAUCER, LAWRENCE. MCR 1850; age 26; b. Germany; cabinetmaker; Galveston, Galveston County.

SCHAEPER, CHRISTOF. MCR 1850, 1860, 1870; age 40 in 1850; b. Hanover; cabinetmaker; Fredericksburg, Gillespie County. Schaeper, his wife, and four children migrated from Umstedt, Hanover, to Texas in 1845 on the *Weser* (Chester William Geue and Ethel Hander Geue, *A New Land Beckoned,* p. 140). In 1860 he had a one-man cabinet shop in Fredericksburg which used timber valued at $250 to make "all kinds of furniture" valued at $700. He was still working in Fredericksburg in 1870.

SCHAFFER, PETER. MCR 1860; age 38; b. Prussia; cabinetmaker; Seguin, Guadalupe County.

SCHAFFTER, HENRY. MCR 1860; age 37; b. Switzerland; cabinetmaker; Richmond, Fort Bend County. Schaffter moved to Galveston following the Civil War and advertised in *Flake's Daily Bulletin,* August 3, 1865: "Henry Schaffter, Cabinet Maker, has opened a shop on Tremont Street, opposite the residence of G. Ball, Esq. He is prepared to repair and make Furniture to order, he will also do all kinds of carpenter work."

SCHENCK, JOHN H. MCR 1860. Schenck had a two-man wagon and carriage-building shop at Hookers, Hunt County, in 1860, equipped with a horse-powered lathe. He produced 8 wagons valued at $400, 1 buggy valued at $75, and 10 bedsteads valued at $80.

SCHETTER, HENRY. MCR 1870; age 35; b. Prussia; joiner; Fredericksburg, Gillespie County.

SCHIEGE, CARL JOHANN RUDOLPH. MCR 1860; age 45; b. Prussia; chairmaker; Round Top, Fayette County. Schiege was born June 1, 1805, and came to Round Top before 1860. In September, 1861, he purchased lots 2 and 3 in block 29, Round Top, from G. C. August Bess and located his home and shop on this site. A bed made by Schiege and descended in his family belongs to the Witte Memorial Museum, San Antonio. He died in 1901. (Interview with Mrs. Rudi Legler, Round Top, June 11, 1973; Fayette County Deed Records, vol. R, p. 262.) For an example of his work, see 6.9.

SCHMIDT, HEINRICH. MCR 1870; age 33; b. Bavaria; joiner; New Braunfels, Comal County.

SCHMIDT, JOHANNES. MCR 1850, 1860; age 41 in 1850; b. Germany; cabinetmaker; Seguin, Guadalupe County. Schmidt continued to work in Seguin until his death on June 27, 1875 (Guadalupe County Death Certificates).

SCHMIDTZ, WILLIAM. MCR 1860. In 1860, Schmidtz had a two-man cabinet shop in Austin, Travis County, which used timber valued at $600 and "other articles" valued at $200 to produce furniture valued at $2,000.

SCHNEIDER, JACOB. MCR 1860, 1870; age 37 in 1860; b. Prussia; cabinetmaker; Fredericksburg, Gillespie County. Schneider was born December 5, 1823, in Fronhofen, Prussia. From 1845 to 1850 he served in the Sixteenth Regiment of the Eighth Prussian Army Corps. He and his wife immigrated to Texas on board the *Antoinette* in 1853 and settled in Fredericksburg, where he built a home and cabinet shop on the corner of Kerrville Road and San Antonio Street. In 1860 this shop used timber valued at $400 to produce furniture valued at $1,500. He also made coffins and exterior house trim. Schneider died July 25, 1911. (Mrs. Herman Kuhlman, Houston, June 4, 1973, to LT.) For examples of his work, see 2.2 and 4.25.

SCHOLL, ADAM. MCR 1860; age 26; b. Nassau; joiner; New Braunfels, Comal County. *See also* Scholl, Heinrich.

SCHOLL, HEINRICH. MCR 1850, 1860; age 22 in 1850; b. Nassau; carpenter; New Braunfels, Comal County. Heinrich Scholl and his brother, Adam, were born in Neuholte, near Dillenburg, Nassau, and came to Texas in 1846. Their mother was widowed on the trip from Indianola to New Braunfels, and they learned carpentry while she kept a boarding house. The brothers set up a shop behind their home and made sashes and doors as well as furniture. They were Union sympathizers and remained in hiding during most of the Civil War. Heinrich Scholl died in 1909. ("History of the Scholls in Texas," in possession of Mrs. O. A. Stratemann, New Braunfels.) For examples of Heinrich Scholl's work, see 4.3, 4.24, 6.26, 6.34, and 6.35.

SCHROLERE, AUGUST. MCR 1850; age 30; b. Germany; cabinetmaker; Galveston, Galveston County.

SCHUEDDEMAGEN, CONRAD. Schueddemagen, while primarily a saddler, evidently made furniture for his neighbors in Round Top, Fayette County. He was born June 11, 1811, in Hohenhameln, Hanover, and came to Texas in 1847, settling first at Industry, Austin County. He was working as a saddler and making furniture in Round Top in 1860. He died in 1900. (Gertrude Franke, *A Goodly Heritage*, p. 18.) For examples of his work, see 4.8 and 6.31. A lounge and chair attributed to him are in the possession of his great-granddaughter.

SCHULTZ, WILLIAM. MCR 1860; age 50; b. Prussia; cabinetmaker; Swartout, Polk County.

SCHULZE, FERDINAND. MCR 1860, 1870; age 45 in 1860; b. Prussia; cabinetmaker in 1860; joiner and farmer in 1870; Fredericksburg, Gillespie County. According to his grandsons, Schulze came to Texas in 1846 and was an early settler of Fredericksburg. He was trained as a cabinetmaker in Germany and, upon arrival in Gillespie County, built his own sliding-catch bench from local cypress and pecan. The bench was exhibited at the American Heritage Museum in Fredericksburg until that museum's closing in 1973. Schulze was a freethinker and was known to his neighbors as "Sontag" Schulze because he had no objection to working on Sunday. (Interviews with Ed Schulze, Fredericksburg, June 3, 1973; Hugo Schulze, Hilda, June 3, 1973.)

SCHURLOCK, JOHN. MCR 1850; age 34; b. Iowa; cabinetmaker; Dallas County.

SCHWEERS, SCHWEER. Schweers was born Schweer Balzeen in Germany in 1808. He and his family migrated from Oldenburg to Texas in 1856 and settled at Quihi, Medina County. Soon after this he changed his last name from Balzeen to Schweers, possibly to protect a son who had fled from compulsory military service in Germany. He practiced the trades of butcher and blacksmith in Quihi but retired from active business when he was about seventy. From then until his death at the age of ninety-two he lived alternately with each of his nine children for one month at a time and occupied his time by making chairs (see 4.14, 4.32). These chairs are quite numerous in Medina County, and two were included in the "Index of American Design, Data Report Sheets, Texas" (Tex-Fu-23 and Tex-Fu-24). They are also pictured by Ralph and Terry Kovel, *American Country Furniture 1780–1875*, p. 101. (Interviews with Willie Schweers, Quihi, May 24, 1973; C. F. Schweers, Hondo, May 24, 1973.)

SCOTT, W.B. MCR 1870; age 27; b. Iowa; manufacturer of chairs; Comfort, Kerr County (now Kendall County). Scott was one of the Hill Country Unionists who participated in the battle with Confederate troops on the Nueces River in August, 1862. He escaped the massacre and made his way to Mexico, where he joined the United States Army and served three years with the First Texas Cavalry. (Guido Ransleben, *A Hundred Years of Comfort in Texas: A Centennial History*, pp. 110–114.)

SELLE, ALEXANDER. MCR 1850; age 37; b. Germany; cabinetmaker; Galveston, Galveston County. Alexander Selle was still working in Galveston in 1872, when John H. Heller's *Galveston City Directory 1872* gave his residence as 407 East Avenue K.

SELLE, FRANK A. MCR 1870; age 54; b. Saxony; cabinetmaker; Galveston, Galveston County.

SELLE, HAYMEN. MCR 1870; age 20; b. Saxony; cabinetmaker; Galveston, Galveston County.

SERGER, EMIL. Serger was born in Prussia on March 27, 1831, and came to Comfort, then in Kerr County, in 1856, where he combined farming with cabinetmaking. In May, 1861, the Kerr County Commissioners' Court appointed him to a three-man committee to oversee the building of a courthouse in Comfort. (Guido Ransleben, *A Hundred Years of Comfort in Texas: A Centennial History*, pp. 153, 212; a photograph of a *Schrank* made by Serger follows p. 132.)

SHANAHAN, JAMES B. MCR 1850; age 35; b. New Jersey; mechanic; Clarksville, Red River County. Shanahan was the first of a series of fine cabinetmakers who worked in Clarksville in the mid-nineteenth century; *see also* Brem, John W.; Chute, James; Gaines, William C.; Longe, Jasper; and Milke, August. On June 5, 1844, Shanahan placed an advertisement in the Clarksville *Northern Standard* which read: "CABINET FURNITURE. The undersigned returns his thanks to his old friends and the public in general, for their patronage heretofore, and respectfully solicits a continuance of it. He has established a shop on main street, near the bridge, where he intends manufacturing every article in his line of business for which there may be a demand. He will also act as undertaker for funerals, and will prepare coffins at the shortest notice. The undersigned wishes to purchase 30 or 40,000 feet of black Walnut, Birch, Cherry, and Sycamore lumber, for which he will pay in cabinet ware. James B. Shanahan." His shop must have prospered, for on April 2, 1846, he bought ten acres of land in Red River County and less than three years later, on January 18, 1849, he bought two town lots in Clarksville from George and Isabella Gordon (Red River County Deed Records, vol. H, pp. 63, 305).

An idea of the style in which Shanahan worked and the distribution of his furniture at this period may be gained from an advertisement in the *Northern Standard*, June 24, 1848, in which he announced that "he has lately received a fresh supply of veneer, and that he is prepared as heretofore to do any sort of cabinet work, such as book cases, bureaus, wardrobes, tables, bedsteads, etc. . . . He would refer persons at a distance to the articles made by him for gentlemen in Bowie and Lamar as specimens of the quality of his work. Mahogany, Walnut, Birch and Gum, always on hand for manufacturing purposes." On March 3, 1855, he and his partner, T. J. Brim, advertised in the *Standard* that they had just received a lot of mahogany veneering and were prepared to make bureaus, tables, lounges, sofas, and bedsteads from it.

Like several other Texas cabinetmakers, Shanahan purchased a limited franchise on a Northern furniture patent, paying John Pierce of Racine, Wisconsin, $60 in 1856 for an interest in a patent "for improvements in bedstead fastenings, originally granted to Issac A. Sergeant of Cincinnati on July 13, 1852" (Red River County Deed Records, vol. K, p. 244).

By 1850, Shanahan's shop employed three males and one female and used 15,000 feet of lumber valued at $300 to produce "300 sundries" valued at $2,000. It was the third-largest cabinet shop in Texas that year, and the only cabinet shop in North Texas to produce furniture valued at more than $500. In November, 1856, the shop was destroyed by a fire which started in it and also burned down the county jail and William C. Gaines's cabinet shop (*Southern Intelligencer*, November 19, 1856). In February, 1857, Shanahan announced that, "since the fire which destroyed his old shop, he has rebuilt, and now has a large and commodious house, and is prepared to do all sorts of work in his line, such as Bureaus, Sideboards, Tables, Stands, Bedsteads, etc." (*Standard*, February 21, 1857). He evidently ceased working before 1860, as he does not appear on the 1860 census return for Red River County.

SHATTUCK, FRANK. MCR 1870; age 24; b. Ohio; chairmaker; Hempstead, Austin County (now Waller County).

SHAVER, H.L. MCR 1850; age 38; b. Tennessee; cabinetmaker; Polk County.

SHAW, A.J. MCR 1850; age 40; b. Connecticut; cabinetmaker; Upshur County.

SHAW, JOHN. MCR 1860; age 32; b. Kentucky; cabinetmaker; South Sulphur, Hunt County.

SHAW, JOSIAH. MCR 1870; age 55; b. New York; chairmaker; Brooklyn, Shelby County.

SHELTON, THOMAS W. MCR 1860; age 28; b. Tennessee; cabinetmaker; Tennessee Colony, Anderson County. Shelton closed his shop when he joined the Confederate army in 1861 (Pauline B. Hokes, *Centen-*

nial History of Anderson County, p. 236).

SHEPARD, J. MCR 1860; age 33; b. Ohio; cabinetmaker; Belton, Bell County.

SHEPARD, THOMAS. MCR 1860; age 45; b. New York; cabinetmaker; Burnet, Burnet County.

SHEPPARD, WILLIAM. MCR 1860, 1870; age 30 in 1860; b. Kentucky; cabinetmaker; Tyler, Smith County. William Sheppard first opened his shop in Tyler in December, 1858, when he announced in the *Tyler Reporter:* "NEW CABINET SHOP. WILLIAM SHEPARD would respectfully inform the citizens of Tyler that he has opened a Cabinet Shop in the lower room of the 'Temple Building' where he intends to MANUFACTURE AND PREPARE EVERY DESCRIPTION OF FURNITURE! He also designs, in the future, to keep on hand an extensive variety of CABINET WORK Such as Bureaus, Wardrobes, Tables, Lounges, Bedsteads, Stands, Safes, Book-cases, Desks, &c., &c." (ad dated December 17, 1858, *Tyler Reporter*, February 9, 1859). By 1860, he had gone into partnership with J. C. Rogers in Tyler; *see* Rogers, J. C. His firm survived the Civil War to become a major furniture manufacturer by 1870. In that year Sheppard's shop at Mechanicsville, in the Garden Valley precinct, just outside of Tyler, was equipped with a fifteen-horsepower steam engine operating four lathes, two boring machines, and one "tennant" (tenoning machine?) and employed ten men, who used pine, gum, hickory, and pin oak valued at $3,000 to produce furniture valued at $5,500.

SHROTS, J. MCR 1860; age 22; b. Tennessee; cabinetmaker; Columbus, Colorado County.

SILLS, B.F. MCR 1860; age 45; b. South Carolina; cabinetmaker; Waco, McLennan County.

SIMLER, ALFRED. MCR 1870; age 17; b. Texas; apprentice to cabinetmaker; Houston, Harris County.

SIMON, FERDINAND. MCR 1850, 1860; age 29 in 1850; b. Nassau; cabinetmaker in 1850; joiner in 1860; New Braunfels, Comal County.

SIMONDS, THOMAS. MCR 1860; age 23; b. Arkansas; master cabinetmaker; Denton, Denton County.

SIMPSON, HENRY E. MCR 1860; age 29; b. England; cabinet workman; Beaumont, Jefferson County.

SIMS, GARLAND M. MCR 1860; age 26; b. Kentucky; cabinetmaker and chair turner; Livingston, Polk County.

SKEEN, M. MCR 1860; age 41; b. North Carolina; cabinetmaker; Milford, Ellis County.

SKINNER, W.T. MCR 1860; age 32; b. Kentucky; master cabinetmaker; Carter, Denton County. In 1860, Skinner had a two-man shop which used 15,000 feet of pine lumber valued at $600 to produce 100 tables valued at $8 each, 50 safes valued at $15 each, and 100 bedsteads valued at $8 each.

SLAUGHTER, CALVIN. MCR 1850; age 26; b. Alabama; cabinetmaker; Rusk County.

SMITH, B.H. MCR 1860; age 31; b. Tennessee; cabinetmaker; Bright Star (now Sulphur Springs), Hopkins County.

SMITH, C.P. MCR 1860; age 50; b. New York; cabinetmaker; San Antonio, Bexar County.

SMITH, HENRY. MCR 1870; age 36; b. England; cabinetmaker; Bastrop, Bastrop County.

SMITH, J.C. MCR 1860; age 19; b. Alabama; cabinetmaker; Pittsburg, Upshur County.

SMITH, JAMES H. James H. Smith was an early partner of Clarksville cabinetmaker William C. Gaines. On December 18, 1852, Gaines and Smith purchased a town lot in Clarksville from J. D. H. Epperson, and on July 12, 1853, Smith sold his interest in the lot to Gaines (Red River County Deed Records, vol. J, pp. 41, 177).

SMITH, JOHN N. MCR 1870; age 26; b. South Carolina; cabinetmaker; Athens, Henderson County.

SMITH, LEMUEL. MCR 1850; age 40; b. Virginia; cabinetmaker; Walker County.

SMITH, WILLIAM W. MCR 1850, 1860; age 24 in 1850; b. Tennessee; cabinetmaker; White Oak, Hopkins County. By 1860, William W. Smith had a fairly large cabinetmaking establishment on the banks of White Oak Bayou. His shop used a horse and inclined wheel as motive power, employed five men, and used 20,000 feet of plank valued at $500 to produce furniture valued at $3,500.

SNIDER, HARMON. MCR 1850; age 26; b. Germany; cabinetmaker; Austin County.

SNIDER, JOHN. MCR 1870; age 24; b. Württemberg; cabinetmaker; Jefferson, Marion County.

SONNEKSEN, C.N. Sonneksen advertised in the *Tyler Reporter* (Smith County), November 17, 1855: "FURNITURE MANUFACTURE, The undersigned begs leave to inform the citizens of Tyler and vicinity, he has opened a HOUSE FURNITURE ESTABLISHMENT where he is prepared to execute all orders which may be intrusted to him, he flatters himself that he is competent to please the most fastidious with his workmanship, his Shop is on the South side of Public Square. Dec. 3, 1854." Nothing more is known of him.

SOULNIA, P. MCR 1860; age 42; b. France; cabinetmaker; Houston, Harris County.

SOUTHWOOD, THOMAS J. MCR 1860; age 44; b. Tennessee; cabinet workman; Gainesville, Cooke County.

SPALDING, JOHN H. MCR 1870; age 35; b. Missouri; cabinetmaker; Waxahachie, Ellis County. John H. Spalding was born in Ralls County, Missouri, on April 29, 1835. He learned the trade of cabinetmaking from an uncle in Missouri and moved to Waxahachie in 1860 to open a cabinet shop. He was in business there on May 12, 1861, when Robert Minor Wyatt noted in his diary: "Money can scarcely be had. I put my old lathe in partnership with Mr. Spalding." However, Spalding closed his shop shortly afterward to join the Confederate army and served through the war with Parson's Brigade, Nineteenth Texas Cavalry. He returned to Waxahachie after the war and prospered in business. In 1870, his shop employed three men and used materials valued at $4,000 to produce furniture valued at $7,500, making him the third-largest producer of furniture in Texas that year. During the early 1870's, he invested his profits in farmland around Waxahachie, and in 1871 he served as a city alderman. About 1878, however, he suffered personal financial reverses and sold his business. He was then elected city marshal of Waxahachie and was killed making an arrest on December 17, 1882. His descendants in Waxahachie have several examples of his work, including a side chair, two drop-front desks, and a circular dining table with attached lazy susan. ("Texas Genealogical Records, Ellis County, 1784–1955," VI, 31, Ellis County Public Library, Waxahachie; Robert Minor Wyatt, Diary, Ellis County Public Library, Waxahachie; interview with William Spalding, Waxahachie, June 3, 1973.)

SPALDING, ROBERT. MCR 1870; age 23; b. Kentucky; cabinetmaker; Waxahachie, Ellis County.

SPENCER, JOSEPH. MCR 1870; age 21; b. Georgia; cabinetmaker; McKinney, Collin County.

SPIKES, WILLIAM. MCR 1870; age 29; b. Mississippi; cabinetmaker; Pinetree, Upshur County.

SPRALING, JOHN. MCR 1860; age 24; b. Missouri; cabinetmaker; San Antonio, Bexar County.

STAATS, CHRISTIAN. MCR 1850, 1860, 1870; age 28 in 1850; b. Nassau; carpenter in 1850; cabinetmaker in 1860 and 1870; Fredericksburg, Gillespie County. Christian Staats immigrated from Harzburg am Harz to Texas on the *B. Bohlen* in 1845 (Chester William Geue and Ethel Hander Geue, *A New Land Beckoned*, p. 150). In 1860 his one-man shop used timber valued at $500 to produce furniture valued at $1,500. By 1870 his annual production had dropped below $500, but he continued in business until the late 1880's, when he was killed in a wagon accident (interview with Eddie Staats, Llano, June 3, 1973).

STAATS, S.D. S. D. Staats advertised in the Houston *Morning Star*, March 23, 1843: "CABINET MAKER AND JOINER. The subscriber has on hand and is constantly manufacturing All kinds of cabinet ware on the lowest and most reasonable terms of the following description: Double Bedsteads, Single Bedsteads, Trundle Bedsteads, Column bureaus, half column bureaus, plain bureaus, wash stand, dining tables, breakfast tables, dressing tables, work stands, candle stands, writing desks, armors [sic], &c., &c. CONSTANTLY ON HAND. Bedsteads, tables, dining and breakfast tables, hair bottom stools, chairs, bureaus—column, half column, and plain—all of his own manufacture, which he offers for sale cheap for cash or country produce. S. D. Staats, Main st." Nothing more is known of him.

STALCUP, JOSEPH. MCR 1850; age 37; b. North Carolina; cabinetmaker; Anderson County.

STALLINGS, JAMES A. MCR 1860, 1870; age 22 in 1860; b. Georgia; cabinetmaker; Cherino, Nacogdoches County, in 1860. In 1870, Stallings was working in Rusk, Cherokee County, where he was in partnership with William Hughes; see Hughes, William.

STAMPER, WILLIAM. MCR 1870; age 26; b. Tennessee; Clarksville, Red

River County.

STAUTZENBERGER, FRANZ. Stautzenberger came to Texas with his brother's family about 1845 from Nassau, where he had been employed as a cabinetmaker by the Duke of Nassau. He was a bachelor and lived in the home of his niece, Magdalene, and her husband, Konrad Oelkers, at Clear Spring in Guadalupe County. He helped them build their house there, a half-timbered, three-room structure which is still standing, and made the furniture for it (see 2.15, 3.1, 5.11, 6.43). He also made furniture for other members of his family but seems not to have engaged in the cabinetmaking business in Texas.

STEADHAM, JOHN. MCR 1860; age 34; b. Alabama; chairmaker; Huntsville, Walker County.

STEEL, WILLIAM. MCR 1870; age 50; b. Maryland; works in cabinet shop; Bonham, Fannin County.

STEGEMANN, FREDERICK. MCR 1860, 1870; age 33 in 1860; b. Prussia; cabinetmaker; Houston, Harris County. Stegemann's name is Anglicized as *Stagman* on the 1870 Harris County census return.

STEINHAGEN, CHRISTOFER FRIDERICH CARL. MCR 1860; age 45; b. Mecklenburg; wagonmaker; Anderson, Grimes County. According to the pencil inscription on a wardrobe he made (2.32), Carl Steinhagen was born on December 21, 1814, in the village of Warckdorff, near the Baltic port of Wismar in the Grand Duchy of Mecklenburg-Schwerin. Wismar was a Swedish possession until ten years before Steinhagen's birth, which may account for the Scandinavian tone of some of his designs (see particularly 5.1). Steinhagen came to Texas in 1847 and settled in Anderson, which was an important crossroads for several stage lines. These lines provided Steinhagen with an opportunity to practice the trades of wheelwright and wagon builder. He designed and made furniture for his family, building, according to family legend, a piece for each of his twelve children. In 1872 he built and patented a self-regulating water wheel to power the machinery in his woodworking shop, which is still standing, although much altered, in Anderson. (Irene Taylor Allen, *Saga of Anderson*, p. 202.) Steinhagen died February 19, 1893, according to his tombstone. A number of his tools and several examples of his furniture are in the Winedale collection. For examples of his work, see 1.3, 2.32, 4.1, 5.1, 6.25,

and 6.36.

STEPHEN, ——. *See* Gaines, William C.

STEPHENS, OBADIAH. *See* Longe, Jasper.

STEPHENS AND LONGE. *See* Longe, Jasper.

STERZING, CARL THEODOR. MCR 1870; age 18; b. Texas; joiner's apprentice; Austin, Travis County. Sterzing is listed in S. A. Gray and W. D. Moore's *Mercantile and General City Directory of Austin, Texas, 1872–73*, as residing near the Military Institute and being a partner in the firm of Kempen and Sterzing. *See* Kempen, Adolph.

STETSON, P.M. MCR 1860; age 42; b. Massachusetts; carpenter; Jefferson, Marion County. Stetson was a partner in the firm of Stetson and Stewart of Jefferson, which advertised in the Clarksville *Standard*, April 9, 1859: "STETSON & STEWART, SASH, BLIND, AND DOOR MANUFACTORY, JEFFERSON, TEXAS Have in operation, the most approved machinery for the speedy manufactory of Sash, Blinds, Doors, etc., for building and also PLAIN furniture, such as Safes, Wardrobes, Bedsteads, and other articles of that class, which they can afford to sell at less price than they can be procured elsewhere in Northern and Eastern Texas." Stetson was subsequently a partner with J. T. Warner in a steam-powered grist and planing mill in Jefferson whose equipment included a planer, a circular saw and table, and an iron lathe. This partnership was dissolved in March, 1863. (Marion County District Court Minutes, book A, p. 211.)

STEVES, EDUARD. Eduard Steves was born at Barmen, Eberfeld, Germany, on December 14, 1829. He came to Texas in 1848 and settled in New Braunfels, where he learned the trade of cabinetmaking in the shop of Karl Floege. In 1850, he moved to San Antonio and worked for two years as a house carpenter, returning to his father's farm in Comal County in 1852. In 1857, he married and moved to the Comfort area, where he engaged in farming and cabinetmaking. In 1866 he moved to San Antonio and founded the Eduard Steves Lumber Yard (known as the Ed Steves and Son lumber yard after 1879), which became San Antonio's leading lumber yard and made Steves one of the city's wealthiest citizens. He died on April 20, 1890. (Frederick C. Chabot, *With the Makers of San Antonio*, pp. 399–400.) For an example of his work, see 7.2.

STEVES, SIEGBERT FRANZ. MCR 1870; age 62; b. Prussia; cabinetmaker;

Fayetteville, Fayette County. Siegbert Franz Steves apparently arrived in Fayette County about 1858. On December 21 of that year he purchased 3 1/2 acres of land on Cummins Creek, near Fayetteville (Fayette County Deed Records, vol. Q, p. 96). He died January 24, 1873, leaving a homestead of 20 3/4 acres (adjoining the town of Fayetteville), a widow, eight children, and an estate valued at $4,034 (Fayette County Record of Probate, book N, p. 144).

STEWART, ———. *See* Stetson, P. M.

STINEBOUGH, JACOB. MCR 1870; age 75; b. Tennessee; cabinetmaker; Farmersville, Collin County.

STITH, ABNER H. MCR 1850; age 36; b. Kentucky; master carpenter; Henderson, Rusk County. In 1850, Stith had a two-man cabinet shop in Henderson which used 2,500 feet of sawed lumber valued at $250 to produce "a variety of bureaus and pieces" valued at $2,000.

STOCKER, CHRISTOPHER. MCR 1850; age 54; b. Germany; cabinetmaker; New Braunfels, Comal County.

STREETING, B. MCR 1860; age 24; b. Prussia; cabinetmaker; Austin, Travis County.

STROEMER, LUDWIG. MCR 1870; age 40; b. Prussia; turner; New Braunfels, Comal County. In 1870, Stroemer used timber valued at $300 to manufacture furniture valued at $800.

STUCKE, ADOLF. MCR 1860; age 67; b. Hanover; cabinetmaker; Fredericksburg, Gillespie County. Stucke immigrated from Schulenberg, Hanover, to Texas on the *Gesina* in 1845. He died in 1874. (Chester William Geue and Ethel Hander Geue, *A New Land Beckoned*, p. 151.)

STUKES, WILLIAM. MCR 1850; age 27; b. South Carolina; cabinetmaker; Calhoun County. In 1848, Stukes was working in Galveston, where he and his partner, T. McDonough, advertised that their shop on the corner of Commercial and Mechanic streets made "to order, every species of FURNITURE of the latest fashion, and on the most reasonable terms. They will keep constantly on hand the following articles of furniture, viz.— WARDROBES, BUREAUS, SIDEBOARDS, PRESSES, SAFES, CUPBOARDS, SOFAS, SETTES, COUCHES, CENTRE TABLES, DESKS, BEDSTEADS, &c. &c." (*Corpus Christi Gazette*, January 8, 1848).

STURM, LEWIS. MCR 1870; age 45; b. Prussia; cabinetmaker; Jefferson, Marion County. Sturm was working in Jefferson as early as 1854, when he filed suit against Hugo Fox for payment of a bill totaling $306, including "1 cherry table, folding leaf, $12," and "95 1/2 days labor as a master workman at $2.50 a day, plus pay for a journeyman workman named Otto" (Marion County District Court Minutes, docket 82). He married Eveline Dwyer on July 7, 1859, but was granted a divorce from her on November 21, 1861, the court finding that "her general character for chastity since marriage was bad" (ibid., docket 132). He later remarried and had one son by his second wife (ibid., dockets 701, 884).

In 1870, the census marshal reported that Sturm had a furniture factory in Jefferson equipped with a twenty-four–horsepower steam engine which employed fifteen hands to produce $95,000 worth of furniture. These figures seem absurdly large and are entered on the census return just above a set of equally large figures for a Jefferson mattress factory which have been marked, in a hand other than that of the census marshal, "omit." No traces of Sturm's factory can be found in the Marion County courthouse records; so it seems quite likely that the census entry is grossly inaccurate, perhaps the result of a practical joke. Sturm died before April 20, 1871 (Marion County District Court Minutes, dockets 701, 884).

SUMMERS, WILLIAM S. MCR 1850; age 36; b. Tennessee; cabinetmaker; Sabine County. In 1850, Summers used 2,000 feet of assorted lumber valued at $90 to produce furniture valued at $500.

SUNDERLAND, SETH. MCR 1860; age 25; b. Yorkshire, England; cabinet workman; Greenville, Hunt County.

SWANN, ROBERT. MCR 1850; age 45; b. Indiana; cabinetmaker; Jackson County.

SWEET, JOSEPH. MCR 1860; age 77; b. New York; chairmaker; Dallas County.

SWIFT, JONATHAN. MCR 1860; age 68; b. South Carolina; cabinetmaker; Melrose, Nacogdoches County.

SWINGLE, ALFRED. MCR 1850; age 40; b. Maryland; cabinetmaker; Galveston, Galveston County. Swingle was evidently both a furniture importer and a cabinetmaker. In an advertisement in the *Galvestonian*, April 3, 1840, he states: "The subscribers have opened a ware room in their new building, one block south of the Tremont House, where they have on hand, and for sale, a general assortment of furniture, consisting in part of Mahogany sideboards and Bureaus, Black walnut sideboards, Mahogany and Black Walnut Washstands with Marbletops, Black Walnut sofas, Cherry dining and breakfast tables, cherry washstands, bedsteads, etc. We will also make to order and repair furniture on the shortest notice. Turning in all its varieties executed with neatness and despatch. SWINGLE & WILLIAMSON."

TALLEY, ———. *See* Outlaw, John C.

TANNER, J.R. MCR 1850; age 45; b. Delaware; cabinetmaker; Bastrop, Bastrop County.

TANNER, JAKOB. MCR 1870; age 57; b. Switzerland; works in joiner shop; New Braunfels, Comal County.

TARDY, JOHN. MCR 1870; age 69; b. Virginia; cabinetmaker; Boling, Leon County.

TATSCH, JOHANN PETER. MCR 1860, 1870; age 34 in 1860; b. Prussia; cabinetmaker; Fredericksburg, Gillespie County. Johann Peter Tatsch was one of the first Texas cabinetmakers whose furniture became known to collectors. Some of his work was recorded in the Texas survey made for *The Index of American Design* between 1939 and 1942, and he was included in a survey by Esther Mueller, "Some Craftsmen of Early Fredericksburg," in "A Group of Themes on the Architecture and Culture of Early Texas by Students in Course A.350," ed. Samuel E. Gideon. Many examples of his work still survive in Fredericksburg (see 1.7, 1.26, 2.28, 2.29, 2.30, 2.31, 4.5, 4.6, 4.13, and 4.33).

Tatsch was born in Irmenach, near the Mosel River, July 26, 1822. He and his family migrated to Texas in 1852 and settled at Fredericksburg, where the house he built is still standing. In a shop beside his house he set up a turning lathe, workbench, and shaving horse, and made not only cabinet furniture but also wooden bowls, trays, ladles, mousetraps, wooden laying eggs, chairs, bedsteads, and spinning wheels. He also cut and shaved staves for coopers to form into churns, buckets, tubs, and barrels. In 1860, he reported that he used timber valued at $200 to produce furniture valued at $700. His grandchildren have described him as "above medium height, thin and active . . . he had dark hair and eyes. Being a man of intelligence and pride, touched with humor and irony, he joked often." He died on May 1, 1907. (Gil-lespie County Historical Society, *Pioneers in God's Hills*, pp. 213–215.)

TATSCH, WILLIAM. MCR 1870; age 17; b. Texas; apprentice to joiner; Fredericksburg, Gillespie County.

TAYLOR, ARMSTED J. MCR 1860, 1870; age 29 in 1860; b. Tennessee; cabinetmaker; McKinney, Collin County.

TAYLOR, JOHN. MCR 1860; age 35; b. Connecticut; chairmaker; Gay Hill, Washington County. John Taylor may have been associated with some sort of manufacturing establishment at Gay Hill. The census return lists him as a single adult living in the household of Eli Kittridge, an engineer from Massachusetts, along with Kittridge's family and three other single adults—two carpenters and a wheelwright.

TAYLOR, WILLIAM. MCR 1860; age 27; b. Georgia; master cabinetmaker; Homer, Angelina County.

TEETERS, R.P. MCR 1860; age 39; b. Kentucky; chairmaker; Decatur, Wise County.

THACKER, GEORGE. MCR 1870; age 67; b. Missouri; chairmaker; Farmersville, Collin County.

THIELE, KARL. MCR 1850, 1860, 1870; age 56 in 1850; b. Braunschweig; joiner; New Braunfels, Comal County. Thiele was born in Hendessen, Braunschweig, and immigrated to Texas in 1846. He was working in New Braunfels on November 21, 1849, when he declared his intention to become a United States citizen. (Comal County District Court Minutes, vol. A, p. 217.) In 1870 his one-man joinery used timber valued at $200 to produce furniture valued at $500.

THOMAS, J.D. MCR 1870; age 21; b. Texas; cabinet manufacturer; Paris, Lamar County.

THOMAS, JOHN J. MCR 1870; age 56; b. Pennsylvania; chairmaker; Hempstead, Austin County (now Waller County).

THOMAS, PETER. MCR 1870; age 20; b. Germany; apprentice cabinetmaker; Victoria, Victoria County.

THOMAS, SHADRACH. MCR 1850; age 57; b. North Carolina; cabinetmaker; San Augustine County.

THOMASON, DAVID. MCR 1870; age 71; b. Virginia; chairmaker; Melrose, Nacogdoches County.

THORNTON, S.C. MCR 1860; age 28; b. Tennessee; cabinetmaker; Bonham, Fannin County.

THURM, J. MCR 1860; age 24; b. France; cabinetmaker; Waco, McLennan County.

TIDWELL, JOHN. MCR 1870; age 35; b. Georgia; cabinetmaker; Garden Valley, Smith County.

TIETZE, FRIEDRICH WILHELM. MCR 1860, 1870; age 40 in 1860; b. Saxony; joiner; New Braunfels, Comal County. Tietze became a United States citizen in New Braunfels on April 17, 1858, at which time he had lived in the United States for five years (Comal County District Court Minutes, vol. C, p. 115). For an example of his work, see 1.15.

TINKE, CHARLES. MCR 1850; age 28; b. Germany; cabinetmaker; Houston, Harris County.

TITSWORTH, LEMUEL B. MCR 1860, 1870; age 18 in 1860; b. Arkansas; cabinet workman; Tidwell Creek, Hunt County, in 1860. In 1870, Titsworth had a cabinet shop near Bright Star Post Office, Hopkins County, which in eight months of operation used timber valued at $75 and 500 feet of lumber valued at $50 to produce 500 chairs valued at $500, 3 spinning wheels valued at $15, and 8 bedsteads valued at $64.

TITSWORTH, LEVI. MCR 1870; age 39; b. Tennessee; chairmaker; Bonham, Fannin County.

TITSWORTH, THOMAS P. MCR 1870; age 35; b. Tennessee; cabinet business; Bonham, Fannin County.

TRAVIS, ALEXANDER. MCR 1870; age 24; b. Louisiana; upholsterer; Houston, Harris County. Travis was the partner of Edward O'Reilly in a Houston upholstery and cabinet shop in 1870. *See* O'Reilly, Edward.

TUCKER, JOHN. MCR 1870; age 28; b. Georgia; cabinetmaker; Garden Valley, Smith County. According to Smith County historian Edna L. Hatcher, "John Tucker lived at one time at Mechanicsville, three miles southwest of Mt. Sylvan. He operated a furniture manufacturing establishment there which was later bought by a Mr. Lange" ("An Economic History of Smith County, 1846–1940" [M.S. thesis, East Texas State Teachers College, 1940], p. 38).

TUDER, JAMES. MCR 1870; age 19; b. Kentucky; cabinet workman; Aiken, Bell County.

TUDER, WILLIAM. MCR 1870; age 49; b. Tennessee; cabinet workman; Aiken, Bell County. In 1870, William Tuder's cabinet shop used 3,000 feet of lumber valued at $100 to make 25 bedsteads valued at $200, 100 chairs valued at $150, 20 tables valued at $100, 50 lounges valued at $300, and "other items" valued at $200.

TUDER, WILLIAM. MCR 1870; age 21; b. Kentucky; cabinet workman; Aiken, Bell County.

TUKELS, NEHEMIAH. MCR 1860; age 41; b. Louisiana; chairmaker; Hempstead, Austin County (now Waller County).

TUMEY, T.H. From his two extant advertisements, Tumey, of Austin, Travis County, appears to have been both a cabinetmaker and a furniture dealer. In the Austin *Tri-Weekly Times*, October 3, 1856, he advertised that "he has on hand, and continues to make, a large assortment of all kinds of furniture. All orders promptly filled. I have a good turning lathe, and will do every variety of turning that may be wanted at reasonable prices ... Persons calling at night can find me at my residence a few yards in the rear of my shop, on Pecan Street." The *Southern Intelligencer*, February 1, 1860, carries a second advertisement, in which Tumey states that he has received a splendid lot of furniture, "to wit: Sofas, Tete-a-Tetes, Easy, Parlor, Reclining, and Fine Rocking Chairs, as well as wood seat do., Centre and extension tables, Music Stools, Hall Stands, Clock Cradles (a beautiful and novel article), Basket Stands, Single and Double Bedsteads, Brass Cornices, Fire-Boards, and other articles too numerous to mention. Every description of cabinet work kept and made to order."

TURNEY, DANIEL. MCR 1860; age 31; b. Tennessee; cabinetwork; Rusk, Cherokee County.

TURNEY, THOMAS H. MCR 1860; age 39; b. Kentucky; cabinetmaker; Austin, Travis County.

UMLAND, CLAUS. MCR 1870; age 19; b. Hanover; cabinetmaker; Chappell Hill, Washington County. Claus Umland, son of Johann Umland, was born January 11, 1851. He came to Texas with his father in 1854 and was presumably trained by him as a cabinetmaker. In March, 1870, the Masonic Lodge at Chappell Hill paid Claus Umland $10.00 for hanging canvas in the lodge's meeting room. In 1873, when he was admitted to the lodge as a member, he gave his occupation as "merchant." He died October 13, 1878. (Hubert Lodge No. 67, A.F. of A.M. Lodge Records, Chappell Hill.)

UMLAND, HEINRICH. MCR 1850, 1860; age 45 *[sic]* in 1850; b. Germany; cabinetmaker; Bellville, Austin County. Heinrich Umland, brother of Johann Umland, was born January 23, 1807. He became a master cabinetmaker in the city of Hamburg and owned a shop there which employed from six to twelve hands. His business was ruined in the economic depression following the fire of 1848, and in September, 1849, he and his family and his brother-in-law, August Heinzelmann, and his family migrated to Texas. In September, 1850, Heinrich Umland purchased 125 acres in the Thomas Bell League, three miles west of Bellville on Pines Creek, and began farming. He was killed in an accident on the Houston and Texas Central Railroad in 1869, leaving his widow and nine children an estate consisting of 175 acres of land, a gin house and cotton press, 1 wagon and 4 yoke of oxen, 6 horses, 75 head of cattle, house and kitchen furniture, $35 worth of carpenter's tools, 1 buggy, 100 head of sheep, and a growing crop. (William Umland, "A Kind of Family Record Made up the Best I Know How," University of Texas at Austin Winedale Museum, Round Top; Waller County Historical Survey Committee, *A History of Waller County*, p. 679; Waller County Deed Records, vol. D–E, p. 199; vol. R, p. 280.) Heinrich Umland is listed on the census forms as Henry Umland.

UMLAND, JACOB. MCR 1860; age 16; b. Hanover; cabinetmaker; Chappell Hill, Washington County. Jacob Umland, son of Johann Umland, was born September 19, 1843. He came to Texas with his father and worked with him in Chappell Hill; he died July 7, 1868.

UMLAND, JOHANN. MCR 1860, 1870; b. Hanover; cabinetmaker; Chappell Hill, Washington County. Johann Umland was born November 21, 1811. He came to Texas in 1854 with his father, Jacob Umland, a glassmaker from Freiburg. He purchased a one-acre lot in Chappell Hill from John Glass on August 8, 1854. Although he made furniture in Chappell Hill from that date until his retirement in 1881, a very few examples of his work have been located. Umland purchased a number of town lots in Chappell Hill in the 1860's and served as an alderman there in 1866. He was tyler of Hubert Lodge No. 67, A.F. of A.M., in 1867 and 1868, and the lodge records include several payments to him for making coffins, making a gate, and repairing a staircase. In 1870 his shop used 3,000 feet of cedar valued at $120, 100 feet of walnut valued at $8, and 100 feet of ash valued at $4 to produce 3 wardrobes valued at $90, 2 safes valued at $50, 6 bedsteads valued at $60, and repairing valued at $25. In December, 1881, he sold his property in Chappell Hill and moved to Bellville, where he died on June 13, 1886. (William Umland, "A Kind of Family Record Made up the Best I Know How," University of Texas at Austin Winedale Museum, Round Top; Washington County Deed Records, vol. P, p. 450; vol. T, pp. 375, 484; vol. W, p. 93; Hubert Lodge No. 67, A.F. of A.M. Lodge Records, Chappell Hill.)

For examples of Johann Umland's work, see 1.1 and 1.2.

URBAN, EMIL. MCR 1870; age 23; b. Prussia; cabinetmaker; Victoria, Victoria County.

VANCLEVE, L. *See* Leach, A. W.

VAUGHN, CHRISTOPHER. MCR 1870; age 37; b. Tennessee; chairmaker; Seguin, Guadalupe County.

VERSE, A. An advertisement in the *Round Rock Sentinel* (Williamson County), August 3, 1871, reads: "NOTICE. The undersigned would respectfully inform the public of Round Rock, and vicinity, that he has opened a FURNITURE SHOP in the old Masonic Hall, over the Baptist Church, and is prepared to build from Kitchen Safes, Wardrobes, Book and Show Cases, Bedsteads, and Tables down to a Baby Crib at moderate prices. Furniture repaired and revarnished. Orders solicited. A. Verse." Nothing more is known of him.

VOEGELSANG, GUS. MCR 1870; age 35; b. Prussia; cabinetmaker; San Marcos, Hays County.

VOIGHT, F.F. MCR 1860; age 25; b. Prussia; cabinetmaker; Waco, McLennan County.

VORRHEES, G.W. MCR 1860; age 30; b. Pennsylvania; cabinetmaker; Dallas, Dallas County.

VOSBURG, W.H. MCR 1870; age 55; b. New York; cabinetmaker; Sabine Pass, Jefferson County.

WAGNER, J. On August 31, 1860, J. Wagner advertised in the *Navarro Express* (Corsicana, Navarro County): "FURNITURE! FURNITURE! The undersigned having established himself in Corsicana, offers for sale a choice lot of furniture of the most approved styles and patterns. He is well prepared to manufacture cabinet work in all its various branches, as well as doors, sash, and blinds . . . Shop in front of Mr. Bright's residence." Nothing more is known of him.

WAGNER, P. MCR 1860; age 42; b. Germany; cabinetmaker; Galveston, Galveston County.

WALKER, A.A. MCR 1860, 1870; age 21 in 1860; b. Tennessee; cabinetmaker; Paris, Lamar County. In 1860 A. A. Walker was a partner of Willet Babcock in the Paris cabinetmaking firm of Walker and Babcock; *see* Babcock, Willet. That partnership was later dissolved, and in 1870 Walker had his own shop in Paris, where he used horse power and 3,300 feet of wood valued at $105 to produce tables, beds, bookcases, and washstands valued at $1,350. He was a veteran of the Mexican War and in later years abandoned the trade of cabinetmaking to practice dentistry in Paris. He died about 1900. (A. W. Neville, *The History of Lamar County*, p. 108.)

WALKER, H. MCR 1860; age 29; b. Germany; cabinetmaker; Galveston, Galveston County.

WALKER AND BABCOCK. *See* Babcock, Willet.

WALKER AND HARR. MCR 1860. The carpentry firm of Walker and Harr, in Kaufman, Kaufman County, was capitalized at $500 in 1860 and employed two men. The firm used 2,000 feet of lumber valued at $600 to produce 2 houses valued at $425, 7 bureaus valued at $177, 7 wardrobes valued at $105, 10 tables valued at $40, and miscellaneous articles valued at $300.

WALLACE, ELLIS A. MCR 1860; age 59; b. South Carolina; wheelwright; Angelina County. In 1860, Ellis A. Wallace had a chair factory which used 25,000 feet of lumber valued at $170 to make chairs and "other articles" valued at $720.

WALLACE, THOMAS P. MCR 1870; age 17; b. Texas; apprentice to cabinetmaker; Gonzales, Gonzales County.

WARD, C.J. The *San Marcos Weekly Pioneer*, June 5, 1869, carried an advertisement from C. J. Ward and his brother, W. D. Ward: "C. J. WARD AND BROTHER, Manufacturers of Furniture, San Marcos, Texas, Are prepared at all times, to make to order, at lowest cash rates, the following articles in their line, viz: Sofas, Ottomans, Bedsteads, Bureaus, Tables, Lounges, Wardrobes, Chairs, Cribs, Mattresses, etc., etc., etc. Repairing done neatly and with dispatch. N.B.—undertaking

done in the best style, at short notice." Nothing more is known of these two men.

WARD, H. H. Ward was an early Austin entrepreneur whose enterprises included house carpentry and cabinetmaking. He announced in the *Texas Sentinel*, April 29, 1840, that he had opened the "CITY CABINET WARE HOUSE AND JOINERS SHOP in Austin. The subscriber has located himself in this city for the sole purpose of carrying on the house carpenter and joiner's business in all its branches, as also building in general of every description and material. His shop is large and commodious and can accomodate 15 or 20 workmen. Having thirteen years experience on the public works in the state of New York (for which the best evidence can be produced from the State authorities) he feels himself fully competent as an undertaker or contractor, to go through with any work which he may venture to engage in. Relying solely on his own exertions, he is determined not to be thrown from the track or outdistanced by any, and therefore only asks from a generous public that share of patronage which merit alone may entitle him to. H. Ward. N.B. One or two benches will be constantly employed at the cabinet work." Three months later, he advertised again in the *Texas Sentinel* (August 15, 1840) that "tables, stands and desks, China presses, bedsteads and cots, wardrobes and book cases and drawers, milk and meat safes, cupboards and lockers, will be made to order, at the City Ware Room, by calling on H. Ward. August 1." Nothing more is known of him.

WARD, W.D. *See* Ward, C. J.

WARMMOCK, JOHN. MCR 1870; age 26; b. Tennessee; works in cabinet shop; Centreville, Leon County.

WASSEN, SAMUEL. MCR 1850; age 45; b. South Carolina; cabinetmaker; Rusk County.

WASSENICH, JOSEPH. MCR 1870; age 44; b. Prussia; furniture merchant; Seguin, Guadalupe County. Although he is listed on the population schedule of the census return as a furniture merchant, Joseph Wassenich's entry on the products-of-industry schedule for the same year indicates that he used materials valued at $200 to produce furniture valued at $600. His advertisement in the *Guadalupe Times*, August 14, 1875, confirms that he was both a cabinetmaker and a furniture importer: "JOSEPH WASSENICH, MANUFACTURER and dealer in FURNITURE, Keeps constantly on hand a large assortment of well-made furniture; consisting in part of Parlor Furniture, Hat Racks, Bureaus, Wardrobes, Extension Tables, Safes, &c. A large assortment of HOME-MADE bedsteads, chairs, and tables always on hand. JUST RECEIVED: A large assortment of Wall Paper, Window Shades, Clocks, Looking Glasses, Children's Carriages, Oval, Square, and Rustic Picture Frames, Picture Nails, Cords and Tassels, Picture Glass any size up to 26 by 39 inches, Mouldings and backing, Enamelled Cloth for Table covers, Woollen Table covers, Wall Brackets &c. If you would buy CHEAP AND GOOD FURNITURE, etc., go to JOSEPH WASSENICH, West of Masonic Building, Seguin, Texas."

WEAVER, HENRY H. MCR 1870; age 30; b. Kentucky; cabinetmaker; Mount Vernon, Titus County.

WEBBER, HENRY C. MCR 1850; age 35; b. Germany; cabinetmaker; Liberty County.

WEIBERG, F. MCR 1860; age 35; b. Germany; cabinetmaker; Galveston, Galveston County.

WEIGHLY, WILLIAM. MCR 1860; age 36; b. Germany; cabinetmaker; Galveston, Galveston County.

WELLKEG, R.J. MCR 1860; age 32; b. Poland; cabinet work; Rusk, Cherokee County.

WENDLER, CARL. MCR 1860; age 56; b. Prussia; joiner; Fredericksburg, Gillespie County. In 1860, Wendler had a one-man shop which used timber valued at $250 to produce furniture valued at $700.

WESSENDORF, ANTON. MCR 1870; age 34; b. Prussia; cabinetmaker; Stafford, Fort Bend County.

WESSENDORF, B. MCR 1860; age 30; b. Germany; cabinetmaker; Galveston, Galveston County. In the mid-1850's, Wessendorf worked in Richmond, Fort Bend County. He advertised in the *Richmond Reporter*, August 2, 1856: "FURNITURE &c., The subscriber keeps constantly on hand Wardrobes, Safes, Tables, Washstands, Lounges, &c., which will be sold cheap. He is also prepared to execute any order of work in his line. Repairing done on shortest notice. B. Wessendorf, opposite Mrs. Battle's." A desk attributed to Wessendorf is in the Fort Bend County Historical Museum.

WEST, JOHN. MCR 1870; age 23; b. Kentucky; cabinetmaker; Jefferson, Marion County.

WESTERFIELD, G.W. MCR 1860; age 33; b. Germany; cabinetmaker; San Marcos, Hays County.

WESTFALL, ———. Rusk County historian Garland R. Farmer says in *The Realm of Rusk County*, p. 39, that "Mr. Westfall came to Mount Enterprise from Germany . . . About 1840 the Westfalls operated a factory making furniture, farm implements, and caskets. This factory stood by a mound between the old and new highway at the Laneville and Shiloh crossing." Nothing more is known of this man.

WETSEL, LEWIS. MCR 1850, 1860, 1870; age 23 in 1850; b. Illinois; cabinetmaker; McKinney, Collin County. According to Land Certificate Number 79, issued by the commissioners of Peters Colony, Lewis Wetsel came to Texas as a twenty-year-old widower in 1847 (Collin County Deed Records, book C, p. 43). He purchased lot 10, block 2, in McKinney on March 30, 1850 (ibid., book B, p. 69), and opened his cabinet shop on that site. In 1856 he received a belated headright grant of 320 acres in Collin County (Collin County Deed Records, vol. E, p. 162), but he continued to live and work in McKinney. In the late sixties and early seventies he was associated in business with cabinetmaker Isaac Crouch, and in 1870 their firm, Crouch and Wetsel, produced $7,000 worth of furniture, making it one of the major cabinetmaking firms in Texas. On June 3, 1871, the *McKinney Weekly Enquirer* reported that "the handsome store-house of Lew Wetsel on the East side of the square is nearly completed, and presents a beautiful appearance, adding much to the looks of our square." Wetsel seems to have suffered financial reverses in the mid-seventies, when several suits were filed against him by tool and wholesale furniture companies (Collin County Deed Records, vol. F, p. 151; vol. G, p. 213; vol. H, p. 350). On January 1, 1876, he mortgaged a "sixteen-inch swing Victor lathe and attachments" for $58.75 (ibid., vol. H, p. 350). The date of his death is not known.

WETSEL, PETER. MCR 1860; age 42; b. Pennsylvania; cabinet workman; McKinney, Collin County. Peter Wetsel or Wetzel was in Collin County as early as April 9, 1849, when he purchased 40 acres of land from William Davis (Collin County Deed Records, book A, p. 267).

WHITE, C.R. MCR 1860; age 28; b. Prussia; cabinetmaker; Belton, Bell County.

WHITEHEAD, J.M. MCR 1860. Whitehead, of Jamestown, Smith County, advertised in the *Tyler Reporter*, February 9, 1859: "WORK! WORK! WORK! The undersigned take this method of informing the public that they have this day associated together as partners in the manufacture of HOUSEHOLD FURNITURE, Such as Bureaus, Wardrobes, Secretaries, Safes, Bedsteads, Centre, Dressing, Dining, and Folding Tables; together with any and all other articles of Furniture usually manufactured in a Southern Cabinet Shop. All of which they propose to sell as low or lower than any other establishment in the State—FOR CASH!—or cash arrangements, only. Call and examine our stock. WHITEHEAD, HALTOM & Co., Jamestown, January 18th, 1859." The next year Whitehead reported that his shop employed three men and used 8,000 feet of pine valued at $160 and 2,000 feet of oak valued at $100 to produce 50 bedsteads valued at $600, 5 bureaus valued at $100, 6 safes valued at $100, and "other work" valued at $100.

WICKER, E.W. MCR 1860; age 44; b. Kentucky; cabinetmaker; Pilot Point, Denton County.

WILCOX AND COMPANY. The La Grange *True Issue*, February 12, 1859, carried an advertisement for "Wilcox & Co., Cabinet Makers and Carriage Manufacturers," that reads in part: "They keep in their employment the best workmen, and are prepared to make bureaus with or without mirrors, dressing stands, wardrobes, tables, sofas, etc., and coaches, hacks, carriages, buggies, sulkies, etc. . . . Shop on Colorado Street, east of the La Grange Hotel." Nothing more is known about this firm.

WILEY, LEROY. MCR 1850; age 19; b. Alabama; cabinetmaker; Rusk County.

WILEY, TAYLOR. MCR 1850; age 57; b. North Carolina; cabinetmaker; Rusk County.

WILKINS, JOHN. MCR 1850; age 37; b. Virginia; cabinetmaker; Jackson County. A note on the census return says that Wilkins was "deaf and dumb."

WILLIAMS, CHRISTIAN. MCR 1850; age 27; b. Germany; cabinetmaker; Austin, Travis County.

WILLIAMS, COMMORDORE. MCR 1870; age 45; b. Tennessee; cabinetmaker; White Rock, Hunt County.

WILLIAMS, J. MCR 1850; age 50; b. Pennsylvania; cabinetmaker; Upshur County.

WILLIAMS, JOHN W. MCR 1860; age 27; b. Kentucky; cabinetmaker; Dallas, Dallas County.

WILLIAMS, L.R. MCR 1860; age 34; b. Mississippi; cabinetmaker; Paris, Lamar County.

WILLIAMS, MONROE. MCR 1870; age 22; b. Mississippi; apprentice cabinet manufactory; Paris, Lamar County.

WILLIAMSON, ——. *See* Swingle, Alfred.

WILLIAMSON, BOB. A note in the Corsicana *Navarro Express* (Navarro County), January 7, 1860, reads: "We are glad to learn that Bob Williamson and 'Dan' Rice are going to establish a cabinet shop soon in our town. One has long been needed, and they certainly will make money." Nothing else is known about these men.

WILLIAMSON, DALE. MCR 1860; age 39; b. Tennessee; cabinetmaker; Palestine, Anderson County.

WILLIAMSON, MARCUS. MCR 1850; age 33; b. New York; cabinetmaker; Houston, Harris County. Marcus Williamson advertised in the Houston *Democratic Telegraph and Texas Register*, January 18, 1847: "FURNITURE WARE ROOM. The Subscriber has just opened a Furniture Ware Room, on Main Street, a few doors below the Houston House, where he has a general assortment of furniture, consisting in part of Mahogany, Cane, and Wood-Seat Chairs, Sofas, Divans, Plain and Toilet Bureaus, Mahogany, Black Walnut, and Cherry Dining Tables; Marble Top Centre Tables; Card and Work Tables; Office Desks; Office Stools; Piano Stools; Bedsteads, Hat Stands, Looking-escapes, Looking-plates, &c. &c."

WILLITIER, C. MCR 1860; age 33; b. France; cabinetmaker; Galveston, Galveston County.

WINDIKER, F. MCR 1860; age 36; b. Hesse; cabinetmaker; Houston, Harris County.

WINKEL, FREDERICK. MCR 1850; age 23; b. Germany; cabinetmaker; Fredericksburg, Gillespie County. Frederick Winkel of Peine, Hanover, came to Texas on the *Hercules* in 1845 (Chester William Geue and

Ethel Hander Geue, *A New Land Beckoned*, p. 162). In 1850, he was Fredericksburg's most important cabinetmaker, employing three hands and using timber valued at $150 to produce bedsteads, chairs, and furniture valued at $1,784. Curiously, no examples of his furniture seem to have survived.

WINKEL, HENRY. MCR 1850; age 26; b. Germany; cabinetmaker; Fredericksburg, Gillespie County.

WISSEMAN, CONRAD. MCR 1850, 1860, 1870; age 33 in 1850; carpenter in 1850; cabinetmaker in 1860 and 1870; Fredericksburg, Gillespie County. Conrad Wisseman was born January 1, 1816, in Raboldshausen, Hesse-Nassau, the son of an Evangelical minister. He left Germany in January, 1846, and arrived in Galveston on April 11, 1846. He proceeded directly to Fredericksburg, where he built his house and shop on Lot 247, Main Street. About 1885 he moved to Beaver Creek, Mason County, where he died on March 31, 1903. (C. L. Wisseman, Kerrville, July 13, 1973, to LT.)

WITTEBORG, CASPAR. MCR 1870; age 49; b. Prussia; cabinetmaker; Brenham, Washington County. Witteborg was a prominent Washington County cabinetmaker for a number of years. He was at Chappell Hill on August 1, 1854, when he advertised in the *Texas Advertiser* (Columbia) as "C. Whitteberg, Cabinet Maker, Chappell Hill," saying he was "prepared to do work in the best style, and will always be found in his shop, opposite the hotel." Two years later he advertised in the *Brenham Enquirer*, December 5, 1856, that "C. WITTEBORG, Cabinet Manufacturer, Chappell Hill, Texas, manufactures all articles of general utility, which he warrants." He sold his town lot in Chappell Hill to fellow cabinetmaker Johann Umland in 1866 and moved to Brenham, where he reported in 1870 that his shop employed two hands and used 8,000 feet of pine valued at $260, 200 feet of walnut valued at $14, 200 feet of cedar valued at $10, and 200 feet of ash valued at $10 to produce 12 bedsteads valued at $96, 12 wardrobes valued at $300, 25 tables valued at $125, bureaus valued at $200, and "repairing and other furniture valued at $1,000." The *Brenham Banner*, January 8, 1874, carried an advertisement for his shop on Ant Street, describing him as "Manufacturer and Dealer in Furniture, such as Bedsteads, Wardrobes, Sofas, Lounges, Chairs, Bureaus, in fact every article de-

sired by housekeepers," and added that "UNDERTAKING will continue to receive prompt attention." Later in that same year, on September 24, the *Banner* noted that "Mr. C. Witteborg has bought out Mr. J. L. Compton, and can now be found at his old stand, next door to R. Hoffman, with a full and choice selection of furniture on hand." On November 10, 1876, Witteborg advertised in the *Banner* that, "on account of ill health, I am offering my entire stock of furniture at cost, in order to close out my business." However, his store was still open when he died in March, 1877. At that time his letterhead read, "C. Witteborg, Cabinet Maker and Dealer in Furniture, Paints, Oils, Turpentine, Varnish, Etc." The inventory of his estate lists his tools: "1 turning lathe; 33 wooden vices, 5 wooden vices, 10 framing saws, 1 paint mill, 1 saw sett, 1 grind stone, 3 hand saws, 1 mitre box, 1 lot cabinet tools, benches, and chest, 1 lot pine lumber, 1 lot walnut lumber." It also lists the contents of his store, which included pigments, oils, bedsteads, chairs, safes, wardrobes, lounges, rocking chairs, extension tables, saloon tables, folding tables, secretaries, sofa lounges, bed lounges, oval lounges, wash stands, cribs, coffins, glass, and mirror frames. (Washington County Probate Records, file 363.)

WOBBE, HENRY. MCR 1870; age 40; b. Prussia; cabinetmaker; Frelsburg, Colorado County.

WOLDERT, EDWARD. MCR 1850, 1870; age 19 in 1850; b. Germany; cabinetmaker; San Augustine, San Augustine County, in 1850. In 1870, Edward Woldert was working at Etna, Smith County. He was probably a relative of J. George Woldert.

WOLDERT, J. GEORGE. MCR 1850; age 35; b. Germany; cabinetmaker; San Augustine, San Augustine County. J. George Woldert first advertised in the San Augustine *Red-Lander* on May 19, 1842, saying that he had "established a permanent furniture establishment in this city . . . Orders for any description of furniture will be promptly filled, and any peculiarity of pattern desired will be faithfully executed. His furniture ware-room is on Main Street, within a short distance of the printing office, where he now has on hand and for sale low, for ready cash, the following articles, to wit: SETTEES, SIDE-BOARDS, TABLES, ROCKING CHAIRS, WASH-STANDS, CUPBOARDS, PRESSES, WARDROBES, CENTRE-TABLES, BUREAUS, SOFAS, WRITING DESKS, &c, &c, together with many other articles for House Keepers and new Married people; who are respectfully invited to call and examine for themselves. Corn and Cotton will be taken in payment for all furniture." In 1850, Woldert was one of two cabinetmakers in San Augustine whose annual product exceeded $500. (The other was George W. Blake.) He reported that, in that year, he employed two men and used $100 worth of walnut and $100 worth of cherry to produce furniture valued at $1,500. Woldert apparently left San Augustine in the mid-1850's and lived for a while in San Antonio, for an advertisement in the *San Antonio Ledger*, August 23, 1858, says: "Circumstances compel me to move to the Eastern part of the state. Selling all goods. J. G. Woldert." San Augustine historian George L. Crockett says that Woldert lived at the corner of Main and Congress streets in San Augustine and that he later moved to Tyler, Smith County (*Two Centuries in East Texas*, p. 117).

WOLFGANG, WILLIAM. MCR 1870; age 42; b. Hanover; works for cabinetmaker; Galveston, Galveston County. W. Richardson and Co.'s *Galveston Directory for 1866–7* lists Wolfgang as a cabinetmaker with Root and Davis; John H. Heller's *Galveston City Directory 1872* lists him as an employee of B. R. Davis and Bro., 66 Strand.

WOLZ, FREDERICK. MCR 1860; age 32; b. Germany; cabinet workman; Marshall, Harrison County. Wolz migrated from Germany to New Orleans in 1845 and came to Marshall to practice his trade in 1851. In 1860, his shop employed two men and produced 50 bedsteads valued at $650, 6 cribs valued at $72, 4 wardrobes valued at $100, and 12 washstands valued at $60. The shop was on the first floor of a two-story building on West Houston Avenue, with the Wolz family living quarters on the second floor. Wolz served in the Confederate army and was wounded at the battle of Mansfield, Louisiana, after which he was detailed to work in the Confederate arsenal at Marshall, making gun stocks. He was a prominent citizen of Marshall, owned a considerable amount of property, and was active in county Democratic politics. He died in 1871. (Harrison County Conservation Society, *Heritage Sketch and Cook Book*.)

WOOD, B.D. MCR 1860; age 30; b. Tennessee; cabinet workman; Orange, Orange County.

WOOD, DAVIS H. MCR 1870; age 36; b. Tennessee; cabinet workman; Henderson, Rusk County.

WOODISON, WILLIAM. MCR 1850; age 38; b. Pennsylvania; cabinetmaker; Walker County.

WOODS, J.W. MCR 1860; age 35; b. North Carolina; cabinetmaker; Prairie Point, Wise County.

WOOFTER, E. MCR 1860; age 30; b. Virginia; cabinetmaker; Austin, Travis County. Woofter was a partner in 1859 with J. W. England in the Austin cabinetmaking firm of England and Woofter; *see* England, J. W.

WRIGHT, FRANCIS. Francis Wright advertised in the *Huntsville Recorder* (Walker County), October 15, 1857, as "Francis Wright, Cabinet Maker, Huntsville, Texas," saying that he had "opened a furniture shop in the house formerly occupied by M. Moore, where he is prepared on short notice to make Tables, Wardrobes, Safes, Bureaus, Writing desks, Sofas, Black walnut chairs, mattrasses, and in fact every article usually kept in furniture establishments." Nothing more is known of him.

WRIGHT, GLASSBERRY. MCR 1870; age 23; b. Arkansas; chairmaker; Ladonia, Fannin County.

WRIGHT, HOLLAND. MCR 1860; age 36; b. New Hampshire; cabinetmaker; Liberty, Liberty County.

WRIGHT, SIMON. MCR 1850; age 48; b. Ohio; cabinetmaker; Hunt County.

ZERBST, CHARLES W. MCR 1860; age 60; b. Prussia; cabinetmaker; Wheelock, Brazos County.

ZIMBERHAUSEN, JOSEPH. MCR 1870; age 40; b. Prussia; cabinetmaker; Pedernales, Travis County.

ZINRAM, ADOLPH. MCR 1860, 1870; age 48 in 1860; b. Braunschweig; farmer in 1860; joiner in 1870; New Braunfels, Comal County. A draw-leaf extension table signed "A. Zinram / 1871 / 23 December" is pictured by Cecilia Steinfeldt and Donald L. Stover, *Early Texas Furniture and Decorative Arts*, p. 76, where it is said that Zinram immigrated from Walkenried, Braunschweig, in 1854.

ZUENT, JOSEPH. MCR 1870; age 24; b. Switzerland; joiner; New Braunfels, Comal County.

ZWETSCH, FRANK. MCR 1870; age 44; b. Prussia; cabinetmaker; Galveston, Galveston County. Frank Zwetsch is listed in John H. Heller's *Galveston City Directory 1872* as a cabinet workman living at 513 East Avenue L.

Appendix

The following tables are summaries of the information on Texas cabinet-makers contained in the manuscript census returns for schedule 5 of the United States censuses of 1850, 1860, and 1870. This schedule, referred to as the schedule of products of industry, was an innovation of the 1850 census. It included all "productive" industries except firms producing less than five hundred dollars' worth of goods and the usual household manufactures. The schedule contained blanks for the answers to fourteen different questions concerning the operation of each shop. Because of the use of printed instructions to the enumerators concerning each of the fourteen inquiries, the 1850 census of manufactures is much more accurate than previous census schedules had been. The 1860 census, the returns of which were tabulated under the pressures of wartime Washington, is less accurate than its predecessor, but the inaccuracies lie mainly in discrepancies between the manuscript returns and the printed census and are the results of errors in tabulating the manuscript returns. The manuscript returns for the 1860 census contain much more specific information about the forms of furniture produced in each shop than the 1850 returns, and this information is included in Table 2.

Francis Amasa Walker, the superintendent of the 1870 census, wished to reform the entire method of taking that census in order to place it on a sounder statistical basis, but his efforts were defeated in Congress. He was, however, able to effect some alterations in the questions on schedule 5. These alterations are reflected in Table 3 in reference to numbers of machines and number of months in operation. In some cases the enumerators made a note on the types of machines used in the shop. This information is contained in the entries in the Checklist of Texas Cabinetmakers under the names of the appropriate cabinetmakers.

The answers to the question on capital are generally considered unreliable by census scholars, and they have been omitted from all three tables. As Francis Amasa Walker said, "No man in business knows what he is worth—far less can he say what portion of his estate is to be treated as capital" (quoted by Meyer H. Fishbein, "The Censuses of Manufacturers: 1810–1890," *National Archives Accessions* 57 [1963]:12). In a few cases it is difficult to tell what portion of the annual product of a particular craftsman represents furniture and what portion represents coffins, repairing, wagon building, or some other activity. Where the census enumerator's notations have made it possible to separate these, we have done so on the table, placing the non-furniture-producing activities in brackets and omitting their value from the column headed "Value and Kind of Furniture," except for coffins, which are regularly included with furniture. In cases where the residences of cabinetmakers as given on the schedule of population differ from the location of their shops as recorded on schedule 5, the residences have been placed in brackets. On the 1870 census, it is obvious that some furniture dealers who assembled cases of knocked-down furniture were listed as manufacturers, although this was contrary to the spirit of the enumerators' instructions; such furniture had already been tabulated at its original place of manufacture. With the exception of these few pitfalls, we feel that the statistics in schedule 5 give an accurate picture of the cabinetmaker's trade as it was carried on in the larger shops in Texas during the middle decades of the nineteenth century.

TABLE 1. *Texas Cabinet Shops with an Annual Product Exceeding $500 in 1850*

	Total Value of Furniture Produced	Feet of Wood Used	Value of Wood Used	Kind of Motive Power	Number of Male Hands[a]	Average Monthly Wage, Male	Number of Female Hands	Average Monthly Wage, Female	Value of Annual Product
Galveston County	$7,000								
Helmut Conrad Kroll, Galveston		40,000	$1,200	Hand	2	$40	—	—	$3,000
Daniel Lochied, Galveston		60,000	1,500	Hand	3	40	—	—	4,000
Gillespie County	2,676								
Joseph D. Goodall and Co.		—	100	Water	1	30	—	—	892
Frederick Winkel, Fredericksburg		—	150	Hand	3	25	—	—	1,784
Harrison County	?								
A. D. Burress, Marshall		3,000	500	Hand	4	25	—	—	[4,500—wagons and furniture][b]
Montgomery County	700								
Irvin and Irvin, Montgomery		3,000	60	Horse	2	25	—	—	700
Red River County	2,000								
James B. Shanahan, Clarksville		15,000	300	Hand	3	40	1	$8	2,000
Rusk County	?								
Job A. Dean		2,000	200	Hand	1	50	—	—	—
Abner H. Stith, Henderson		2,500	250	Hand	2	50	—	—	2,000
Sabine County	2,400								
George Bartlett		3,000	115	Hand	2	40	—	—	600
Martin J. Brown		2,000	50	Hand	1	40	—	—	500
Henry Meyers		1,300	40	Hand	1	40	—	—	800
William S. Summers		2,000	90	Hand	1	40	—	—	500
San Augustine County	2,300								
George W. Blake, San Augustine		—	200	Hand	2	35	—	—	800
J. George Woldert, San Augustine		—	200	Hand	2	25	—	—	1,500

Source: United States Census, manuscript census returns for Texas, schedule 5 (products of industry), 1850.

[a]This usually refers to the number of people working in the shop, including the owner.

[b]Bracketed items are not included in furniture totals.

TABLE 2. *Texas Cabinet Shops with an Annual Product Exceeding $500 in 1860*

	Total Value of Furniture Produced	Feet of Wood Used	Value of Wood Used	Kind of Motive Power	Number of Hands[a]	Average Monthly Wage	Value and Kind of Furniture Produced during Census Year
Angelina County	$ 1,920						
Charles Guinn		20,000	$150	Hand	1	$60	$ 600—chairs
James M. Jones		12,000	80	Hand	1	40	600—chairs
Ellis A. Wallace		25,000	170	Hand	1	40	720—chairs
Austin County	2,000						
H. Spencer Huby, Hempstead		—	800	Hand	2	50	2,000
Bell County	1,500						
Alonzo Beeman, Belton		3,000	120	Hand	1[b]	35	1,500—1,000 chairs
Caldwell County	1,475						
Anderson and John E. Dorris, Lockhart		—	135	Hand	2	25	675—450 common chairs
Stephen J. Dorris, Lockhart		—	160	Hand	1	25	800—600 common chairs
Cooke County	850						
William G. Fisher, Gainesville		8,000	320	Hand	3	50	850—500 pieces
Denton County	2,350						
W. T. Skinner, Denton [Carter]		15,000	600	Hand	2	50	2,350—100 tables, $800; 50 safes, $750; 100 bedsteads, $800
Freestone County	?						
H. P. Daviss, Fairfield		10,000	300	Hand	2½	50	[2,400—furniture and sash][c]
Galveston County	1,692						
J. F. W. Ahrens, Galveston		8,000	480	Hand	2	60	1,692—24 desks, $960; 18 bookcases, $540; 48 tables, $192
Gillespie County	10,100						
Friedrich Gentmann, Fredericksburg		—	300	Hand	1	40	900—all kinds of furniture
Johann Adam Kunz, Fredericksburg		—	500	Hand	1	40	1,500—all kinds of furniture
William Leilich, Fredericksburg		—	350	Hand	1	40	1,200—all kinds of furniture
Johann Martin Loeffler, Fredericksburg		—	300	Hand	1	40	800—all kinds of furniture
John Petri, Fredericksburg		—	150	Hand	1	40	600—all kinds of furniture

TABLE 2. *Continued*

	Total Value of Furniture Produced	Feet of Wood Used	Value of Wood Used	Kind of Motive Power	Number of Hands[a]	Average Monthly Wage	Value and Kind of Furniture Produced during Census Year
Christof Schaeper, Fredericksburg		—	$250	Hand	1	$40	$ 700—all kinds of furniture
Jacob Schneider, Fredericksburg		—	400	Hand	1	40	1,500—all kinds of furniture
Christian Staats, Fredericksburg		—	500	Hand	1	40	1,500—all kinds of furniture
Johann Peter Tatsch, Fredericksburg		—	200	Hand	1	40	700—all kinds of furniture
Carl Wendler, Fredericksburg		—	250	Hand	1	40	700—all kinds of furniture
Grayson County	$ 800						
Samuel F. Gault, Sherman		2,000	80	Oxen	1	35	800—100 articles furniture
Guadalupe County	3,550						
John M. Brem, Seguin		4,000	120	Horse	2	50	2,550—1,500 chairs, $2,250; miscellaneous, $300
Bartholemew Buerger, Seguin		2,800	160	Hand	1	50	1,000—furniture
Harrison County	882						
Frederick Wolz, Marshall		—	300	Hand	2	39	882—50 bedsteads, $650; 6 cribs, $72; 4 wardrobes, $100; 12 washstands, $60
Hopkins County	3,500						
William W. Smith, White Oak		20,000	500	Horse	5	30	3,500
Houston County	3,888						
W. J. Foster, Crockett		3,000	675	Horse	3	50	3,300—house furniture, $3,000; coffin making, $300 [repairing gins, $500]
H. T. Sanders, Beat 1		1,500	30	Hand	2	50	588—350 chairs, $400; 7 bedsteads, $77; 3 tables, $12; 10 spinning wheels, $50; other work, $25; 4 coffins, $24

TABLE 2. *Continued*

	Total Value of Furniture Produced	Feet of Wood Used	Value of Wood Used	Kind of Motive Power	Number of Hands[a]	Average Monthly Wage	Value and Kind of Furniture Produced during Census Year
Kaufman County	$ 1,122						
J. D. Hall, Kaufman		5,000	$ 150	Hand	1	$40	$ 500—14 bedsteads, $140; 1 wardrobe, $20; 10 tables, $40; other articles, $300
Walker and Harr, Kaufman		2,000	600	Hand	2	50	622—7 bureaus, $177; 7 wardrobes, $105; 10 tables, $40; miscellaneous, $300 [2 houses, $425]
Lamar County	10,500						
Overstreet and Rodgers, Paris		25,000	800	Hand	5	33	4,500—400 articles furniture
Walker and Babcock, Paris		35,000	1,250	Hand	6	35	6,000—500 articles furniture
Lavaca County	1,200						
Valentin Riemenschnider, Hallettsville		3,000	100	Hand	2[d]	50	1,200—20 bedsteads, bureaus, safes, and other articles
McLennan County	4,032						
William H. Anderson, Waco		5,000	235	Hand	2	25	1,390—6 wardrobes, $210; 24 safes, $480; mixed articles, $700
Andrew J. Conrow, Waco		13,588	655	Horse	7	21	2,642—mixed furniture [sash and doors, $848; blinds, $261]
Navarro County	4,000						
Crawford and Porter, Corsicana [Muskite]		2,000	600	Steam	5	39	4,000—cabinet work
Rusk County	1,152						
F. Lemuel Duncan, Henderson		—	100	Horse	1	75	1,152—96 bedsteads
San Augustine County	2,500						
[Ransom] Horn and Brother, San Augustine		20,000	300	Horse	1	32	2,500—250 pieces cabinet work [6 guns, $180]
Smith County	5,150						
S. C. Crone, Tyler		12,000	260	Horse	1	40	630—30 bedsteads, $240; 3 safes, $30; 60 chairs, $60; wardrobes, bureaus, etc., $300

TABLE 2. *Continued*

	Total Value of Furniture Produced	Feet of Wood Used	Value of Wood Used	Kind of Motive Power	Number of Hands[a]	Average Monthly Wage	Value and Kind of Furniture Produced during Census Year
Joshua McClung, Mount Carmel		9,000	$200	Horse	1	$50	$ 620—30 bedsteads, $300; 6 bureaus, $120; 4 safes, $100; 80 chairs, $100
Rogers and Sheppard, Tyler		20,000	400	Horse	3	40	3,000—75 bedsteads, $1,000; bureaus, wardrobes, etc., $1,200; other furniture, $800
J. M. Whitehead, Jamestown		10,000	260	Hand	3	50	900—50 bedsteads, $600; 5 bureaus, $100; 6 safes, $100; other work, $100
Travis County	$2,000						
William Schmidtz, Austin		—	600	Hand	2	50	2,000—furniture
Van Zandt County	1,000						
Josh Ballard, Canton		—	150	Hand	1	40	1,000—1,248 chairs and 200 wheels[e]
Walker County	4,700						
Hopkins and Creager, Huntsville		5,800	116	Hand	2	45	1,600
Outlaw and Talley, Huntsville		7,000	140	Hand	3	30	1,800—coffins, furniture, and sundries
State Penitentiary, Huntsville		26,000	400	Hand	4	19	1,300
Wood County	1,000						
J. W. Davenport, Quitman		6,000	300	Hand	3	25	1,000—cabinet work

Source: United States Census, manuscript census returns for Texas, schedule 5 (products of industry), 1860.

[a]This usually refers to the number of people working in the shop, including the owner.

[b]Beeman had one employee in addition to himself, according to the population schedule; his name was D. McNall, and he lived in Beeman's household.

[c]Bracketed items are not included in furniture totals.

[d]One of Riemenschnider's two hands was female; she earned an average of $12 per month.

[e]The value here seems low and may be an error, as the average price of a common chair in 1860 was between $1.00 and $1.25. "Wheels" probably means wagon wheels.

TABLE 3. *Texas Cabinet Shops with an Annual Product Exceeding $500 in 1870*

	Total Value of Furniture Produced	Feet of Wood Used	Value of Wood Used	Kind of Motive Power	Number of Machines	Horse-power	Number of Hands[a]	Value and Kind of Furniture
Austin County	$3,075							
Rudolph Blaschke, Cat Spring		—	$ 150	Hand	—	—	1	$ 600—20 tables, $200; 10 cabinets, $400
Gottfried Buescher, Industry [New Ulm]		—	375	Hand	—	—	2	1,500—furniture, $1,000; 300 chairs, $500
Frederick Buntzel, Cat Spring		—	175	Hand	—	—	1	700—15 cabinets, $600; 4 desks, $100
Leander Mosscross, Hempstead		2,000	60	Steam	5	10	3	275—200 hidebottom chairs (in operation for one month)[b]
Bell County	950							
William Tuder, Belton [Aiken]		3,000	100	Hand	—	—	1	950—25 bedsteads, $200; 100 chairs, $150; 20 tables, $100; 50 lounges, $300; other items, $200 (in operation for ten months)
Caldwell County	734							
John Lyles, Lockhart		3,000	150	Horse	2	2	1	734—42 bedsteads, $504; 9 tables, $90; 9 candlestands, $140
Cherokee County	600							
Hughes and Stallings, Rusk		—	250	Horse	1	—	2	600 (in operation for nine months)
Collin County	9,000							
Crouch and Wetsel, McKinney		—	—	Hand	—	—	3	7,000
James Foster, Highland [Mantua]		—	1,000	Hand	—	—	1	2,000

TABLE 3. *Continued*

	Total Value of Furniture Produced	Feet of Wood Used	Value of Wood Used	Kind of Motive Power	Number of Machines	Horse-power	Number of Hands[a]	Value and Kind of Furniture
Comal County	$3,700							
Eugen Benno Ebensberger, New Braunfels		—	$ 400	Hand	—	—	2	$1,200
Edward Eberhard, New Braunfels		—	150	Hand	1	—	1	600
Johann Michael Jahn, New Braunfels		—	100	Hand	—	—	1	600—furniture
Ludwig Stroemer, New Braunfels		—	300	Hand	1	—	1	800—furniture
Karl Thiele, New Braunfels		—	200	Hand	—	—	1	500
Dallas County	2,850							
Joshua Addington, Dallas		—	1,100	Hand	—	—	2	1,800—furniture [repairs, $400][c]
Asa W. Morton, Dallas		—	500	Hand	—	—	1	1,050—furniture
Ellis County	7,500							
John H. Spalding, Waxahachie		—	4,000	Hand	—	—	3	7,500
Fannin County	800							
Theodore B. Revell, Bonham		—	300	Hand	—	—	2	800
Fayette County	2,400							
Heinrich Harigel, La Grange		2,000	90	Hand	—	—	1	2,400—bedsteads, bureaus, tables [repairs, $300]
Freestone County	2,500							
John J. Cullison, Fairfield		—	600	Hand	—	—	3	1,000
Charlie Miller, Fairfield		—	500	Hand	—	—	2	1,500

TABLE 3. *Continued*

	Total Value of Furniture Produced	Feet of Wood Used	Value of Wood Used	Kind of Motive Power	Number of Machines	Horse-power	Number of Hands[a]	Value and Kind of Furniture
Galveston County	$3,935							
E. Beck and C. Miller, Galveston		3,500	$170	Hand	—	—	2	$1,175—20 desks, $300; 10 wardrobes, $375; 20 safes, $500 [repairs, $500]
C. H. L. Gerloff, Galveston		—	600	Hand	1	—	1	1,000—turning [billiard balls and fancy articles, $100]
William F. Howe, Galveston		5,000	150	Hand	1	—	1	1,325—75 cots, $300; tables, desks, etc., $1,025 [150 mattresses, $700; repairs, $575]
William W. Patch, Galveston		3,000	120	Hand	—	—	2	435—30 cots, $35; 10 desks, $200; 20 tables, $200 [50 mattresses, $200; repairs, $1,000][d]
Gonzales County	1,786							
John William August Kleine, Gonzales		5,000	250	Hand	1	—	1	1,786—3–4 bureaus, $140; 12–15 tables, $96; 60–70 bedsteads, $660; 3–4 wardrobes, $140; 50–60 coffins, $750
Grayson County	1,500							
A. Harrington, Sherman		5,000	250	Hand	—	—	3	1,500
Guadalupe County	1,300							
Bartholemew Buerger, Seguin		—	250	Hand	—	—	1	700 (in operation for eleven months)
Joseph Wassenich, Seguin		—	200	Hand	—	—	1	600 (in operation for eleven months)

TABLE 3. *Continued*

	Total Value of Furniture Produced	Feet of Wood Used	Value of Wood Used	Kind of Motive Power	Number of Machines	Horse-power	Number of Hands[a]	Value and Kind of Furniture
Harrison County	$1,200							
George Moffat, Marshall		—	$ 600	Hand	—	—	1	$1,200—chairs, coffins, and repairs
Hill County	2,500							
Moses A. Mock, Hillsboro		—	1,000	Hand	—	—	1	2,500
Hopkins County	2,579							
James R. Manning, Bright Star		1,500	525	Steam	—	4	—	2,000 (in operation for ten months)
Lemuel B. Titsworth, Bright Star		500+	125	Hand	1	—	1	579—500 chairs, $500; 3 spinning wheels, $15; 8 bedsteads, $64 (in operation for eight months)
Hunt County	1,426							
Albert McArt, Greenville		2,000	80	Hand	—	—	1	855—300 chairs, $375; 50 tables, $250; 2 bureaus, $50; 3 safes, $30; 1 wardrobe, $25; 5 whatnots, $25; other objects, $100
Marshall and Herberger, Greenville		1,000	115	Hand	—	—	1	571 (in operation for one month)
Jefferson County	500							
William Harris, Sabine Pass		2,000	60	Hand	—	—	1	500—safes and tables (in operation for eight months)

TABLE 3. *Continued*

	Total Value of Furniture Produced	Feet of Wood Used	Value of Wood Used	Kind of Motive Power	Number of Machines	Horse-power	Number of Hands[a]	Value and Kind of Furniture
Lamar County	$11,850							
Willet Babcock, Paris		77,000	$2,720	Horse	1	—	15	$ 7,900—400 bedsteads, etc.
James W. Rodgers, Paris		70,000	700	Horse	2	—	4	2,600 (in operation for ten months)
A. A. Walker, Paris		3,300	105	Horse	1	—	1	1,350—tables, beds, bookcases, washstands (in operation for eight months)
Madison County	500							
Greenwood W. Dean, Madisonville		—	100	Hand	—	—	1	500 (in operation for eleven months)
McLennan County	11,000							
William H. Anderson, Waco		—	3,300	Hand	—	—	6	11,000—5,000 pieces furniture (this figure probably includes knocked-down furniture assembled in Anderson's shop)
Milam County	1,580							
A. Lindstein, Port Sullivan		2,300	126	Horse	1	—	2	680—20 bedsteads, $200; 25 tables, $175; 3 wardrobes, $105; other articles, $200
David Meyers, Cameron		—	400	Hand	1	—	2	900 (in operation for 5 months)
Polk County	?							
Theophilus Reece, Livingston		500	20	Hand	—	—	1	[600—cabinetware and wagon repairing]

TABLE 3. *Continued*

	Total Value of Furniture Produced	*Feet of Wood Used*	*Value of Wood Used*	*Kind of Motive Power*	*Number of Machines*	*Horse-power*	*Number of Hands*[a]	*Value and Kind of Furniture*
Red River County	$5,300							
August Milke, Clarksville		—	$ 400	Hand	—	—	4	$ 800—bureaus and bedsteads (in operation for nine months)
Stephens and Longe, Clarksville		2,500	500	Steam	—	20	6	4,500—200 bedsteads, $2,000; 1,000 chairs, $2,500 (in operation for four months)
Smith County	5,500							
William Sheppard, Garden Valley [Tyler]		—	3,000	Steam	7	15	10	5,500
Travis County	9,000							
W. W. Evans, Austin		3,000	225	Hand	—	—	2	3,000—coffins and furniture
Joseph W. Hannig, Austin		10,000	750	Hand	—	—	3	6,000—coffins and furniture
Upshur County	790							
John Duphrate, Pinetree		—	100	Hand	1	—	1	790—20 bedsteads, $400; 10 wardrobes, $150; 10 safes, $200; 10 chairs, $15; 1 bureau, $25
Van Zandt County	1,200							
Cade and Robin, Canton		—	400	Hand	—	—	2	1,200 (in operation for three months)
Victoria County	1,300							
Izadore Locherer, Victoria		—	300	Hand	—	—	1	1,300

TABLE 3. *Continued*

	Total Value of Furniture Produced	Feet of Wood Used	Value of Wood Used	Kind of Motive Power	Number of Machines	Horse-power	Number of Hands[a]	Value and Kind of Furniture
Washington County	$3,497							
Charles Blank, Brenham		2,000	$ 60	Hand	—	—	1	$ 105 (in operation for three months)[b]
Joseph Massanari, Brenham		6,000	400	Hand	—	—	1	1,446 (in operation for ten months)
Johann Umland, Brenham [Chappell Hill]		3,200	132	Hand	—	—	2	225—3 wardrobes, $90; 2 safes, $50; 6 bedsteads, $60; repairing, $25 (number of months in operation not given)[b]
Caspar Witteborg, Brenham		8,600	294	Hand	—	—	2	1,721—12 bedsteads, $96; 12 wardrobes, $300; 25 tables, $125; bureaus, $200; repairing, $1,000
Wood County	600							
William G. Fisher, Quitman		2,000	200	Hand	1	—	1	600

Source: United States Census, manuscript census returns for Texas, schedule 5 (products of industry), 1870.

[a]This usually refers to the number of people working in the shop, including the owner.

[b]The annual production presumably would have been over $500 if the shop had been in operation the entire year.

[c]Bracketed items are not included in furniture totals.

[d]Total is over $500 if mattresses are included as furniture.

Notes

MID-NINETEENTH-CENTURY TEXAS: THE COAST AND THE HINTERLAND

1. A. A. Parker, *Trip to the West and Texas*, pp. 143–148; Frederick Law Olmsted, *Journey through Texas: A Saddle-Trip on the Southwestern Frontier*, pp. 1–2, 9–11; William Fairfax Gray, *From Virginia to Texas, 1835: Diary of Col. Wm. F. Gray*, pp. 83–89; Moritz Tiling, *History of the German Element in Texas from 1820–1850*, pp. 25–26; [?] Lewis, "The Adventures of the 'Lively' Immigrants," *Quarterly of the Texas State Historical Association* 3 (1899):15–16; Marilyn McAdams Sibley, *Travelers in Texas, 1761–1860*, pp. 32–35.

2. John Holmes Jenkins III, ed., *Recollections of Early Texas: The Memoirs of John Holland Jenkins*, pp. 43–44. See also Earl Fornell, *The Galveston Era: The Texas Crescent on the Eve of Secession*, pp. 92–93.

3. *Texas Almanac, 1860*, unpaginated advertisement; see also p. 251. For freight wagons on the wet prairies, see William Ransom Hogan, *The Texas Republic: A Social and Economic History*, pp. 66–68; Ferdinand Roemer, *Texas, with Particular Reference to the German Immigration and the Physical Appearance of the Country*, trans. Oswald Mueller, pp. 70–80.

4. J. H. Young, *A New Map of Texas* (1837); *Richardson's New Map of the State of Texas* (1860); Barbara Overton Chandler and J. Ed Howe, *History of Texarkana and Bowie and Miller Counties*, pp. 9–12; Walter Prescott Webb, ed., *The Handbook of Texas*, I, 321.

5. Hogan, *Texas Republic*, p. 61; Abigail Curlee Holbrook, "Cotton Marketing in Antebellum Texas," *Southwestern Historical Quarterly* 73 (1970):431–455.

6. The term *beat* was used by both English- and German-speaking residents of Fayette County until the 1940's to denote a justice precinct or a commissioner's precinct. In German, the reference was to "Beat Eins, Beat Zwei," and so on. See F. Lotto, *Fayette County: Her History and People*, p. 121; Dennis Sacks, interview, Round Top, April 11, 1975.

7. United States Census, manuscript census returns (MCR), schedule of population, Fayette County, 1860; "Inventory of J. R. Edwards' Store, Round Top," Fayette County Record of Probate, book D, p. 487; Fayette County Deed Records, book N, p. 64.

8. Until 1836, the Nueces River was the southern boundary of first Spanish and then Mexican Texas. After the Texas Revolution, the Republic of Texas claimed the Rio Grande as its southern boundary but was unable to exercise effective control over the territory between the Nueces and the Rio Grande. The Treaty of Guadalupe Hidalgo established the Rio Grande as Texas's southern boundary in 1848. See D. W. Meinig, *Imperial Texas: An Interpretive Essay in Cultural Geography*, pp. 23, 39–40.

9. Meinig, *Imperial Texas*, pp. 54–58; Carey McWilliams, *North from Mexico: The Spanish-Speaking People of the United States*, pp. 85–88; José San Ramón Papers, Barker History Center, University of Texas at Austin; Le Roy P. Graf, "The Economic History of the Lower Rio Grande Valley, 1820–1875" (M.A. thesis, Harvard University, 1942), pp. 273–290.

10. Webb, ed., *Handbook of Texas*, II, 289–290.

11. Olmsted, *Journey through Texas*, pp. 167–168.

12. Mack Walker, *Germany and the Emigration, 1816–1885*, pp. 9–16, 37–41, 43–69, 153–174; Rudolph Biesele, *The History of the German*

Settlements in Texas, 1831–1861, pp. 1–41; Karl Postl [pseud. Charles Sealsfield], *Nathan, der Squatter-Regulator, oder Der erste Amerikaner in Texas*; idem, *The Cabin Book*.

13. Olmsted, *Journey through Texas*, pp. 73–76.

14. Biesele, *German Settlements in Texas*; Terry G. Jordan, *German Seed in Texas Soil: Immigrant Farmers in Nineteenth-Century Texas*; Walker, *Germany and the Emigration*; Fornell, *Galveston Era*, pp. 125–139; W. Maury Darst, ed., "September 8, 1900: An Account by a Mother to Her Daughters," *Southwestern Historical Quarterly* 73 (1969):57–66; T. Herbert Etzler, "German-American Newspapers in Texas with Special Reference to the Texas Volksblatt, 1877–1879," *Southwestern Historical Quarterly* 57 (1954):423–431; Ferdinand Peter Herff, *The Doctors Herff*; Frederick C. Chabot, *With the Makers of San Antonio*, pp. 315–412; Webb, ed., *Handbook of Texas*, I, 968.

15. Ralph A. Wooster, "Wealthy Texans, 1860," *Southwestern Historical Quarterly* 71 (1967):163.

16. For extensive descriptions of Texas-German homes, see especially Ottilie Fuchs Goethe, *Memoirs of a Texas Pioneer Grandmother (Was Grossmutter Erzaehlt), 1805–1915*; Caroline Mackensen Romberg, *The Story of My Life Written for My Children*; Heinrich Otto Mackensen, *Experiences Recorded for His Descendants*, trans. Annie Romberg; Annie Romberg, *History of the Romberg Family*; Rosa Kleberg, "Some of My Early Experiences in Texas," *Quarterly of the Texas State Historical Association* 1 (1898):170–173; Louis Reinhardt, "The Communistic Colony of Bettina," *Quarterly of the Texas State Historical Association* 3 (1899):33–40; William Trenckmann, "Die Lateiner am Possum Creek," *Das Wochenblatt* (Austin), December 25, 1907; August Siemering, "Die Lateinische Anseidlung in Texas," *Texana* 5 (1967): 126–131.

17. Mattie Austin Hatcher, *Letters of an Early American Traveller: Mary Austin Holley, Her Life and Works, 1784–1846*, p. 166.

18. Fayette County Record of Probate, book C, pp. 298–299. See also Alice Killman, "Furniture Used during the Days of the Republic of Texas," p. 10, Barker History Center, University of Texas at Austin.

19. Frances Jane Leathers, ed., "Christopher Columbus Goodman: Soldier, Indian Fighter, Farmer, 1818–1861," *Southwestern Historical Quarterly* 69 (1966):356, 364–365.

20. Fisher's inventory is quoted in full by Killman, "Furniture," pp. 21–25.

21. Amelia W. Williams and Eugene C. Barker, eds., *The Writings of Sam Houston, 1813–1863*, III, 304–305.

22. L. Tuffly Ellis, "The Revolutionizing of the Texas Cotton Trade, 1865–1885," *Southwestern Historical Quarterly* 73 (1970):478–508.

CABINETMAKING IN THE HINTERLAND

1. See Carl Bridenbaugh, *The Colonial Craftsman*, pp. 126–129, 147–148; Charles F. Hummel, "The Dominys of East Hampton, Long Island, and Their Furniture," in *Country Cabinetwork and Simple City Furniture*, ed. John D. Morse, pp. 36–48; Berry B. Tracy et al., *Nineteenth-Century America: Furniture and Other Decorative Arts*, p. xiv; Elizabeth A. Ingerman, "Personal Experiences of an Old New York Cabinetmaker," *Antiques* 84 (1963):577–578.

2. See the Checklist of Texas Cabinetmakers, above, based on the United States Census, manuscript census returns (hereafter cited as MCR) for Texas in 1850, 1860, and 1870.

3. The Galveston firms of L. A. Hitchcock, H. A. Cobb, and J. A. Sauter were leading furniture importers of the 1840's and 1850's; Sauter continued to import furniture during the Civil War. See the *Civilian and Galveston Gazette*, November 4, 1840; June 12, 1844; November 21, 1854; *Tri-Weekly Telegraph* (Houston), February 16, 1863.

4. *Civilian and Galveston Gazette*, November 9, 1847.

5. James H. Cooke (92 Broadway), G. Ebbinghausen (88–92 Attorney Street), and Henry Weil were all New York cabinetmakers who specialized in furniture for the Southern market. In 1847, Cooke offered furniture to Texas merchants "at the following low rates (in lots of a dozen): sofas, $20 to $150; mahogany chairs, $36 to $120; mahogany rocking chairs, $5 to $35; card tables, $10 to $25 each; center tables, $15 to $60 each, and French bedsteads, $18 to $50 each" (*Civilian and Galveston Gazette*, April 21, 1847). For Ebbinghausen, see the *San*

Antonio Ledger, October 9, 1858. Another New York cabinetmaker remembered that Weil made a fortune in the 1840's by manufacturing "those ugly heavy veneered eight cornered high post bedsteads of which you find so many down South, also large mahogany wardrobes, dressing bureaus, and other large case work" (Ingerman, "Personal Experiences," p. 577).

Galveston was not the only furniture-importing city in Texas. John B. Burke and William Chrysler of Lavaca (now Port Lavaca) and R. E. Hyde of Marshall all advertised during the fifties that they purchased furniture directly from manufacturers in New York, Cincinnati, and New Orleans. See the *Texan Mercury* (Seguin), February 4, 1854; *Lavaca Herald,* September 13, 1856; *Star State Patriot* (Marshall), June 10, 1851. John Cox of Gonzales, Vance and Brother in San Antonio, and England and Woofter in Austin also advertised before the Civil War that they carried New York furniture. See the *Gonzales Inquirer,* July 2, 1853; *San Antonio Ledger,* December 30, 1852; *Southern Intelligencer* (Austin), February 1, 1860. For furniture imports in the 1870's, see Ben Harigel, *Leaflets from the Book of Life,* pp. 10–11.

6. Alfred Swingle's advertisement, *Galvestonian,* April 3, 1848.

7. William Stukes's advertisement, *Corpus Christi Gazette,* January 8, 1848.

8. See Andrew Forest Muir, "Inventions Patented by Texans, 1846–1861," *Southwestern Historical Quarterly* 62 (1959):522.

9. MCR, schedule of products of industry, Galveston County, 1850.

10. MCR, schedules of population and products of industry, Galveston County, 1850.

11. MCR, schedule of products of industry, Galveston County, 1850.

12. Earl Fornell, *The Galveston Era: The Texas Crescent on the Eve of Secession,* pp. 27–28, 33; *Telegraph and Texas Register* (Houston), June 16, 1838.

13. MCR, schedule of products of industry, Galveston County, 1850, 1860, 1870, 1880.

14. Frederick Law Olmsted, *Journey through Texas: A Saddle-Trip on the Southwestern Frontier,* pp. 50–53; Walter Prescott Webb, ed., *Handbook of Texas,* I, 85.

15. *Texas Sentinel* (Austin), February 19, 1840. The firm was that of A. W. Leach and L. Vancleve.

16. Ibid., April 29, 1840.

17. Ibid., August 15, 1840.

18. MCR, schedule of population, Travis County, 1850.

19. *Southern Intelligencer,* February 1, 1860.

20. See ibid. for articles imported from Galveston by Thomas H. Tumey and J. W. England and the *Tri-Weekly Times* (Austin), October 3, 1856, for Tumey's undertaking enterprise. Advertisements for furniture made to order by Thomas M. Bostick, J. W. England, and E. Woofter can be found in the *Tri-Weekly Times,* October 3, 1856; *Daily State Gazette and General Advertiser* (Austin), October 12, 1859; *Southern Intelligencer,* October 14, 1857; January 20, 1858; October 20, 1858. A good short biography of Charles Nitschke is "The Nitschke Family: Early Austin Citizens," Austin–Travis County Collection, Austin Public Library. Bills to state agencies from Thomas M. Bostick are in the Elisha Pease Papers, Austin–Travis County Collection, Austin Public Library, and in the Comptroller's Papers, Archives, Texas State Library, Austin.

21. For the production level and employees of Austin cabinet shops in 1870, see MCR, schedule of products of industry, Travis County, 1870. Hannig is mentioned by Mary Starr Barkley, *History of Travis County and Austin, 1839–1899,* p. 79; his advertisements can be found in the *Georgetown Watchman,* March 20, 1869; *Southern Intelligencer,* March 15, 1866; and S. A. Gray and W. D. Moore, *Mercantile and General City Directory of Austin, Texas, 1872–73,* p. 56.

22. Webb, ed., *Handbook of Texas,* I, 85.

23. Gray and Moore, *Mercantile and General City Directory,* p. 56.

24. MCR, schedule of population, Travis County, 1880.

25. William Seale, "San Augustine: In the Texas Republic," *Southwestern Historical Quarterly* 72 (1969):347–358; D. W. Meinig, *Imperial Texas: An Interpretive Essay in Cultural Geography,* pp. 33–34; Webb, ed., *Handbook of Texas,* II, 524; Dorman W. Winfrey, *Julien Sidney Devereux and His Monte Verdi Plantation.*

26. Information on cabinet shops in the San Augustine area is from MCR,

schedules of population and products of industry, Sabine, Rusk, and San Augustine counties, 1850, 1860. Whitehead's advertisement is in the *Tyler Reporter*, February 9, 1859; Woldert's is in the *Red-Lander* (San Augustine), May 19, 1842.

27. Webb, ed., *Handbook of Texas*, I, 436, 849, 867; II, 627; Harry F. Estill, "The Old Town of Huntsville," *Quarterly of the Texas State Historical Association* 3 (1900):265–278.

28. *Northern Standard* (Clarksville), January 13, 1844.

29. MCR, schedules of population and products of industry, Smith, Houston, and Walker counties, 1860.

30. *Tyler Reporter*, February 9, 1859.

31. Estate Inventory of Joseph Jones, Walker County Probate Minutes, book A, pp. 478–479.

32. Estate Inventory of Daniel Ellison, Walker County Probate Minutes, book D, p. 581.

33. Estate Inventory of George Wilson, Fayette County Record of Probate, book 1, March 25, 1839. For general discussions of nineteenth-century cabinetmakers' tools and machines, see Henry C. Mercer, *Ancient Carpenters' Tools*; W. L. Goodman, *A History of Woodworking Tools*; Alex Bealer, *Old Ways of Working Wood*; Polly Ann Earle, "Craftsmen and Machines: The Nineteenth-Century Furniture Industry," in *Technological Innovation and the Decorative Arts*, ed. Ian M. G. Quimby and Polly Ann Earle, pp. 307–329. Mortising machines were fairly common in Texas; one was offered for sale in the *Crockett Printer*, November 14, 1860, and another turns up on the estate inventory of a Brenham cabinetmaker who died in 1854 (Washington County Probate Records, book B, p. 43).

34. Bill from Thomas W. Ward to Elisha Pease, May 2, 1854, Elisha Pease Papers; Estate Inventory of S. F. Steves, Probate Case No. 1084, Fayette County Record of Probate.

35. Albert A. Hopkins, ed., *The Scientific American Cyclopedia of Receipts, Notes and Queries*, p. 571. For information on painted furniture, see, for instance, the bill dated May 2, 1854, in the Elisha Pease Papers, which lists several painted pine tables. Both John Duphrate of Upshur County and A. Harrington of Sherman listed paint and varnish among the materials used in their cabinet shops on the 1870 MCR, schedule of products of industry. A number of recipes for cabinetmakers' copal varnish can be found in the *Scientific American Cyclopedia*, ed. Hopkins.

36. *Report of the State Penitentiary for 1854–1855*, pp. 20, 25–26, 40.

37. MCR, schedule of products of industry, Walker County, 1860.

38. See N. A. M. Dudley, *Report on the Condition of the State Penitentiary, Huntsville, Feb. 10, 1870*.

39. A transcription of Robert Minor Wyatt's diary is in the Ellis County Public Library, Waxahachie. Wyatt also made looms and clock reels and served as county surveyor of Ellis County. He says in the diary that he was trained in "tailoring and designing."

40. *Crockett Printer*, November 14, 1860.

41. MCR, schedule of products of industry, Houston County, 1860.

42. Knight Parker, interview, San Augustine, February 10, 1974. See also MCR, schedule of products of industry, San Augustine County, 1860.

43. *Northern Standard* (Clarksville), February 5, 1853.

44. File 24, Austin County Civil Dockets.

45. For a discussion of cabinetmakers as "partial craftsmen," see Bruce Buckley, "A Folklorist Looks at the Traditional Craftsman," in *Country Cabinetwork*, ed. Morse, p. 273. Z. N. Morrel of Washington advertised in the Houston *Telegraph and Texas Register*, May 19, 1838, that he turned house columns. L. C. Richardson in Crockett and the firm of Elkins and Fields in Troup, Smith County, made both furniture and wagons (*Crockett Printer*, November 14, 1860; MCR, schedule of products of industry, Smith County, 1860). James Chute of Red River County advertised in the Clarksville *Northern Standard*, June 14, 1845, that he did white- and blacksmithing, gunsmithing, cabinet work, and wagonmaking and made spinning wheels and chairs.

46. MCR, schedule of products of industry, Smith, Houston, San Augustine, and Rusk counties, 1860. The cabinetmaker who had both a lathe and a slitting saw was John Lyles of Lockhart, who used two horses harnessed to a horse power (MCR, schedule of products of industry, Caldwell County, 1870). An examination of the products-of-industry schedules for the entire state shows that by 1860 twelve of the fifty-one

cabinet shops listed used some sort of power source. Eleven reported animal power and one, in Corsicana, used a 2 1/2-horsepower steam engine. Of the eleven horse powers, six were in East Texas, and all but one, in Waco, were in rural areas.

47. *Tyler Reporter*, February 9, 1859.

48. Ibid., August 1, 1861. See also MCR, schedule of products of industry, Smith County, 1860.

49. MCR, schedule of products of industry, Smith County, 1870; Edna L. Hatcher, "An Economic History of Smith County, 1846–1940" (M.S. thesis, East Texas State Teachers College, 1940), p. 38.

50. Blewett Kerbow, "The Early History of Red River County, 1817–1865" (M.A. thesis, University of Texas, 1936), pp. 3–42; A. W. Neville, *The History of Lamar County*, pp. 12–14; Webb, ed., *Handbook of Texas*, I, 366–367, 835; II, 15; Meinig, *Imperial Texas*, pp. 48–60.

51. Meinig, *Imperial Texas*, p. 60; J. Lee Stambaugh and Lillian J. Stambaugh, *A History of Collin County, Texas*, p. 64; William J. Hammond and Margaret F. Hammond, *La Réunion: A French Settlement in Texas*, pp. 85–115; Annie Carpenter Love, *History of Navarro County*, pp. 24, 79–112; *A Memorial and Biographical History of Ellis County, Texas*, pp. 173–176.

52. MCR, schedules of population and products of industry, Red River, Lamar, Hopkins, Navarro, Collin, Dallas, and Ellis counties, 1850, 1860, 1870.

53. Ibid.

54. Ibid.

55. MCR, schedule of products of industry, Ellis County, 1870.

56. Sample entries from different places in Spalding's ledger. The ledger is in the University of Texas at Austin Winedale Museum library; it and much information about Spalding's cabinet shop came from his grandson, William Spalding, of Waxahachie.

57. MCR, schedule of products of industry, Hill County, 1870.

58. William L. Bray, *Forest Resources of Texas*, p. 18.

59. *Northern Standard*, June 5, 1844.

60. Ibid., June 24, 1848.

61. See the advertisements of Hatley, Gaines, and Stephen, ibid., July 22,

1854, and of Shanahan and Brim, ibid., March 3, 1855. The Spalding ledger records numerous purchases of lumber from sawmills.

62. MCR, schedule of products of industry, Navarro County, 1860.

63. *Independent Monitor* (Bright Star), December 1, 1860.

64. Red River County Deed Records, vol. Q, p. 16.

65. Ibid.; MCR, schedule of products of industry, Red River County, 1870; Anne Holdaway Eitel, "Red River County, Past and Present" (M.A. thesis, East Texas State Teachers College, 1953), p. 33; Pat B. Clark, *The History of Clarksville and Old Red River County*, p. 241.

66. MCR, schedule of products of industry, Hopkins County, 1870.

67. Ibid., Lamar County, 1860, 1870.

68. *Paris Weekly Press*, September 3, 1875.

69. MCR, schedule of products of industry, Lamar and Red River counties, 1880. Babcock's death date is from his tombstone, Paris cemetery.

70. *North Texan* (Paris), September 6, 1879; "Rodgers-Wade Furniture Company, Statement of Profit and Loss, 1921," mimeographed, Rodgers-Wade Company files, Paris.

71. For general histories of this region, see William Trenckmann, *Austin County*; Mrs. R. E. Pennington, *The History of Brenham and Washington County*; F. Lotto, *Fayette County: Her History and People*.

72. See Morrel's advertisement, *Telegraph and Texas Register*, May 19, 1838; MCR, schedules of population (schedules 1 and 2), Austin, Colorado, Fayette, and Washington counties, 1850, 1860, 1870.

73. Bray, *Forest Resources of Texas*, p. 19; Lotto, *Fayette County*, pp. 26–33.

74. William Umland, "A Kind of Family Record Made up the Best I Know How," University of Texas at Austin Winedale Museum, Round Top.

75. Edward H. Reisner, *Nationalism and Education since 1789*, pp. 121–139.

76. Ibid.

77. MCR, schedule of products of industry, Austin County, 1870.

78. MCR, schedules of population and products of industry, Austin, Waller, and Washington counties, 1870, 1880; Cecilia Steinfeldt and Donald L. Stover, *Early Texas Furniture and Decorative Arts*, pp. 96, 104.

79. Terry G. Jordan, *German Seed in Texas Soil: Immigrant Farmers in Nineteenth-Century Texas*, pp. 118–120.

80. Ibid.; Rudolph Biesele, *The History of the German Settlements in*

Texas, 1831–1861, pp. 120, 134, 139–177.

81. Mack Walker, *Germany and the Emigration, 1816–1885,* p. 69.

82. MCR, schedule of products of industry, Gillespie County, 1850, 1860; Comal County, 1850, 1860, 1870.

83. MCR, schedules of population, Comal and Gillespie counties, 1860, 1870; Gillespie County Historical Society, *Pioneers in God's Hills,* p. 3.

84. Gillespie County Historical Society, *Pioneers in God's Hills,* pp. 4, 214; Samuel E. Gideon, ed., "A Group of Themes on the Architecture and Culture of Early Texas by Students in Course A.350," p. 109. The German-made tools of William Leilich and Johann·Peter Tatsch are preserved in the Pioneer Museum, Fredericksburg (see Plate 2); those of Scholl, as well as his homemade lathe, are preserved in the home of Dr. and Mrs. O. A. Stratemann, New Braunfels (see Plate 1). Schulze's bench was exhibited in 1973 at the American Heritage Museum in Fredericksburg by his grandson, Ed Schulze of Fredericksburg. The information on wood is based largely upon examples of furniture, plus references to Tatsch's local sources in *Pioneers in God's Hills,* p. 214, and Don Biggers's *German Pioneers in Texas,* p. 97, and to Jahn's trips to Bastrop in Pauline Pinckney's "Johann Michael Jahn, Texas Cabinetmaker," *Antiques* 75 (1959):463.

85. MCR, schedule of products of industry, Gillespie and Comal counties, 1850, 1860, 1870; Vance and Brother's advertisement, *San Antonio Ledger,* December 30, 1852; *Neu-Braunfelser Zeitung,* November 5, 1908; Steinfeldt and Stover, *Early Texas Furniture,* pp. 249–250; Gillespie County Historical Society, *Pioneers in God's Hills,* p. 215.

FURNITURE OF THE FRONTIER

1. Estate Inventory of Samuel Rankin, Fayette County Record of Probate, book A, p. 188; Andrew Forest Muir, "Inventions Patented by Texans, 1846–1861," *Southwestern Historical Quarterly* 62 (1959):522.

2. *Lavaca Herald,* September 13, 1856.

3. "Inventory of Furniture and Articles of Governor's House, Nov. 8th, 1861," letter book 4, p. 46, Governor Francis Lubbock Papers, Archives, Texas State Library, Austin; *Weekly Enquirer* (McKinney), April 15, 1871.

4. "Inventory of Furniture and Articles of Governor's House."

5. Andrew Jackson Downing, *The Architecture of Country Houses,* p. 449.

6. Ibid., p. 459.

7. S. D. Staat's advertisement, *Morning Star* (Houston), March 23, 1843.

8. *Standard* (Clarksville), February 20, 1858.

9. *True Issue* (La Grange), February 12, 1859.

10. Muir, "Inventions Patented by Texans."

11. *Democratic Telegraph and Texas Register* (Houston), January 18, 1847.

12. *Texas Ranger and Lone Star* (Washington), December 15, 1853.

13. Louisiana State Museum, *Early Furniture of Louisiana,* nos. 29, 30.

14. Ibid., no. 31.

15. Albert Walzer, "Baden-Württembergische Bauern Möbel," *Der Museumsfreund aus Heimatmuseen und Sämmlungen in Baden-Württemberg* 10–11: plates 86, 88.

16. "Inventory of Furniture and Articles of Governor's House."

17. Frederick Law Olmsted, *Journey through Texas: A Saddle-Trip on the Southwestern Frontier,* pp. 74–75.

18. Council of Europe, *The Age of Neo-Classicism: Fourteenth Exhibition of the Council of Europe,* plate 23.

19. Walzer, "Baden-Württembergische Bauern Möbel," plate 3.

20. *Bastrop Advertiser,* May 27, 1854; *Tyler Reporter,* February 9, 1859; *Standard,* February 20, 1858.

21. Downing, *Architecture of Country Houses,* p. 449.

22. *Texan Mercury* (Seguin), February 4, 1854.

23. McLennan County Deed Records, book J, p. 61.

24. Homer Eaton Keyes, "Echt Biedermeier," *Antiques* 17 (1930):221.

25. Quoted in "History of the Scholls in Texas," manuscript in possession of Mrs. O. A. Stratemann, New Braunfels.

26. Berry B. Tracy et al., *Nineteenth-Century America: Furniture and Other Decorative Arts,* no. 185.

27. Unpaginated, undated notebook in possession of Mrs. Walter D. Kleine, Gonzales.

28. Ibid.

Glossary

Acorn: in ornament, a device resembling an acorn, often used as a finial, occasionally used as the terminal ornament of bed posts. *See* Finial.

Acroterium (pl., acroteria): in classical architecture, a pedestal for ornament placed at the apex or at each corner of a pediment; by extension the term is also applied to that ornament. This classical architectural feature was incorporated into furniture, especially during the Empire and Restauration periods of the early nineteenth century.

Anthemion: in ornament, a conventionalized design of flower and leaf forms used by the Greeks and thought to represent honeysuckle; elements are arranged in a symmetrical pattern radiating from the central motif. It was introduced into furniture design of the second half of the eighteenth century, and popular during the Empire period.

Astragal: in cabinetmaking, a half-round or three-quarter–round profile applied to molding. *See* Ovolo *and* Torus.

Bale: C-shaped handle of a furniture mount.

Baluster: a short pillar or column of vase form, usually pear-shaped.

Beaded: in cabinetmaking, having a half-round profile, usually applied to small convex moldings. *See* Cock beading.

Bevel: in cabinetmaking, a slanting cutting away of an edge of a board to reduce its thickness.

Biedermeier style: term applied to Germanic furniture of the Late Empire, Restauration, and Early Rococo Revival periods (ca. 1825–1860); derived from the name of a caricature in a Vienna newspaper, Herr Biedermeier, who typified affluent but uncultured middle-class Germans. *See* Empire, Restauration, *and* Rococo Revival *styles*.

Bobbin-turned: in furniture, a term applied to lathe-turned moldings and ornament characterized by a repeated ball- or bobbinlike profile.

Burled: in wood, applied to a malformation protruding from the trunk of a tree, containing dense wood with an irregular, highly patterned grain. Burled wood was often used as an ornamental veneer, especially in the Renaissance Revival period (ca. 1855–1875).

Butterfly joint: in cabinetmaking, a small piece of wood in the shape of a butterfly which is let into each of two adjacent planks to bind them together.

Cabriole: in furniture, a distinctive S shape usually utilized in legs; introduced in France during the late Louis XIV style and widely used in the Rococo Louis XV style; used in England after 1700, in Queen Anne and Early Georgian styles; reintroduced in the Rococo Revival period.

Cant: in cabinetwork, to cut off the corner of a rectangle at a forty-five–degree angle, on table tops and carcases of case pieces, such as chests or wardrobes.

Capital: in architecture, the crowning element of a column. Columnar forms are often used as ornament in furniture.

Carcase: in furniture, the framework or body of a case piece, such as a chest, desk, or wardrobe.

Cartouche: in ornament, a French heraldic term applied to an open decorative device surrounded by strap or scroll work, often used as a central crowning ornament; by extension, any central crowning ornament.

Cavetto: in furniture, a concave molding, usually quarter round in section, frequently used in the Restauration period.

Chamfer: in cabinetmaking, to cut away a corner, as on a table leg. The surface thus created is similar to a canted surface, but smaller.

Cheval: in furniture, a term derived from the French word for "horse" or "support," given to a type of fire screen characterized by vertical upright supports on either side of a frame. In the late eighteenth century and during the nineteenth century, a similar frame was used on full-length looking glasses.

Cleat: in cabinetmaking, a strip of wood attached to a flat surface for bracing or to prevent warping.

Cock beading: in cabinetmaking, a small half-round molding often used around drawer edges.

Colonnette: in furniture, a small or miniature column.

Corbel: in architecture, a wall bracket used to support vaulting ribs or roof members; in cabinetmaking, applied to a similar type of bracket.

Cornice: in classical architecture, the crowning element of the entablature; in cabinetmaking, the upper horizontal member of a case piece.

Crocket: in ornament, a projecting decorative element in Gothic architecture in the form of budding leaves, often used on the ridge of a spire or the edge of a gable; in Gothic-style furniture, used in finials or carved ornament.

Cyma: in cabinetmaking, a continuous S shape in profile, usually applied to moldings.

Diaper: in ornament, an overall pattern characterized by repetition of the same small shape, usually a square.

Dowel: in cabinetmaking, a circular wooden pin used to join two pieces of wood.

Draw table: in furniture, a space-saving form introduced during the Renaissance, with a three-section top, consisting of two smaller leaves on runners which can be slid under the larger leaf when not in use.

Elizabethan Revival: a mid-nineteenth-century romantic-revival style (ca. 1845–1875), drawing on seventeenth-century English designs, especially the spiral and bobbin turnings of the Carolean and Jacobean periods.

Empire style: a revival of antique ornament and furniture design (ca. 1805–1825), characterized by an archaeological approach, developed during the First French Empire of Napoleon I, combining elements of Classical Greek, Roman, and Egyptian styles.

Entablature: in architecture, the horizontal member resting upon columns; in furniture, the same or, in classically derived furniture, the horizontal member below a cornice.

Escutcheon: in furniture mounts, the decorative plate, usually metal, surrounding a keyhole.

Extension table: in furniture, a table with a split top and sliding skirt capable of being opened to receive extra leaves.

Fiche: a French term meaning "hook" or "pin"; in furniture hardware, applied to large ornamental hinges used in French and Continental case pieces of the eighteenth century.

Fielded panel: in furniture, a panel with beveled edges and a projecting flat field in the center.

Fillister plane: in cabinetmaking, a rabbet plane with a movable fence on one side, usually attached to the body of the plane by adjustable screws, so that the plane may be used to cut a groove in a board at any given distance from the board's edge.

Finial: in ornament, a carved or turned ornament at the upper terminal of a chair stile or bed post or crowning a case piece or mirror, often in the shape of a vase, urn, or acorn.

Frieze: in architecture, the part of the entablature located beneath the cornice; in furniture, the horizontal member located below the cornice. *See* Entablature.

Gothic Revival style: a mid-nineteenth-century romantic-revival style (ca. 1830–1870), drawing on medieval architecture, characterized chiefly by the use of pointed arches, but also incorporating crockets, quatrefoils, trefoils, and cluster columns.

Klismos: in furniture, a type of chair made in the Empire period, based on antique Greek prototypes characterized by a sweeping curve from the front legs into the seat frame and up into the stiles. The stiles are often capped with a large rectangular tablet.

Miter: in cabinetmaking, a joint cut at an angle, usually forty-five degrees.

Mortise and tenon: in cabinetmaking, a type of joinery consisting of a rectangular hole, the mortise, into which a tongue, the tenon, is inserted.

Muntin: in architecture, the small vertical or horizontal member that retains a pane of glass within a window; in furniture, the same in a desk or cupboard door.

Ogee: in cabinetmaking, an **S** curve convex above and concave below.

Ovolo: in cabinetmaking, a convex molding, often half round.

Palmette: in ornament, a conventionalized design of palm fronds arranged in a symmetrical fan-shaped form, similar in appearance to an anthemion.

Pediment: in architecture, the triangular termination above the cornice, at the upper end of a building; in furniture, architectural detail used in case pieces as a crowning ornament above the cornice.

Pied de biche: in furniture, a form of terminal on a cabriole leg resembling a cloven hoof; a French term, meaning literally "deer foot."

Pilaster: in architecture, a flat column or pier engaged to the wall, with a columnlike base and capital; in furniture, a similar architectural detail often employed on case pieces.

Plinth: in architecture, the lowest square member of a column; in furniture, a similar architectural detail or pedestal-like element above a cornice within a pediment.

Quatrefoil: in ornament, a conventionalized four-lobed motif, often in leaf or foil form and peculiar to the Gothic style.

Rabbet: in cabinetmaking, a rectangular slot or groove.

Rail: in cabinetmaking, a horizontal connecting member between two supports.

Raking: set at an angle.

Ratchet: in cabinetmaking, a toothlike device which enables forward or backward adjustment with numerous small variations.

Renaissance Revival: a mid-nineteenth-century romantic-revival style (ca. 1855–1875), drawing loosely on Renaissance architecture and characterized by flat surfaces with applied panels, medallions, moldings, and strapwork.

Reserve: in ornament, a defined area, clearly separated from its surroundings, usually with an ornamental border, within which is often a contrasting design or texture.

Restauration style: the second and final stage of revived archaeological classical style (ca. 1825–1850), evolved at the French court of the restored Bourbon monarchy, characterized by simplified flat, unornamented surfaces, often employing scrolled lines.

Rococo Revival: a mid-nineteenth-century romantic-revival style (ca. 1850–1870), drawing on the French style of the eighteenth century and characterized by curved lines; naturalistic flower, shell, and rock ornament, often arranged in asymmetry; and cabriole legs.

Rosette: a circular ornament, usually small in scale, with decorative motifs arranged around its center or in concentric bandings.

Sheraton style: a late-eighteenth- and early-nineteenth-century neoclassical style (ca. 1790–1815), based nonarchaeologically on antique Roman sources and originally evolved by Robert Adam (1728–1792); named for Thomas Sheraton (1751–1806), English furniture designer and author of various publications on furniture design including *The Cabinet-Maker and Upholsterer's Drawing Book* (1791–1794), which was widely circulated in America.

Spandrel: in architecture and furniture, the triangular space formed by the curve of an arch and the horizontal and vertical lines enclosing it.

Spindle: in furniture, a lathe-turned member tapering at either end, usually decorative.

Splat: in furniture, the central vertical member within an open chair back; in the nineteenth century, also applied to the horizontal members.

Spool-turned: in furniture, applied to lathe-turned members resembling a series of spools.

Stiles: in furniture, the vertical upright members of the framework at the sides or corners of case pieces; in chairs, the back posts.

Strapwork: in ornament, a shallow, narrow band of straplike ornament, bent, folded, crossed, and interlaced, often used in the Renaissance Revival style.

Stretcher: in furniture, the strengthening horizontal member placed between the legs of chairs, stools, settees, and tables.

Template: in cabinetmaking, a cut-out pattern used by the cabinetmaker as a model to create repeatedly the same design, such as a chair leg or arm.

Tenon. *See* Mortise and tenon.

Tester: in furniture, a rectangular framework, occasionally cloth-covered, that crowns the tall posts of a bed; also called a canopy.

Torus: in cabinetmaking, a small incised molding which in section tapers downward in a concave curve.

Trefoil: in ornament, a conventionalized three-lobed motif often in leaf or foil form and peculiar to the Gothic style.

Vase: in furniture, a member resembling a vase in form.

Vernacular style: an indigenous style whose antecedents are long forgotten and whose forms and ornament are utilized out of tradition rather than mode or fashion.

Voltaire chair: in the Restauration period, a name ascribed to chairs with curved backs and elaborately scrolled arms.

Bibliography

UNPUBLISHED WORKS

Baldwin, John W. "An Early History of Walker County." M.A. thesis, Sam Houston State Teachers College, 1957.

Curlee, Abigail. "A Study of Texas Slave Plantations, 1822 to 1865." Ph.D. dissertation, University of Texas, 1932.

Devereux, Julien L. Day Book, 1851–1852. Barker History Center, University of Texas at Austin.

Duval, Thomas H. Diary, October–November, 1857. Barker History Center, University of Texas at Austin.

Eitel, Anne Holdaway. "Red River County, Past and Present." M.A. thesis, East Texas State Teachers College, 1953.

Embree, Mrs. J. W. Diary, 1858–1860. Barker History Center, University of Texas at Austin.

First German Protestant Church of New Braunfels. Register. New Braunfels.

Gideon, Samuel E., ed. "A Group of Themes on the Architecture and Culture of Early Texas by Students in Course A.350." Mimeographed. Austin: University of Texas College of Engineering, Department of Architecture, n.d.

Graf, Le Roy P. "The Economic History of the Lower Rio Grande Valley, 1820–1875." M.A. thesis, Harvard University, 1942.

Gupton, Thurman M. "Biography of Heinrich Jansen (1819–1900)." University of Texas at Austin Winedale Museum, Round Top.

Haas, Oscar. "Henry Rochau, Sr., My Maternal Grandfather's Civil War Story." Haas Collection, New Braunfels.

Hatcher, Edna L. "An Economic History of Smith County, 1846–1940." M.S. thesis, East Texas State Teachers College, 1940.

"History of the Scholls in Texas." In possession of Mrs. O. A. Stratemann, New Braunfels.

Hubert Lodge No. 67, A.F. of A.M. Lodge Records. Chappell Hill.

"Index of American Design, Data Report Sheets, Texas." University of Texas at Austin Winedale Museum, Round Top.

Kerbow, Blewett. "The Early History of Red River County, 1817–1865." M.A. thesis, University of Texas, 1936.

Killman, Alice. "Furniture Used during the Days of the Republic of Texas." Barker History Center, University of Texas at Austin.

Kleine, John William August. Notebook. In possession of Mrs. Walter D. Kleine, Gonzales.

"Life History of Frank C. Kaiser, Old Texas Ranger." Haas Collection, New Braunfels.

Lubbock, Governor Francis, Papers. Archives, Texas State Library, Austin.

Mueller, Esther. "Some Craftsmen of Early Fredericksburg." In "A Group of Themes on the Architecture and Culture of Early Texas by Students in Course A.350," edited by Samuel E. Gideon. Mimeographed. Austin: University of Texas College of Engineering, Department of Architecture, n.d.

"The Nitschke Family: Early Austin Citizens." Austin–Travis County Collection, Austin Public Library.

Pease, Elisha, Papers. Austin–Travis County Collection, Austin Public Library.

"Rodgers-Wade Furniture Company, Statement of Profit and Loss, 1921." Mimeographed. Rodgers-Wade Company files, Paris.

San Ramón, José, Papers. Barker History Center, University of Texas at Austin.

Spalding, John H. Ledger. University of Texas at Austin Winedale Museum, Round Top.

"Texas Genealogical Records, Ellis County, 1784–1955." Ellis County Public Library, Waxahachie.

Thompson, Hiram, and Sons. Business Ledger. Winfield Collection, Chappell Hill.

Umland, William. "A Kind of Family Record Made up the Best I Know How." University of Texas at Austin Winedale Museum, Round Top.

Woldert, Will. Memoirs. In possession of Smith County Historical Society, Tyler.

Wyatt, Robert Minor. Diary. Ellis County Public Library, Waxahachie.

PUBLIC RECORDS

Alphabetical Index of Naturalization Record. District Court, Washington County. Brenham.
Austin County Civil Dockets. Bellville.
Austin County Deed Records. Bellville.
Caldwell County Deed Records. Lockhart.
Caldwell County Marriage Records. Lockhart.
Caldwell County Probate Minutes. Lockhart.
Collin County Deed Records. McKinney.
Colorado County Death Certificates. Columbus.
Colorado County Deed Records. Columbus.
Colorado County District Court Minutes. Columbus.
Comal County Commissioners' Minutes. New Braunfels.
Comal County District Court Minutes. New Braunfels.
Comal County Probate Records. New Braunfels.
Comptroller's Papers. Archives, Texas State Library, Austin.
Ellis County Deed Records. Waxahachie.
Ellis County Record of Probate. Waxahachie.
Fayette County Deed Records. La Grange.
Fayette County Record of Probate. La Grange.
Guadalupe County Death Certificates. Seguin.
Guadalupe County Deed Records. Seguin.

Lamar County Deed Records. Paris.
McLennan County Deed Records. Waco.
Marion County District Court Minutes. Jefferson.
MCR. *See* United States Census.
Red River County Deed Records. Clarksville.
United States Census. Manuscript census returns (MCR) for Texas, schedules 1, 2, and 5, 1850, 1860, 1870. Archives, Texas State Library, Austin.
Walker County Deed Records. Huntsville.
Walker County Probate Records. Huntsville.
Waller County Deed Records. Hempstead.
Washington County Deed Records. Brenham.
Washington County District Court Records. Brenham.
Washington County Probate Records. Brenham.

BOOKS AND ARTICLES

Allen, Irene Taylor. *Saga of Anderson.* New York: Greenwich Book Publishers, 1957.

Barkley, Mary Starr. *History of Travis County and Austin, 1839–1899.* Austin, 1963.

Bealer, Alex. *Old Ways of Working Wood.* Barre, Mass.: Barre Publishers, 1972.

Biesele, Rudolph. *The History of the German Settlements in Texas, 1831–1861.* Austin: Von Boeckmann–Jones, 1930.

Biggers, Don. *German Pioneers in Texas.* Fredericksburg: Press of the Fredericksburg Publishing Co., 1925.

Bray, William L. *Forest Resources of Texas.* Bureau of Forestry Bulletin, no. 47. Washington, D.C.: United States Department of Agriculture, 1904.

Bridenbaugh, Carl. *The Colonial Craftsman.* Chicago: University of Chicago Press, 1961.

Buckley, Bruce. "A Folklorist Looks at the Traditional Craftsman." In *Country Cabinetwork and Simple City Furniture,* edited by John D. Morse. Charlottesville: University Press of Virginia, 1970.

Cat Spring Agricultural Society. *The Cat Spring Story.* San Antonio: Lone Star Printing Company, 1956.

Chabot, Frederick C. *With the Makers of San Antonio.* San Antonio: Artes Gráficas, 1937.

Chandler, Barbara Overton, and J. Ed Howe. *History of Texarkana and Bowie and Miller Counties.* Texarkana, Texas: J. Ed Howe, 1939.

Christensen, Erwin O., ed. *The Index of American Design.* New York: Macmillan, 1950.

Clark, Pat B. *The History of Clarksville and Old Red River County.* Dallas: Mathis, Van Nort, and Co., 1937.

Council of Europe. *The Age of Neo-Classicism: Fourteenth Exhibition of the Council of Europe.* London: Arts Council of Great Britain, 1972.

Crockett, George L. *Two Centuries in East Texas.* Dallas: Southwest Press, 1932.

Darst, W. Maury, ed. "September 8, 1900: An Account by a Mother to Her Daughters." *Southwestern Historical Quarterly* 73 (1969):57–66.

Delono, A. *Galveston Directory 1856–7.* Galveston: News Book and Job Office, 1856.

Dielmann, Henry B. "Emma Altgelt's Sketches of Life in Texas." *Southwestern Historical Quarterly* 63 (1960):363–384.

Downing, Andrew Jackson. *The Architecture of Country Houses.* New York: Dover Publications, 1969.

Dudley, N. A. M. *Report on the Condition of the State Penitentiary, Huntsville, Feb. 10, 1870.* N.p., n.d.

Dugas, Vera Lea. "Texas Industry, 1860–1880." *Southwestern Historical Quarterly* 59 (1955):151–183.

Earle, Polly Ann. "Craftsmen and Machines: The Nineteenth-Century Furniture Industry." In *Technological Innovation and the Decorative Arts,* edited by Ian M. G. Quimby and Polly Ann Earle, pp. 307–329. Charlottesville: University Press of Virginia, 1974.

Ellis, L. Tuffly. "The Revolutionizing of the Texas Cotton Trade, 1865–1885." *Southwestern Historical Quarterly* 73 (1970):478–508.

Estill, Harry F. "The Old Town of Huntsville." *Quarterly of the Texas State Historical Association* 3 (1900):265–278.

Etzler, T. Herbert. "German-American Newspapers in Texas with Special Reference to the Texas Volksblatt, 1877–1879." *Southwestern Historical Quarterly* 57 (1954):423–431.

Farmer, Garland R. *The Realm of Rusk County.* Henderson: Henderson Times, 1951.

Fishbein, Meyer H. "The Censuses of Manufacturers: 1810–1890." *National Archives Accessions* 57 (1963):1–20.

Ford, John Salmon. *Rip Ford's Texas.* Austin: University of Texas Press, 1963.

Fornell, Earl. *The Galveston Era: The Texas Crescent on the Eve of Secession.* Austin: University of Texas Press, 1961.

——. "Texans and Filibusters in the 1850's." *Southwestern Historical Quarterly* 59 (1956):411–428.

Franke, Gertrude. *A Goodly Heritage.* Uvalde: Printit Office Supplies, 1959.

Friend, Llerena B. "The Texan of 1860." *Southwestern Historical Quarterly* 62 (1958):1–17.

Gage, Larry Jay. "The City of Austin on the Eve of the Civil War." *Southwestern Historical Quarterly* 63 (1960):428–438.

Galveston Directory for 1859–1860. Galveston, 1859.

Geiser, Samuel Ward. *Naturalists of the Frontier.* Dallas: Southern Methodist University Press, 1937.

Geue, Chester William, and Ethel Hander Geue. *A New Land Beckoned.* Waco, 1966.

Gillespie County Historical Society. *Pioneers in God's Hills.* Austin: Von Boeckmann–Jones, 1960.

Goethe, Ottilie Fuchs. *Memoirs of a Texas Pioneer Grandmother (Was Grossmutter Erzaehlt), 1805–1915.* Austin, 1969.

Goodman, W. L. *A History of Woodworking Tools.* London: G. Bell and Son, 1954.

Gray, S. A., and W. D. Moore. *Mercantile and General City Directory of Austin, Texas, 1872–73.* Austin, 1872.

Gray, William Fairfax. *From Virginia to Texas, 1835: Diary of Col. Wm. F. Gray.* Houston: Fletcher Young Publishing Co., 1965.

Haas, Oscar. *History of New Braunfels and Comal County, Texas, 1844–1946.* Austin: Steck, 1968.

Hammond, William J., and Margaret F. Hammond. *La Réunion: A French Settlement in Texas.* Dallas: Royal Publishing Co., 1958.

Harigel, Ben. *Leaflets from the Book of Life.* La Grange: La Grange Journal, 1946.

Harrison County Conservation Society. *Heritage Sketch and Cook Book.* Marshall, n.d.

Hatcher, Mattie Austin. *Letters of an Early American Traveller: Mary Austin Holley, Her Life and Works, 1784–1846.* Dallas: Southwest Press, 1933.

Heller, John H. *Galveston City Directory 1872.* Galveston: News Office, 1872.

Herff, Ferdinand Peter. *The Doctors Herff.* San Antonio: Trinity University Press, 1973.

Hogan, William Ransom. *The Texas Republic: A Social and Economic History.* Austin: University of Texas Press, 1969.

Hokes, Pauline B. *Centennial History of Anderson County.* San Antonio: Naylor, 1936.

Holbrook, Abigail Curlee. "Cotton Marketing in Antebellum Texas." *Southwestern Historical Quarterly* 73 (1970):431–455.

Hopkins, Albert A., ed. *The Scientific American Cyclopedia of Receipts, Notes and Queries.* New York: Munn and Co., 1893.

Hummel, Charles F. "The Dominys of East Hampton, Long Island, and Their Furniture." In *Country Cabinetwork and Simple City Furniture,* edited by John D. Morse, pp. 36–48. Charlottesville: University Press of Virginia, 1970.

Ingerman, Elizabeth A. "Personal Experiences of an Old New York Cabinetmaker." *Antiques* 84 (1963):577–578.

Jenkins, John Holmes, III, ed. *Recollections of Early Texas: The Memoirs of John Holland Jenkins.* Austin: University of Texas Press, 1958.

Jenson, Martin F. *History of Four Mile Settlement and Church, Established 1848.* Canton, Texas: Four Mile Lutheran Church, 1972.

Johnson, Frank W. *History of Texas and Texans, 1799–1884.* 5 vols. Chicago: American Historical Society, 1914.

Jordan, Terry G. *German Seed in Texas Soil: Immigrant Farmers in Nineteenth-Century Texas.* Austin: University of Texas Press, 1966.

Kendall, Dorothy Steinbomer. *Gentilz: Artist of the Old Southwest.* Elma Dill Russell Spencer Foundation Series, no. 6. Austin: University of Texas Press, 1974.

Keyes, Homer Eaton. "Echt Biedermeier." *Antiques* 17 (1930):221.

King, Dick. *Ghost Towns of Texas.* San Antonio: Naylor, 1955.

Kleberg, Rosa. "Some of My Early Experiences in Texas." *Quarterly of the Texas State Historical Association* 1 (1898):170–173.

Kovel, Ralph, and Terry Kovel. *American Country Furniture 1780–1875.* New York: Crown Publishers, 1966.

Krueger, Max. *Pioneer Life in Texas.* San Antonio: Clegg, 1930.

Landrum, Graham. *An Illustrated History of Grayson County, Texas.* Fort Worth: Historical Publishers, 1967.

Langermann, A. B., comp. *The Railroad System of Texas on September 1, 1881.* Chicago: Rand McNally and Co., 1881.

Lathrop, Barnes. *Migration into East Texas, 1835–1860.* Austin: Texas State Historical Association, 1949.

Leathers, Frances Jane, ed. "Christopher Columbus Goodman: Soldier, Indian Fighter, Farmer, 1818–1861." *Southwestern Historical Quarterly* 69 (1966):353–376.

Lewis, [?]. "The Adventures of the 'Lively' Immigrants." *Quarterly of the Texas State Historical Association* 3 (1899):1–32.

Lotto, F. *Fayette County: Her History and People.* Schulenberg: Sticker Steam Press, 1902.

Louisiana State Museum. *Early Furniture of Louisiana.* New Orleans: Louisiana State Museum, 1972.

Love, Annie Carpenter. *History of Navarro County.* Dallas: Southwest Press, 1933.

Mackensen, Heinrich Otto. *Experiences Recorded for His Descendants.* Translated by Annie Romberg. N.p., n.d.

McWilliams, Carey. *North from Mexico: The Spanish-Speaking People of the United States.* New York: Greenwood Press, 1968.

Maudslay, Robert. *Texas Sheepman: The Reminiscences of Robert Maudslay.* Edited by Winifred Kupper. Austin: University of Texas Press, 1951.

Meinig, D. W. *Imperial Texas: An Interpretive Essay in Cultural Geography.* Austin: University of Texas Press, 1969.

A Memorial and Biographical History of Ellis County, Texas. Chicago: Lewis Publishing Co., 1892.

Memorial and Genealogical Record of Southwest Texas. Chicago: Goodspeed Brothers, 1894.

Mercer, Henry C. *Ancient Carpenters' Tools.* Doylestown, Pa.: Bucks County Historical Society, 1960.

Miller, Susan E. *Sixty Years in the Nueces Valley*. San Antonio: Naylor, 1930.

Morgan, Ruth. "The Crafts of Early Texas." *Southwest Review* (Winter 1945):155–160.

Morrel, Z. N. *Flowers and Fruits from the Wilderness*. Boston: Gould and Lincoln, 1872.

Morse, John D., ed. *Country Cabinetwork and Simple City Furniture*. Charlottesville: University Press of Virginia, 1970.

Muir, Andrew Forest. "Inventions Patented by Texans, 1846–1861." *Southwestern Historical Quarterly* 62 (1959):522.

——. "Railroads Come to Houston, 1852–1861." *Southwestern Historical Quarterly* 64 (1960):42–63.

Neville, A. W. *The History of Lamar County*. Paris: North Texas Publishing Co., 1937.

Olmsted, Frederick Law. *Journey through Texas: A Saddle-Trip on the Southwestern Frontier*. Austin: Von Boeckmann-Jones, 1962.

Parker, A. A. *Trip to the West and Texas*. Austin: Pemberton Press, 1968.

"Paul Maureaux, Early Texas Cabinetmaker." *Frontier Times* 13 (1936): 282–284.

Pennington, Mrs. R. E. *The History of Brenham and Washington County*. Houston, 1915.

Pinckney, Pauline. "Johann Michael Jahn, Texas Cabinetmaker." *Antiques* 75 (1959):462–463.

Postl, Karl [pseud. Charles Sealsfield]. *The Cabin Book*. London: Ingram, Cooke and Co., 1852.

——. *Nathan, der Squatter-Regulator, oder Der erste Amerikaner in Texas*. Zurich: Friedrich Schulthess, 1837.

Quimby, Ian M. G., and Polly Ann Earle, eds. *Technological Innovation and the Decorative Arts*. Charlottesville: University Press of Virginia, 1974.

Rankin, Melinda. *Texas in 1850*. Waco: Texian Press, 1966.

Ransleben, Guido. *A Hundred Years of Comfort in Texas: A Centennial History*. San Antonio: Naylor, 1954.

Reed, S. G. A. *A History of Texas Railroads*. Houston: St. Clair Publishing Co., 1941.

Reinhardt, Louis. "The Communistic Colony of Bettina." *Quarterly of the Texas State Historical Association* 3 (1899):33–40.

Reisner, Edward H. *Nationalism and Education since 1789*. New York: Macmillan, 1923.

Report of the State Penitentiary for 1854–1855. Austin: Marshall and Oldham, 1856.

Richardson, W., and Co. *Galveston Directory for 1866–7*. Galveston: News Book Office, 1866.

——. *Galveston Directory for 1868–9*. Galveston, 1868.

Richardson's New Map of the State of Texas. Philadelphia: Charles Desilver, 1860.

Robinson, Willard B. *Texas Public Buildings of the Nineteenth Century*. Texas Architectural Survey, no. 2. Austin: University of Texas Press, 1974.

Roemer, Ferdinand. *Texas, with Particular Reference to the German Immigration and the Physical Appearance of the Country*. Translated by Oswald Mueller. San Antonio: Standard Printing Co., 1935.

Romberg, Annie. *History of the Romberg Family*. Belton: Peter Hansborough Bell Press, n.d.

Romberg, Caroline Mackensen. *The Story of My Life Written for My Children*. N.p., 1970.

Santleben, August. *A Texas Pioneer*. New York: I. D. Affleck, 1910.

Seale, William. "San Augustine: In the Texas Republic." *Southwestern Historical Quarterly* 72 (1969):347–358.

Sibley, Marilyn McAdams. *Travelers in Texas, 1761–1860*. Austin: University of Texas Press, 1967.

Siemering, August. "Die Lateinische Anseidlung in Texas." *Texana* 5 (1967):126–131.

Smith, Ophia D. "A Trip to Texas in 1855." *Southwestern Historical Quarterly* 59 (1955):24–39.

Smithwick, Noah. *The Evolution of a State*. Austin: Gammel Book Co., 1900.

Stambaugh, J. Lee, and Lillian J. Stambaugh. *A History of Collin County, Texas*. Austin: Texas State Historical Association, 1958.

Steinfeldt, Cecilia, and Donald L. Stover. *Early Texas Furniture and Decorative Arts*. San Antonio: Trinity University Press, 1973.

Tiling, Moritz. *History of the German Element in Texas from 1820–1850*. Houston, 1913.

Tracy, Berry B., Marilynn Johnson, Marvin D. Schwarz, and Suzanne Boorsch. *Nineteenth-Century America: Furniture and Other Decorative Arts.* New York: Metropolitan Museum of Art, 1970.

Trenckmann, William. *Austin County.* Bellville: Wochenblatt, 1898.

———. "Die Lateiner am Possum Creek." *Das Wochenblatt* (Austin), December 25, 1907.

Tyler, George W. *The History of Bell County.* Belton: D. Kelley, 1966.

Walker, Mack. *Germany and the Emigration, 1816–1885.* Cambridge: Harvard University Press, 1964.

Waller County Historical Survey Committee. *A History of Waller County.* Waco, 1973.

Wallis, Johnie Lockhart, and Laurence L. Hill. *Sixty Years on the Brazos: The Life and Letters of Dr. John Washington Lockhart.* Waco: Texian Press, 1967.

Walzer, Albert. "Baden-Württembergische Bauern Möbel." *Der Museumsfreund aus Heimatmuseen und Sämmlungen in Baden-Württemberg* 10–11 (n.d.).

Webb, Walter Prescott, ed. *The Handbook of Texas.* 2 vols. Austin: Texas State Historical Association, 1952.

Williams, Amelia W., and Eugene C. Barker, eds. *The Writings of Sam Houston, 1813–1863.* 8 vols. Austin: University of Texas, 1938–1943.

Winfield, Nath. "A Letter from Texas." *Southwestern Historical Quarterly* 71 (1968):425–429.

Winfrey, Dorman W. *Julien Sidney Devereux and His Monte Verdi Plantation.* Waco: Texian Press, 1964.

Wooster, Ralph A. "Foreigners in the Principal Towns of Ante-Bellum Texas." *Southwestern Historical Quarterly* 66 (1962):208–220.

———. "Notes on Texas' Largest Slaveholders, 1860." *Southwestern Historical Quarterly* 65 (1961):72–79.

———. "Wealthy Texans, 1860." *Southwestern Historical Quarterly* 71 (1967):163–180.

Young, J. H. *A New Map of Texas.* Philadelphia: S. Augustus Mitchell, 1837.

NEWSPAPERS

Bastrop Advertiser. 1854–1858.

Bejareño, El (San Antonio). 1855–1856.

Belton Weekly Journal. 1870–1880.

Brenham Banner. 1866–1876.

Brenham Enquirer. 1854, 1856, 1858.

Civilian and Galveston Gazette. SEE *Civilian and Gazette.*

Civilian and Gazette (Galveston); sometimes called *Civilian and Galveston Gazette.* 1838–1840, 1843–1856, 1858–1862, 1865, 1872–1873.

Colorado Citizen (Columbus). 1858, 1860.

Colorado Tribune (Matagorda). 1848, 1851.

Corpus Christi Gazette. 1846, 1848.

Corsicana Observer. 1867.

Crockett Printer. 1853, 1860.

Daily Austin Republican. 1868–1871.

Daily State Gazette and General Advertiser (Austin). 1859.

Democratic Telegraph and Texas Register. SEE *Telegraph and Texas Register.*

Flake's Daily Bulletin (Galveston). 1865–1872.

Fredericksburg Standard. 1955.

Frontier News (Weatherford). 1858.

Galveston Daily News. 1857–1873.

Galvestonian. 1839–1841, 1848.

Galveston Weekly News. 1844–1868, 1871–1880.

Georgetown Watchman. 1867, 1869–1871.

Goliad Messenger. 1860, 1864.

Gonzales Inquirer. 1853–1854, 1859, 1864.

Guadalupe Times (Seguin). 1875.

Huntsville Item. 1853, 1858, 1864, 1941.

Huntsville Recorder. 1857.

Independent Monitor (Bright Star [Sulphur Springs]). 1860.

Indianola Courier. 1859–1861.

Indianola Weekly Bulletin. 1871–1872.

Lavaca Herald. 1856–1857.

Lone Star (Washington). 1851–1852.

McKinney Messenger. 1860–1861, 1865–1874.

McKinney Weekly Enquirer. 1869, 1871, 1878.

Morning Star (Houston). 1839–1846.

Navarro Express (Corsicana). 1859–1864.

Neu-Braunfelser Zeitung (New Braunfels). 1852–1853, 1855, 1859, 1868, 1870, 1908.

Northern Standard. SEE *Standard.*

North Texan (Paris). 1876, 1879.

Nueces Valley (Corpus Christi). 1850, 1854, 1857–1858, 1870–1872.

Paris Weekly Press. 1875.

Rambler (Lockhart). 1859.

Red-Lander (San Augustine). 1839, 1841–1842, 1845–1846.

Reformer (Austin). 1871.

Richmond Reporter. 1856–1857, 1859.

Round Rock Sentinel. 1870–1871.

San Antonio Express. 1865, 1867–1880.

San Antonio Herald. 1855–1861, 1866–1880.

San Antonio Ledger. 1851–1859.

San Antonio Ledger and Texan. 1859–1861.

San Antonio Reporter. 1856.

San Marcos Weekly Pioneer. 1869.

Seguin Journal and General Advertiser. 1858.

Seguin Mercury. 1857–1860.

Southern Beacon (Henderson). 1855–1857, 1859.

Southern Democrat (Waco). 1858.

Southern Intelligencer (Austin); sometimes called *Weekly Southern Intelligencer.* 1855–1861, 1865–1867.

South-West Quarter Sheet (Waco). 1860–1861.

Standard (Clarksville); before 1857, usually called *Northern Standard.* 1842–1865, 1868–1874.

Star State Patriot (Marshall). 1851–1853.

Telegraph and Texas Register (Houston); sometimes called *Democratic Telegraph and Texas Register.* 1835–1853.

Texan Mercury (Seguin). 1853–1855.

Texas Advertiser (Columbia). 1854.

Texas Plowboy (Lockhart). 1869, 1871.

Texas Ranger and Lone Star (Washington). 1849, 1851–1854, 1856.

Texas Republican (Marshall). 1849–1869.

Texas Sentinel (Austin). 1840–1841.

Texas Weekly Quid Nunc (Crockett). 1865.

Texian and Brazos Farmer (Washington). 1843.

Trinity Advocate (Palestine). 1853, 1857.

Tri-Weekly Telegraph (Houston). 1856–1870.

Tri-Weekly Times (Austin). 1854–1857.

True Issue (La Grange). 1857–1859, 1863–1864.

Tyler Reporter. 1855, 1859, 1861–1862, 1864.

Waco Daily Advance. 1872.

Weekly Enquirer. SEE *McKinney Weekly Enquirer.*

Weekly Southern Intelligencer. SEE *Southern Intelligencer.*

Western Texan (San Antonio). 1848–1854.

Wochenblatt, Das (Austin). 1879, 1881, 1886, 1907, 1909–1938.

LETTERS AND INTERVIEWS

Baird, Mrs. James. Letter, Paris, March 12, 1970, to Lonn Taylor (LT).

Biesele, Mrs. Hugo. Interview, New Braunfels, November 20, 1974.

Collin, Shirley Insall. Letter, San Antonio, August 8, 1973, to LT.

Conger, Roger. Letter, Waco, March 10, 1973, to LT.

Haas, Oscar. Interview, New Braunfels, February 10, 1973.

Jahn, Ben. Interview, New Braunfels, February 14, 1973.

Kuhlman, Mrs. Herman. Letter, Houston, June 4, 1973, to LT.

Legler, Mrs. Rudi. Interview, Round Top, June 11, 1973.

Meitzen, Warren C. Interview, Houston, February 10, 1973.

Parker, Knight. Interview, San Augustine, February 10, 1974.

Sacks, Dennis. Interview, Round Top, April 11, 1975.

Schulze, Ed. Interview, Fredericksburg, June 3, 1973.

Schulze, Hugo. Interview, Hilda, June 3, 1973.

Schweers, C. F. Interview, Hondo, May 24, 1973.

Schweers, Willie. Interview, Quihi, May 24, 1973.

Spalding, William. Interview, Waxahachie, June 3, 1973.

Staats, Eddie. Interview, Llano, June 3, 1973.

Winfield, Nath. Letter, Chappell Hill, June 13, 1972, to LT.

———. Letter, Chappell Hill, October 17, 1973, to LT.

Wisseman, C. L. Letter, Kerrville, July 13, 1973, to LT.

Index